Silver Burdett

MATHEMATICS

AUTHORS

SENIOR SERIES AUTHORS
Lucy J. Orfan • Bruce R. Vogeli

SENIOR PROBLEM SOLVING AUTHORS
Stephen Krulik • Jesse A. Rudnick

Sadie C. Bragg • Ruth I. Champagne • Gerald A. Goldin • Edith E. Grimsley
Deborah B. Gustafson • John F. LeBlanc • William D. McKillip • Fernand J. Prevost

SILVER BURDETT COMPANY
MORRISTOWN, NJ

Atlanta, GA   •   Cincinnati, OH   •   Dallas, TX   •   Northfield, IL   •   San Carlos, CA   •   Agincourt, Ontario

ISBN 0-382-01710-2

Table of Contents

13 Geometry

Theme: School Day

Addition Facts Through 10

How many children are getting ready for the school play?

COMMUNITY HELPERS

We add to find how many in all.

$$4 + 2 = 6$$

4 ← addend
+2 ← addend
6 ← sum

addend   addend   sum

We say, "Four plus two equals six."

There are 6 children getting ready for the play.

CLASSWORK

Find each sum.

1. 2
   +3

2. 4
   +4

3. 5
   +1

4. 9
   +1

5. 0
   +4

6. 6 + 3 = ☐

7. 2 + 7 = ☐

8. 3 + 4 = ☐

2

Find each sum.

1. 2 +2	2. 4 +1	3. 1 +7	4. 2 +1	5. 3 +3	6. 3 +2	7. 1 +5
8. 6 +1	9. 0 +8	10. 2 +4	11. 4 +3	12. 1 +9	13. 4 +6	14. 3 +1
15. 1 +8	16. 5 +3	17. 6 +4	18. 7 +2	19. 2 +5	20. 4 +5	21. 1 +1
22. 7 +3	23. 2 +8	24. 5 +4	25. 3 +6	26. 7 +1	27. 3 +5	28. 1 +6

29. $1 + 3 = \square$ 30. $6 + 0 = \square$ 31. $3 + 7 = \square$ 32. $2 + 6 = \square$

33. $5 + 2 = \square$ 34. $8 + 1 = \square$ 35. $5 + 5 = \square$ 36. $8 + 2 = \square$

37. $2 + 6 = \square$ 38. $7 + 3 = \square$ 39. $0 + 5 = \square$

40. $\square = 1 + 3$ 41. $\square = 7 + 0$ 42. $\square = 1 + 4$

43. $\square = 3 + 7$ 44. $\square = 1 + 2$ 45. $\square = 6 + 2$

Find the missing numbers.

★ 46. $\triangle + \square = 8$

★ 47. $\triangle + \square = 10$

APPLICATION

48. Six children made costumes. Two children collected tickets. How many children worked?

49. Alan sold 3 tickets to the play. Rita sold 2 tickets. How many tickets did they sell in all?

★ 50. Make up a story about this fact.
$5 + 5 = 10$

MENTAL ARITHMETIC

Find the hidden addends.

1. $1 + \hexagon = 3$

2. $1 + \hexagon = 4$

3. $1 + \hexagon = 5$

4. $1 + \hexagon = 6$

5. $1 + \hexagon = 7$

3

Order in Addition

How many fish does Lisa have altogether in her science project?

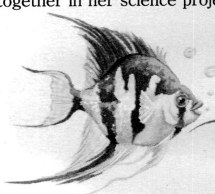

We can add in any order.

$$5 \qquad 3$$
$$\underline{+3} \qquad \underline{+5}$$
$$8 \qquad 8$$

Lisa has 8 fish altogether.

▶ The order in which numbers are added does not change the sum.

$$5 + 3 = 8$$
$$3 + 5 = 8$$

▶ The sum of any number and 0 is that number.

$$6 \qquad 0$$
$$\underline{+0} \qquad \underline{+3}$$
$$6 \qquad 3$$

$$4 + 0 = 4$$
$$0 + 5 = 5$$

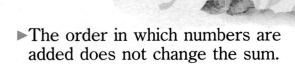

When we know one fact we know another fact.

CLASSWORK

Find each sum.

1. $\quad 4 \qquad 2$
    $\quad \underline{+2} \quad \underline{+4}$

2. $\quad 2 \qquad 1$
    $\quad \underline{+1} \quad \underline{+2}$

3. $\quad 8 \qquad 0$
    $\quad \underline{+0} \quad \underline{+8}$

4. $\quad 6 \qquad 3$
    $\quad \underline{+3} \quad \underline{+6}$

5. $8 + 2 = \square$
    $2 + 8 = \square$

6. $6 + 1 = \square$
    $1 + 6 = \square$

7. $7 + 3 = \square$
    $3 + 7 = \square$

8. $9 + 0 = \square$
    $0 + 9 = \square$

9. $7 + 0 = \square$

10. $0 + 1 = \square$

11. $0 + 6 = \square$

12. $3 + 0 = \square$

4

PRACTICE

Find each sum.

1. 3 1
   $+1$ $+3$

2. 2 0
   $+0$ $+2$

3. 3 2
   $+2$ $+3$

4. 5 1
   $+1$ $+5$

5. 9
   $+1$

6. 7
   $+2$

7. 3
   $+3$

8. 4
   $+5$

9. 2
   $+2$

10. 1
    $+4$

11. 7
    $+1$

12. 4
    $+3$

13. 5
    $+5$

14. 2
    $+4$

15. 2
    $+8$

16. 3
    $+4$

17. 2
    $+7$

18. 1
    $+6$

19. $5 + 0 = \square$
    $0 + 5 = \square$

20. $6 + 2 = \square$
    $2 + 6 = \square$

21. $8 + 1 = \square$
    $1 + 8 = \square$

22. $6 + 4 = \square$
    $4 + 6 = \square$

23. $1 + 0 = \square$

24. $0 + 4 = \square$

25. $4 + 6 = \square$

26. $3 + 5 = \square$

27. $5 + 4 = \square$

28. $4 + 1 = \square$

29. $2 + 5 = \square$

30. $0 + 0 = \square$

31. $1 + 7 = \square$

32. $5 + 2 = \square$

33. $4 + 4 = \square$

34. $3 + 6 = \square$

Find each missing number.

★ 35. $5 + 2 = 2 + \square$

★ 36. $3 + 7 = 7 + \square$

★ 37. $\square + 4 = 4 + 0$

APPLICATION

38. For their science project, Mark collected 6 leaves and Shana collected 4. How many leaves did they collect in all?

39. Jim planted seeds for his project. In one box, no plants came up. In another box, 3 plants came up. How many plants were there in all?

★ 40. Write an addition fact for each snail that shows a sum of 7.

5

Addition Facts Through 18

How many jars of paint did
Mr. Mendez give to the children?

$$4 + 8 = 12 \qquad \begin{array}{r} 4 \\ +8 \\ \hline 12 \end{array}$$

Mr. Mendez gave 12 jars of paint to the children.

We can show addition on a number line.

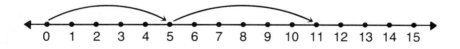

$$5 + 6 = 11 \qquad \begin{array}{r} 5 \\ +6 \\ \hline 11 \end{array}$$

CLASSWORK

Add. You may use a number line to help you.

1. $\begin{array}{r} 6 \\ +6 \\ \hline \end{array}$
2. $\begin{array}{r} 9 \\ +2 \\ \hline \end{array}$
3. $\begin{array}{r} 8 \\ +7 \\ \hline \end{array}$
4. $\begin{array}{r} 7 \\ +6 \\ \hline \end{array}$
5. $\begin{array}{r} 9 \\ +5 \\ \hline \end{array}$
6. $\begin{array}{r} 6 \\ +9 \\ \hline \end{array}$
7. $\begin{array}{r} 8 \\ +4 \\ \hline \end{array}$

8. $9 + 4 = \square$ 9. $5 + 7 = \square$ 10. $7 + 4 = \square$ 11. $8 + 8 = \square$

Add.

1.	2.	3.	4.	5.	6.	7.
7 +8	6 +5	5 +9	9 +7	8 +5	2 +7	8 +2

8.	9.	10.	11.	12.	13.	14.
5 +8	9 +3	7 +7	4 +9	8 +9	6 +4	7 +3

15.	16.	17.	18.	19.	20.	21.
9 +8	7 +9	7 +5	5 +5	4 +7	3 +8	9 +1

22. $6 + 8 = \square$ 23. $2 + 9 = \square$ 24. $9 + 6 = \square$ 25. $8 + 6 = \square$

26. $8 + 3 = \square$ 27. $4 + 6 = \square$ 28. $\square = 9 + 9$ 29. $\square = 7 + 6$

Write the fact shown on each number line.

30.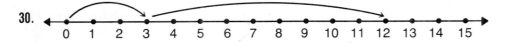

31.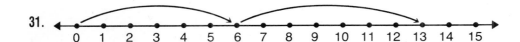

Write two addition facts for each.

★ 32. 9, 5, 14   ★ 33. 7, 5, 12   ★ 34. 8, 5, 13

APPLICATION

35. In art class, children made 9 funny masks and 3 scary masks. How many masks did they make in all?

★ 36. Make up a funny story to go with this fact.
$$7 + 4 = 11$$

★ 37. Make up a scary story to go with this fact.
$$8 + 4 = 12$$

Missing Addends

Knowing the addition facts can help
us find a missing addend.

14

$\begin{array}{r} 9 \\ +5 \\ \hline 14 \end{array}$ $\begin{array}{r} 5 \\ +9 \\ \hline 14 \end{array}$ $\begin{array}{r} 8 \\ +6 \\ \hline 14 \end{array}$ $\begin{array}{r} 6 \\ +8 \\ \hline 14 \end{array}$ $\begin{array}{r} 7 \\ +7 \\ \hline 14 \end{array}$

15

$\begin{array}{r} 9 \\ +6 \\ \hline 15 \end{array}$ $\begin{array}{r} 6 \\ +9 \\ \hline 15 \end{array}$ $\begin{array}{r} 8 \\ +7 \\ \hline 15 \end{array}$ $\begin{array}{r} 7 \\ +8 \\ \hline 15 \end{array}$

16

$\begin{array}{r} 9 \\ +7 \\ \hline 16 \end{array}$ $\begin{array}{r} 7 \\ +9 \\ \hline 16 \end{array}$ $\begin{array}{r} 8 \\ +8 \\ \hline 16 \end{array}$

17

$\begin{array}{r} 9 \\ +8 \\ \hline 17 \end{array}$ $\begin{array}{r} 8 \\ +9 \\ \hline 17 \end{array}$

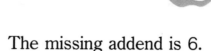

18

$\begin{array}{r} 9 \\ +9 \\ \hline 18 \end{array}$

The missing addend is 6.

CLASSWORK

Find each missing addend.

1. $\begin{array}{r} 7 \\ +\square \\ \hline 14 \end{array}$ 2. $\begin{array}{r} 5 \\ +\square \\ \hline 9 \end{array}$ 3. $\begin{array}{r} 9 \\ +\square \\ \hline 17 \end{array}$ 4. $\begin{array}{r} 6 \\ +\square \\ \hline 9 \end{array}$ 5. $\begin{array}{r} 4 \\ +\square \\ \hline 12 \end{array}$ 6. $\begin{array}{r} 2 \\ +\square \\ \hline 11 \end{array}$ 7. $\begin{array}{r} 5 \\ +\square \\ \hline 10 \end{array}$

8. $7 + \square = 15$ 9. $8 + \square = 14$ 10. $9 + \square = 18$ 11. $6 + \square = 11$

12. $8 + \square = 17$ 13. $5 + \square = 7$ 14. $4 + \square = 11$ 15. $3 + \square = 12$

8

Find each missing addend.

1. 8
   +□
   ‾‾‾
   12

2. 5
   +□
   ‾‾‾
   14

3. 6
   +□
   ‾‾‾
   8

4. 9
   +□
   ‾‾‾
   13

5. 8
   +□
   ‾‾‾
   15

6. 3
   +□
   ‾‾‾
   7

7. 6
   +□
   ‾‾‾
   10

8. 7
   +□
   ‾‾‾
   11

9. 9
   +□
   ‾‾‾
   15

10. 4
   +□
   ‾‾‾
   10

11. 2
   +□
   ‾‾‾
   9

12. 4
   +□
   ‾‾‾
   13

13. 9
   +□
   ‾‾‾
   12

14. 5
   +□
   ‾‾‾
   11

15. 7
   +□
   ‾‾‾
   9

16. 8
   +□
   ‾‾‾
   11

17. □
   +7
   ‾‾‾
   16

18. □
   + 4
   ‾‾‾
   8

19. □
   + 8
   ‾‾‾
   14

20. □
   + 5
   ‾‾‾
   13

21. □
   + 8
   ‾‾‾
   16

22. 8 + □ = 10

23. 7 + □ = 12

24. 9 + □ = 14

25. 7 + □ = 16

26. 3 + □ = 12

27. 9 + □ = 11

28. 5 + □ = 13

29. 1 + □ = 10

30. □ + 7 = 12

31. □ + 7 = 13

32. □ + 9 = 15

33. □ + 7 = 10

34. □ + 6 = 12

35. □ + 5 = 9

36. □ + 5 = 8

37. □ + 8 = 17

★ 38. 4 + 7 = 8 + □

★ 39. 7 + □ = 9 + 6

★ 40. 8 + 5 = 7 + □

★ 41. 6 + □ = 2 + 8

★ 42. 5 + 9 = 8 + □

★ 43. 4 + □ = 5 + 7

APPLICATION

44. Faye cut out 6 red apples and some green apples. Now she has 15 apples. How many green apples are there?

45. Larry put 5 pink stars and 8 orange stars on the felt board. How many stars are there altogether?

★ 46. Find each missing addend above.

9

Adding Three Numbers

How many balls are there in all?

We can group the
numbers in different ways.

$$4 + 2 + 3 = \square$$
$$6 \quad + 3 = 9$$

$$4 + 2 + 3 = \square$$
$$4 + \quad 5 \quad = 9$$

There are 9 balls in all.

We can
add down.

$$\begin{array}{r} 3 \\ 6 \\ +1 \\ \hline \end{array} \quad \begin{array}{r} 9 \\ +1 \\ \hline 10 \end{array}$$

We can
add up.

$$\begin{array}{r} 3 \\ 6 \\ +1 \\ \hline \end{array} \quad \begin{array}{r} 3 \\ +7 \\ \hline 10 \end{array}$$

▶ The way in which numbers are grouped
does not change the sum.

CLASSWORK

Add.

1.
$$\begin{array}{r} 1 \\ 4 \\ +5 \\ \hline \end{array}$$

2.
$$\begin{array}{r} 1 \\ 4 \\ +5 \\ \hline \end{array}$$

3.
$$\begin{array}{r} 1 \\ 7 \\ +0 \\ \hline \end{array}$$

4.
$$\begin{array}{r} 6 \\ 2 \\ +2 \\ \hline \end{array}$$

5.
$$\begin{array}{r} 3 \\ 3 \\ +3 \\ \hline \end{array}$$

6. $8 + 1 + 7 = \square$

7. $6 + 0 + 3 = \square$

8. $3 + 5 + 4 = \square$

9. $1 + 5 + 2 = \square$

10

PRACTICE

Add.

1.	2	2.	3	3.	3	4.	4	5.	1	6.	4	7.	4
	1		2		3		4		2		0		1
	+8		+7		+4		+2		+7		+5		+8

8.	7	9.	5	10.	3	11.	8	12.	1	13.	7	14.	2
	1		2		5		0		4		2		7
	+7		+6		+2		+3		+4		+2		+1

15.	2	16.	3	17.	9	18.	0	19.	3	20.	5	21.	6
	2		2		0		3		4		2		3
	+7		+6		+9		+4		+5		+3		+0

22. 6 + 3 + 5 = ☐   **23.** 4 + 4 + 4 = ☐   **24.** 8 + 0 + 8 = ☐

25. 1 + 3 + 4 = ☐   **26.** 2 + 5 + 4 = ☐   **27.** 6 + 0 + 9 = ☐

Choose the correct sum.

28. 1 + 4 + 2 + 2 = ☐
   a. 10   **b.** 9
   c. 7   **d.** 8

29. 4 + 3 + 2 + 1 = ☐
   a. 7   **b.** 6
   c. 10   **d.** 9

Find each missing addend.

★**30.** 4 + 0 + ☐ + 3 = 10

★**31.** 3 + 0 + ☐ + ☐ = 6

APPLICATION

═══ CALCULATOR ═══

1. Add the numbers. What is the sum?

2. Now add the numbers another way. Is the sum the same?

3. Add three numbers to get a sum of 12.

4. Add four numbers to get a sum of 12.

Problem Solving

FINDING FACTS FROM PICTURES

Being a good problem solver can be helpful in school and at home. There are four steps you should follow to become a good problem solver.

THINK
PLAN
SOLVE
LOOK
BACK

Six students brought their pets to school. Lee and Peter both brought their kittens. How many kittens did Lee and Peter bring?

Use the four steps to help solve the problem.

THINK **What is the question?**

How many kittens did Lee and Peter bring in all?

What are the facts?

Look at the picture to find out. Lee brought 4 kittens. Peter brought 3 kittens.

PLAN **How can you find the answer?**

Add the number of Lee's kittens and the number of Peter's kittens.

$$4 + 3 = \square$$

SOLVE **Carry out the plan. Do the work and find the answer.**

$$\begin{array}{r} 4 \\ +3 \\ \hline 7 \end{array}$$ Lee and Peter brought 7 kittens in all.

LOOK BACK **Did you answer the question? Is your arithmetic correct?**

There are 7 kittens. Count the kittens to check your arithmetic.

Use the picture on page 12 to answer questions 1–10.

1. Who brought goldfish?

2. How many dogs did Bert bring?

3. Who brought the fewest pets?

4. Who brought the most pets?

5. How many birds did Pat and Carlos bring in all?

6. How many kittens and dogs were there in all?

7. Who brought more kittens, Lee or Peter?

8. Were there more goldfish or more dogs?

9. Who brought the same number of pets?

10. How many pets did the students bring in all?

Use the picture to answer questions 11–16.

11. How many basketballs are there?

12. How many baseballs are there?

13. How many soccer balls are there?

14. How many basketballs and footballs are there in all?

15. How many balls are there in all?

★ 16. Are there more basketballs or more baseballs? How many more?

=== CREATE YOUR OWN PROBLEM ===

Tina brought stickers to school.
Use the picture to make up 2 addition problems.

13

Subtraction Facts Through 10

Scott took 1 book from the display. How many books are left?

We subtract to find how many are left.

FABLES

$$6 - 1 = 5 \qquad \begin{array}{r} 6 \\ -1 \\ \hline 5 \end{array} \leftarrow \text{difference}$$

difference

We say, "Six minus one equals five."

There are 5 books left.

▶ When we subtract 0 from a number, the difference is that number.

$$\begin{array}{r} 9 \\ -0 \\ \hline 9 \end{array} \qquad \begin{array}{r} 2 \\ -0 \\ \hline 2 \end{array}$$

▶ When we subtract a number from itself, the difference is 0.

$$\begin{array}{r} 7 \\ -7 \\ \hline 0 \end{array} \qquad \begin{array}{r} 3 \\ -3 \\ \hline 0 \end{array}$$

CLASSWORK

Find each difference.

1. $\begin{array}{r} 5 \\ -1 \\ \hline \end{array}$ 2. $\begin{array}{r} 4 \\ -3 \\ \hline \end{array}$ 3. $\begin{array}{r} 6 \\ -3 \\ \hline \end{array}$ 4. $\begin{array}{r} 8 \\ -6 \\ \hline \end{array}$ 5. $\begin{array}{r} 0 \\ -0 \\ \hline \end{array}$ 6. $\begin{array}{r} 10 \\ -5 \\ \hline \end{array}$ 7. $\begin{array}{r} 9 \\ -4 \\ \hline \end{array}$

8. $9 - 2 = \square$ 9. $10 - 1 = \square$ 10. $7 - 3 = \square$ 11. $8 - 5 = \square$

Find each difference.

1. 3 −1	**2.** 5 −2	**3.** 4 −2	**4.** 1 −1	**5.** 6 −5	**6.** 5 −4	**7.** 2 −1
8. 6 −2	**9.** 9 −9	**10.** 8 −1	**11.** 7 −4	**12.** 10 − 3	**13.** 7 −2	**14.** 5 −5
15. 10 − 9	**16.** 8 −4	**17.** 10 − 4	**18.** 6 −0	**19.** 9 −3	**20.** 5 −3	**21.** 8 −2
22. 8 −3	**23.** 7 −6	**24.** 9 −5	**25.** 9 −7	**26.** 10 − 8	**27.** 6 −4	**28.** 10 − 6

29. 9 − 1 = ☐   **30.** 7 − 5 = ☐   **31.** ☐ = 8 − 7   **32.** ☐ = 10 − 7

Follow the rule to complete.

Rule:
Subtract 2.

33.	10
34.	9
35.	8
36.	7
37.	6

Rule:
Subtract 3.

38.	8
39.	5
40.	6
41.	7
42.	10

Rule:
Subtract 4 and add 3.

★ **43.**	10
★ **44.**	9
★ **45.**	8
★ **46.**	7
★ **47.**	6

APPLICATION

LOGICAL THINKING

1. I am the difference when 1 is subtracted from 4. What number am I?

2. I am the difference when 2 is subtracted from 10. What number am I?

3. I give a difference of 6 when I am subtracted from 7. What number am I?

4. I give a difference of 4 when I am subtracted from 9. What number am I?

15

Subtraction Facts Through 13

In a fable the ant wants to store 12 seeds.
How many more seeds does the ant need?

We subtract to find how many more are needed.

$$12 - 8 = 4 \qquad \begin{array}{r} 12 \\ -\ 8 \\ \hline 4 \end{array}$$

The ant needs 4 more seeds.

We can show subtraction on a number line.

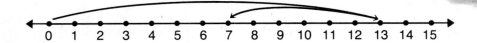

$$13 - 6 = 7 \qquad \begin{array}{r} 13 \\ -\ 6 \\ \hline 7 \end{array}$$

CLASSWORK

Subtract. You may use a number line to help you.

1. $\begin{array}{r} 11 \\ -\ 2 \\ \hline \end{array}$
2. $\begin{array}{r} 13 \\ -\ 8 \\ \hline \end{array}$
3. $\begin{array}{r} 12 \\ -\ 6 \\ \hline \end{array}$
4. $\begin{array}{r} 13 \\ -\ 9 \\ \hline \end{array}$
5. $\begin{array}{r} 11 \\ -\ 3 \\ \hline \end{array}$
6. $\begin{array}{r} 12 \\ -\ 4 \\ \hline \end{array}$

7. $13 - 5 = \square$ 8. $12 - 7 = \square$ 9. $11 - 9 = \square$ 10. $11 - 6 = \square$

PRACTICE

Subtract.

1.	2.	3.	4.	5.	6.
12 − 3	13 − 4	8 −2	11 − 2	12 − 5	13 − 6

7.	8.	9.	10.	11.	12.
11 − 4	6 −6	13 − 5	12 − 4	11 − 5	10 − 1

13.	14.	15.	16.	17.	18.
11 − 6	11 − 8	9 −6	12 − 7	13 − 9	13 − 7

19. $13 - 4 = \square$ **20.** $10 - 6 = \square$ **21.** $12 - 9 = \square$ **22.** $13 - 8 = \square$

23. $12 - 8 = \square$ **24.** $11 - 9 = \square$ **25.** $\square = 9 - 8$ **26.** $\square = 11 - 7$

Find each missing number.

27.  $11 - \square = 5$

28. 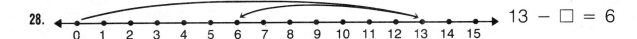 $13 - \square = 6$

Write two subtraction facts for each.

★ **29.** 8, 5, 13   ★ **30.** 12, 3, 9   ★ **31.** 4, 11, 7

APPLICATION

32. It takes 12 jumps to get to the seeds. The grasshopper made 3 jumps. How many more jumps must the grasshopper make?

★ **33.** Make up a story about the ant or the grasshopper to show this fact. $13 - 4 = 9$

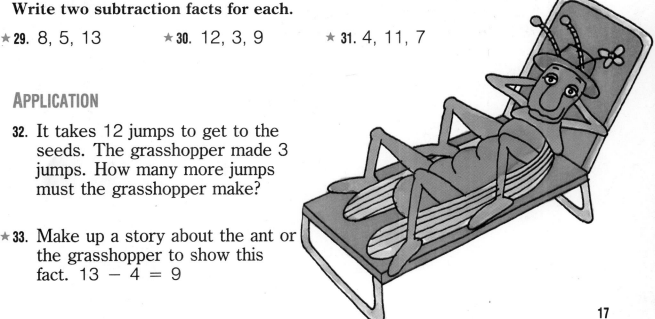

17

Subtraction Facts Through 18

How many more recorders than bells are there?

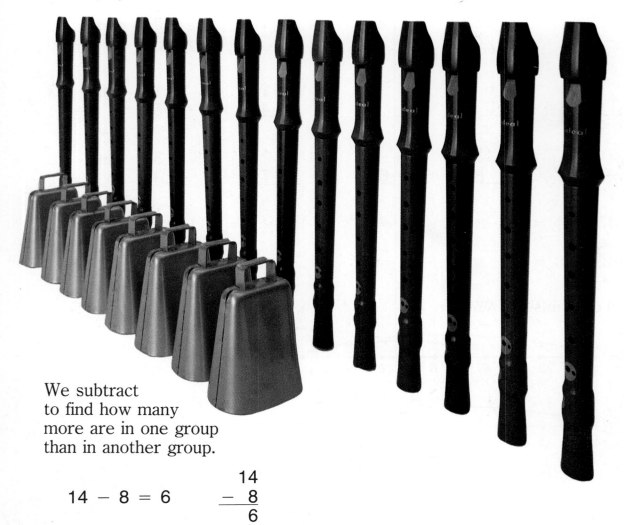

We subtract
to find how many
more are in one group
than in another group.

$$14 - 8 = 6 \qquad \begin{array}{r} 14 \\ -\ 8 \\ \hline 6 \end{array}$$

There are 6 more recorders than bells.

CLASSWORK

Subtract.

1. $\begin{array}{r} 14 \\ -\ 7 \\ \hline \end{array}$
2. $\begin{array}{r} 16 \\ -\ 8 \\ \hline \end{array}$
3. $\begin{array}{r} 15 \\ -\ 6 \\ \hline \end{array}$
4. $\begin{array}{r} 16 \\ -\ 9 \\ \hline \end{array}$
5. $\begin{array}{r} 14 \\ -\ 5 \\ \hline \end{array}$
6. $\begin{array}{r} 15 \\ -\ 7 \\ \hline \end{array}$

7. $18 - 9 = \square$
8. $14 - 6 = \square$
9. $17 - 8 = \square$
10. $15 - 9 = \square$

PRACTICE

Subtract.

1. 11
    − 4

2. 15
    − 8

3. 13
    − 6

4. 14
    − 9

5. 17
    − 9

6. 14
    − 8

7. 16
    − 7

8. 18
    − 9

9. 15
    − 9

10. 17
    − 8

11. 14
    − 5

12. 16
    − 8

13. 15 − 6 = ☐

14. 16 − 9 = ☐

15. 15 − 7 = ☐

16. 14 − 7 = ☐

Find each missing number.

★ 17. ☐
      −9
      ───
      9

★ 18. ☐
      −9
      ───
      6

★ 19. ☐
      −7
      ───
      8

★ 20. 13
      −☐
      ───
      4

APPLICATION

21. How many more children than recorders are there?

22. There are 13 music books. Miss Mark gave 8 of them to the children. How many music books are left?

★ 23. Write a subtraction fact that tells about the children and recorders.

MIXED PRACTICE

1. 6
    +9

2. 12
    − 5

3. 4
    +7

4. 16
    − 7

5. 11
    − 8

6. 9
    +4

7. 5
    +0

8. 7
    −0

9. 0
    +3

10. 8
    +0

11. 4
    2
    +3

12. 6
    0
    +2

13. 3 + 2 = ☐

14. 17 − ☐ = 9

15. 7 − 5 = ☐

16. ☐ + 9 = 9

17. 6 + ☐ = 9

18. 9 + ☐ = 15

19. ☐ + 5 = 13

20. 1 + 0 + 8 = ☐

21. 5 + 2 + 1 = ☐

Fast Facts

Add as fast as you can.

1. 6
   +7

2. 8
   +5

3. 3
   +4

4. 7
   +9

5. 9
   +6

6. 2
   +8

7. 5
   +2

8. 4
   +6

9. 9
   +8

10. 6
    +5

11. 0
    +3

12. 8
    +7

13. 7
    +4

14. 1
    +9

15. 6
    +4

16. 2
    +9

17. 5
    +8

18. 9
    +7

19. 6
    +6

20. 4
    +8

21. 3
    +9

22. 7
    +1

23. 2
    +3

24. 8
    +8

25. 5
    +5

26. 1
    +7

27. 2
    +6

28. 6
    +1

29. 4
    +2

30. 9
    +5

31. 8
    +4

32. 0
    +9

33. 6
    +9

34. 3
    +3

35. 8
    +2

36. 2
    +5

37. 1
    +3

38. 3
    +8

39. 0
    +5

40. 9
    +4

41. 7
    +3

42. 9
    +9

43. 3
    +5

44. 7
    +2

45. 4
    +5

46. 9
    +1

47. 8
    +6

48. 6
    +3

49. 7
    +8

50. 5
    +9

Subtract as fast as you can.

1. $9 - 7$	2. $6 - 2$	3. $12 - 8$	4. $16 - 7$	5. $8 - 5$	6. $17 - 9$
7. $5 - 3$	8. $2 - 1$	9. $18 - 9$	10. $13 - 6$	11. $7 - 7$	12. $6 - 5$
13. $4 - 4$	14. $10 - 3$	15. $9 - 6$	16. $15 - 9$	17. $3 - 1$	18. $12 - 6$
19. $14 - 6$	20. $9 - 8$	21. $7 - 5$	22. $11 - 5$	23. $6 - 0$	24. $16 - 9$
25. $4 - 2$	26. $7 - 6$	27. $10 - 7$	28. $8 - 3$	29. $12 - 9$	30. $5 - 2$
31. $13 - 8$	32. $6 - 3$	33. $9 - 4$	34. $8 - 6$	35. $5 - 5$	36. $10 - 9$
37. $5 - 0$	38. $8 - 4$	39. $11 - 4$	40. $10 - 8$	41. $9 - 2$	42. $7 - 1$
43. $12 - 3$	44. $14 - 9$	45. $13 - 7$	46. $10 - 2$	47. $11 - 6$	48. $15 - 8$
49. $17 - 8$	50. $13 - 4$				

Fact Families

Some facts use the same numbers.
Together they make up a fact family.
This fact family uses 5, 9, and 14.

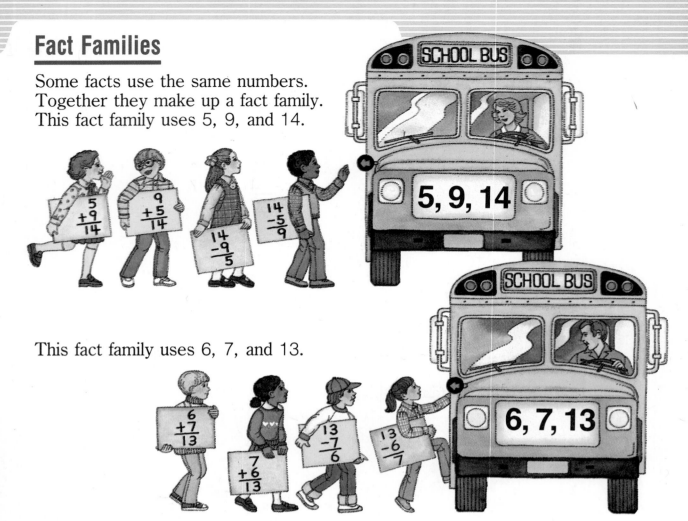

This fact family uses 6, 7, and 13.

Fact families help us remember
our addition and subtraction facts.

CLASSWORK

Add or subtract. Watch the signs.

1. $\begin{array}{r} 8 \\ +7 \\ \hline \end{array}$ $\begin{array}{r} 7 \\ +8 \\ \hline \end{array}$ $\begin{array}{r} 15 \\ -\ 7 \\ \hline \end{array}$ $\begin{array}{r} 15 \\ -\ 8 \\ \hline \end{array}$ 2. $\begin{array}{r} 6 \\ +5 \\ \hline \end{array}$ $\begin{array}{r} 5 \\ +6 \\ \hline \end{array}$ $\begin{array}{r} 11 \\ -\ 5 \\ \hline \end{array}$ $\begin{array}{r} 11 \\ -\ 6 \\ \hline \end{array}$

3. $\begin{array}{r} 5 \\ +4 \\ \hline \end{array}$ $\begin{array}{r} 4 \\ +5 \\ \hline \end{array}$ $\begin{array}{r} 9 \\ -4 \\ \hline \end{array}$ $\begin{array}{r} 9 \\ -5 \\ \hline \end{array}$ 4. $\begin{array}{r} 17 \\ -\ 9 \\ \hline \end{array}$ $\begin{array}{r} 17 \\ -\ 8 \\ \hline \end{array}$ $\begin{array}{r} 8 \\ +9 \\ \hline \end{array}$ $\begin{array}{r} 9 \\ +8 \\ \hline \end{array}$

Give the other facts in each family.

5. $9 + 6 = 15$ 6. $7 - 2 = 5$ 7. $8 + 4 = 12$

Add or subtract. Watch the signs.

1.　　8　　　3　　　11　　　11
　　　+3　　+8　　－ 3　　－ 8

2.　　14　　　14　　　6　　　8
　　　－ 8　　－ 6　　+8　　+6

3.　　2　　　8　　　6　　　8
　　　+6　　－2　　+2　　－6

4.　　11　　　4　　　7　　　11
　　　－ 4　　+7　　+4　　－ 7

Add or subtract. Then write another fact using the same numbers.

5.　　4　　6.　　9　　7.　　3　　8.　　2　　9.　　12　　10.　　6　　11.　　9
　　+6　　　　+4　　　　+5　　　　+8　　　　－ 6　　　　－4　　　　－7

12. 3 + 4 = ☐　　13. 1 + 6 = ☐　　14. 5 − 3 = ☐　　15. 10 − 7 = ☐

Tell which facts form a family.

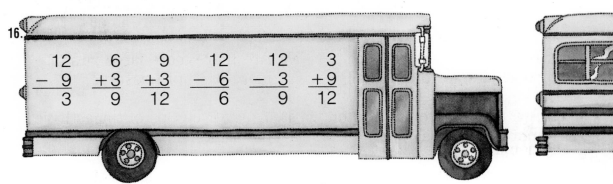

16.
12	6	9	12	12	3
− 9	+3	+3	− 6	− 3	+9
3	9	12	6	9	12

Write the fact family for each.

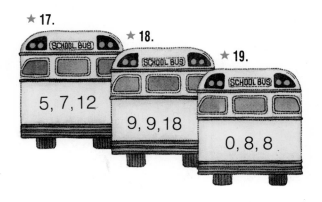

★ 17.　5, 7, 12

★ 18.　9, 9, 18

★ 19.　0, 8, 8

APPLICATION

=== LOGICAL THINKING ===

Choose the pair that fits.

5 and 4　　6 and 3　　7 and 2

1. The sum is 9. The difference is 3.
2. The sum is 9. The difference is 5.
3. The sum is 9. The difference is 1.

Problem Solving

SKILLS AND STRATEGIES REVIEW

Use the pictures to answer each question.

1. How many large jars of paint are there?

2. How many small jars of paint are there?

3. How many crayons are there?

4. How many brushes are there?

5. How many masks are there?

6. How many brushes and pairs of scissors are there in all?

7. How many large jars and small jars are there in all?

8. Are there more large jars or more pairs of scissors?

9. Are there more crayons or more small jars?

10. Which 2 groups of things have the same number?

11. Eight children want to use scissors. Tad brought one pair. How many pairs are still needed?

★12. Which two groups of things, when added together, equal a sum of 12?

Problem Solving

WHAT IF . . . ?

5 for $1

$3 each

$2 each

Students in third grade are having a sale to raise money for their field trip.

Use the pictures to answer each question.

1. How much do pumpkins cost?

2. How much do 5 apples cost?

3. How much does cider cost?

4. How much does corn cost?

5. Which costs more, a pumpkin or a bunch of corn?

6. Which costs more, 5 apples or a jug of cider?

7. How many more jugs of cider are there than pumpkins?

8. How many more bunches of corn are there than pumpkins?

What if Carlos bought 2 jugs of cider?

9. How much would he pay?

10. How many jugs would be left?

What if Karen bought 1 pumpkin and 1 bunch of corn?

11. How much would she pay?

12. How many bunches of corn would be left?

What if pumpkins cost $6 and jugs of cider cost $4?

★ 13. How much would Bonnie pay for 1 pumpkin and 2 jugs of cider?

★ 14. How much would Marlon pay for 10 apples and 1 jug of cider?

$5 each

Add. pages 2–11

1. $\begin{array}{r} 3 \\ +5 \\ \hline \end{array}$	2. $\begin{array}{r} 7 \\ +2 \\ \hline \end{array}$	3. $\begin{array}{r} 9 \\ +7 \\ \hline \end{array}$	4. $\begin{array}{r} 9 \\ +0 \\ \hline \end{array}$	5. $\begin{array}{r} 4 \\ +6 \\ \hline \end{array}$	6. $\begin{array}{r} 3 \\ +4 \\ \hline \end{array}$

7. $5 + 6 = \square$ 8. $3 + 9 = \square$ 9. $7 + 4 = \square$ 10. $6 + 8 = \square$

$6 + 5 = \square$ $9 + 3 = \square$ $4 + 7 = \square$ $8 + 6 = \square$

11. $8 + 0 + 8 = \square$ 12. $2 + 4 + 3 = \square$ 13. $5 + 4 + 5 = \square$

Find each missing addend. pages 8–9

14. $\begin{array}{r} 8 \\ +\square \\ \hline 15 \end{array}$	15. $\begin{array}{r} 7 \\ +\square \\ \hline 14 \end{array}$	16. $\begin{array}{r} \square \\ +8 \\ \hline 16 \end{array}$	17. $\begin{array}{r} \square \\ +8 \\ \hline 17 \end{array}$	18. $\begin{array}{r} 6 \\ +\square \\ \hline 15 \end{array}$	19. $\begin{array}{r} \square \\ +9 \\ \hline 18 \end{array}$

Subtract. pages 14–19

20. $\begin{array}{r} 8 \\ -3 \\ \hline \end{array}$	21. $\begin{array}{r} 9 \\ -8 \\ \hline \end{array}$	22. $\begin{array}{r} 7 \\ -0 \\ \hline \end{array}$	23. $\begin{array}{r} 6 \\ -6 \\ \hline \end{array}$	24. $\begin{array}{r} 10 \\ -\ 4 \\ \hline \end{array}$	25. $\begin{array}{r} 9 \\ -2 \\ \hline \end{array}$

26. $13 - 6 = \square$ 27. $15 - 8 = \square$ 28. $12 - 7 = \square$ 29. $14 - 5 = \square$

30. $17 - 9 = \square$ 31. $11 - 3 = \square$ 32. $16 - 9 = \square$ 33. $15 - 6 = \square$

Write the other facts for each family. pages 22–23

34. $9 + 4 = 13$ 35. $6 + 8 = 14$ 36. $9 - 4 = 5$ 37. $3 + 2 = 5$

Solve. pages 12–13, 24–25

38. Third graders made puppets. How many animal puppets did they make in all?

39. Gilbert brought 11 books to share. Kelly brought 7. How many more books did Gilbert bring?

Find each sum.

1. $4 + 3$
2. $7 + 8$
3. $6 + 2$
4. $2 + 7$
5. $5 + 1$
6. $9 + 5$

7. $2 + 9 = \square$
   $9 + 2 = \square$

8. $9 + 8 = \square$
   $8 + 9 = \square$

9. $6 + 7 = \square$
   $7 + 6 = \square$

10. $6 + 1 + 2 = \square$
11. $4 + 3 + 5 = \square$
12. $7 + 0 + 3 = \square$

Find each missing addend.

13. $7 + \square = 16$
14. $9 + \square = 15$
15. $\square + 7 = 16$
16. $8 + \square = 17$
17. $\square + 6 = 12$

Find each difference.

18. $6 - 3$
19. $10 - 6$
20. $8 - 2$
21. $9 - 1$
22. $7 - 6$

23. $14 - 8$
24. $16 - 7$
25. $15 - 7$
26. $17 - 8$
27. $14 - 7$

28. $11 - 6 = \square$
29. $13 - 5 = \square$

Write the other facts for each family.

30. $7 + 5 = 12$
31. $10 - 3 = 7$

Solve.

32. Ray needs 10 boxes for his lima bean plants. He found 8. How many more boxes does hé need?

33. Max counted the flowers. How many flowers did Max count in all?

There were 12 books. Fred borrowed 3. Lia returned 2. Sue borrowed 5. Now how many books are there?

LOGICAL THINKING

1. Start with a set of alphabet blocks. There are 6 letters on each block. If you put one block on the table, how many letters are showing? How many letters are hidden?

There are 5 letters showing. There is 1 letter that is hidden. $5 + 1 = 6$

2. Now use two blocks. There are 12 letters altogether. Put the two blocks end to end on the table. How many letters are showing? How many letters are hidden?

3. Put three blocks end to end. How many letters are showing?

Put the third block on top of the D block above. Now how many letters are showing?

4. Place four blocks so the least number of letters show. Then place them so the greatest number of letters show.

USING PARENTHESES

Complete each exercise. Do the part in
( ) first. Then use your answers and the
letter code to finish the limerick below.

Example: $2 + (9 - 5) = S$
$2 + 4 = S$
$6 = S$

1. $8 + (8 - 0) = A$
2. $(6 + 6) - 9 = B$
3. $(18 - 9) - 9 = C$
4. $16 - (7 + 2) = D$
5. $(7 + 6) - 5 = E$
6. $(16 - 7) + 2 = H$
7. $(15 - 8) + 6 = I$
8. $(8 + 1) + 5 = K$
9. $6 - (9 - 4) = L$
10. $(13 - 5) - 4 = N$
11. $7 + (9 - 6) = O$
12. $5 + (1 + 6) = P$
13. $(17 - 9) + 1 = R$
14. $(9 + 5) - 8 = S$
15. $8 + (6 + 1) = T$
16. $9 + (8 - 0) = W$

There was an old man with a beard,

Who said, "It is just as I feared!

Two ___ ___ ___ ___ and a ___ ___ ___,
     10 17 1 6   11 8 4

Four ___ ___ ___ ___ ___ and a ___ ___ ___ ___,
    1 16 9 14 6   17 9 8 4

Have all built their nests in my beard!"

—Edward Lear

INTRODUCING THE CALCULATOR

A calculator is a tool. We can use a calculator to help us do mathematics problems.

When the calculator is on, we enter numbers and commands by pressing keys. The numbers and commands that we enter are **input.**

The calculator shows the answer, or **output,** in a display.

When we press 8 + 3 = , we see **11** in the display.

```
              11
```

When we press 1 3 − 7 = , we see **6** in the display.

```
               6
```

Tell what the output will be.

1. 5 + 3 =
2. 4 + 7 =
3. 11 − 4 =
4. 6 + 3 + 2 =
5. 13 − 4 =
6. 12 − 9 =

WITH A CALCULATOR

1. Try **1–6** with a calculator.

2. Compare each output with your answer.

3. Were your answers correct?

★ 4. On Your Own: Try adding and subtracting greater numbers.

INTRODUCING THE COMPUTER

We can use a computer to
help us solve many different
kinds of problems.

We give instructions, or **input,** to a
computer by using a keyboard.
The keys look like keys on a
typewriter.

Monitor →

Screen

The computer shows the answer, or
output, on a screen. It looks like
the screen of a television set.

Keyboard →

To do the addition 6 + 8,
we type PRINT 6 + 8.

`PRINT 6 + 8`

When we press ⎡RETURN⎤ or ⎡ENTER⎤,
the computer computes and prints
the answer 14.

`14`

When we type PRINT 17 − 8,
the computer output is 9.

`PRINT 17 - 8`
`9`

Tell what the output will be.

1. `PRINT 9 + 6`   2. `PRINT 3 + 7`   3. `PRINT 18 - 9`

4. `PRINT 12 - 7`   5. `PRINT 4 + 2 + 9`   6. `PRINT 3 + 5 + 6`

AT THE COMPUTER

1. Try **1–6** on a computer.

2. Compare each output with your answer.

3. Were your answers correct?

★4. On Your Own: Try adding and subtracting greater numbers.
Try adding more than three numbers.

Choose the correct answer. Write A, B, C or D.

1. 7
    $+1$

    A 7   C 8

    B 9   D not given

2. $9 + \square = 11$

    A 3   C 1

    B 2   D not given

3. $4 + \square = 13$

    A 6   C 8

    B 7   D not given

4. $6 + 3 + 1 = \square$

    A 9   C 8

    B 10   D not given

5. $10 - 4 = \square$

    A 6   C 8

    B 7   D not given

6. 14
    $- \ 5$

    A 8   C 9

    B 7   D not given

7. 17
    $- \ 9$

    A 8   C 4

    B 9   D not given

8. What is another fact in the family? $14 - 8 = 6$

    A $6 + 2 = 8$ C $8 + 6 = 14$

    B $8 - 6 = 2$ D not given

9. What is another fact in the family? $9 + 6 = 15$

    A $9 - 6 = 3$ C $6 + 3 = 9$

    B $15 - 9 = 6$ D not given

Use the picture for 10 and 11.

10. How many puppies are there?

    A 3   C 5

    B 4   D not given

11. How many more kittens are there than puppies?

    A 1   C 3

    B 2   D not given

Theme: Fairs and Shows

Tens and Ones

The Navajo Nation Fair is next month. Joe Cly will sell bracelets that he makes. He uses 10 beads to make each bracelet.

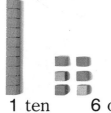

10 ones = 1 ten

We use the digits 0, 1, 2, 3, 4, 5, 6, 7, 8, and 9 to write numbers.

1 ten   6 ones

tens	ones
1	6

10 + 6 = 16

- number 16
- word name sixteen

4 tens   3 ones

tens	ones
4	3

40 + 3 = 43

- number 43
- word name forty-three

CLASSWORK
Complete.

1.

_____ tens _____ ones

2.
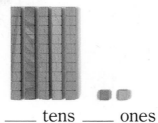
_____ tens _____ ones

3.
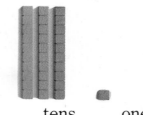
_____ tens _____ one

Write the number. Then read it.

4. 3 tens 8 ones
7. 20 + 2
10. ninety-six

5. 9 tens 2 ones
8. 80 + 9
11. seventy-one

6. 5 tens 4 ones
9. 60 + 7
12. forty-eight

34

Complete.

1.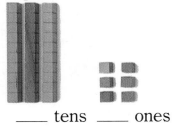
____ tens ____ ones

2.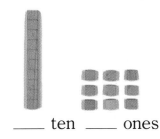
____ ten ____ ones

3.
____ tens ____ ones

Write the number.

4. 2 tens 7 ones

5. 1 ten 2 ones

6. 5 tens 0 ones

7. 8 tens 8 ones

8. 9 tens 4 ones

9. 3 tens 3 ones

10. 4 tens 6 ones

11. 6 tens 1 one

12. 7 tens 5 ones

13. 60 + 3

14. 40 + 0

15. 80 + 5

16. 50 + 1

17. 90 + 8

18. 30 + 4

19. eighty-three

20. forty-six

21. eighteen

22. ninety-nine

23. thirteen

24. fifty-seven

25. sixty-four

26. thirty-eight

27. twenty

★ 28. 4 tens more than 46

★ 29. 6 ones more than 32

★ 30. 3 tens more than 61

APPLICATION

31. Which road numbers have 3 in ones place?

32. Which road numbers have 6 in tens place?

★ 33. Which road numbers have no ones?

★ 34. Which road numbers have more than 6 tens?

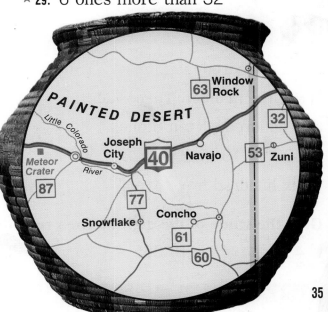

Hundreds

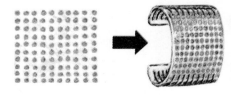

Joe Cly helped his grandfather make a bracelet of 100 beads.

10 tens   =   1 hundred

This drawing shows a greater number.

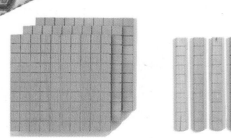

3 hundreds   4 tens   7 ones

hundreds	tens	ones
3	4	7

300   +   40   +   7 = 347

The value of the digit 3 is 300.
The value of the digit 4 is 40.
The value of the digit 7 is   7.

number   347
- word name   three hundred forty-seven

CLASSWORK

Complete.

1.

____ hundred ____ tens ____ ones

2.

____ hundreds ____ tens ____ ones

Write the number. Then read it.

3. 5 hundreds 1 ten 6 ones

4. 8 hundreds 9 tens 0 ones

5. 300 + 10 + 2

6. 700 + 30 + 9

7. six hundred fifty-seven

8. four hundred eleven

Give the value of the digit 3. Then read the number.

9. 432   10. 365   11. 39   12. 318   13. 73

Complete.

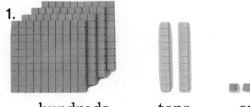

1. ___ hundreds ___ tens ___ ones

2. ___ hundreds ___ tens ___ ones

Write the number.

3. 7 hundreds 4 tens 5 ones

4. 6 hundreds 0 tens 2 ones

5. 5 hundreds 9 tens 3 ones

6. 9 hundreds 1 ten 0 ones

7. 400 + 30 + 8

8. 100 + 70 + 5

9. 600 + 90 + 9

10. 700 + 80 + 2

11. nine hundred twenty-six

12. one hundred forty-four

13. six hundred ninety

14. seven hundred seven

Give the value of the digit 4.

15. 84

16. 704

17. 451

18. 47

19. 949

Write the number.

★20. 1 ten more than 360

★21. 2 tens more than 245

APPLICATION

22. Find how many bracelets were sold at the fair. Place the digits below in the correct order.

tens	ones	hundreds
6	4	2

★24. List all possible 3-digit numbers that can be named using 1, 7, and 5.

★23. Write a number. Put 0 in tens place, 4 in ones place, and 7 in hundreds place. What is the number?

LOGICAL THINKING

1. What is the greatest 3-digit number that can be named?

2. What is the least 3-digit number that can be named?

37

Counting

The children are waiting their turn for Moon Bounce. Each child has a number.

A number line shows the order of numbers.

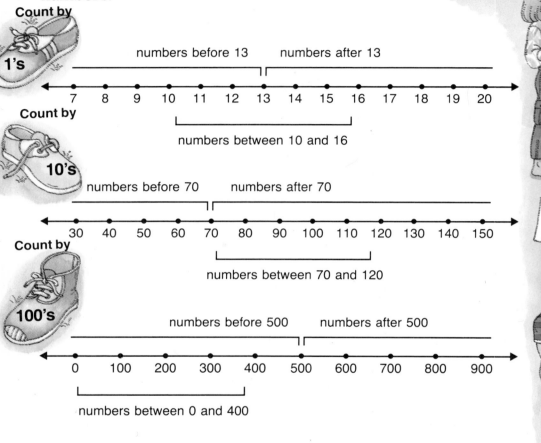

Count by 1's

numbers before 13 | numbers after 13

7 8 9 10 11 12 13 14 15 16 17 18 19 20

numbers between 10 and 16

Count by 10's

numbers before 70 | numbers after 70

30 40 50 60 70 80 90 100 110 120 130 140 150

numbers between 70 and 120

Count by 100's

numbers before 500 | numbers after 500

0 100 200 300 400 500 600 700 800 900

numbers between 0 and 400

CLASSWORK
Write the missing numbers.

1. 54, 55, _____, _____, _____

2. _____, 80, 90, _____, _____

3. _____, _____, _____, 39, 40

4. _____, _____, 600, 700, _____

5. 67, _____, _____, 97, _____

6. 290, _____, 490, _____, 690

7. 0, _____, _____, _____, 400

8. _____, 344, _____, 364, _____

PRACTICE

Write the missing numbers.

1. _____, 19, 20, _____, _____   2. _____, 36, _____, _____, 66

3. 500, 600, _____, _____, _____   4. _____, _____, 91, 92, _____

5. 845, _____, _____, 875, 885   6. _____ 512, _____, 712, _____

7. 910, _____, _____, _____, 950   8. 347, _____, 367, _____, _____

Give the numbers that come between.

9. 21 and 25   10. 73 and 76   11. 58 and 62

12. 378 and 382   13. 634 and 638   14. 510 and 514

15. 829 and 833   16. 907 and 910   17. 797 and 801

Give the number that comes just before and the number that comes just after.

18. 45   19. 60   20. 82   21. 9   22. 14

23. 226   24. 132   25. 540   26. 317   27. 751

28. 483   29. 978   30. 695   31. 800   32. 989

Write the missing numbers.

★ 33. _____, 847, _____, 647, _____   ★ 34. 313, _____, _____, _____, 273

APPLICATION

CALCULATOR

1. Start with 11. Add 10. Keep adding 10 to complete this pattern.

   11, 21, _____, _____, _____

2. Start with 137. Add 100. Keep adding 100 to complete this pattern.

   137, _____, _____, _____, _____

Comparing and Ordering Numbers

Russ counted 21 Model T's and 18 Model A's. Did he count more Model T's or Model A's?

Compare the numbers.

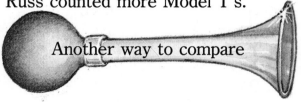

21 is greater than 18

    21 > 18

Russ counted more Model T's.

>	means	is greater than
<	means	is less than

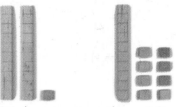

Another way to compare

Compare **637** and **635**.

Begin at the left and compare the digits in each place.

hundreds	tens	ones
6	3	7
6	3	5

    ↑   ↑

  same   same 7 > 5

    so **637 > 635**

We can write these numbers in order from least to greatest. Compare them two at a time.

527   466   473   541

       466 < 473

       473 < 527

       527 < 541

The numbers are in order from least to greatest.

466 < 473 < 527 < 541

CLASSWORK

Compare. Use > or < for ●.

1. 31 ● 13   **2.** 89 ● 91   **3.** 151 ● 115   **4.** 624 ● 397

Write the numbers in order from least to greatest.

5. 57, 81, 59, 63   **6.** 692, 618, 803, 740   **7.** 920, 720, 870, 640

Antique Car Show

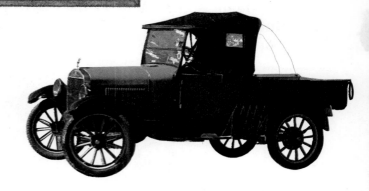

Compare. Use > or < for ●.

1. 3 ● 7
2. 11 ● 9
3. 36 ● 28
4. 25 ● 52

5. 45 ● 42
6. 97 ● 79
7. 68 ● 86
8. 10 ● 100

9. 361 ● 321
10. 275 ● 263
11. 149 ● 139
12. 520 ● 552

13. 789 ● 840
14. 644 ● 464
15. 943 ● 934
16. 613 ● 316

Write the numbers in order from least to greatest.

17. 24, 17, 29, 15
18. 81, 88, 83, 75
19. 147, 139, 116, 125

20. 346, 539, 378, 548
21. 781, 776, 747, 906
22. 814, 896, 823, 841

Write the numbers in order from greatest to least.

23. 4, 19, 32, 27
24. 56, 62, 74, 51
25. 190, 175, 282, 209

26. 307, 298, 317, 321
27. 715, 701, 726, 761
28. 602, 599, 598, 612

★29. 647, 98, 295, 802
★30. 813, 929, 770, 81
★31. 930, 903, 39, 93

APPLICATION

32. The first automobile trip across the United States took 63 days. Last week the Kritz family drove across the United States in 7 days. Which trip took the greater number of days?

★33. There were 40 carmakers in the first automobile show in 1900. There were 212 in the show in 1905. Compare the number of carmakers. (Use > and then <.)

Dollars, Dimes, and Pennies

Tanya bought some shells at the seashore festival. This is the amount of money she gave the salesperson.

2 dollars   5 dimes   3 pennies

write **$2.53**

● word name   two dollars and fifty-three cents

$.79

write $.79 or 79¢

● word name   seventy-nine cents

 dollar
100¢ or $1.00

dime
10¢ or $.10

penny
1¢ or $.01

We use the dollar sign ($) and decimal point (.) to write amounts of money.

CLASSWORK

Read each amount.

1. $3.67   2. 50¢   3. $.72   4. $4.08   5. 19¢

Write each amount. Use a dollar sign and decimal point.

6. six dollars and five cents   7. 9 dollars, 4 dimes, 1 penny

8.

9.

Write each amount. Use a dollar sign and decimal point.

1. two dollars and ten cents

2. twenty-seven cents

3. 6 dollars 3 dimes

4. 1 dollar 3 pennies

5. 5 dollars

6. 4 dimes 1 penny

7.

8.

Find the output that equals the input.

	Input	Output
9.	1 dollar	☐ dimes
10.	1 dollar	☐ pennies

	Input	Output
11.	2 dollars	☐ dimes
12.	2 dollars	☐ pennies

Write *yes* or *no*.

13. Is there enough money for the shell?

★ 14. Is there enough money for two sand dollars?

$3.50

$1.50

MENTAL ARITHMETIC

Take one dollar and one dime from each amount.

What is the new amount?

1. $2.86

2. $6.41

3. $8.76

4. $9.57

5. $1.10

6. $9.12

Problem Solving

WHICH OPERATION?

THINK
PLAN
SOLVE
LOOK
BACK

You make a plan to solve a problem. To plan, you must know which operation to use.

There were 6 wooden bottles on a table. John threw the ball and knocked some down. There were 2 bottles left. How many did John knock down?

THINK   **What is the question?**

How many bottles did John knock down?

What are the facts?

There were 6 bottles to start.
There were 2 bottles left.

PLAN   **How can you find the answer?**

Subtract the number of bottles left from the number of bottles started with.

$$6 - 2 = \square$$

SOLVE   **Carry out the plan. Do the work and find the answer.**

$$\begin{array}{r} 6 \\ -2 \\ \hline 4 \end{array}$$ John knocked down 4 bottles.

LOOK BACK   **Did you answer the question? Is your arithmetic correct? Does your answer make sense?**

Add the number of bottles knocked down to the number left on the table. The answer should be the number started with.

$$\begin{array}{r} 4 \\ +2 \\ \hline 6 \end{array}$$ There were 6 bottles to start. Your answer makes sense.

Mary won 5 prizes.
Sally won 8 prizes.

**Read the problem. Tell
whether you would add
or subtract. Then solve
the problem.**

1. How many prizes did Mary and
Sally win in all?

2. How many more prizes did Sally
win than Mary?

3. If Mary won 2 more prizes, how
many prizes would she have in
all?

4. There are 16 clowns at the fair.
Of these, 9 are women. The rest
are men. How many are men?

5. There are 13 cars on the Ferris
wheel. The roller coaster has 6.
How many more cars are on the
Ferris wheel?

6. Paul rode the roller coaster 4
times. Terry rode it 8 times.
How many times did Paul and
Terry ride the roller coaster?

■, ▲, ● take the place of numbers in each
problem below. You can't solve the problems. Just
decide whether to add or subtract.

There are ■ cows, ▲ horses, and ● pigs in
the 4-H show.

7. How many more cows than
horses are there?

8. How many horses and pigs are
there in all?

9. How many animals are there in
all?

★10. Write a number sentence to
show the total number of cows
and pigs.

CREATE YOUR OWN PROBLEM

The Ferris wheel has gone around 4 times.
It will go around 3 more times
before the ride is over. Make up
a problem using addition.

Rounding to the Nearest Ten

About 70 projects can be displayed in Franklin Hall. Students have 68 projects to display.

FRANKLIN SCIENCE FAIR

We round a number to tell *about* how many.

Round 68 to the nearest ten.

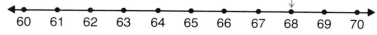

68 is between 60 and 70.
68 is closer to 70.
68 rounded to the nearest ten is 70.

Round 42 to the nearest ten.

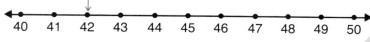

42 is between 40 and 50.
42 is closer to 40.
42 rounded to the nearest ten is 40.

Round 35 to the nearest ten.

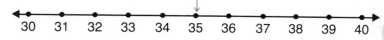

35 is halfway between 30 and 40.
When a number is halfway, round it to the greater number.
35 rounded to the nearest ten is 40.

CLASSWORK

Round to the nearest ten.

1. 21
2. 26
3. 29
4. 25
5. 22
6. 24
7. 33
8. 66
9. 28
10. 82
11. 12
12. 91

Round to the nearest ten.

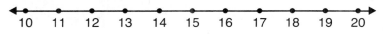

```
10  11  12  13  14  15  16  17  18  19  20
```

1. 14   2. 18   3. 11   4. 19   5. 15   6. 13

```
50  51  52  53  54  55  56  57  58  59  60
```

7. 55   8. 52   9. 53   10. 58   11. 56   12. 59

13. 94   14. 87   15. 62   16. 78   17. 53   18. 77

19. 16   20. 88   21. 54   22. 37   23. 64   24. 89

25. 43   26. 31   27. 86   ★28. 135   ★29. 122   ★30. 147

Give the numbers on the frog's banner that round to 70.

★31.

67   78
64   74
75
72   65

APPLICATION

25 PRIZES to be Awarded

32. Rounded to the nearest ten, how many prizes will be awarded at the science fair?

★33. A scientist gave a talk about space travel. About 90 students attended. What is the least number and the greatest number that could have attended?

Rounding to the Nearest Hundred

About how many people in each group attended the Old World Festival?

Men 317
Women 350
Children 383

Round each number to the nearest hundred.

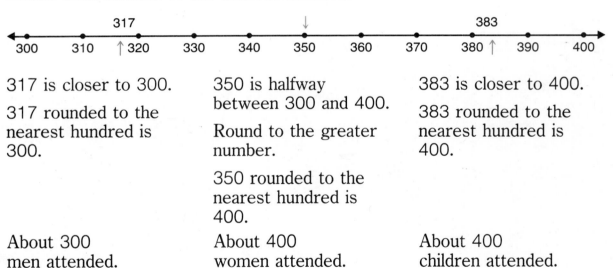

317 is closer to 300.

317 rounded to the nearest hundred is 300.

About 300 men attended.

350 is halfway between 300 and 400.

Round to the greater number.

350 rounded to the nearest hundred is 400.

About 400 women attended.

383 is closer to 400.

383 rounded to the nearest hundred is 400.

About 400 children attended.

CLASSWORK

Round to the nearest hundred.

```
←——•——————•——————•——————•——————•——————•——————•——————•——————•——————•——————•——→
  600    610    620    630    640    650    660    670    680    690    700
```

1. 610   2. 650   3. 623   4. 672   5. 695

6. 432   7. 278   8. 550   9. 749   10. 910

48

Round to the nearest hundred.

```
  200   210   220   230   240   250   260   270   280   290   300
```

1. 225   2. 240   3. 281   4. 250   5. 266   6. 248

7. 175   8. 335   9. 192   10. 353   11. 314   12. 197

13. 736   14. 145   15. 150   16. 885   17. 370   18. 419

19. 243   20. 456   21. 213   22. 585   23. 747   24. 564

25. 938   26. 245   27. 761   28. 914   29. 520   30. 889

Give the numbers that round to 500.

★31.

472 563 450 419 549

APPLICATION

32. Use the digits 7, 2, and 5. Give a number that rounds to 500.

★33. Use the digits 7, 2, and 5. Give a number that rounds to 260.

Tell whether you would add or subtract. Then solve.

34. Judges gave 8 first prizes and 6 second prizes. How many prizes did the judges give?

35. How many more first prizes than second prizes did the judges give?

49

Thousands

Children let 2,134 balloons go at the start of the Indiana State Fair.

10 hundreds = 1 thousand

2 thousands   1 hundred   3 tens   4 ones

thousands	hundreds	tens	ones
2,	1	3	4

The value of the digit 2 is 2,000.
The value of the digit 1 is 100.
The value of the digit 3 is   30.
The value of the digit 4 is   4.

2,000 + 100 + 30 + 4 = 2,134

We place a comma between the thousands and hundreds to make the number easier to read.

number   2,134
● word name   two thousand, one hundred thirty-four

CLASSWORK

Write the number. Then read it.

1. 4 thousands 6 hundreds 7 tens 8 ones

2. 2,000 + 800 + 20 + 5   3. 7,000 + 100 + 60 + 1

4. five thousand, nine hundred eighty-four

Give the value of the digit 5. Then read the number.

5. 2,504   6. 5,183   7. 459   8. 3,025

PRACTICE

Write the number.

1. 3 thousands 6 hundreds 4 tens 2 ones

2. 5 thousands 1 hundred 5 tens 0 ones

3. 1,000 + 400 + 60 + 1

4. 4,000 + 70 + 4

5. eight thousand, one hundred fifteen

6. seven thousand, six hundred ninety-nine

Give the value of the digit 7.

7. 1,070   8. 4,007   9. 7,528   10. 739

Write the missing numbers.

11. 1,215   1,216   _____   1,218   _____

12. 8,000   8,100   _____   _____   8,400

★ 13. _____   _____   1,800   1,810   _____

APPLICATION

14. How many children attended the fair in one day? Place the balloons in correct order to find out.

    tens 5   thousands 1   ones 7   hundreds 2

Use the digits below.

★ 15. Make the greatest 4-digit number.

★ 16. Make the least 4-digit number.

    5   7   3   9

Mixed Practice

1. $\begin{array}{r} 13 \\ -\ 7 \\ \hline \end{array}$ 2. $\begin{array}{r} 1 \\ +9 \\ \hline \end{array}$

3. $\begin{array}{r} 7 \\ +9 \\ \hline \end{array}$ 4. $\begin{array}{r} 14 \\ -\ 8 \\ \hline \end{array}$

5. $\begin{array}{r} \square \\ -5 \\ \hline 9 \end{array}$ 6. $\begin{array}{r} 8 \\ +7 \\ \hline \end{array}$

7. $\begin{array}{r} \square \\ -5 \\ \hline 0 \end{array}$ 8. $\begin{array}{r} 11 \\ -\ 9 \\ \hline \end{array}$

9. $\begin{array}{r} 4 \\ +8 \\ \hline \end{array}$ 10. $\begin{array}{r} 0 \\ +\square \\ \hline 7 \end{array}$

11. $\begin{array}{r} 2 \\ 7 \\ +4 \\ \hline \end{array}$ 12. $\begin{array}{r} 8 \\ 0 \\ +3 \\ \hline \end{array}$

13. $7 + 5 = \square$

14. $8 - \square = 0$

15. $\square - 9 = 4$

16. $9 + \square = 17$

17. $4 + 5 = \square$

18. $6 + \square = 12$

19. $15 - 9 = \square$

20. $\square + 6 = 11$

21. $6 + 2 + 4 = \square$

22. $4 + 3 + 7 = \square$

Comparing and Ordering Thousands

On Friday, 986 people rode the racing cars at the world's fair. On Saturday, 3,457 people rode the cars. Compare the number of riders on the two days.

thousands	hundreds	tens	ones
	9	8	6
3,	4	5	7

The number with more digits is greater.

$$3,457 > 986$$
$$986 < 3,457$$

The number of riders was greater on Saturday than on Friday.

When two numbers have the same number of places, begin at the left and compare the digits in each place.

Compare **6,835** and **7,342**.

thousands	hundreds	tens	ones
6,	8	3	5
7,	3	4	2

6 < 7

so **6,835 < 7,342**

Compare **7,151** and **7,129**.

thousands	hundreds	tens	ones
7,	1	5	1
7,	1	2	9

same   same   5 > 2

so **7,151 > 7,129**

We can write these numbers in order from least to greatest.

8,799   8,910   8,641

Compare them two at a time.

8,641 < 8,799
8,799 < 8,910

The numbers are in order from least to greatest.

8,641 < 8,799 < 8,910

CLASSWORK

Compare. Use > or < for ●.

1. 1,654 ● 2,368

2. 2,035 ● 948

3. 1,463 ● 1,470

Write the numbers in order from least to greatest.

4. 5,291   4,826   5,106

5. 3,452   3,680   3,397

Compare. Use > or < for ●.

1. 3,115 ● 2,515
2. 7,104 ● 6,835
3. 4,998 ● 5,100

4. 6,031 ● 2,879
5. 3,691 ● 9,613
6. 4,215 ● 4,517

7. 1,826 ● 827
8. 8,514 ● 8,539
9. 110 ● 1,010

Write the numbers in order from least to greatest.

10. 3,482   1,406   6,013
11. 2,117   3,217   5,117

12. 6,701   6,790   6,738
13. 2,753   1,773   1,753

Write the numbers in order from greatest to least.

14. 2,997   4,793   4,812
15. 9,352   9,519   9,261

★ 16. 5,010   587   5,001
★ 17. 4,850   4,085   485

APPLICATION

Make a time line like the one below.

18. Write the date of the London fair below the name of the city.

19. Write the date of the New Orleans fair below the name of the city.

★ 20. Write the dates and places of the other world's fairs.

WORLD'S FAIRS

Montreal 1967
London 1851
Paris 1889
New York 1939
New Orleans 1984

LONDON

NEW ORLEANS

Ten Thousands and Hundred Thousands

A record was set at the air show.
The winner flew his hot air balloon
at 23,415 feet.

thousands		ones		
tens	ones	hundreds	tens	ones
2	3,	4	1	5

- **number** 23,415
- **word name** twenty-three thousand, four hundred fifteen

The value of the digit 2 is 20,000.
The value of the digit 3 is 3,000.

thousands			ones		
h	t	o	h	t	o
9	1	7,	8	6	0

- **number** 917,860
- **word name** nine hundred seventeen thousand, eight hundred sixty

The value of the digit 9 is 900,000.
The value of the digit 1 is 10,000.
The value of the digit 7 is   7,000.

CLASSWORK

Write the number. Then read it.

1. forty-four thousand, three hundred fifty

2. seventy-two thousand, six hundred

3. five hundred sixty thousand, eight hundred nineteen

4. nine hundred twenty thousand

Give the value of the digit 8. Then read the number.

5. 584,067   6. 800,363   7. 79,821   8. 98,130

PRACTICE

Write the number.

1. eighty-five thousand, nine hundred thirty-one
2. fifty-two thousand, one hundred eighteen
3. twenty-seven thousand, two hundred
4. thirty thousand
5. six hundred forty-one thousand, nine hundred fifty-six
6. two hundred eleven thousand, eight hundred four
7. eight hundred thousand, five hundred twelve
8. seven hundred one thousand

Give the value of the digit 6.

9. 32,160   10. 506,852   11. 64,917   12. 673,034

Give the value of the digit 1.

13. 220,166   14. 387,241

15. 510,809   16. 179,000

Write the number.

★ 17. two ten thousands more than 51,977
★ 18. one hundred thousand more than 100,843
★ 19. two hundred thousand more than 40,713

APPLICATION

PATTERNS

Give the next number in the pattern.

1. 12,345   23,456   34,567   _____

2. 66,004   66,104   66,204   _____

3. 587,121   487,121   387,121   _____

Problem Solving

SKILLS AND STRATEGIES REVIEW

Leon drives a horse cart at the fair. The cart can hold 4 people and Leon. The ride downhill to the clown show takes 7 minutes. The ride back uphill takes 9 minutes.

RIDES

ADULTS $2.75
CHILDREN...$2.00
(UNDER 12)

Solve each problem.

1. Aretha is 10 years old. How much will the cart ride cost her?

2. Felipe is 15 years old. How much will the cart ride cost him?

3. Laura, Maggie, Jeff, and Stan want to take the ride. Can they all go together?

4. Mr. and Mrs. Sarro and their 3 children want to take the ride. Can they all go together?

5. Ken, Paula, and Ron went on the ride together. How many minutes did it take them to get to the clown show?

6. After the show Ken, Paula, and Ron rode back uphill. How many minutes was the ride, round trip?

Leon took 3 adults and 5 children to the first clown show. He took 2 adults and 4 children to the second clown show.

Solve each problem.

7. How many adults in all did Leon take to the clown shows?

8. How many children in all did Leon take to both clown shows?

★ 9. How many people in all did Leon take?

★ 10. How many more children than adults did Leon take?

Read and solve each problem.

11. Little Clown gave away 389 buttons. Big Clown gave away 510 buttons. Who gave away more buttons?

12. There were 1,000 tickets on sale. By 1:00 P.M., 925 people had bought tickets. Were all the tickets sold by 1:00 P.M.?

13. Scores are rounded to the nearest hundred at one game booth. Jack scored 461 points. What was his score rounded to?

14. Scores higher than 350 points win prizes at another game booth. Lydia scored 407 points. Did she win a prize?

15. Children at the fair get blue buttons. Adults get red buttons. There were 500 people wearing blue buttons. There were 400 people wearing red buttons. Were there more children or more adults at the fair?

16. There were 1,726 people at the fair on Saturday. There were 2,671 people at the fair on Sunday. Were there more people at the fair on Saturday or on Sunday?

★ 17. Homemade bread costs $2.65. Maria has 2 dollars and 2 dimes. Can she buy the bread?

★ 18. The printer only prints orders in groups of hundreds. The fair needs 852 posters. How many posters should be ordered?

Tell whether you would add or subtract in each problem.

19. The prize hog weighed 1,861 pounds. The runner-up hog weighed 1,681 pounds. How much more did the prize hog weigh?

20. There were 4 blue ribbons, 3 yellow ribbons, and 2 red ribbons awarded. How many ribbons were awarded?

CHAPTER REVIEW

Write the number. pages 34–37, 50–51

1. 8 tens 9 ones
2. 5 hundreds 0 tens 3 ones
3. 700 + 60 + 8
4. 9,000 + 500 + 20 + 6

Write the value of the digit 9. pages 36–37, 50–51, 54–55

5. 197,202
6. 4,966
7. 9,216
8. 980,317

Write the missing numbers. pages 50–51

9. 2,870   2,880   2,890   2,900
10. 5,100   5,200   5,300   5,400

Compare. Use > or < for ●. pages 40–41, 52–53

11. 780 ● 817
12. 8,500 ● 8,150
13. 3,208 ● 3,214

Write the numbers in order from least to greatest. pages 40–41, 52–53

14. 764   761   660   702
15. 3,295   3,287   3,292   3,411

Write each amount. Use a dollar sign and decimal point. pages 42–43

16. seven dollars and five cents
17. fifty-nine cents
18. 2 dollars 4 dimes 1 penny
19. 3 dimes 6 pennies

Round to the nearest ten. pages 46–47

20. 22
21. 75
22. 89
23. 93
24. 41
25. 57

Round to the nearest hundred. pages 48–49

26. 167
27. 580
28. 426
29. 317
30. 252

Tell whether you would add or subtract. Then solve. pages 44–45, 56–57

31. On Monday, 6 baskets were sold. On Tuesday, 9 baskets were sold. How many baskets were sold on both days?

32. How many more baskets were sold on Tuesday than on Monday?

Write the number.

1. 2,000 + 800 + 10 + 6

2. ten thousand, two hundred

Write the value of the digit 4.

3. 462,008

4. 54,979

5. 6,455

6. 894

Write the missing numbers.

7. 1,340 1,440 _____ _____

8. 4,500 _____ 4,520 _____

Compare. Use > or < for ●.

9. 7,500 ● 7,000

10. 920 ● 2,009

11. 6,480 ● 6,814

Write the numbers in order from least to greatest.

12. 475   510   347   380

13. 1,920   1,890   2,900   1,931

Write each amount. Use a dollar sign and decimal point.

14. six dollars and ten cents

15. thirty-five cents

Round to the nearest ten.

16. 58

17. 63

18. 17

19. 46

Round to the nearest hundred.

20. 630

21. 271

22. 839

23. 756

Tell whether you would add or subtract. Then solve.

24. Mr. Gomez bought 8 pennants. Mrs. Gomez bought 9. How many fewer pennants did Mr. Gomez buy than Mrs. Gomez?

25. How many pennants in all did Mr. and Mrs. Gomez buy?

Trisha had $8.45. She spent 1 dollar. Her brother gave her 2 dimes. How much money does Trisha have now?

The Dig-In-and-Build-a-Number Game

You will need:
- a set of large cards numbered 0 through 9
- a set of small matching cards for each player
- a paper bag
- paper and pencils

Each player makes a table like this one.

hundred thousands	ten thousands	thousands	hundreds	tens	ones

1. The large cards are put into the bag. One player is chosen to be the digger.

2. The digger digs into the bag and pulls out a number. The players put their matching number in any place on their table.

3. The digger pulls another number from the bag. The players put their matching number in another place on their table.

4. The players keep playing until the digger has pulled six numbers. The players will have built a six-digit number.

The player who has built the greatest number is the winner.

The game can be played another way. The player who can build the least number is the winner.

ROMAN NUMERALS

Many years ago the Romans used symbols for numbers that were different from our symbols. We call their symbols *Roman numerals*.

The numbers 1 to 39 can be written with only these symbols:

I V X

Find the Roman numeral for each.

1. 4   2. 7   3. 18

4. 15   5. 19   6. 20

Find the number for each.

7. III   8. VI   9. XII

10. XVI   11. XIV   12. XVII

Write the Roman numerals from 21 to 39. Use the chart to help you.

Number	Roman Numeral	What it means
1	I	1
2	II	1 + 1
3	III	1 + 1 + 1
4	IV	5 − 1
5	V	5
6	VI	5 + 1
7	VII	5 + 2
8	VIII	5 + 3
9	IX	10 − 1
10	X	10
11	XI	10 + 1
12	XII	10 + 2
13	XIII	10 + 3
14	XIV	10 + 4
15	XV	10 + 5
16	XVI	10 + 6
17	XVII	10 + 7
18	XVIII	10 + 8
19	XIX	10 + 9
20	XX	10 + 10

Choose the correct answer. Write A, B, C or D.

1. $9 + 8 = \square$

   A 17   C 16

   B 18   D not given

2. $6 + \square = 15$

   A 4   C 7

   B 9   D not given

3. $2 + 4 + 3 = \square$

   A 10   C 9

   B 8   D not given

4.
$$\begin{array}{r} 12 \\ -\ 3 \\ \hline \end{array}$$

   A 9   C 5

   B 8   D not given

5. Choose the number for 2 hundreds 3 tens 6 ones.

   A 326   C 236

   B 632   D not given

6. Compare. 537 ● 573

   A >   C =

   B <   D not given

7. What is the value?

   A $1.53   C $1.23

   B $1.43   D not given

Use the picture to solve **8** and **9**.

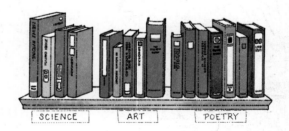

SCIENCE   ART   POETRY

8. How many science books and poetry books are there?

   A 10   C 12

   B 11   D not given

9. How many more art books are there than science books?

   A 1   C 2

   B 3   D not given

Theme: Forests

Adding Two-Digit Numbers

A chipmunk stored 25 acorns for the winter. It collected 32 more. How many acorns did the chipmunk store in all?

We add to find how many in all.

Step 1
Add ones.

tens	ones
2	5
+3	2
	7

Step 2
Add tens.

tens	ones
2	5
+3	2
5	7

The chipmunk stored 57 acorns in all.

Find 21 + 8.

Line up ones and tens.	Add ones.	Add tens.
21	21	21
+ 8	+ 8	+ 8
	9	29

CLASSWORK

Add.

1. 43
   +20

2. 22
   +67

3. 92
   + 4

4.   3
   +45

5. 17
   +60

6. 35
   +21

7. 24 + 13 = ☐

8. 34 + 5 = ☐

9. 6 + 40 = ☐

10. 58 + 20 = ☐

11. 71 + 17 = ☐

12. 49 + 50 = ☐

64

Add.

1.	tens	ones
	2	3
+3	1	

2.	tens	ones
	6	2
+3	5	

3.	tens	ones
	1	6
+2	0	

4.	tens	ones
	2	5
+1	4	

5. 70
   +10

6. 16
   +12

7. 41
   +37

8. 70
   +18

9. 71
   + 4

10. 16
    +51

11. 43
    +40

12. 7
    +32

13. 35
    +60

14. 32
    +40

15. 2
    +62

16. 9
    +50

17. 48 + 11 = □

18. 1 + 13 = □

19. 9 + 30 = □

Choose the number sentence that answers the question.

20. Two chipmunks each stored 43 acorns. How many did they store in all?

a. 2 + 43 = 45
b. 43 + 2 = 45
c. 43 + 43 = 86
d. 43 − 2 = 41

21. One chipmunk found 31 acorns. Another found 47 acorns. How many did they find in all?

a. 1 + 31 + 47 = 79
b. 31 + 47 = 78
c. 47 − 31 = 16
d. 47 + 2 = 49

Add across and down.

★22.

32	13	
21	11	

★23.

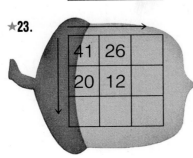

41	26	
20	12	

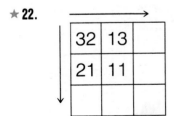

APPLICATION

========== MENTAL ARITHMETIC ==========

Add 2-digit numbers in your head.

70 + 20 = □

Think 7 tens + 2 tens = 9 tens.
   So   70 + 20 = 90.

Try these.

1. 30 + 40 = □
2. 40 + 50 = □
3. 10 + 20 = □
4. 10 + 50 = □
5. 30 + 20 = □
6. 60 + 30 = □

Regrouping Ones

Giant dinosaurs roamed the forests of long ago. This dinosaur is called a brontosaurus.

38 feet   **29 feet**

We add to find how long this dinosaur was.

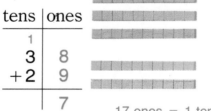

Step 1 Add ones. Regroup.		Step 2 Add tens.	

tens | ones
1
3 | 8
+2 | 9
  | 7

17 ones = 1 ten 7 ones

tens | ones
1
3 | 8
+2 | 9
6 | 7

5 tens + 1 ten = 6 tens

The dinosaur was 67 feet long.

More Examples

a.
```
  1
  47
+28
  75
```

b.
```
  1
  85
+ 7
  92
```

c.
```
  1
  67
+19
  86
```

CLASSWORK

Add.

1.
```
  24
+18
```

2.
```
  36
+27
```

3.
```
  65
+15
```

4.
```
  24
+27
```

5.
```
  15
+ 9
```

6.
```
   8
+37
```

7. 39 + 16 = ☐

8. 26 + 5 = ☐

9. 6 + 54 = ☐

Add.

1. tens	ones
1	8
+1	6

2. tens	ones
4	7
+1	7

3. tens	ones
3	1
+3	9

4. tens	ones
	7
+2	3

5. 12
+49

6. 16
+19

7. 28
+59

8. 21
+48

9. 29
+ 9

10. 53
+36

11. 46
+36

12. 5
+86

13. 79
+13

14. 56
+ 8

15. 15
+68

16. 51
+23

17. 78
+ 7

18. 40
+24

19. 9
+64

20. 35
+44

21. 8
+35

22. 47
+ 8

23. 38 + 13 = □

24. 3 + 49 = □

25. 14 + 74 = □

26. 18 + 6 = □

27. 57 + 16 = □

28. 7 + 64 = □

Compare. Write >, <, or = for ●.

29. 16 + 12 ● 8 + 20

30. 25 + 3 ● 11 + 16

★31. 9 + 51 ● 26 + 14

★32. 57 + 38 ● 29 + 68

APPLICATION

Scientists used the bones they found to build a dinosaur skeleton.

Tell whether you would add or subtract. Then solve.

	West Dig	East Dig
September	25 bones	17 bones
October	38 bones	6 bones
November	20 bones	19 bones

33. How many bones were found in September?

34. How many bones were found in all in October?

35. In September, 17 bones were found in the East Dig. The scientists used 9 of them. How many bones were left?

★36. The scientists used all the bones from the West Dig and 8 bones from the East Dig. How many were used altogether?

Regrouping Tens

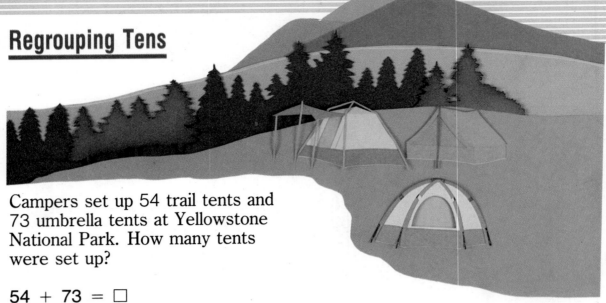

Campers set up 54 trail tents and 73 umbrella tents at Yellowstone National Park. How many tents were set up?

54 + 73 = ☐

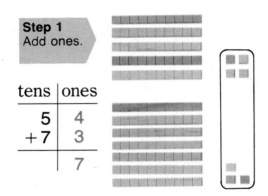

Step 1
Add ones.

tens	ones
5	4
+7	3
	7

Step 2
Add tens.
Regroup.

hundreds	tens	ones
	5	4
+	7	3
1	2	7

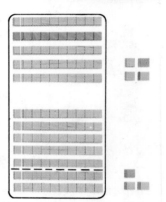

5 tens + 7 tens = 12 tens
12 tens = 1 hundred 2 tens

Check by adding up.

```
  54  ↑    The sum is the same.
 +73  |    127 = 127
 127  |    The addition is correct.
```

There were 127 tents set up.

CLASSWORK

Add. Check by adding up.

1. 82
    +62

2. 61
    +58

3. 95
    +34

4. 60
    +78

5. 92
    +63

6. 13
    +95

7. 84 + 75 = ☐

8. 65 + 81 = ☐

9. 91 + 82 = ☐

10. 42 + 97 = ☐

11. 88 + 70 = ☐

12. 76 + 87 = ☐

PRACTICE

Add. Check by adding up.

1.
h	t	o
	5	2
+	5	1

2.
h	t	o
	4	1
+	6	3

3.
h	t	o
	7	2
+	7	5

4.
h	t	o
	5	5
+	9	3

5. 94
 +22

6. 32
 +76

7. 97
 +71

8. 96
 +42

9. 78
 +21

10. 60
 +52

11. 85
 +90

12. 74
 +45

13. 43
 +86

14. 64
 +61

15. 24
 +68

16. 56
 +29

17. 90 + 16 = ☐

18. 83 + 14 = ☐

19. 84 + 54 = ☐

20. 72 + 80 = ☐

21. 7 + 59 = ☐

22. 31 + 85 = ☐

Follow each rule to complete.

Rule: Add 25.

	Input	Output
23.	20	
24.	54	
25.	63	
26.	81	

Rule: Add 51.

	Input	Output
27.	8	
28.	62	
29.	75	
30.	47	

Rule: Add 74.

	Input	Output
31.	6	
32.	17	
33.	34	
34.	76	

Write each sum in words.

★ 35. eighty-seven plus forty-one

★ 36. sixty-three plus ninety

★ 37. thirty-two plus seventy-seven

APPLICATION

38. On Monday 62 campers saw the wildlife movie. On Tuesday 45 campers saw the movie. How many campers in all saw the movie?

★ 39. The Yellowstone camping area has 95 parking spaces. There are 52 cars parked. Is there room for 29 more cars?

69

Regrouping Ones and Tens

Ash tree

How many bats were made in all?

We add to find how many in all.

Number of Bats	
Machine #1	68
Machine #2	56

Step 1
Add ones.
Regroup.

$$\begin{array}{r} 1 \\ 68 \\ +56 \\ \hline 4 \end{array}$$

14 ones = 1 ten 4 ones

Step 2
Add tens.
Regroup.

$$\begin{array}{r} 1 \\ 68 \\ +56 \\ \hline 124 \end{array}$$

12 tens = 1 hundred 2 tens

Check by
adding up.

$$\begin{array}{r} 1 \\ 68 \\ +56 \\ \hline 124 \end{array}$$

There were 124
bats made in all.

CLASSWORK

Add. Check by adding up.

1. $\begin{array}{r} 67 \\ +64 \\ \hline \end{array}$
2. $\begin{array}{r} 97 \\ +75 \\ \hline \end{array}$
3. $\begin{array}{r} 57 \\ +83 \\ \hline \end{array}$
4. $\begin{array}{r} 5 \\ +95 \\ \hline \end{array}$

5. $\begin{array}{r} 35 \\ +76 \\ \hline \end{array}$
6. $\begin{array}{r} 46 \\ +87 \\ \hline \end{array}$
7. $\begin{array}{r} 36 \\ +99 \\ \hline \end{array}$
8. $\begin{array}{r} 7 \\ +98 \\ \hline \end{array}$

9. $92 + 9 = \square$

10. $82 + 38 = \square$

PRACTICE

Add. Check by adding up.

1.	h	t	o
		3	9
+		6	2

2.	h	t	o
		8	5
+		2	9

3.	h	t	o
		7	9
+		7	3

4.	h	t	o
		6	9
+		4	8

5. 36
  +96

6. 72
  +47

7. 57
  +46

8. 44
  +76

9. 78
  +84

10. 91
   + 9

11. 86
   +58

12. 87
   +73

13. 99
   + 9

14. 63
   +17

15.   5
   +97

16. 72
   +38

17. 26
   +74

18. 98
   +79

19. 40
   +88

20. 18
   +86

21. 28
   +83

22. 49
   +51

23. 94 + 59 = □   24. 11 + 89 = □

25. 8 + 96 = □   26. 66 + 54 = □

★ 27. Which 2-digit number when added to itself gives the greatest sum?

★ 28. Which 2-digit number when added to itself gives the least sum?

APPLICATION

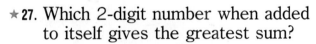

Order Form	Grand Slams	64
	Big Sluggers	78
	All Pros	46

Coach Lang ordered bats for the city baseball teams.

29. What is the total of Grand Slams and Big Sluggers ordered?

30. What is the total of Big Sluggers and All Pros ordered?

31. What is the total of All Pros and Grand Slams ordered?

★ 32. What is the total of all the bats ordered?

71

Addition Patterns

The Nature Center displayed 18 plant fossils and 6 animal fossils. How many fossils were displayed in all?

We can add 18 + 6 mentally (in our heads) by thinking of basic facts.

Since 8 + 6 = 14,
then 18 + 6 = 24.

There were 24 fossils in all.

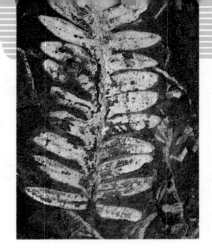

fos sil (FOS uhl), the hardened remains of a plant or an animal of a past age.

Another Example

Since
$$\begin{array}{r} 3 \\ +9 \\ \hline 12 \end{array}$$
then
$$\begin{array}{r} 13 \\ +\ 9 \\ \hline 22 \end{array} \quad \begin{array}{r} 23 \\ +\ 9 \\ \hline 32 \end{array} \quad \begin{array}{r} 33 \\ +\ 9 \\ \hline 42 \end{array}$$

We use patterns like these to find sums.

$$\begin{array}{c} 7 \\ 6 \end{array} > 13 \qquad \begin{array}{c} 5 \\ 9 \end{array} > 14$$
$$\begin{array}{r} +9 \\ \end{array} \quad \begin{array}{r} +\ 9 \\ \hline 22 \end{array} \qquad \begin{array}{r} +7 \\ \end{array} \quad \begin{array}{r} +\ 7 \\ \hline 21 \end{array}$$

CLASSWORK

Add mentally.

1. 4 + 2 = ☐
    14 + 2 = ☐
    24 + 2 = ☐
    34 + 2 = ☐

2. 6 + 5 = ☐
    16 + 5 = ☐
    26 + 5 = ☐
    36 + 5 = ☐

3. 8 + 7 = ☐
    18 + 7 = ☐
    28 + 7 = ☐
    38 + 7 = ☐

4.
$$\begin{array}{r} 2 \\ +7 \end{array} \quad \begin{array}{r} 12 \\ +\ 7 \end{array} \quad \begin{array}{r} 22 \\ +\ 7 \end{array} \quad \begin{array}{r} 32 \\ +\ 7 \end{array}$$

5.
$$\begin{array}{r} 5 \\ +3 \end{array} \quad \begin{array}{r} 15 \\ +\ 3 \end{array} \quad \begin{array}{r} 25 \\ +\ 3 \end{array} \quad \begin{array}{r} 35 \\ +\ 3 \end{array}$$

6.
$$\begin{array}{r} 8 \\ 7 \\ +6 \end{array}$$

7.
$$\begin{array}{r} 9 \\ 5 \\ +9 \end{array}$$

8.
$$\begin{array}{r} 4 \\ 7 \\ +5 \end{array}$$

9.
$$\begin{array}{r} 7 \\ 6 \\ +4 \end{array}$$

10.
$$\begin{array}{r} 3 \\ 8 \\ +9 \end{array}$$

11.
$$\begin{array}{r} 5 \\ 7 \\ +7 \end{array}$$

Add mentally. Then write the answer.

1. $3 + 3 = \square$
   $13 + 3 = \square$
   $23 + 3 = \square$
   $33 + 3 = \square$

2. $4 + 5 = \square$
   $14 + 5 = \square$
   $24 + 5 = \square$
   $34 + 5 = \square$

3.
$$\begin{array}{r} 1 \\ +3 \\ \hline \end{array} \qquad \begin{array}{r} 11 \\ +\ 3 \\ \hline \end{array} \qquad \begin{array}{r} 21 \\ +\ 3 \\ \hline \end{array} \qquad \begin{array}{r} 31 \\ +\ 3 \\ \hline \end{array}$$

4.
$$\begin{array}{r} 8 \\ +4 \\ \hline \end{array} \qquad \begin{array}{r} 18 \\ +\ 4 \\ \hline \end{array} \qquad \begin{array}{r} 28 \\ +\ 4 \\ \hline \end{array} \qquad \begin{array}{r} 38 \\ +\ 4 \\ \hline \end{array}$$

5.
$$\begin{array}{r} 9 \\ 3 \\ +2 \\ \hline \end{array}$$
6.
$$\begin{array}{r} 5 \\ 7 \\ +3 \\ \hline \end{array}$$
7.
$$\begin{array}{r} 3 \\ 7 \\ +8 \\ \hline \end{array}$$
8.
$$\begin{array}{r} 6 \\ 9 \\ +7 \\ \hline \end{array}$$

9. $7 + 67 = \square$

10. $53 + 6 = \square$

11. $2 + 8 + 3 = \square$

12. $4 + 8 + 9 = \square$

★13. $5 + 3 + 4 = \square$
   $5 + 3 + 14 = \square$
   $5 + 3 + 24 = \square$

★14. $6 + 2 + 7 = \square$
   $6 + 2 + 17 = \square$
   $6 + 2 + 27 = \square$

APPLICATION

≡ LOGICAL THINKING ≡

Tell what number must be added to give the next number in each.

1. 4, 8, 12, 16, 20, 24, 28

2. 5, 10, 20, 25, 35, 40, 50

3. 6, 13, 16, 23, 26, 33, 36

4. 10, 14, 15, 20, 24, 25, 30

1.
$$\begin{array}{r} 8 \\ +7 \\ \hline \end{array}$$
2.
$$\begin{array}{r} 11 \\ -\ 6 \\ \hline \end{array}$$

3.
$$\begin{array}{r} 5 \\ +7 \\ \hline \end{array}$$
4.
$$\begin{array}{r} 14 \\ -\ 8 \\ \hline \end{array}$$

5.
$$\begin{array}{r} 9 \\ +8 \\ \hline \end{array}$$
6.
$$\begin{array}{r} 16 \\ -\ 9 \\ \hline \end{array}$$

7.
$$\begin{array}{r} 15 \\ -\ 8 \\ \hline \end{array}$$
8.
$$\begin{array}{r} 7 \\ +7 \\ \hline \end{array}$$

9.
$$\begin{array}{r} 3 \\ 3 \\ +1 \\ \hline \end{array}$$
10.
$$\begin{array}{r} 2 \\ 5 \\ +3 \\ \hline \end{array}$$

11. $7 + 9 = \square$

12. $9 - 3 = \square$

13. $10 - 6 = \square$

14. $5 + 6 = \square$

15. $6 + 3 + 1 = \square$

Compare. Use >, <, or = for ●.

16. 77 ● 67

17. 128 ● 128

18. 16 ● 19

19. 43 ● 41

20. 156 ● 175

Adding Three Numbers

How many steps will Carlos take from Cedar Path to the canoe landing? Add to find how many steps.

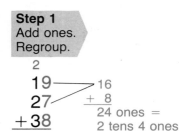

Step 1
Add ones.
Regroup.

$$
\begin{array}{r}
2 \\
19 \\
27 \\
+38 \\
\hline
4
\end{array}
\qquad
\begin{array}{r}
16 \\
+\ 8 \\
\hline
24 \text{ ones} = \\
2 \text{ tens } 4 \text{ ones}
\end{array}
$$

Step 2
Add tens.

$$
\begin{array}{r}
2 \\
19 \\
27 \\
+38 \\
\hline
84
\end{array}
$$

Check by adding up.

$$
\begin{array}{r}
2 \\
19 \\
27 \\
+38 \\
\hline
84
\end{array}
$$

Carlos will take 84 steps.

Find $35 + 8 + 63$.
Line up ones and tens.

Add ones.
Regroup.

$$
\begin{array}{r}
1 \\
35 \\
8 \\
+63 \\
\hline
6
\end{array}
\qquad
\begin{array}{r}
13 \\
+\ 3 \\
\hline
16
\end{array}
$$

Add tens.
Regroup.

$$
\begin{array}{r}
1 \\
35 \\
8 \\
+63 \\
\hline
106
\end{array}
$$

Check

$$
\begin{array}{r}
1 \\
35 \\
8 \\
+63 \\
\hline
106
\end{array}
\qquad
\begin{array}{r}
5 \\
+11 \\
\hline
16
\end{array}
$$

CLASSWORK

Add. Check by adding up.

1.	2.	3.	4.	5.	6.
60	84	49	13	94	15
16	30	17	21	6	63
+13	+12	+ 5	+28	+24	+34

7. $47 + 9 + 78 = \square$

8. $86 + 75 + 50 = \square$

PRACTICE

Add. Check by adding up.

1. $\begin{array}{r} 31 \\ 24 \\ +43 \\ \hline \end{array}$
2. $\begin{array}{r} 16 \\ 50 \\ +21 \\ \hline \end{array}$
3. $\begin{array}{r} 17 \\ 11 \\ +16 \\ \hline \end{array}$
4. $\begin{array}{r} 51 \\ 7 \\ +36 \\ \hline \end{array}$
5. $\begin{array}{r} 34 \\ 23 \\ +14 \\ \hline \end{array}$
6. $\begin{array}{r} 43 \\ 73 \\ +22 \\ \hline \end{array}$

7. $\begin{array}{r} 22 \\ 94 \\ +51 \\ \hline \end{array}$
8. $\begin{array}{r} 58 \\ 62 \\ +51 \\ \hline \end{array}$
9. $\begin{array}{r} 8 \\ 96 \\ +\ 3 \\ \hline \end{array}$
10. $\begin{array}{r} 66 \\ 23 \\ +77 \\ \hline \end{array}$
11. $\begin{array}{r} 99 \\ 21 \\ +31 \\ \hline \end{array}$
12. $\begin{array}{r} 28 \\ 25 \\ +27 \\ \hline \end{array}$

13. $\begin{array}{r} 67 \\ 46 \\ +17 \\ \hline \end{array}$
14. $\begin{array}{r} 29 \\ 54 \\ +18 \\ \hline \end{array}$
15. $\begin{array}{r} 6 \\ 49 \\ +39 \\ \hline \end{array}$
16. $\begin{array}{r} 36 \\ 62 \\ +20 \\ \hline \end{array}$
★17. $\begin{array}{r} 55 \\ 86 \\ 47 \\ +38 \\ \hline \end{array}$
★18. $\begin{array}{r} 96 \\ 4 \\ 79 \\ +62 \\ \hline \end{array}$

19. $9 + 89 + 65 = \square$

20. $92 + 46 + 90 = \square$

★21. $47 + 52 + 6 + 98 = \square$

★22. $73 + 45 + 89 + 56 = \square$

APPLICATION

ANIMALS CARLOS SAW			
	Friday	Saturday	Sunday
Chipmunk	4	8	3
Raccoon	3	2	1
Rabbit	6	7	8
Squirrel	9	10	4

23. How many animals in all did Carlos see on Friday?

24. What was the total number of animals he saw on Saturday and Sunday?

★25. On which day did Carlos see the most animals?

★26. How many animals did Carlos see in all?

MENTAL ARITHMETIC

Add 13, 24, and 17 mentally.

Look for 2 numbers with a sum of 10 in ones place.

$13 + 17 = 30$

Add the other number.

$30 + 24 = 54$

Try these.

1. $24 + 21 + 16 = \square$

2. $32 + 21 + 18 = \square$

3. $25 + 25 + 36 = \square$

4. $33 + 47 + 15 = \square$

Problem Solving

WHAT IS MISSING?

You cannot solve a problem if a fact is missing. There are 3 cabins. All of them are filled. How many people are camping?

THINK   **What is the question?**

How many people are camping?

What are the facts?

There are 3 cabins. All of them are filled.

Are there any facts missing?

the number of people in each cabin

Suppose each cabin has 5 people in it. Now solve the problem.

PLAN   **How can you find the answer?**

Add to find the number of people.

$$5 + 5 + 5 = \square$$

SOLVE   **Carry out the plan. Do the work and find the answer.**

$$\begin{array}{r} 5 \\ 5 \\ +5 \\ \hline 15 \end{array}$$

There are 15 people camping.

LOOK BACK   **Did you answer the question? Is your arithmetic correct? Does the answer make sense?**

Add another way to check.

$$(5 + 5) + 5$$
$$10 \quad + 5 = 15$$

The answer makes sense.

Tell what fact is missing in each problem.

1. The children saw 2 bears eating fish from a little stream. How many fish did the bears eat?

2. Students from 8 schools were in the national forest that day. How many students were there in all?

3. Susan's family stayed at the campground 3 days longer than Alicia's family. How long did Susan's family stay at the campground?

4. Susan's family had a barbecue one day for lunch. Each member of Susan's family ate 2 hamburgers. How many hamburgers did they eat in all?

Make up a fact that is missing in each problem. Then solve the problem.

5. The children went on a hike. They saw 5 squirrels and some chipmunks. How many animals did they see?

6. Susan, Barb, and David picked berries. Susan filled 4 cans and David filled 3. How many cans did the children fill?

★7. Barb said, "The oak tree is the tallest." David said, "No, the pine tree is the tallest." Susan said, "You are both wrong. The spruce tree is the tallest. It is 14 feet tall." Who was right?

★8. The children walked past the lake. There were people sailing and windsurfing on the lake. Barb saw 5 windsurfers. Susan saw 4 sailboats. How many people did they see in all?

=== CREATE YOUR OWN PROBLEM ===

Make up a problem that has a fact missing. Ask a friend to make up a fact and solve the problem.

Adding Three-Digit Numbers

Susan Davis stocked Eagle Brook with 156 rainbow trout and 242 brown trout. How many trout did she put in the brook?

156 + 242 = ☐

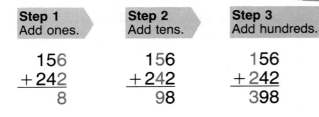

Step 1 Add ones.	Step 2 Add tens.	Step 3 Add hundreds.
156 +242 8	156 +242 98	156 +242 398

Susan put 398 trout in the brook.

These examples show regrouping in ones, or tens, or hundreds places.

a. Regroup ones.
```
  1
 659
+214
 873
```

b. Regroup tens.
```
  1
 371
+155
 526
```

c. Regroup hundreds.
```
 741
+853
1,594
```
15 hundreds =
1 thousand 5 hundreds

CLASSWORK

Add. Check by adding up.

1. 327
   +161

2. 529
   +346

3. 642
   +743

4.   51
   +816

5. 475
   + 34

6. 736
   +201

7. 418 + 514 = ☐

8. 116 + 23 = ☐

9. 71 + 234 = ☐

10. 637 + 421 = ☐

11. 404 + 93 = ☐

12. 742 + 536 = ☐

Add. Check by adding up.

1. 631 $+237$	2. 141 $+325$	3. 316 $+645$	4. 438 $+158$

5. 725 $+59$ 6. 214 $+431$

7. 382 $+562$ 8. 43 $+372$ 9. 470 $+181$ 10. 825 $+732$ 11. 612 $+880$ 12. 143 $+226$

13. 641 $+88$ 14. 976 $+921$ 15. 702 $+147$ 16. 530 $+749$ 17. 68 $+291$ 18. 996 $+352$

19. 202 143 $+532$ 20. 134 25 $+312$ 21. 425 73 $+61$ 22. 431 942 $+225$ 23. 424 63 $+150$ 24. 764 372 $+430$

25. $263 + 165 = \square$

26. $705 + 82 = \square$

27. $307 + 403 = \square$

28. $126 + 41 + 72 = \square$

29. $8 + 57 + 205 = \square$

30. $231 + 524 + 602 = \square$

★ 31. $26 + 9 + 347 + 110 = \square$

★ 32. $465 + 3 + 170 + 281 = \square$

APPLICATION

LOGICAL THINKING

How many do you need to make 1,000?

1. 200 $+\blacksquare\blacksquare\blacksquare$ $1,000$ 2. 700 $+\blacksquare\blacksquare\blacksquare$ $1,000$ 3. 100 500 $+\blacksquare\blacksquare\blacksquare$ $1,000$

4. 300 200 $+\blacksquare\blacksquare\blacksquare$ $1,000$ 5. 600 300 $+\blacksquare\blacksquare\blacksquare$ $1,000$ 6. 400 400 $+\blacksquare\blacksquare\blacksquare$ $1,000$

Regrouping Twice

A lumber company in Georgia planted 459 white pine seedlings and 387 spruce seedlings. How many seedlings did the company plant?

459 + 387 = ☐

Step 1
Add ones.
Regroup.

```
  1
  459
+ 387
    6
```
16 ones =
1 ten 6 ones

Step 2
Add tens.
Regroup.

```
 1 1
  459
+ 387
   46
```
14 tens =
1 hundred 4 tens

Step 3
Add hundreds.

```
 1 1
  459
+ 387
  846
```

The company planted 846 seedlings.

Find 928 + 815.

Regroup ones and hundreds.

```
  1
  928
+ 815
1,743
```

Find 562 + 970.

Regroup tens and hundreds.

```
  1
  562
+ 970
1,532
```

CLASSWORK

Add. Check by adding up.

1.
```
  435
+ 297
```

2.
```
  548
+  68
```

3.
```
  739
+ 816
```

4.
```
  982
+ 456
```

5.
```
  807
+ 465
```

6. 573 + 645 = ☐

7. 328 + 92 = ☐

8. 857 + 691 = ☐

80

PRACTICE

Add. Check by adding up.

1.	2.	3.	4.	5.	6.
329 +287	136 + 78	826 +904	707 +748	619 +590	482 +364

7.	8.	9.	10.	11.	12.
453 +837	971 +534	568 + 97	357 +852	827 +669	735 +296

13.	14.	15.	16.	17.	18.
176 +512	649 +179	735 +638	984 + 54	486 +930	663 +587

19.	20.	21.	22.	★ 23.	★ 24.
214 22 +305	430 918 + 30	23 400 +351	615 39 +543	842 835 890 +261	918 304 726 +581

25. $96 + 386 = \square$ 26. $865 + 121 = \square$ 27. $936 + 708 + 45 = \square$

28. $919 + 62 = \square$ 29. $796 + 9 = \square$ 30. $82 + 654 + 793 = \square$

Find each missing digit.

★31.	★32.	★33.	★34.
2∎6 +∎71 587	7∎∎ +∎48 984	∎5∎ +6∎5 1,025	4∎1 +∎3∎ 1,017

APPLICATION

Use the map to find a number for each □.

35. The forest ranger checked a map of seedlings planted. He found that a total of □ pine and cedar were planted. A total of □ hemlock and Douglas fir were planted.

★ 36. A total of □ seedlings in all were planted.

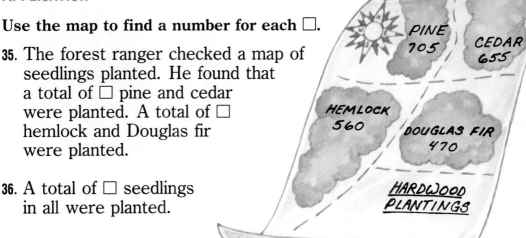

PINE
705

CEDAR
655

HEMLOCK
560

DOUGLAS FIR
470

HARDWOOD PLANTINGS

81

Regrouping Three Times

Last season Jake collected 572 pails of maple sap. This season he collected 648 pails. How many pails did he collect altogether?

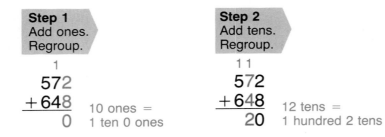

572 + 648 = □

<table>
<tr>
<td>

Step 1
Add ones.
Regroup.

```
  1
  572
+ 648
────────
    0
```
10 ones =
1 ten 0 ones

</td>
<td>

Step 2
Add tens.
Regroup.

```
 1 1
  572
+ 648
────────
   20
```
12 tens =
1 hundred 2 tens

</td>
<td>

Step 3
Add hundreds.
Regroup.

```
 1 1
  572
+ 648
────────
1,220
```
12 hundreds =
1 thousand 2 hundreds

</td>
</tr>
</table>

Check by adding up.

```
 1 1
  572
+ 648
────────
1,220
```

Jake collected 1,220 pails altogether.

CLASSWORK

Add. Check by adding up.

1. 319
   +897

2. 453
   +967

3. 986
   + 76

4. 647
   +754

5. 859
   +952

6. 268
   +883

7. 957 + 85 = □

8. 586 + 969 = □

9. 35 + 899 = □

10. 945 + 675 = □

PRACTICE

Add. Check by adding up.

1. 269
  +942

2. 753
  +949

3. 928
  + 95

4. 506
  +423

5. 813
  +595

6. 764
  +158

7. 376
  +975

8. 259
  +874

9. 624
  +576

10. 322
  +789

11. 934
  +476

12. 639
  +897

13. 596
  +817

14. 459
  +763

15. 879
  +468

16. 681
  +539

17. 985
  +326

18. 975
  +648

19. $935 + 765 = \square$

20. $926 + 86 = \square$

21. $756 + 658 = \square$

22. $98 + 908 = \square$

23. $937 + 87 = \square$

24. $906 + 87 = \square$

25. 489
  163
  +418

26. 93
  504
  +865

27. 893
  958
  +765

28. 23
  415
  +632

29. 172
  543
  +818

30. 578
  365
  +946

Find the last number.

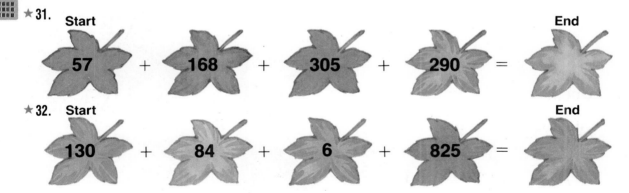

★31. Start ... 57 + 168 + 305 + 290 = End

★32. Start ... 130 + 84 + 6 + 825 = End

APPLICATION

33. Trucks delivered 895 cans of maple syrup to New York and 755 cans to Ohio. How many cans were delivered in all?

★34. Two restaurant owners each bought 250 cans of syrup. Another bought 370 cans. How many cans were bought in all?

83

Adding Four-Digit Numbers

Many birds fly south for the winter and return in the spring. How many miles do the hummingbirds fly altogether?

2,455 + 3,076 = □

Step 1 Add ones. Regroup.	Step 2 Add tens. Regroup.	Step 3 Add hundreds.	Step 4 Add thousands.
1	1 1	1 1	
2,455	2,455	2,455	2,455
+3,076	+3,076	+3,076	+3,076
1	31	531	5,531

The hummingbirds fly 5,531 miles altogether.

More Examples

a.
```
  3,410
+ 4,562
  7,972
```

b.
```
    1
  1,915
+ 3,450
  5,365
```

c.
```
  1 11
  7,689
+ 9,745
 17,434
```

CLASSWORK

Add. Check by adding up.

1.
```
  3,607
+ 2,819
```

2.
```
  5,792
+ 1,683
```

3.
```
  8,274
+   956
```

4.
```
  3,468
+ 7,529
```

5.
```
  2,076
+    92
```

6.
```
  4,135
+ 1,848
```

7. 926 + 1,587 = □

8. 1,254 + 3,298 = □

9. 4,662 + 4,791 = □

10. 3,942 + 7,186 = □

11. 2,964 + 3,157 = □

12. 8,942 + 1,379 = □

84

PRACTICE

Add. Check by adding up.

1. 3,206
+ 4,581

2. 8,251
+ 1,507

3. 6,543
+ 2,125

4. 2,381
+ 7,146

5. 7,521
+ 4,313

6. 9,304
+ 363

7. 3,694
+ 5,417

8. 2,851
+ 4,672

9. 7,468
+ 1,438

10. 5,732
+ 486

11. 8,629
+ 624

12. 4,573
+ 8,329

13. 1,987
+ 5,937

14. 5,443
+ 8,960

15. 6,567
+ 9,637

16. 9,742
+ 7,538

17. 7,539
+ 66

★18. 4,261
1,003
+ 745

★19. 2,859
5,104
+ 1,953

★20. 279
3
+ 4,865

21. $658 + 9{,}142 = \square$

22. $4{,}498 + 2{,}935 = \square$

Choose the correct sum for each.

23. $7{,}486 + 68 = \square$
  a. 7,444   b. 7,654
  c. 7,454   d. 7,554

24. $76 + 9{,}975 = \square$
  a. 10,041   b. 10,051
  c. 10,151   d. 9,051

APPLICATION

In December, New Jersey birdwatchers counted these birds.

Type of Bird	Number
Canada Goose	2,437
Mallard	1,457
Ring-billed Gull	1,407

25. How many Canada geese and mallards did they count?

26. How many mallards and ring-billed gulls did they count?

★27. How many birds did they count in all?

Adding Money

The Boy Scouts collected old newspapers to earn money. How much money did the two Scout troops earn?

We add money the way we add other numbers.

Line up the decimal points. Then add.

$4.50
+ 3.25
$7.75

Write the dollar sign and decimal point in the answer.

The Boy Scouts earned $7.75.

Save Trees!
Recycle Newspapers

Troop 342	Troop 426
$4.50	$3.25

Another Example

Check

```
 1 1 1            1 1 1
$58.75          $58.75  ↑
+  9.79         +  9.79
$68.54          $68.54
```

CLASSWORK

Add. Check by adding up.

1. $2.66
   + 8.13

2. $.85
   + .13

3. $1.74
   + 6.50

4. $19.98
   + 39.00

5. $50.43
   + 2.87

6. $7.27
   + .46

7. $25.00 + $45.00 = ☐

8. $3.42 + $3.68 = ☐

9. $40.00 + $17.25 = ☐

10. $36.14 + $2.05 = ☐

PRACTICE

Add. Check by adding up.

1.	2.	3.	4.	5.
$5.17 + 1.10	$2.04 + 2.89	$.28 + .37	$.60 + .29	$7.38 + 8.62

6.	7.	8.	9.	10.
$84.07 + 5.60	$34.63 + 35.84	$35.18 + 21.71	$68.71 + 53.78	$23.60 + 8.20

11.	12.	13.	★14.	★15.
$.12 .50 + .04	$6.37 3.01 + .89	$2.53 3.20 + 1.67	$24.32 78.55 + 46.47	$59.56 63.24 + 87.16

16. $7.16 + $2.59 = ☐

17. $8.29 + $5.72 = ☐

18. $65.39 + $40.96 = ☐

19. $82.70 + $86.94 = ☐

20. $9.90 + $18.56 = ☐

21. $54.65 + $9.75 = ☐

22. $95.67 + $65.49 = ☐

★23. $.96 + $4.57 + $96.89 = ☐

APPLICATION

24. Troop 98 sold stacks 1 and 6. How much did it earn?

25. Troop 426 sold stacks 2 and 3. How much did it earn?

★26. Troop 342 earned $4.50. Which two stacks did it sell?

★27. How much money did the troops earn in all?

1 — $2.50

2 — $1.65

3 — $1.60

4 — $1.50

5 — $3.00

6 — $2.50

=== VISUAL THINKING ===

Move only 3 circles to change Figure **A** to Figure **B**.

A

B

Estimating Sums

One helicopter poured 13 buckets of water to put out a fire. Another helicopter poured 28 buckets. About how many buckets did it take to put out the fire?

Sometimes we do not need an exact number, so we **estimate** to find the answer.

▶To **estimate** the sum, round each addend to the nearest ten. Then add.

$$
\begin{array}{r}
13 \quad \text{rounds to} \quad 10 \\
+28 \quad \text{rounds to} \quad +30 \\
\hline
40 \quad \text{estimated sum}
\end{array}
$$

It took about 40 buckets of water.

Estimate 186 + 327.

▶To estimate this sum, round each addend to the nearest hundred. Then add.

$$
\begin{array}{r}
186 \quad \text{rounds to} \quad 200 \\
+327 \quad \text{rounds to} \quad +300 \\
\hline
500 \quad \text{estimated sum}
\end{array}
$$

CLASSWORK

Round to the nearest ten and estimate each sum.

1.	2.	3.	4.	5.	6.
62 +27	39 +14	85 +31	50 +18	71 +46	56 +87

Round to the nearest hundred and estimate each sum.

7.	8.	9.	10.	11.	12.
205 +398	779 +512	419 +850	100 +264	357 +706	624 +189

Round to the nearest ten and estimate each sum.

1. 21 +58	**2.** 45 +93	**3.** 19 +33	**4.** 78 +59	**5.** 16 +25	**6.** 37 +48
7. 63 +86	**8.** 35 +28	**9.** 68 +95	**10.** 54 +47	**11.** 62 +43	**12.** 75 +84

Round to the nearest hundred and estimate each sum.

13. 362 +371	**14.** 635 +680	**15.** 482 +239	**16.** 952 +840	**17.** 619 +262	**18.** 456 +587
19. 237 +182	**20.** 728 +857	**21.** 546 +552	**22.** 149 +966	**23.** 962 +971	**24.** 647 +853

Estimate each sum.

25. 242 + 276 = ☐   **26.** 350 + 416 = ☐   ★**27.** 52 + 36 + 19 = ☐

APPLICATION

What facts are missing?

28. Two helicopters carried people. One carried 27 people. Rounded to the nearest ten, how many people did both helicopters carry?

29. There were 33 people waiting to ride the helicopter. Others joined them. Rounded to the nearest ten, how many people were waiting?

CALCULATOR

Estimate this sum.   562 +319   600 +300 = 900

Find the exact sum.   5 6 2 + 3 1 9 = **881**

Find the difference between the estimate and the exact sum.   9 0 0 - 8 8 1 = **19**

How close are you? Now do exercises **25** and **26** in this way.

Problem Solving

SKILLS AND STRATEGIES REVIEW Planting Trees

Cub Scout Pack 56 and Brownie Scout Troop 41 were planting pine trees in the forest.

Read the problem.
Tell whether you would add or subtract.
Then solve the problem.

1. The Cub Scouts planted 52 trees and the Brownie Scouts planted 49 trees. Together, how many trees did both groups plant?

2. Tony planted 8 trees. Joan planted 5 trees. How many more trees did Tony plant than Joan?

3. There were 17 Cub Scouts. There were 14 Brownies and 2 leaders. How many people were there in all?

4. The Cub Scouts worked 9 hours. The Brownies worked 6 hours. How much longer did the Cub Scouts work than the Brownies?

Read the problem. Make up a fact if one is missing. Then solve the problem.

5. The Scouts went to stock the lake. They put 875 trout and almost as many bass in the lake. How many fish did they put in the lake?

6. Max and Luis watered seedlings. Max watered 6, and Luis watered 8. How many more seedlings did Luis water than Max?

7. There were 35 egg sandwiches, 25 cheese sandwiches, and some ham sandwiches for lunch. How many sandwiches were there in all?

★8. Pine seedlings come in bundles of 3. Each seedling costs $2.75. How much does a bundle of seedlings cost?

9. How many pinecones and acorns are there in all?

10. How many more pinecones than acorns are there?

Read the problem. Make up a fact if one is missing. Then solve the problem.

MAXIMUM
WEIGHT
16,000
POUNDS

11. The logs on the truck weigh 2,000 pounds each. How much do they weigh in all?

12. The truck in the picture weighs 8,000 pounds. Can it go across the bridge?

13. The loggers cut down a tree. They cut it into 3 parts. Each part was the same size. Was the tree more or less than 20 feet tall?

14. On Tuesday, the cut logs were taken to the sawmill. Eight trucks carried the logs away. How many logs were carried away on Tuesday?

★ 15. One tree was cut into 4 pieces. How many cuts were made in it?

★ 16. How many cuts would it take to cut a tree into 6 pieces?

═══SOMETHING EXTRA═══

A Domino Puzzle

Use the dominoes pictured here.

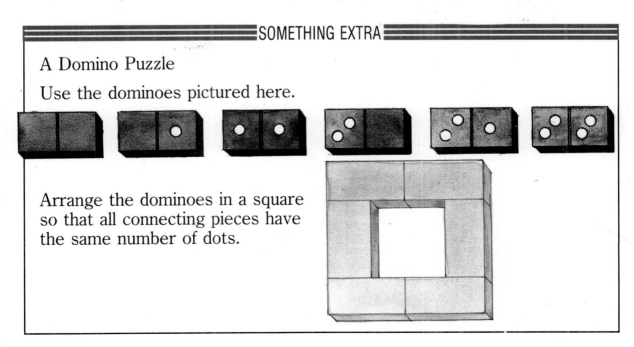

Arrange the dominoes in a square so that all connecting pieces have the same number of dots.

Add. pages 64–75

1. 56
    +23

2. 48
    +19

3. 46
    +37

4. 63
    +92

5. 75
    +64

6. 9
    7
    +3

7. 26
    12
    + 5

8. 54
    27
    +62

9. 85
    6
    +39

10.   4
      98
    +11

11. 5 + 8 + 2 = □

12. 14 + 26 + 9 = □

13. 27 + 59 + 4 = □

14. 7 + 65 + 6 = □

Find each sum. pages 78–87

15.   186
    +201

16.   437
    +238

17.   925
    +187

18.   364
    +959

19. 1,076
    +3,120

20. 2,754
    +3,097

21. 6,248
    +1,956

22. 5,876
    +9,354

23. 8,175
    +7,995

24. 5,946
    +7,829

25. $4.60
    + .98

26. $1.87
    + 3.59

27. $16.20
    + 8.95

28. $ 7.86
    + 18.46

29. $95.88
    + 69.57

30. 329 + 190 = □

31. 473 + 78 = □

32. $5.14 + $4.69 = □

33. $89.67 + $3.56 = □

Estimate each sum. pages 88–89

34.   17
    +72

35.   78
    +35

36.   345
    +568

37.   156
    +412

38.   349
    +125

39. 59 + 35 = □

40. 254 + 213 = □

Solve. If a fact is missing, tell what it is. pages 76–77, 90–91

41. Birdwatchers counted 2,079 starlings and 403 song sparrows. How many birds did they count in all?

42. While on a hike, Carla and Bert took photos. Carla took 24 photos. How many photos did they both take?

Add.

1. 12
   +35

2. 42
   +38

3. 67
   +96

4. 174
   + 85

5. 157
   +194

6. 8
    9
   +3

7. 29
    2
   +18

8. 65
    37
   +46

Find each sum.

9. 168
   +521

10. 247
    +319

11. 763
    + 82

12. 849
    +677

13. 4,306
    +1,192

14. 1,625
    + 318

15. 8,967
    +3,437

16. 5,009
    +3,993

17. $6.53
    + 2.68

18. $1.27
    +   .15

19. $18.35
    + 9.65

20. $26.51
    + 54.69

21. 954 + 68 = □

22. 7,306 + 2,998 = □

23. $26.53 + $1.97 = □

24. $.59 + $3.85 = □

Estimate each sum.

25. 65
   +18

26. 309
    +486

27. 135
    +549

28. 752
    +936

29. 42 + 75 = □

30. 36 + 21 = □

31. 149 + 128 = □

Solve. If a fact is missing, tell what it is.

32. The nursery grew 595 red maples and 4,480 Norway maples from seedlings. How many trees were grown in all?

33. There are 265 small pines. Nearby are elm trees. How many pine trees and elm trees are there altogether?

Justine bought 2 wood duck decoys for $9.25 each. She bought a birdfeeder for $10.00. How much did she spend in all?

MAKING A COUNTING FRAME

You will need:
- 5 pipe cleaners
- 27 pieces of macaroni

Place 9 pieces of macaroni on each of 3 pipe cleaners. Attach the ends of each pipe cleaner to the remaining pipe cleaners as shown. Now you have a counting frame!

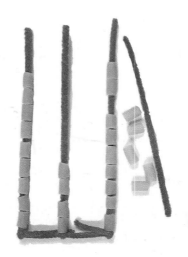

Use the frame to show place value.

Show 316.

Push up 6 ones, 1 ten, and 3 hundreds.

Use the frame to add.

316 + 412 = □

Push up 2 more ones, 1 more ten, and 4 more hundreds.
316 + 412 = 728

Try some addition on your counting frame.

1. 314 + 223 = □   2. 144 + 555 = □   3. 74 + 122 = □

4. 216 + 582 = □   5. 325 + 352 = □   6. 673 + 15 = □

CROSS-NUMBER PUZZLES

Trace each puzzle. Do each operation.
Write your answers in the puzzle.

ACROSS

1. 21 + 21
2. 87 + 9
5. 109 + 139
8. 19 + 37
9. 9 + 29

DOWN

1. 22 + 18
3. 48 + 14
4. 50 + 99
6. 27 + 8
7. 13 + 5

ACROSS

1. 248 + 105
3. 200 + 12
5. 428 + 428
7. 214 + 218
9. 80 + 159
11. 545 + 147
13. 299 + 562
14. 22 + 104

DOWN

1. 205 + 123
2. 91 + 255
3. 104 + 100
4. 227 + 65
6. 253 + 250
8. 41 + 308
9. 112 + 156
10. 268 + 653
11. 528 + 103
12. 189 + 57

FLOWCHARTS

When we have a big job to do, it is easier to do the job one step at a time.

Sometimes a **flowchart** is used to show each small step.

This flowchart shows the steps for the addition 426 + 312.

The ⬭ shape is used for **START** or **STOP**.

The ▭ shape is used for giving instructions.

The arrow ↓ is used to show which instruction to follow next.

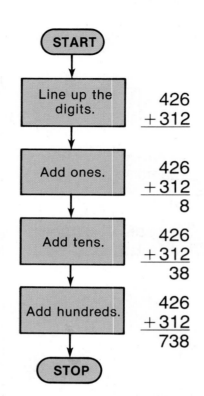

Use the flowchart to find each sum.

1. 823 + 154 = □
2. 641 + 248 = □
3. 600 + 339 = □
4. 145 + 632 = □
5. 216 + 350 = □
6. 775 + 21 = □
7. Draw a flowchart to show how to add 25 + 32.
★ 8. Draw a flowchart to show how to add 16 + 67.

Add this step to your flowchart. | Regroup ones. |

A flowchart can help us prepare instructions for the computer.

This flowchart tells us to add 5 to a number, and then to subtract 4.

The 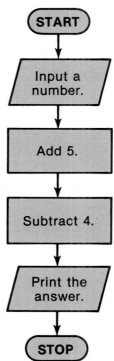 shape is used to enter numbers or display results.

When you enter a number, it is called **input.**

START

Input a number.

Add 5.

Subtract 4.

Print the answer.

STOP

Use the flowchart. Tell what output a computer will print for each input.

9. 7   **10.** 15

11. 89   **12.** 203

13. 764   **14.** 382

15. Arrange the steps of this flowchart in correct order.

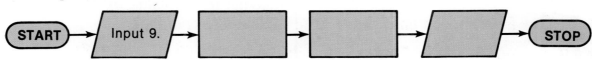

STOP   Input a number.   Print the answer.   START   Subtract 5.

16. Complete this flowchart for $9 - 5 + 7 = \Box$.

START → Input 9. → ☐ → ☐ → ☐ → STOP

CUMULATIVE REVIEW

Choose the correct answer. Write A, B, C, or D.

1.
$$4$$
$$+6$$
A 12   C 14
B 10   D not given

2. $5 + 9 = \square$
A 11   C 14
B 13   D not given

3. $6 + \square = 14$
A 8   C 7
B 9   D not given

4. $8 + 0 + 2 = \square$
A 11   C 10
B 12   D not given

5. $10 - 6 = \square$
A 3   C 2
B 4   D not given

6.
$$13$$
$$- 8$$
A 6   C 4
B 5   D not given

7.
$$15$$
$$- 6$$
A 9   C 5
B 7   D not given

8. $17 - 9 = \square$
A 8   C 6
B 9   D not given

9. What is another fact in the family? $16 - 7 = 9$
A $9 - 7 = 2$ C $7 + 9 = 16$
B $7 + 2 = 9$ D not given

10. What is the number for 4 hundreds 7 tens 2 ones?
A 427   C 407
B 472   D not given

11. Compare. 397 ● 386
A $<$ C $=$
B $>$ D not given

12. What is the value of 3 dollars, 6 dimes, 4 pennies?
A $3.44   C $3.64
B $3.04   D not given

CUMULATIVE REVIEW

Choose the correct answer. Write A, B, C, or D.

13. Round 436 to the nearest hundred.

A 300　　　　C 500

B 400　　　　D not given

14. What is the number for 1 thousand 2 hundreds 1 ten 3 ones?

A 123　　　　C 1,213

B 1,223　　　D not given

15. 3,000 + 400 + 10 + 2

A 3,241　　　C 342

B 3,412　　　D not given

16. Compare. 9,800 ● 9,008

A <　　　　C =

B >　　　　D not given

17. What is the number for nine hundred forty-one thousand?

A 900,410　　C 941,000

B 904,100　　D not given

18. 42 + 23 = ☐

A 85　　　　C 65

B 56　　　　D not given

19. 65 + 89 + 9 = ☐

A 163　　　　C 153

B 136　　　　D not given

20. 548
+465

A 1,103　　　C 903

B 1,013　　　D not given

21. 268 + 873 = ☐

A 1,141　　　C 1,031

B 1,041　　　D not given

22. 6,046 + 1,358 = ☐

A 7,094　　　C 7,404

B 8,104　　　D not given

23. $32.72 + $13.79 = ☐

A $45.41　　C $46.41

B $46.51　　D not given

24. Estimate. 347 + 239 = ☐

A 500　　　　C 300

B 400　　　　D not given

Choose the correct answer. Write A, B, C, or D.

Use the picture for **25** and **26**.

25. How much more does the train cost than the doll?

  A $6.90   **C** $5.88

  B $7.90   **D** not given

26. How much do the two toys cost?

  A $37.10   **C** $32.90

  B $37.88   **D** not given

Solve.

29. Dora saw 4 boats in the toy store. She saw 9 toy trucks. How many more trucks than boats did she see?

  A 13   **C** 14

  B 4   **D** not given

30. Ted wanted to buy 9 stickers. Sam wanted to buy 8. How many stickers did they want to buy in all?

  A 17   **C** 18

  B 1   **D** not given

Tell whether you would add or subtract. Then solve **27** and **28**.

27. Erin has 25 coupons for the carnival rides. Pete has 19. How many more does Erin have than Pete?

  A subtract; 4   **C** add; 5

  B subtract; 6   **D** not given

28. One booth had stuffed animals for prizes. There were 56 bears, 42 dogs, and 15 elephants. How many prizes were there in all?

  A add; 113   **C** add; 13

  B subtract; 1   **D** not given

What facts are missing in **31** and **32**?

31. Sue has a new coat and hat. The hat cost $5.49. How much did her outfit cost in all?

  A the cost of the hat   **C** the number of hats

  B the cost of the coat   **D** not given

32. Dan lives 2 blocks from school. Is he closer to school or town?

  A distance from school to town   **C** distance from home to school

  B distance from home to town   **D** not given

Theme: Communications

Subtracting Two-Digit Numbers

The children in Judy's class tied messages to 38 balloons. They let 23 balloons go and saved the rest for another day. How many balloons were left?

We subtract to find how many were left.

Step 1
Subtract ones.

tens	ones
3	8
−2	3
	5

Step 2
Subtract tens.

tens	ones
3	8
−2	3
1	5

There were 15 balloons left.

Find 26 − 5.

Step 1
Line up ones and tens.

```
  26
-  5
```

Step 2
Subtract ones.

```
  26
-  5
   1
```

Step 3
Subtract tens.

```
  26
-  5
  21
```

CLASSWORK

Subtract.

1. $\begin{array}{r} 56 \\ -24 \end{array}$
2. $\begin{array}{r} 77 \\ -50 \end{array}$
3. $\begin{array}{r} 82 \\ -61 \end{array}$
4. $\begin{array}{r} 95 \\ -85 \end{array}$
5. $\begin{array}{r} 48 \\ -3 \end{array}$
6. $\begin{array}{r} 65 \\ -4 \end{array}$

7. $99 - 78 = \square$

8. $58 - 18 = \square$

9. $37 - 5 = \square$

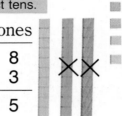

Finder,
Please return this card and tell me where you found my message.
Thank you,
Judy Burnet

PRACTICE

Subtract.

1. tens	ones		2. tens	ones		3. tens	ones		4. tens	ones
4	5		6	7		5	6		3	9
−3	2		−2	4		−1	0		−	7

5. 30
  − 20

6. 48
  − 35

7. 75
  − 15

8. 94
  − 20

9. 79
  − 5

10. 70
  − 70

11. 32
  − 22

12. 54
  − 21

13. 67
  − 6

14. 86
  − 43

15. 96
  − 4

16. 49
  − 25

17. 58
  − 50

18. 68
  − 42

19. 97
  − 66

20. 88
  − 7

21. 97
  − 93

22. 82
  − 82

23. 98 − 18 = ☐

24. 80 − 60 = ☐

25. 59 − 7 = ☐

26. 64 − 51 = ☐

27. 72 − 22 = ☐

28. 39 − 13 = ☐

Subtract across and down.

★ 29. ⟶

29	18	
16	10	

★ 30. ⟶

48	31	
25	11	

★ 31. ⟶

99	68	
17	16	

APPLICATION

32. The children in Judy's class sent 23 balloon messages. So far the children received 11 answers. How many messages were not answered?

★ 33. A sailor sent a message in a bottle. The first day the bottle floated 37 miles. The next day it floated 15 miles. How far did the bottle float?

103

Regrouping to Subtract

Laura Egan is a travel agent. She has a list of 45 telephone calls to make. She has made 29 of them. How many more calls must Laura make?

We subtract to find how many more are needed.

Step 1
Subtract ones.
Not enough ones.

tens	ones
4	5
−2	9

Step 2
Regroup 1 ten as 10 ones.

tens	ones
3	15
4̸	5̸
−2	9

Step 3
Subtract ones.

tens	ones
3	15
4̸	5̸
−2	9
	6

Step 4
Subtract tens.

tens	ones
3	15
4̸	5̸
−2	9
1	6

Laura must make 16 more calls.

CLASSWORK

Subtract.

1. 73
   −48

2. 41
   −39

3. 82
   −37

4. 70
   −26

5. 94
   − 8

6. 65
   − 5

7. 64 − 46 = □

8. 45 − 9 = □

9. 27 − 8 = □

PRACTICE

Subtract.

1. tens	ones
6	4
− 2	7

2. tens	ones
8	5
− 1	6

3. tens	ones
5	3
− 1	9

4. tens	ones
5	1
−	8

5. 34
  − 15

6. 90
  − 30

7. 85
  − 28

8. 70
  − 15

9. 52
  − 49

10. 32
  − 8

11. 80
  − 44

12. 52
  − 5

13. 73
  − 62

14. 61
  − 18

15. 51
  − 37

16. 42
  − 7

17. 96
  − 27

18. 26
  − 9

19. 83
  − 76

20. 36
  − 5

21. 47
  − 39

22. 94
  − 19

23. $98 - 88 = \square$

24. $70 - 2 = \square$

25. $92 - 56 = \square$

Compare. Use >, <, or = for ●.

26. $36 \bullet 54 - 26$

27. $97 - 59 \bullet 41$

28. $55 - 23 \bullet 32$

★29. $49 - 31 \bullet 72 - 57$

★30. $63 + 9 \bullet 90 - 18$

APPLICATION

MENTAL ARITHMETIC

Subtract 2-digit numbers in your head.
$80 - 30 = \square$

Think   8 tens − 3 tens = 5 tens
   So $80 - 30 = 50.$

Try these.

1. $50 - 30 = \square$

2. $70 - 40 = \square$

3. $80 - 10 = \square$

4. $90 - 60 = \square$

5. $60 - 20 = \square$

6. $40 - 30 = \square$

Subtracting Three-Digit Numbers

A radio station did a show to find homes for 257 animals. By the middle of the week, 104 cats and dogs had found homes. How many cats and dogs are still waiting for homes?

$257 - 104 = \square$

Step 1 Subtract ones.	**Step 2** Subtract tens.	**Step 3** Subtract hundreds.
257 − 104 3	257 − 104 53	257 − 104 153

We can check subtraction by adding.

$$\begin{array}{r} 257 \\ -104 \\ \hline 153 \end{array} \quad \text{same} \quad \begin{array}{r} 153 \\ +104 \\ \hline 257 \end{array}$$

There are 153 cats and dogs still waiting for homes.

CLASSWORK

Subtract. Check by adding.

1. $\begin{array}{r} 575 \\ -321 \end{array}$
2. $\begin{array}{r} 486 \\ -254 \end{array}$
3. $\begin{array}{r} 689 \\ -154 \end{array}$
4. $\begin{array}{r} 185 \\ -73 \end{array}$
5. $\begin{array}{r} 996 \\ -962 \end{array}$

6. $658 - 642 = \square$ 7. $361 - 51 = \square$ 8. $436 - 24 = \square$

Subtract. Check by adding.

1. 456
   − 332

2. 673
   − 131

3. 847
   − 624

4. 589
   − 565

5. 919
   − 14

6. 384
   − 72

7. 320
   − 120

8. 347
   − 121

9. 753
   − 443

10. 865
    − 714

11. 248
    − 35

12. 957
    − 631

13. 676
    − 314

14. 985
    − 260

15. 578
    − 21

16. 947
    − 436

17. 799
    − 654

18. 618
    − 312

19. 268 − 51 = ☐

20. 129 − 16 = ☐

21. 684 − 243 = ☐

22. 842 − 610 = ☐

23. 581 − 561 = ☐

24. 763 − 132 = ☐

Find each answer.

25. 798 − 103 − 462 = ☐

26. 434 − 124 − 100 = ☐

★27. 235 + 158 − 71 − 210 = ☐

★28. 672 + 316 − 231 + 6 − 763 = ☐

Make up a fact if one is missing. Then solve.

29. When the radio show started, there were 257 cats and dogs at the shelters. How many animals were left when the show ended?

★30. People donated 85 cans of pet food to the shelters. Local shops donated 125 cans. How many more cans of food are needed to meet the goal?

107

Regrouping Once

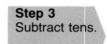

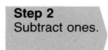

first day
139 miles

second day
251 miles

This pony-express rider traveled many miles each day. How many more miles did he travel on the second day than on the first day?

We subtract to find how many more are in one group than in another group.

Step 1 Subtract ones. Not enough ones. Regroup.	Step 2 Subtract ones.	Step 3 Subtract tens.	Step 4 Subtract hundreds.
4 11 2 5̸ 1̸ 5 tens 1 one = − 1 3 9 4 tens 11 ones	4 11 2 5̸ 1̸ − 1 3 9 2	4 11 2 5̸ 1̸ − 1 3 9 1 2	4 11 2 5̸ 1̸ − 1 3 9 1 1 2

The rider traveled 112 more miles on the second day than on the first day.

Find 226 − 145.

Step 1 Subtract ones.	Step 2 Subtract tens. Not enough tens. Regroup 1 hundred as 10 tens.	Step 3 Subtract tens.	Step 4 Subtract hundreds.
2 2 6 − 1 4 5 1	1 12 2̸ 2̸ 6 2 hundreds 2 tens = − 1 4 5 1 hundred 12 tens 1	1 12 2̸ 2̸ 6 − 1 4 5 8 1	1 12 2̸ 2̸ 6 − 1 4 5 8 1

CLASSWORK

Subtract. Check by adding.

1. 573
   − 258

2. 419
   − 267

3. 864
   − 772

4. 294
   − 68

5. 770
   − 213

6. 645 − 592 = □   7. 544 − 73 = □   8. 983 − 275 = □

Subtract. Check by adding.

1. 362 −125	2. 485 −229	3. 758 −463	4. 524 −442	5. 995 −494	6. 246 −182
7. 540 − 60	8. 939 −784	9. 367 − 57	10. 537 −509	11. 832 −614	12. 407 − 32
13. 129 − 82	14. 298 −172	15. 516 −420	16. 808 −215	17. 326 − 92	18. 915 −345

19. $365 - 327 = \square$ 20. $754 - 38 = \square$ 21. $697 - 189 = \square$

★22. $685 - 147 - 29 = \square$ ★23. $842 - 390 - 117 = \square$

Choose the correct number sentence and solve it.

24. A pony-express rider rode 144 miles to Carson City. Then he rode 290 miles to San Francisco. How many miles did he ride altogether?

    a. $290 - 144 = \square$
    b. $144 + 290 = \square$
    c. $144 - 290 = \square$
    d. $144 + 29 = \square$

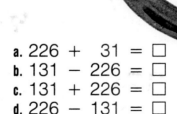

25. A pony-express rider rode 226 miles in one day. He rode along the stagecoach route for 131 miles. The rest of the trip was through the Bad Lands. How many miles did he ride through the Bad Lands?

    a. $226 + 31 = \square$
    b. $131 - 226 = \square$
    c. $131 + 226 = \square$
    d. $226 - 131 = \square$

APPLICATION

26. How many more miles did Wild Willie ride than Brave Bob?

★27. How many more miles did Saddle Sam ride than the other riders together?

PONY-EXPRESS LOG	
Rider	**Miles**
Wild Willie	219
Brave Bob	175
Saddle Sam	404

Regrouping Twice

The telegraph was the first method used to send messages by electricity. Operators tapped out words letter by letter using Morse code.

How many more words did operator A send than operator B?

Telegraph Operator	Number of Words Sent
Operator A	375
Operator B	198

375 − 198 = ☐

Step 1
Subtract ones.
Not enough ones.
Regroup.

```
    6 15
  3 7̸ 5̸
− 1 9 8
```
7 tens 5 ones =
6 tens 15 ones

Step 2
Subtract ones.

```
    6 15
  3 7̸ 5̸
− 1 9 8
        7
```

Step 3
Subtract tens.
Not enough tens.
Regroup.

```
  16
  2 6̸ 15
  3̸ 7̸ 5̸
− 1 9 8
        7
```
3 hundreds 6 tens =
2 hundreds 16 tens

Step 4
Subtract tens.

```
  16
  2 6̸ 15
  3̸ 7̸ 5̸
− 1 9 8
      7 7
```

Step 5
Subtract hundreds.

```
  16
  2 6̸ 15
  3̸ 7̸ 5̸
− 1 9 8
    1 7 7
```

Operator A sent 177 more words than operator B.

CLASSWORK

Subtract.

1. 431
   −263

2. 672
   − 187

3. 734
   − 359

4. 920
   −267

5. 561
   − 84

6. 845 − 399 = ☐

7. 310 − 38 = ☐

8. 912 − 178 = ☐

110

PRACTICE

Subtract.

1. 431 −154	2. 614 −276	3. 740 −583	4. 672 −381	5. 865 −477	6. 532 −164
7. 920 −732	8. 514 −101	9. 983 −194	10. 857 − 99	11. 526 −126	12. 713 − 79
13. 843 −686	14. 644 −352	15. 125 − 66	16. 730 −285	17. 431 −178	18. 902 −645

19. $685 - 496 = \square$ 20. $240 - 75 = \square$ 21. $615 - 387 = \square$

22. $822 - 44 = \square$ 23. $911 - 911 = \square$ 24. $920 - 368 = \square$

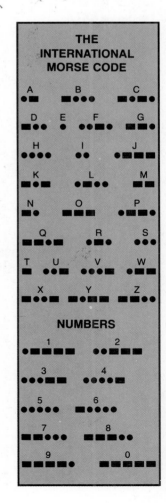

THE INTERNATIONAL MORSE CODE

Find each answer.

25. five hundred eight minus four hundred sixty-seven

26. three hundred forty-one minus two hundred twenty

27. seven hundred minus thirty-five

★ 28. eight hundred minus six, plus twenty-four

★ 29. one hundred thirty plus sixteen, minus eighty

APPLICATION

MENTAL ARITHMETIC

Subtract numbers in your head.

$65 - 19 = \square$

Think 19 is 1 less than 20.

$65 - 20 = 45$

So $65 - 19 = 45 + 1$, or 46.

Try these.

1. $74 - 19 = \square$ 2. $83 - 19 = \square$

3. $57 - 19 = \square$ 4. $41 - 19 = \square$

Subtracting Across Zeros

A homing pigeon must deliver a message 300 miles away. So far it has flown 135 miles of the trip. How many more miles must the pigeon fly?

$300 - 135 = \square$

Step 1
Subtract.
No ones.
No tens.

```
  3 0 0
- 1 3 5
```

Step 2
Regroup hundreds.

```
  2 10
  3̷ 0̷ 0
- 1 3 5
```
3 hundreds 0 tens =
2 hundreds 10 tens

Step 3
Regroup tens.

```
     9
  2 1̷0̷ 10
  3̷ 0̷ 0̷
- 1 3 5
```
10 tens 0 ones =
9 tens 10 ones

Step 4
Subtract ones.

```
     9
  2 1̷0̷ 10
  3̷ 0̷ 0̷
- 1 3 5
      5
```

Step 5
Subtract tens.

```
     9
  2 1̷0̷ 10
  3̷ 0̷ 0̷
- 1 3 5
    6 5
```

Step 6
Subtract hundreds.

```
     9
  2 1̷0̷ 10
  3̷ 0̷ 0̷
- 1 3 5
  1 6 5
```

The pigeon must fly 165 more miles.

CLASSWORK

Subtract.

1.
```
  400
- 225
```

2.
```
  900
- 647
```

3.
```
  802
- 428
```

4.
```
  307
-  89
```

5.
```
  205
- 146
```

6. $800 - 151 = \square$

7. $704 - 85 = \square$

8. $602 - 599 = \square$

9. $900 - 246 = \square$

10. $503 - 117 = \square$

11. $307 - 225 = \square$

112

Subtract.

1. $\begin{array}{r} 500 \\ -328 \end{array}$ 2. $\begin{array}{r} 300 \\ -244 \end{array}$ 3. $\begin{array}{r} 605 \\ -175 \end{array}$ 4. $\begin{array}{r} 723 \\ -356 \end{array}$ 5. $\begin{array}{r} 408 \\ -\ 99 \end{array}$ 6. $\begin{array}{r} 200 \\ -145 \end{array}$

7. $\begin{array}{r} 800 \\ -512 \end{array}$ 8. $\begin{array}{r} 900 \\ -631 \end{array}$ 9. $\begin{array}{r} 203 \\ -\ 25 \end{array}$ 10. $\begin{array}{r} 501 \\ -\ 9 \end{array}$ 11. $\begin{array}{r} 900 \\ -431 \end{array}$ 12. $\begin{array}{r} 703 \\ -647 \end{array}$

13. $\begin{array}{r} 605 \\ -487 \end{array}$ 14. $\begin{array}{r} 908 \\ -179 \end{array}$ 15. $\begin{array}{r} 755 \\ -\ 45 \end{array}$ 16. $\begin{array}{r} 600 \\ -133 \end{array}$ 17. $\begin{array}{r} 502 \\ -395 \end{array}$ 18. $\begin{array}{r} 900 \\ -312 \end{array}$

19. $800 - 631 = \square$ 20. $700 - 89 = \square$ 21. $100 - 37 = \square$

22. $906 - 98 = \square$ 23. $494 - 391 = \square$ 24. $302 - 175 = \square$

25. $400 - 217 = \square$ 26. $507 - 239 = \square$ 27. $630 - 189 = \square$

Find each rule.

28. Rule:
Subtract $\square$.

Input	Output
500	400
344	244
701	601
845	745
423	323

★29. Rule:
Subtract $\square$.

Input	Output
450	200
700	450
925	675
250	0
873	623

★30. Rule: $\square$.

Input	Output
165	300
640	775
250	385
862	997
541	676

APPLICATION

31. Ed is training his pigeon to fly back home. Yesterday the pigeon returned home from 75 miles away. Today it returned from 100 miles away. How many more miles did the pigeon fly today than yesterday?

★32. Eva's homing pigeon must carry a message 700 miles. The pigeon flew 253 miles the first day. The second day's flight was 198 miles. How many more miles must the pigeon fly to deliver the message?

Problem Solving

TOO MUCH INFORMATION

A problem may have extra facts. Read carefully and choose the facts you need to solve the problem.

Jamie spoke to Robert for 12 minutes. Later, she spoke to Li for 18 minutes. Jamie lives 5 miles from Li and 9 miles from Robert. How much longer did Jamie speak to Li than to Robert?

THINK   **What is the question?**

How much longer did Jamie speak to Li than to Robert?

Which facts do you need?

Jamie spoke to Li for 18 minutes.
Jamie spoke to Robert for 12 minutes.

Which facts are extra?

Jamie lives 5 miles from Li and 9 miles from Robert.

PLAN   **How can you find the answer?**

Subtract to find how much longer Jamie spoke to Li than to Robert.

$$18 - 12 = \square$$

SOLVE   **Carry out the plan. Do the work and find the answer.**

$$\begin{array}{r} 18 \\ -12 \\ \hline 6 \end{array}$$ Jamie spoke 6 minutes longer to Li than to Robert.

LOOK BACK   **Did you answer the question? Is your arithmetic correct? Does the answer make sense?**

Check by adding.

$12 + 6 = 18$ The answer makes sense.

Read the problem. Tell which facts are extra.

1. You take 15 minutes to deliver a message. Bernie takes 8 minutes, and Joe takes 11 minutes. How much more time do you take than Joe?

2. Janet delivered 48 papers, Bob delivered 86, and Karen delivered 132. How many papers did Janet and Karen deliver in all?

3. Marlene made a long-distance call for 4 minutes. It cost $.80. Jill made a long-distance call for 5 minutes. It cost $2.00. How long did both girls talk?

4. A record album cost $9.95. Patricia saved $3.85. Harold saved $4.22. How much money did Patricia and Harold save altogether?

Read the problem. Tell which fact in the picture is extra. Then solve the problem.

5. How much more does it cost to send package C than package A by Speed-Mail service?

6. How much less does it cost to send package A than package B?

$7.00 A $12.00 B $28.00 C

===CREATE YOUR OWN PROBLEM===

Laura and Stan are reporters for the school newspaper.

1. Make up an addition problem about Laura and Stan.

2. Make up a subtraction problem about Laura and Stan.

3. Make up a problem about Laura and Stan where the answer is 14.

Subtracting Four-Digit Numbers

The television show *Whiz Kids* was starting a new season. There were 5,378 children who tried out to be on the show. From these, 4,236 were not chosen. How many children were chosen?

$$5,378 - 4,236 = \square$$

Step 1 Subtract ones.	Step 2 Subtract tens.	Step 3 Subtract hundreds.	Step 4 Subtract thousands.
5,378 −4,236 2	5,378 −4,236 42	5,378 −4,236 142	5,378 −4,236 1,142

There were 1,142 children chosen.

These examples show regrouping in each place.

Regrouping tens

$$\begin{array}{r} \text{5 12} \\ \text{a.} \quad 4,3\,\cancel{6}\,\cancel{2} \\ -2,1\,5\,7 \\ \hline 2,2\,0\,5 \end{array}$$

Regrouping hundreds

$$\begin{array}{r} \text{2 11} \\ \text{b.} \quad 5,\cancel{3}\,\cancel{1}\,7 \\ -2,1\,8\,6 \\ \hline 3,1\,3\,1 \end{array}$$

Regrouping thousands

$$\begin{array}{r} \text{5 12} \\ \text{c.} \quad \cancel{6},2\,9\,4 \\ -\quad 8\,7\,0 \\ \hline 5,4\,2\,4 \end{array}$$

CLASSWORK

Subtract.

1. 4,787
   − 1,556

2. 8,196
   − 3,204

3. 5,861
   − 5,453

4. 3,524
   − 1,234

5. 6,999
   − 799

6. $8,782 - 8,561 = \square$

7. $9,035 - 421 = \square$

8. $7,512 - 2,408 = \square$

9. $6,925 - 4,732 = \square$

Subtract.

1. 9,634 − 4,521	2. 5,828 − 1,503	3. 6,981 − 3,871	4. 8,653 − 6,433	5. 1,499 − 1,298
6. 7,498 − 1,327	7. 6,719 − 4,268	8. 5,278 − 1,358	9. 3,492 − 1,327	10. 6,776 − 2,361
11. 6,963 − 3,716	12. 8,918 − 6,543	13. 2,644 − 1,634	14. 7,963 − 129	15. 5,760 − 3,960

16. $9,542 - 812 = \square$ 17. $8,444 - 1,632 = \square$

★ 18. $3,199 - 953 - 1,237 = \square$ ★ 19. $8,002 - 4,015 - 2,906 = \square$

APPLICATION

Tell which facts are extra. Then solve.

20. The first week, 225 people watched *Whiz Kids* in the studio. More than half of them were children. The second week, 340 people watched the show. How many more people watched the second week?

★ 21. Tony watches 1 hour of television each weekday. On Saturday and Sunday he watches 2 hours each day. How many hours does he watch in all on weekends?

LOGICAL THINKING

DD C BB A D C BB	means 3,241.		D CC A C A	means 1,302.

What does each of these mean?

1. D C B AAA D B AAA	2. D B A B	3. DD AAA DD AA

Regrouping More Than Once

Students read 2,134 books. Upper grade students read 1,259 of them. Lower grade students read the rest. How many books did lower grade students read?

$2,134 - 1,259 = \square$

Step 1
Regroup.
Subtract ones.

$$\begin{array}{r} {\scriptstyle 2\ 14} \\ 2,1\,3\,4 \\ -\,1,2\,5\,9 \\ \hline 5 \end{array}$$

3 tens 4 ones =
2 tens 14 ones

Step 2
Regroup.
Subtract tens.

$$\begin{array}{r} {\scriptstyle 12} \\ {\scriptstyle 0\ 2\ 14} \\ 2,1\,3\,4 \\ -\,1,2\,5\,9 \\ \hline 7\ 5 \end{array}$$

1 hundred
2 tens =
0 hundreds
12 tens

Step 3
Regroup.
Subtract hundreds.
Subtract thousands.

$$\begin{array}{r} {\scriptstyle 10\ 12} \\ {\scriptstyle 1\ \cancel{0}\ \cancel{2}\ 14} \\ 2,1\,3\,4 \\ -\,1,2\,5\,9 \\ \hline 8\ 7\ 5 \end{array}$$

2 thousands
0 hundreds =
1 thousand
10 hundreds

Lower grade students read 875 books.

Find $3,000 - 1,645$.

Step 1
Not enough
ones, tens, or
hundreds.

$$\begin{array}{r} 3,0\,0\,0 \\ -\,1,6\,4\,5 \\ \hline \end{array}$$

Step 2
Regroup thousands.

$$\begin{array}{r} {\scriptstyle 2\ 10} \\ 3,\cancel{0}\,0\,0 \\ -\,1,6\,4\,5 \\ \hline \end{array}$$

Step 3
Regroup hundreds.
Regroup tens.
Subtract.

$$\begin{array}{r} {\scriptstyle 9\ 9} \\ {\scriptstyle 2\ \cancel{10}\ \cancel{10}\ 10} \\ 3,\cancel{0}\,\cancel{0}\,\cancel{0} \\ -\,1,6\,4\,5 \\ \hline 1,3\,5\,5 \end{array}$$

CLASSWORK

Subtract.

1. $\begin{array}{r} 9,845 \\ -\,4,379 \\ \hline \end{array}$

2. $\begin{array}{r} 6,061 \\ -\,1,724 \\ \hline \end{array}$

3. $\begin{array}{r} 7,375 \\ -\,4,486 \\ \hline \end{array}$

4. $\begin{array}{r} 4,000 \\ -\,2,658 \\ \hline \end{array}$

5. $\begin{array}{r} 8,009 \\ -\ \ \ 486 \\ \hline \end{array}$

6. $7,331 - 7,229 = \square$

7. $4,680 - 2,589 = \square$

Subtract.

1.   4,825
  −3,216
	2. 9,752
	  −1,673
		3. 8,597
		  −3,565
			4. 7,863
			  −2,486
				5. 5,632
				  − 753

6.   5,734
  −1,518
	7. 6,913
	  −3,578
		8. 9,614
		  −2,632
			9. 8,350
			  −1,250
				10. 1,000
				  − 411

11.   3,085
  −1,762
	12. 7,506
	  − 219
		13. 9,300
		  −8,473
			14. 6,471
			  −1,198
				15. 5,270
				  −3,796

16. $8{,}000 - 5{,}249 = \square$

17. $4{,}322 - 303 = \square$

★18. $9{,}920 - \square = 9{,}205$

★19. $7{,}000 - \square = 5{,}766$

APPLICATION

NUMBER OF BOOKS STUDENTS READ THIS YEAR			
First Week	Second Week	Third Week	Fourth Week
617	516	449	552

20. Did students read more books the first two weeks or the last two weeks?

★21. Last year students read 1,789 books during Super Reader Month. How many more did they read this year?

CALCULATOR

Find the missing number.

$9{,}258 - \square = 2{,}132$

Press:  9 2 5 8 − 2 1 3 2 =   7126

Find each missing number.

1. $5{,}270 - \square = 3{,}210$

2. $9{,}865 - \square = 444$

3. $3{,}772 - \square = 2{,}529$

4. $6{,}909 - \square = 2{,}763$

Subtracting Money

Carrie has $4.75. It will cost $3.50 to mail a package to her grandmother. How much money will Carrie have left?

We subtract money the same way we subtract other numbers.

Line up the decimal points.

$$\begin{array}{r} \$4.75 \\ -\ 3.50 \end{array}$$

Subtract.

$$\begin{array}{r} \$4.75 \\ -\ 3.50 \\ \hline \$1.25 \end{array}$$

Write the dollar sign and decimal point in the answer.

Carrie will have $1.25 left.

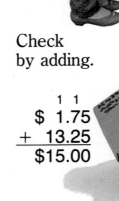

Find $15.00 − $13.25.

Line up the decimal points.

$$\begin{array}{r} \$15.00 \\ -\ 13.25 \end{array}$$

Regroup. Subtract.

$$\begin{array}{r} {}^{9} \\ 4\ \overset{10}{\cancel{10}}\ 10 \\ \$\ 1\ \cancel{5}.\cancel{0}\ \cancel{0} \\ -\ \ 1\ 3.2\ 5 \\ \hline \$\ \ \ 1.7\ 5 \end{array}$$

Check by adding.

$$\begin{array}{r} {}^{1\ \ 1} \\ \$\ 1.75 \\ +\ 13.25 \\ \hline \$15.00 \end{array}$$

CLASSWORK

Subtract. Check by adding.

1. $\begin{array}{r} \$4.69 \\ -\ 2.50 \end{array}$
2. $\begin{array}{r} \$15.65 \\ -\ \ 4.35 \end{array}$
3. $\begin{array}{r} \$.73 \\ -\ .59 \end{array}$
4. $\begin{array}{r} \$8.00 \\ -\ 1.67 \end{array}$
5. $\begin{array}{r} \$28.32 \\ -\ 19.46 \end{array}$

6. $\$4.25 - \$1.80 = \square$

7. $\$30.16 - \$2.87 = \square$

8. $\$16.00 - \$9.95 = \square$

9. $\$56.25 - \$9.30 = \square$

120

PRACTICE

Subtract. Check by adding.

1. $5.50
   − 1.40

2. $10.98
   − 10.50

3. $16.38
   − 5.28

4. $.65
   − .17

5. $7.84
   − 2.38

6. $66.85
   − 31.73

7. $90.79
   − 79.41

8. $9.20
   − 1.16

9. $1.59
   − .75

10. $25.49
   − 6.72

11. $28.31
   − 10.68

12. $78.00
   − 39.40

13. $39.87 − $16.25 = □

14. $17.75 − $2.30 = □

15. $26.34 − $.75 = □

16. $74.92 − $46.87 = □

Find each missing number.

17. $29.50 + □ = $59.50

18. □ + $.98 = $1.98

19. $10.00 + □ = $50.60

★ 20. □ + $.29 = $5.00

★ 21. $1.39 + □ = $17.20

APPLICATION

22. Sara spent $2.75 at the post office. How much change did she receive from $5.00?

★ 23. Mitchell had $5.00. He bought six 9-cent stamps. How much money did he get back?

1. 2
   +4

2. 10
   − 5

3. 2
   +8

4. 9
   −4

5. 8
   +7

6. 15
   − 9

7. 4
   +6

8. 12
   − 3

9. 8
   +9

10. 25
   +34

11. 61
   +27

12. 36
   +75

13. 88
   +75

14. 361
   +225

Compare. Use >, <, or = for ●.

15. 6 ● 7

16. 18 ● 18

17. 49 ● 39

18. 0 ● 40

19. 631 ● 655

20. 763 ● 736

Estimating Differences

About how many more points did Phil score than Amy in the spelling game?

We do not need an exact number. We can estimate to find the answer.

▶To estimate the difference, round each number to the nearest ten. Then subtract.

87	rounds to	90
−71	rounds to	−70
		20 estimated difference

Phil scored about 20 more points than Amy.

▶To estimate this difference, round each number to the nearest hundred. Then subtract.

216	rounds to	200
−109	rounds to	−100
		100 estimated difference

CLASSWORK

Round to the nearest ten and estimate each difference.

1. 76	2. 34	3. 85	4. 53	5. 92	6. 57
−21	−19	−62	−44	−17	−34

Round to the nearest hundred and estimate each difference.

7. 245	8. 836	9. 251	10. 882	11. 748	12. 418
−121	−597	−183	−366	−634	−179

PRACTICE

Round to the nearest ten and estimate each difference.

1. 68
   − 21

2. 93
   − 32

3. 59
   − 38

4. 73
   − 25

5. 45
   − 16

6. 83
   − 41

7. 94
   − 37

8. 81
   − 19

9. 64
   − 48

10. 51
    − 47

11. 26
    − 13

12. 57
    − 26

13. 71 − 25 = ☐

14. 89 − 32 = ☐

15. 43 − 34 = ☐

Round to the nearest hundred and estimate each difference.

16. 368
    − 217

17. 774
    − 153

18. 493
    − 101

19. 835
    − 352

20. 471
    − 435

21. 236
    − 145

22. 921
    − 416

23. 600
    − 574

24. 432
    − 197

25. 329
    − 118

26. 943
    − 630

27. 568
    − 110

28. 898 − 763 = ☐

29. 948 − 651 = ☐

30. 365 − 194 = ☐

Round, then estimate each difference.

★31. 247 − 96 = ☐

★32. 475 − 60 = ☐

★33. 693 − 98 − 348 = ☐

★34. 630 − 351 − 96 = ☐

APPLICATION

Estimate to solve.

About how many points did each team below score?

35. Al and Lee

36. Bob and Linda

37. Al and Bob

38. Lee and Linda

Scores

Al	402
Bob	315
Lee	463
Linda	395

39. Estimate the difference between Al's and Linda's points.

★40. About how many more points did Al and Lee score than Bob and Linda?

Adding and Subtracting

Which is the shorter path to the treasure?

Add to find the length of each path.

$$\begin{array}{r} 85 \\ +129 \\ \hline 214 \end{array}$$ western path $$\begin{array}{r} 172 \\ +59 \\ \hline 231 \end{array}$$ eastern path

Compare the sums.

$$214 < 231$$

The western path is the shorter path.

How much shorter is the western path than the eastern path?

Subtract to find the difference.

$$\begin{array}{r} 231 \\ -214 \\ \hline 17 \end{array}$$

The western path is 17 steps shorter than the eastern path.

CLASSWORK

Add or subtract.

1. $$\begin{array}{r} 67 \\ +42 \end{array}$$
2. $$\begin{array}{r} 98 \\ -9 \end{array}$$
3. $$\begin{array}{r} 50 \\ -31 \end{array}$$
4. $$\begin{array}{r} 194 \\ +657 \end{array}$$
5. $$\begin{array}{r} 683 \\ -584 \end{array}$$

6. $3,035 + 4,227 = \square$ 7. $1,936 - 507 = \square$ 8. $9,990 - 4,316 = \square$

124

Add or subtract.

1. 31
   +68

2. 47
   −42

3. 73
   −13

4. 51
   +36

5. 62
   +37

6. 84
   −59

7. 357
   +428

8. 318
   +205

9. 845
   −379

10. 762
    −573

11. 999
    +205

12. 3,000
    + 950

13. 1,740
    − 894

14. 7,650
    −7,563

15. 8,796
    −2,846

16. 1,500
    +1,949

17. 6,025
    −2,460

18. 2,484
    +1,576

19. $58.13
    − 39.08

20. $72.18
    + 17.99

21. 507 − 63 = ☐

22. 7,435 − 4,752 = ☐

23. 1,764 + 979 = ☐

24. $58.75 − $9.25 = ☐

25. $16.32 + $47.48 = ☐

26. $36.50 + $82.89 = ☐

27. $82.89 − $36.50 = ☐

★28. 1,346 + 719 − 800 = ☐

★29. 4,298 − 374 + 374 = ☐

Choose the letter of each sentence that is true.

30. a. 23 + 47 = 70
    b. 40 − 9 < 30
    c. 125 < 100 + 50
    d. 500 > 450 + 39

APPLICATION

LOGICAL THINKING

1. Name the paths in order from the shortest to the longest.

2. How would you know which path is the shortest path without looking at the numbers?

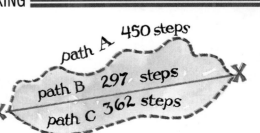

path A 450 steps

path B 297 steps

path C 362 steps

Problem Solving

Pat and Roberta are talking on their cup phones. The string between their phones is 18 feet long. Selma and Joyce are talking on their cup phones. The string between their phones is 25 feet long.

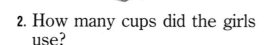

Solve each problem below. Decide which facts you need from the story above. Make up a fact if one is missing.

1. How many feet of string did the girls use?

2. How many cups did the girls use?

3. How many pieces of string did the girls use for the cup phones?

4. How much longer is the string from Joyce to Selma than from Pat to Roberta?

5. The girls bought a ball of string which cost $.75. Together, Pat and Roberta gave $.40. How much was needed from Selma and Joyce to pay for the string?

6. The girls talked for 37 minutes on Monday. They talked for 13 minutes on Tuesday, and 21 minutes on Wednesday. How much longer did they talk on Monday than on Wednesday?

7. It took Pat and Roberta 25 minutes to make their phone. How much longer did it take Selma and Joyce than Pat and Roberta to make theirs?

8. When the girls bought the string, there were 225 feet of string in the ball. How much string did the girls have left after the phones were made?

Problem Solving

WHAT IF . . . ?

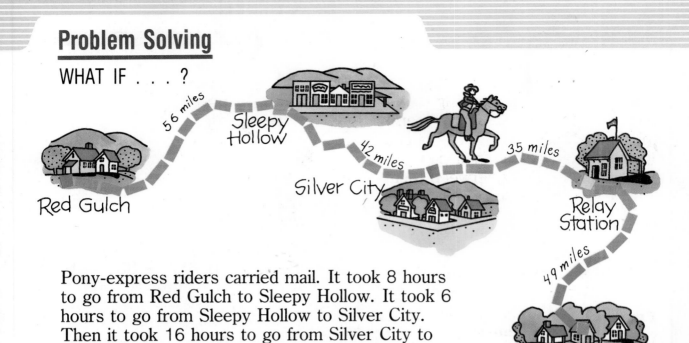

Pony-express riders carried mail. It took 8 hours to go from Red Gulch to Sleepy Hollow. It took 6 hours to go from Sleepy Hollow to Silver City. Then it took 16 hours to go from Silver City to Pine Ridge.

Read and solve each problem.

1. How many hours did it take to go from Red Gulch to Silver City?

2. How many miles did riders travel from Sleepy Hollow to Pine Ridge?

3. How many more miles was it from Pine Ridge to the relay station than from the relay station to Silver City?

4. How many fewer hours did it take to go from Red Gulch to Silver City than from Silver City to Pine Ridge?

What if the riders stopped at Sleepy Hollow for 1 hour on their way to Silver City?

5. How many hours would it take to go from Red Gulch to Silver City?

6. How many hours would it take to go from Red Gulch to Sleepy Hollow?

What if the trip back from Pine Ridge to Silver City took 2 hours less?

★ 7. How long would the return trip from Pine Ridge to Silver City take?

★ 8. How long would the return trip from Pine Ridge to Sleepy Hollow take?

CHAPTER REVIEW

Subtract. pages 102–111

1. 56
    − 23

2. 75
    − 41

3. 72
    − 29

4. 96
    − 38

5. 84
    − 56

6. 267
    − 123

7. 486
    − 295

8. 377
    − 368

9. 621
    − 197

10. 541
    − 263

11. 98 − 21 = □

12. 378 − 149 = □

13. 617 − 330 = □

Find each difference. pages 112–113, 116–121

14. 2,046
    − 1,879

15. 6,800
    − 4,358

16. 3,825
    − 1,704

17. 4,705
    − 2,716

18. 2,600
    − 1,032

19. $9.50
    − 3.25

20. $8.14
    − 7.17

21. $23.36
    − 6.48

22. $30.00
    − 21.74

23. $80.50
    − 50.79

24. 7,500 − 1,274 = □

25. $15.45 − $10.49 = □

Round to the nearest ten and estimate each difference. pages 122–123

26. 33 − 19 = □

27. 85 − 36 = □

28. 73 − 48 = □

Round to the nearest hundred and estimate each difference. pages 122–123

29. 922 − 687 = □

30. 397 − 302 = □

31. 548 − 217 = □

Tell which facts are extra. Then solve. pages 114–115, 126–127

32. The librarian ordered 128 story books and 110 books of facts. He also ordered 30 filmstrips. How many books did he order in all?

33. Paolo bought a book for $5.98, a record for $7.39, and a tape for $6.65. How much more did the record cost than the tape?

Subtract.

1. 79 -64	2. 91 -52	3. 80 -53	4. 693 -420	5. 880 -656

6. $500 - 425 = \square$ **7.** $92 - 38 = \square$ **8.** $600 - 258 = \square$

Find each difference.

9. $7{,}983$ $-3{,}375$	10. $8{,}437$ $-6{,}525$	11. $6{,}590$ $-3{,}034$	12. $8{,}399$ $-7{,}525$	13. $9{,}020$ $-4{,}168$

14. $\$5.15$ -2.75	15. $\$21.05$ -7.78	16. $\$40.00$ -9.16	17. $\$35.80$ -20.93	18. $\$98.76$ -56.48

19. $\$31.50 - \$29.06 = \square$ **20.** $\$92.35 - \$76.50 = \square$

Choose the best estimate.

21. $91 - 33 = \square$

   a. 50   **b.** 70

   c. 60   **d.** 80

22. $839 - 354 = \square$

   a. 300   **b.** 500

   c. 400   **d.** 600

23. $761 - 208 = \square$

   a. 400   **b.** 600

   c. 500   **d.** 700

Find the extra facts. Then solve.

24. The first week, students watched 294 hours of television. The second week, they watched 256 hours. The third week, they watched 263 hours. How many hours did they watch the first two weeks?

25. A ham radio operator made 4,280 contacts last year and 2,796 this year. Her brother made 2,315 contacts this year. How many more contacts did she make last year than this year?

The phone call Brigid made to Ireland during the day cost $12.40. Two calls in the evening cost $4.32 and $5.65. How much less did Brigid spend in the evening than in the morning?

SLIDING SUBTRACTIONS

You will need: · two strips of oaktag
· a ruler
· a marking pen

You can make a tool to help you subtract.

1. Use the ruler. Make evenly-spaced marks along the bottom of one strip. Start with 0 on the left. Number the marks from 0 through 20.

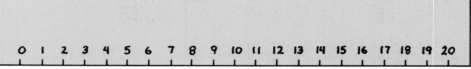

2. Use the first strip to make evenly-spaced marks along the top of the second strip. Number those marks from 0 through 20.

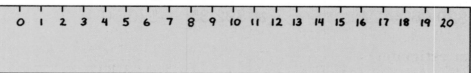

Now you are ready to subtract.

3. To subtract 6 from 13, slide the strips until 6 on the bottom strip is lined up with 13 on the top strip. The answer appears on the top strip above the 0 on the bottom strip. The answer is 7. $13 - 6 = 7$

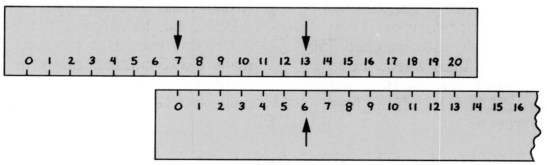

Try these subtraction examples.

1. $8 - 4 = \square$ 2. $19 - 15 = \square$ 3. $17 - 9 = \square$

4. $11 - 8 = \square$ 5. $16 - 5 = \square$ 6. $14 - 5 = \square$

A DIFFERENT WAY TO SUBTRACT

We know how to regroup to subtract.

$$\begin{array}{r} \overset{\scriptstyle 9}{\cancel{6}\,\cancel{10}\,11} \\ \cancel{7}\,0\,\cancel{1} \\ -1\,9\,8 \\ \hline 5\,0\,3 \end{array}$$

Here is another way to subtract.
Add 2 to each number. Then subtract.

$$\begin{array}{r} 701 + 2 = 703 \\ -198 + 2 = 200 \\ \hline 503 \end{array}$$

Your answer is the same as the first way!

Try another example.
This time add 4 to each number.
Then subtract.

$$\begin{array}{r} 2,500 + 4 = 2,504 \\ -\quad 396 + 4 = \quad 400 \\ \hline 2,104 \end{array}$$

Do you see how to choose which number to add?
You want to make the number you are subtracting
end in zero. That way, you do not need to
regroup. This makes subtracting easier.

Now try these.

1. $\begin{array}{r} 1,205 \\ -\quad 97 \\ \hline \end{array}$ 2. $\begin{array}{r} 800 \\ -\ 95 \\ \hline \end{array}$ 3. $\begin{array}{r} 413 \\ -293 \\ \hline \end{array}$

4. $\begin{array}{r} 5,473 \\ -\ 394 \\ \hline \end{array}$ 5. $\begin{array}{r} 8,315 \\ -\quad 99 \\ \hline \end{array}$ 6. $\begin{array}{r} 3,400 \\ -\quad 89 \\ \hline \end{array}$

Did you add 11 to the numbers in exercise 6?
Can you tell why this way of subtracting works?

Choose the correct answer. Write A, B, C, or D.

1. $5 + 3 + 2 = \square$

   A 12   C 14

   B 10   D not given

7. Estimate. $650 + 647 = \square$

   A 1,200   C 1,100

   B 1,300   D not given

2. Round 546 to the nearest hundred.

   A 500   C 600

   B 540   D not given

8. $2,340 - 902 = \square$

   A 1,438   C 2,338

   B 2,448   D not given

3. Choose the number for seven hundred four thousand.

   A 700,400   C 704,000

   B 74,000   D not given

9. Estimate. $435 - 320 = \square$

   A 200   C 300

   B 100   D not given

4. $784 + 137 = \square$

   A 811   C 921

   B 821   D not given

What facts are missing in 10 and 11?

10. Di used 2 rolls of film. How many pictures did she take?

   A cost of film   C 2 rolls

   B number of pictures on both rolls   D not given

5.
$$\begin{array}{r} 8,523 \\ +4,106 \\ \hline \end{array}$$

   A 12,609   C 13,629

   B 12,629   D not given

11. A book has 1 picture on each page. How many pictures are in the book?

6. $\$31.80 + \$47.26 = \square$

   A $78.96   C $79.06

   B $78.06   D not given

   A total pages in book   C number of books

   B number of pictures on page   D not given

Theme: Exploring Space

Hour, Half Hour, Quarter Hour

It is 7 o'clock in the morning.
We are getting ready for lift-off.

The short hand shows hours.

The long hand shows minutes.

- read   seven o'clock
- write   7 o'clock, or 7:00

Now it is quarter after seven.
Everyone is ready.

hours   minutes

- read   seven fifteen, or quarter after seven
- write   7:15

Lift-off takes place at seven thirty.

- read   seven thirty, or half past seven
- write   7:30

▶ 60 minutes = 1 hour
  30 minutes = 1 half hour
  15 minutes = 1 quarter hour

The lift-off was in the morning. It took place at 7:30 A.M.

▶ The hours between 12:00 midnight and 12:00 noon are A.M. hours.
The hours between 12:00 noon and 12:00 midnight are P.M. hours.

CLASSWORK

Write each time, using numbers. Then read.

1.
2.
3.
4.

134

Write each time, using numbers.

1.

2.

3.

4.

5.

6.

7.

8.

Match.

9. seven o'clock in the evening   a. 2:30 P.M.

10. 4:30 A.M.   b. quarter after three

11. 3:15   c. 5:15

12. two thirty in the afternoon   d. half past four in the morning

13. quarter past five   e. 7:00 P.M.

Tell which is the longer time.

★14. 1 half hour or 25 minutes   ★15. 1 hour or 65 minutes

★16. 1 quarter hour or 30 minutes   ★17. 2 hours or 100 minutes

APPLICATION

Write each time another way. Use A.M. or P.M.

18. Jack puts his space suit on at one o'clock in the afternoon.

19. Countdown begins at quarter after six in the evening.

20. Stu works on the rocket. He begins work at half past nine in the morning.

21. Luisa tests machines for the Space Center. She starts work at eight o'clock in the morning.

★22. Read exercises 18–21. Put the following in the order in which they happen.

a. Jack puts space suit on.   b. Countdown begins after 6 P.M.
c. Stu begins work on rocket.   d. Luisa starts work on machines.

Minutes

Edward White was the first American astronaut to walk in space. He walked outside the spacecraft for 21 minutes.

The minute hand moves from one mark to the next mark in 1 minute.

It moves from one number to the next number in 5 minutes.

It moves once around the clock in 60 minutes, or 1 hour.

- read   five minutes after six
- write   6:05

- read   seven minutes after six
- write   6:07

- read   twenty minutes to seven, or six forty
- write   6:40

- read   quarter to seven, fifteen minutes to seven, or six forty-five
- write   6:45

CLASSWORK

Write each time, using numbers. Then read.

1.   2.   3.   4.

5. eight forty   6. six minutes after two   7. one ten

Write each time, using numbers.

1.

2.

3.

4.

5.

6.

7.

8.

9.

10.

11.

12.

13. four minutes after ten

14. thirteen minutes after one

★ 15. four minutes to two

★ 16. nine minutes to eleven

Complete the table.

	Time	4:30	4:40	4:45	4:55
17.	Minutes after 4	30		45	
18.	Minutes to 5	30	20		

APPLICATION

19. Astronaut Clark woke up at eight minutes to six. Astronaut Blake woke up at seven minutes to six. Who woke up first?

★ 20. The first American astronaut went into space at 9:34 A.M. The flight was over 15 minutes later. At what time did the flight end?

CALCULATOR

The astronauts spent 15 minutes doing exercises. They spent 10 minutes eating breakfast. Then they spent 30 minutes cleaning the spacecraft. How much less than 1 hour did these things take?

Elapsed Time

Duane's class saw the movie *Star Trip*. The movie began at 1:00. It lasted 1 hour. At what time did it end?

The minute hand moves once around the clock in 1 hour. The hour hand moves from one number to the next in one hour.

start 1:00  end 2:00

The movie ended at 2:00.

Duane looked at the planet Venus. He started at 2:15. He stopped at 2:25. How much time had passed? Counting by fives can help you.

start 2:15   end 2:25

Ten minutes had passed.

CLASSWORK

Tell what time it will be.

1. in 5 hours

2. in 2 minutes

3. in 8 hours

Tell how much time has passed.

4.

start   end

5.

start   end

138

Tell what time it will be.

1. in 2 hours

2. in 7 hours

3. in 15 minutes

Tell how much time has passed.

4.

start

end

5.

start

end

6. start   8:30
   end   11:30

7. start   11:00
   end   1:00

8. start   4:15
   end   4:45

Complete. Follow the rule, if given.

Rule:
Add 30 minutes.

9. 3:30	
10. 5:00	
11. 12:00	
12. 8:30	

Rule:
Subtract 1 hour.

13. 4:00	
14. 6:15	
15. 9:00	
16. 2:10	

Find the rule.

★17. 1:00	1:12
4:30	4:42
6:00	6:12
7:40	7:52

APPLICATION

18. Rico went to lunch at 11:30 A.M. He finished 1 hour later. What time was it then?

19. Ms. Collins arrived at school at 7:45 A.M. The students arrived at 8:30 A.M. She left school at 4:45 P.M. How long was Ms. Collins in school?

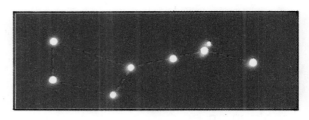

★20. The bus arrived at school at 5:15 P.M. It had left the museum 10 minutes before. At what time had it left?

139

Estimating Time

It took about 8 minutes for the rocket to go into orbit.

▶A **minute** is used to measure a short amount of time.

It takes about 1 minute for a traffic light to change.

It takes about 3 minutes to brush your teeth.

The first people on the moon walked around for about 2 hours.

▶An **hour** is used to measure longer amounts of time.

It takes about 1 hour to listen to both sides of a record album.

It takes about 2 hours to watch a movie.

CLASSWORK

Which unit would you use to measure the time?
Choose minute or hour.

1. cooking an egg

2. sleeping at night

3. drinking some milk

4. working in school

5. watching a ball game

6. getting dressed

Which unit would you use to measure the time?
Choose minute or hour.

1. eating cereal
2. listening to a song
3. reading a page
4. hiking up a mountain
5. taking a plane to France
6. writing your name 20 times

Tell which takes longer.

7. eating breakfast or watching a football game
8. listening to a record album or combing your hair
9. watching a television show or putting on your shoes
10. feeding a pet or making a model airplane

About how long does it take? Choose a or b.

11. playing with your friends	a. 1 minute	b. 1 hour
12. eating a sandwich	a. 10 minutes	b. 10 hours
13. sleeping at night	a. 8 minutes	b. 8 hours
14. staying at the beach	a. 2 minutes	b. 2 hours
★ 15. reading a storybook	a. 25 minutes	b. 5 hours
★ 16. visiting the zoo	a. 40 minutes	b. 4 hours

APPLICATION

Match the space traveler's plans with the times.

Plans for Today
17. Make a phone call.   a. 3 hours
18. Write a letter.   b. 5 minutes
19. Plant a garden.   c. 1 minute
20. Take a vitamin pill.   d. 25 minutes

★ 21. How much time will these activities take in all?

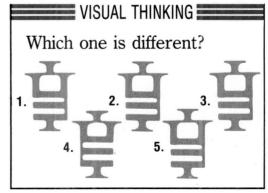

VISUAL THINKING

Which one is different?

1. 2. 3. 4. 5.

Calendar

Jean and Paul will be at the United States Space Camp for two weeks in August.

▶ 1 week = 7 days

Jean and Paul arrive at camp on Sunday, August 7.

- read   August seventh
- write   August 7

SUNDAY	MONDAY	TUESDAY	WEDNESDAY	THURSDAY	FRIDAY	SATURDAY
	1	2	3	4	5	6
7 CAMP	8 ✗	9 ✗	10 ✗	11 ✗	12 ✗	13 ✗
14 ✗	15 ✗	16 ✗	17 ✗	18 ✗	19 ✗	20 ✗
21	22	23	24	25	26	27
28	29	30	31			

AUGUST

Ordinal numbers show order.

A calendar shows the days in order.

The fifth Wednesday is August 31.

The third Monday is August 15.

The first Thursday is August 4.

A calendar also shows the months in order.

CLASSWORK

Use the calendar to answer each question.

1. What is the date of the first Monday in August?
2. What is the date of the second Friday?
3. What is the date of the third Tuesday?
4. What is the date of the fourth Wednesday?
5. On what day and date do Jean and Paul leave the camp?

PRACTICE

Use the August calendar on page 142 to answer each question.

1. What is the date of the second Tuesday?
2. What is the date of the fourth Thursday?
3. What is the date of the first Saturday?
4. What is the date of the third Friday?

What day and date is it? Use the calendar.

5. the day after the sixth
6. the day before the tenth
7. the day before the twentieth

August is the eighth month. Tell which month each of these is.

8. October
9. December
★ 10. May
★ 11. March

APPLICATION

12. Jean tried on a space suit on Tuesday, August 9. The next day she worked with moon rocks. What day was it? What was the date?

13. Paul worked in a lab on Monday, August 15. Two days later he went back to the lab. What day was it? What was the date?

★ 14. Pretend March 2 is a Wednesday. What day in March is the seventeenth?

=== LOGICAL THINKING ===

Pretend the first Sunday in June is June 5. How many Sundays are there in June? What are the dates?

1. $17 + 13 = \square$

2. $10 - 5 = \square$

3. $46 + 57 = \square$

4. $632 + 189 = \square$

5. $408 - 316 = \square$

6. $2,573 - 97 = \square$

7. $\begin{array}{r} 4,735 \\ +\ \ 628 \end{array}$

8. $\begin{array}{r} 7,048 \\ -2,376 \end{array}$

9. $\begin{array}{r} 5,139 \\ +3,876 \end{array}$

10. $\begin{array}{r} 9,304 \\ -6,715 \end{array}$

Round to the nearest hundred.

11. 384
12. 640
13. 198
14. 515
15. 653
16. 938
17. 729

Problem Solving

FINDING PATTERNS

Patterns can help you solve problems. Try to find a pattern.

Susan placed nickels and dimes on a table in a pattern. What coin is under the mouse?

What is the question?

What coin is under the mouse?

What are the facts?

You see dime, nickel, dime, nickel, dime.

How can you find the answer?
What do you do?

Look for a pattern. The nickel follows the dime, the dime follows the nickel. Follow this pattern.

Carry out the plan.
Do the work and solve the problem.

Continue the pattern.

       ?

The next coin should be a nickel.
A nickel is under the mouse.

Did you answer the question?
Does the answer make sense?

Yes. The answer makes sense. Susan's last dime should follow a nickel.

144

Find and complete each pattern.

1. 2, 4, 6, 8, 10, 12, _____

2. 1, 3, 5, 7, _____, 11, _____, 15

3. 18, 15, 12, _____, _____, 3

4. 10¢, 15¢, 20¢, 25¢, _____, _____, 40¢

5.

6.

7.

8.

9. red, blue, yellow, red, blue, yellow, _____

10. A, C, E, G, I, _____, M, O, _____

11.

12. ABA, ACA, ADA, _____, _____, AGA

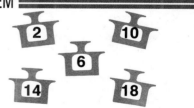

CREATE YOUR OWN PROBLEM

Use these numbers to make a pattern. Find the next number in your pattern.

2   10
6
14   18

Coins, One-Dollar Bill

Anne bought a magazine at the Air and Space Museum. It cost one dollar.

dollar = 100¢ or $1.00

▶   5 pennies = 1 nickel
10 pennies = 1 dime
100 pennies = 1 dollar
2 nickels = 1 dime
5 nickels = 1 quarter
10 dimes = 1 dollar

Anne paid $1.15 for the magazine and one postcard.

one dollar and fifteen cents

Remember to use the dollar sign ($) and decimal point (.) to write amounts of money. You may use just a cents sign (¢) when you have only cents.

penny = 1¢ or $.01

nickel = 5¢ or $.05

dime = 10¢ or $.10

quarter = 25¢ or $.25

half-dollar = 50¢ or $.50

CLASSWORK

Write the value. Use a dollar sign and decimal point. Then read.

1.

2.

PRACTICE

Write the value. Use a cents sign.

1.

2.

Write the value. Use a dollar sign and decimal point.

3.

4.

5. 22 pennies

6. 4 nickels

7. 5 dimes

8. 5 quarters

9. 2 dimes

10. 3 half-dollars

11. 3 dollars, 9 dimes, 2 pennies

12. 4 quarters, 2 dimes, 1 penny

13. 2 dollars, 4 nickels, 2 pennies

14. 1 half-dollar, 2 dimes, 1 nickel

15. 1 dollar, 4 quarters, 10 dimes

★ **16.** 8 dollars, 1 dime, 2 quarters, 1 nickel

★ **17.** 2 dimes, 4 pennies, 1 dollar, 3 nickels

APPLICATION

18. Anne saved a quarter a day for 6 days. Complete the pattern to find the amount she had saved by the sixth day.

$.25, $.50, $.75, ____, ____, ____

★ **19.** Ricky used 8 coins to pay for $1.40-worth of space toys. He used no half-dollars, dimes, or pennies. What coins did he use?

Five-Dollar Bill, Ten-Dollar Bill

Chris saved his allowance until he had $12.95. He wanted to buy a set of NASA patches to wear on his jacket.

twelve dollars and ninety-five cents

Chris changed 10 of his dollars for a ten-dollar bill.

$10.00 $1.00 + $1.00 $.25 + $.25 + $.25 $.10 + $.10

▶ To count money, start with the bill or coin of greatest value. End with the coin of least value.

   five, six dollars,   ten, twenty,   twenty-one cents

$6.21   six dollars and twenty-one cents

CLASSWORK

Write the value. Then read.

1.

2.

Write the value.

1.

2.

3. 7 one-dollar bills, 2 quarters

4. 1 five-dollar bill, 2 one-dollar bills

5. 3 ten-dollar bills, 1 five-dollar bill

6. 1 ten-dollar bill, 3 one-dollar bills, 6 dimes

7. 2 five-dollar bills, 1 one-dollar bill, 1 nickel

8. 5 ten-dollar bills, 2 dimes, 2 pennies

9. 3 five-dollar bills, 2 quarters, 5 dimes

Copy and complete. Use the fewest possible bills and coins.

	Amount	Ten-Dollar Bills	Five-Dollar Bills	One-Dollar Bills	Quarters	Dimes	Nickels	Pennies
★ 10.	$13.25							
★ 11.	$ 6.57							
★ 12.	$34.17							
★ 13.	$25.60							

APPLICATION

14. Chris has 1 bill and 3 coins. He has $5.30. What are the bills and coins he has?

★ 15. Sally was given 2 bills. Each bill was worth less than $10.00. What was the most that Sally could have been given? What was the least?

===== MENTAL ARITHMETIC =====

1. Name 4 coins that equal $.60.

2. Name 3 coins that equal $.31.

3. Name 5 coins that equal $.96.

4. Name 6 coins that equal $.85.

Counting Change

Mr. Chen bought a safety blanket. It cost $2.79. Mr. Chen gave the salesperson $3.00. How much change did the salesperson give Mr. Chen?

First-Aid Thermal Blanket for Home, Car, Boat and Camping

EMERGENCY BLANKET

Reflects and retains up to 80% of radiated body heat. Use to help prevent post-accident shock or to keep warm under emergency cold weather conditions.

weight: 3 oz. approximate size: 32 square feet (7 ft. x 4½ ft.)

The salesperson starts counting with the cost of the blanket. He ends with the amount Mr. Chen gave him.

$2.79	$2.80	$2.90	$3.00

▶To count change, start with the coins of least value.

Add the value of the coins to find the amount of change.

$$\$.01 + \$.10 + \$.10 = \$.21$$

The salesperson gave Mr. Chen $.21 in change.

You can also subtract to find the amount of change.

```
      9
    2 10 10
  $3.0 0
 − 2.7 9
  $ .2 1
```

CLASSWORK

Count the change.

1. Paid 1 dollar.

_____ _____ _____ _____

2. Paid 2 dollars.

_____ _____ _____

150

Count the change.

1. Paid 1 dollar.

_____ _____ _____ _____

2. Paid 3 dollars.

_____ _____ _____

★ 3. Paid 5 dollars.

_____ _____ _____ _____

Count the change. Subtract to check.

Cost	Paid	Total Change
4.		_____
5. 		_____
★ 6.		_____

APPLICATION

7. Mr. Chen bought a wooden glider for $.56. He gave the salesperson $1.00. How much change did he get?

★ 8. Dave bought stickers for $1.80. His change was 2 dimes and 3 dollars. How much did he give the cashier?

151

Comparing Money

Terry wants to buy a book. It costs
$2.29. He has 2 one-dollar bills,
1 quarter, and 3 nickels. Does he
have enough money to buy the book?

Terry has $2.40.
Compare $2.40 and $2.29.

```
          same
      ┌──────────┐
$2.40 .          $2.29
      └────┘
      4 > 2
  so $2.40 > $2.29
```

He has enough money to buy the book.

CLASSWORK

Is there enough money? Answer _yes_ or _no_.

1.

Compare. Use > or < for ●.

2. $1.19 ● $1.21

3. $4.00 ● $3.74

4. $6.88 ● $7.01

5. $2.30 ● $2.03

6. $3.87 ● $5.25

7. $.99 ● $9.20

Is there enough money? Write *yes* or *no*.

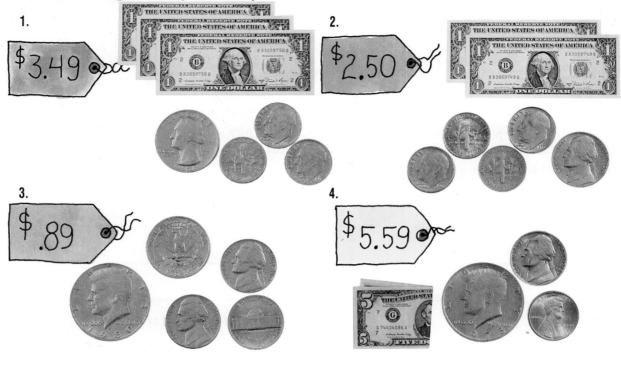

1. $3.49

2. $2.50

3. $.89

4. $5.59

Compare. Use >, <, or = for ⬤

5. $1.50 ⬤ $1.45

6. $2.99 ⬤ $3.10

7. $4.65 ⬤ $5.15

8. $3.01 ⬤ $2.10

★9. 4 dollars, 2 nickels, 1 penny ⬤ 4 dollars, 1 dime

★10. 3 dollars, 1 half-dollar ⬤ 3 dollars, 4 dimes, 2 nickels

APPLICATION

11. Jim has 1 dollar, 2 dimes, 1 nickel, and 2 pennies. Does he have enough money to buy a toy that costs $1.29?

12. Linda has 3 quarters, 1 dime, 1 nickel, and 3 pennies. Does she have enough money to buy a card that costs $.89?

★13. Kate has 2 dollars, 1 dime, 3 nickels, and 4 pennies. How much more does she need to buy a book that costs $2.39?

★14. Mark has 4 dollars, 2 quarters, and 3 dimes. How much change would he get after buying 2 books that cost $2.38 each?

153

Pictographs

Teresa wondered how many students had seen the movie *Moon Walk*. To find out, she and her friends asked students at school.

This **pictograph** shows what they found.

NUMBER OF STUDENTS WHO SAW *MOON WALK*	
Third graders	🧍 🧍
Fourth graders	🧍 🧍 🧍 🧍 🧍
Fifth graders	🧍 🧍 🧍
Sixth graders	🧍 🧍 🧍 🧍

Each 🧍 stands for 10 children.

Count by tens to find how many.

The graph shows that 30 fifth graders saw *Moon Walk*.

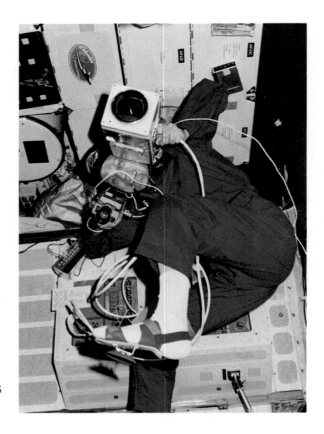

CLASSWORK

Use the pictograph to answer each question.

1. How many third graders saw the movie?

2. How many fourth graders saw the movie?

3. Did more sixth graders or more fifth graders see the movie?

4. Which grade had the most students who had seen the movie?

154

Students planned a trip to Cape Canaveral. They sold raffle tickets to help pay their way. This graph shows how many books were sold.

NUMBER OF BOOKS OF RAFFLE TICKETS SOLD	
Room 321	▭ ▭ ▭ ▭ ▭
Room 322	▭ ▭ ▭ ▭
Room 323	▭ ▭ ▭
Room 324	▭ ▭ ▭ ▭ ▭ ▭ ▭ ▭ ▭ ▭
Room 325	▭ ▭ ▭ ▭

Each ▭ stands for 5 books of tickets.

Use the pictograph to answer each question.

1. Which room sold the most books of tickets?

2. Which room sold the fewest books of tickets?

3. How many books were sold by students in Room 321?

4. How many books were sold by students in Room 325?

5. How many books were sold by students in Room 323?

6. Were more books sold by students in Room 324 or Room 322?

7. Were more books sold by students in Room 321 or Room 323?

8. Which rooms sold an equal number of books?

★ 9. How many more books were sold by students in Room 324 than in Room 325?

★ 10. How many fewer books were sold by students in Room 321 than in Room 324?

APPLICATION

Copy and fill in the pictograph to show each fact.

11. Jon made 8 space capsules.

12. Dot made 6 space capsules.

13. Li made 7 space capsules.

14. Sal made 9 space capsules.

★ 15. How many space capsules did all 4 children make?

NUMBER OF SPACE CAPSULES MADE	
Dot	
Li	
Sal	
Jon	

Each 🚀 stands for 1 space capsule.

Bar Graphs

Third graders wanted to buy a telescope. They sold pencils to make money.

This bar graph shows the number of pencils that were sold.

Each bar shows the number of pencils each student sold.

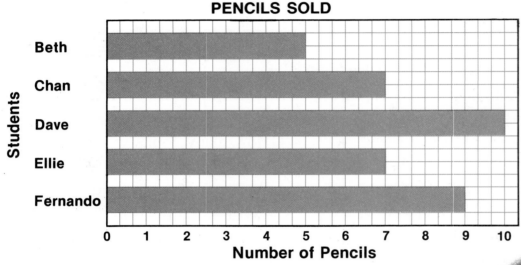

PENCILS SOLD

The graph shows that Chan sold 7 pencils.

CLASSWORK

Use the bar graph to answer each question.

1. Who sold the most pencils?

2. Who sold the fewest pencils?

3. How many pencils did Ellie sell?

4. Did Fernando sell more pencils than Dave?

5. Which two students sold the same number of pencils?

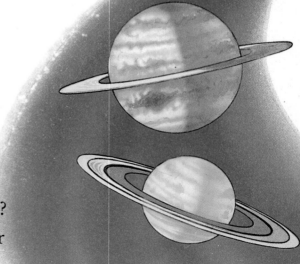
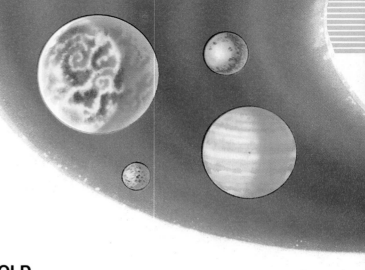

Third graders wrote reports on planets. Each student picked a planet. Mrs. Rose helped them make this graph.

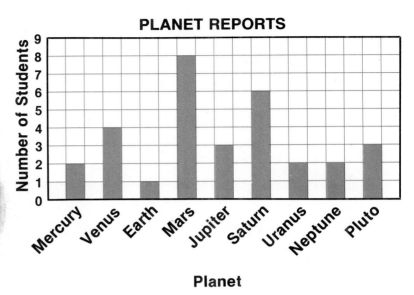

Use the bar graph to answer each question.

1. Which planet was picked by the most students?

2. Which planet was picked by the fewest students?

3. How many students wrote about Jupiter?

4. How many students wrote about Neptune?

5. Did more students write about Pluto or Venus?

6. Did more students write about Saturn or Mercury?

★ 7. How many more students wrote about Mars than about Jupiter?

★ 8. How many fewer students wrote about Pluto than about Saturn?

APPLICATION

The graph shows the number of trips each spacecraft made around the earth.

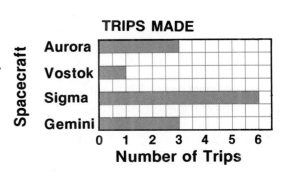

9. Which spacecrafts made the same number of trips?

★ 10. Make up 3 questions about the facts in the graph.

Problem Solving

SKILLS AND STRATEGIES REVIEW Space Travel

The Rocket Club fired 4 rockets. The bar graph
shows how high each one went.

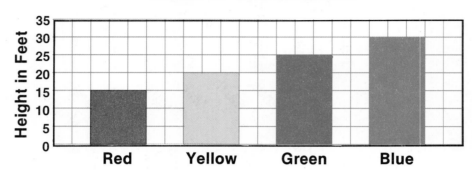

HEIGHT OF ROCKETS FIRED

1. Which rocket went the highest?

2. How high did the highest rocket go?

3. Which went higher, the yellow rocket or the red rocket?

4. How much higher than the yellow rocket did the blue rocket go?

The rockets were fired in the order shown on
the graph. They were fired every 10 minutes.

5. The green rocket was fired at 1:08 P.M. When was the blue rocket fired?

6. The blue rocket stayed in the sky for 6 minutes. What time did it come down?

Each rocket went higher than the one before it in
the same pattern. The club fired an orange rocket
after it fired the blue one.

★ 7. What time was the orange rocket fired?

★ 8. How high would you expect the orange rocket to go?

Problem Solving

WHAT WOULD YOU DO . . . ?

Rex, your dog, is going on a space trip. If he weighs more than 50 pounds, he cannot go. You want to weigh Rex, but he will not stay on the scale.

Answer each question and explain.

1. Could you just guess how much Rex weighs?

2. Could you put Rex in a box and weigh him?

3. Could you hold Rex in your arms and weigh both of you?

4. Do you have a better way?

What would you do?

If you chose **3**, how would you find Rex's weight?

You are going on the space trip, too. You may take up to 12 pounds with you. You would like to take 3 items listed in the chart.

Answer each question and explain.

5. Could you take the stereo, the game, and the camera?

6. Could you take the book, the game, and the camera?

7. What are 3 other items you could take?

Item	Weight
Stereo	6 pounds
Book	2 pounds
Game	4 pounds
Camera	3 pounds

What would you do?

8. Which 3 items would you take? Why?

9. If you could, would you take 4 cameras?

10. If you could, would you take 6 books?

Write what time it will be. pages 134–139

1. in 3 hours

2. in 15 minutes

3. in 1 minute

Tell which takes longer. pages 140–141

4. making your bed or taking a test

5. opening a can or shopping for food

Answer each question about the calendar. pages 142–143

6. July 8 is Friday. July 10 is ____.

7. May 21 is Monday. May 24 is ____.

Count or subtract to find the total change. pages 146–147, 150–151

8. Cost $.72   Paid   1 dollar   Total Change _____

Is there enough money? Write *yes* or *no*. pages 148–149, 152–153

9.

$5.35

Use the pictograph to answer each question. pages 154–155

10. How many magazines were bought by third graders?

11. How many more magazines were bought by fifth graders than sixth graders?

NUMBER OF MAGAZINES BOUGHT	
Third graders	■ ■ ■ ■
Fourth graders	■ ■ ■ ■ ■ ■
Fifth graders	■ ■ ■ ■ ■
Sixth graders	■ ■ ■

■ = 2 magazines

Find the pattern and complete the table. pages 144–145, 158–159

12. Alice saves $1.50 a week. How much money will she save in 8 weeks?

Week	1	2	3	4	5	6	7	8
Savings	$1.50	$3.00	$4.50	$6.00				

Write how much time has passed.

1.
start end

2.
start end

Which unit would you use to measure time?
Choose minute or hour.

3. sharpening some pencils

4. wrapping a package

5. running a marathon

6. waiting for an elevator

May is the fifth month. Tell which month each of these is.

7. June

8. November

9. April

Count the change.

10. Paid 2 dollars.

 $1.68

_____ _____ _____ _____

Compare. Use > or < for ●.

11. $3.39 ● $4.02

12. $.84 ● $1.23

13. $1.19 ● $.99

Solve.

The first bus to Greenville leaves at 7:00 A.M.
Look for the pattern in the times it leaves.

14. Write the next three times.
7:00,   7:20,   7:40,   8:00,   _____,   _____,   _____

Use the bar graph to answer each.

15. Which students received more
pledges than Tim?

How many more pledges
did Lois and Ted get
than Tim and Nina?

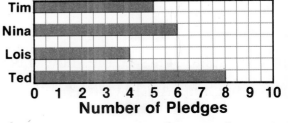

WALKATHON PLEDGES

Tim
Nina
Lois
Ted

0 1 2 3 4 5 6 7 8 9 10
Number of Pledges

THE ALPHA-CENTS GAME

Any number of students can play.

Follow each step.

1. Write your first name. Find the value of each letter from the letters and values below.

2. Add to find the total value of your name.

K · A · T · H · Y
$.11 + $.01 + $.20 + $.08 + $.25 = $.65

3. Compare the value of the name of each player. The player whose name has the greatest value scores 1 point.

4. Find the value of your last name. Add it to the value of your first name. Now who has the name with the greatest value? That player scores 1 point.

5. Find the value of other words. Here are some examples.
   names of pets
   street addresses
   names of best friends

Each time you compare, score 1 point for the word with the greatest value.
The player with the most points at the end of the game wins.

A = $.01   F = $.06   K = $.11   P = $.16   U = $.21
B = $.02   G = $.07   L = $.12   Q = $.17   V = $.22
C = $.03   H = $.08   M = $.13   R = $.18   W = $.23
D = $.04   I = $.09   N = $.14   S = $.19   X = $.24
E = $.05   J = $.10   O = $.15   T = $.20   Y = $.25
                                            Z = $.26

In the Alpha-Cents Game, how much is SILVER worth?

How much is GOLD worth?

FIND THE BEST BUY

There are three stores on Planet FX3.
Each store prints its prices for the week.

Look at the prices.
Then answer the questions below.

STOP and SAVE

Moon milk	$1.69
Venus vegetables	$ .65
Asteroid apples	$1.79
Galaxy grapefruit	$ .79
Jupiter jam	$1.29
Rocket roasts	$3.59
Starship cereal	$ .99
Neptune napkins	$1.99
Mars margarine	$ .99

FOODMART

Moon milk	$1.59
Venus vegetables	$ .69
Asteroid apples	$1.99
Galaxy grapefruit	$ .95
Jupiter jam	$1.19
Rocket roasts	$3.89
Starship cereal	$1.07
Neptune napkins	$1.89
Mars margarine	$1.09

FX3 SHOPMORE

Moon milk	$1.79
Venus vegetables	$ .69
Asteroid apples	$1.80
Galaxy grapefruit	$ .98
Jupiter jam	$1.09
Rocket roasts	$3.55
Starship cereal	$1.09
Neptune napkins	$1.98
Mars margarine	$ .89

1. Which store has the best buy on Moon milk this week?

2. Which store has the best buy on Venus vegetables?

3. Which store has the best buy on Asteroid apples?

4. Which store has the best buy on Galaxy grapefruit?

5. Which store has the best buy on Jupiter jam?

6. Which store has the best buy on Rocket roasts?

7. Which store has the best buy on Starship cereal?

8. Which store has the best buy on Neptune napkins?

9. Which store has the best buy on Mars margarine?

10. Which store has the most good buys?

COMPUTER PROGRAMS

A list of instructions for the computer is called a **program.** A program is usually written in a language so that the computer understands it. We will use the computer language BASIC.

Line numbers tell the computer to do the instructions in that order.

The last instruction should be END.

When we type RUN, the computer follows the instructions one line at a time.

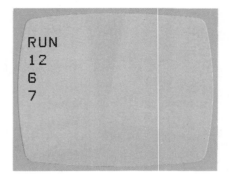

```
10  PRINT 8 + 4
20  PRINT 11 - 5
30  PRINT 26 - 19
40  END
```

```
RUN
12
6
7
```

For each program, tell what the output will be.

1.
```
10  PRINT 4 + 19
20  PRINT 35 - 28
30  END
```

2.
```
10  PRINT 400 + 735
20  PRINT 157 - 131
30  END
```

3.
```
10  PRINT 15 + 23
20  PRINT 88 - 79
30  PRINT 324 - 65
40  END
```

4.
```
10  PRINT 19 - 17
20  PRINT 629 + 765
30  PRINT 347 - 298
40  END
```

The lines of a program are usually numbered by 10's. Then we can add lines in between the 10's without renumbering.

Suppose we want to add a line to print 6 in this program.

We type 25 PRINT 6

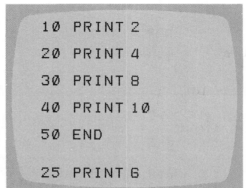

```
10  PRINT 2
20  PRINT 4
30  PRINT 8
40  PRINT 10
50  END

25  PRINT 6
```

The computer follows the instructions in order from least to greatest. It does line 25 after line 20.

```
RUN
2
4
6
8
10
```

For each program, tell what the output will be.

5.
```
10  PRINT 3
30  PRINT 9
20  PRINT 6
40  PRINT 12
50  END
```

6.
```
10  PRINT 439 + 652
20  PRINT 967 - 541
40  PRINT 16 + 35 + 9
50  END
30  PRINT 721 - 60
```

========== AT THE COMPUTER ==========

1. Enter and RUN each program in 1-4, page 164.

2. Compare each output with your answer.

3. Enter and RUN each program on this page.

★ 4. On Your Own: Write a program that will display the numbers as you count by 5's. Start with 5 and stop after 30. Add a line that will print 23 between 20 and 25. Try your program on a computer.

Choose the correct answer. Write A, B, C, or D.

1. What is another fact in the family? $7 + 4 = 11$

    A $8 + 3 = 11$ C $11 - 4 = 7$

    B $7 - 4 = 3$ D not given

2. Compare. $6,012 \bullet 6,021$

    A $>$ C $=$

    B $<$ D not given

3. $5,178 + 3,496 = \square$

    A 7,684   C 8,674

    B 8,647   D not given

4. $\$50.00 - \$39.97 = \square$

    A $10.13   C $10.23

    B $11.13   D not given

5. Estimate. $862 - 193 = \square$

    A 600   C 900

    B 700   D not given

6. What is the time?

    A 8:40   C 8:07

    B 7:35   D not given

Use the graph for **7** and **8**.

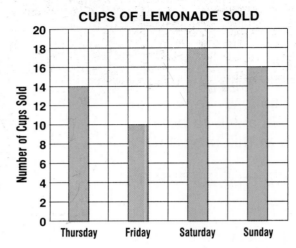

CUPS OF LEMONADE SOLD

7. How many cups of lemonade did Sally sell on Thursday?

    A 16   C 10

    B 12   D not given

8. On what day did Sally sell the most cups of lemonade?

    A Sunday   C Friday

    B Saturday   D not given

Which fact is extra?

9. Bob played softball for 16 days. Todd played for 18 days and Vicki played for 24 days. How many more days did Vicki play than Bob?

    A Todd played 18 days.   C Bob played softball.

    B 24 days   D not given

Theme: The Sea

Understanding Multiplication

How many fish are there in all?

We can count
or we can add.

5 + 5 + 5 = 15

When each group has the same number,
we can multiply.

There are 3 groups.
There are 5 fish in each group.

$$3 \times 5 = 15 \qquad \begin{array}{r} 5 \\ \times 3 \\ \hline 15 \end{array} \begin{array}{l} \text{in each group} \\ \text{groups} \\ \text{in all} \end{array}$$

groups   in each   in all
         group

We say, "Three times five equals fifteen."

There are 15 fish in all.

CLASSWORK

Find how many in all.

1. 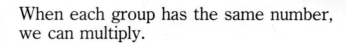   5 + 5 = ☐   2.   2 + 2 + 2 = ☐
                 2 × 5 = ☐   3 × 2 = ☐

3.   4 in each group   4.   3 in each group
            ×3 groups   ×2 groups
               in all   in all

5. 3 + 3 = ☐   6. 5 + 5 + 5 = ☐   7. 4 + 4 + 4 + 4 = ☐
   2 × 3 = ☐   3 × 5 = ☐   4 × 4 = ☐

8. 6 + 6 + 6 = ☐   9. 8 + 8 = ☐   10. 7 + 7 + 7 + 7 = ☐
   3 × 6 = ☐   2 × 8 = ☐   4 × 7 = ☐

Find how many in all.

1. ◆ ◆
   ◆ ◆
   $2 + 2 = \square$
   $2 \times 2 = \square$

2. ◆ ◆ ◆ ◆
   ◆ ◆ ◆ ◆
   $4 + 4 = \square$
   $2 \times 4 = \square$

3. ◆ ◆
   ◆ ◆
   ◆ ◆
   ◆ ◆
   2 in each group
   $\times 4$ groups
   in all

4. ◆ ◆ ◆ ◆
   ◆ ◆ ◆ ◆
   ◆ ◆ ◆ ◆
   ◆ ◆ ◆ ◆
   4 in each group
   $\times 4$ groups
   in all

5. ◆ ◆ ◆ ◆ ◆ ◆
   ◆ ◆ ◆ ◆ ◆ ◆
   6 in each group
   $\times 2$ groups
   in all

6. ◆ ◆ ◆
   ◆ ◆ ◆
   ◆ ◆ ◆
   3 in each group
   $\times 3$ groups
   in all

7. ◆ ◆ ◆
   ◆ ◆ ◆
   ◆ ◆ ◆
   ◆ ◆ ◆
   3 in each group
   $\times 4$ groups
   in all

8. ◆ ◆ ◆
   ◆ ◆ ◆
   ◆ ◆ ◆
   ◆ ◆ ◆
   ◆ ◆ ◆
   3 in each group
   $\times 5$ groups
   in all

Find the missing numbers.

9. 2, 4, 6, ____, ____, ____, ____, ____, ____

10. 5, 10, 15, ____, ____, ____, ____, ____, ____

★11. 3, 6, 9, ____, ____, ____, ____, ____, ____

★12. 4, 8, 12, ____, ____, ____, ____, ____, ____

APPLICATION

13. Write an addition sentence to show the number of seashells.

14. Write a multiplication sentence to show the number of seashells.

★15. The answer to a story problem is 12 snails. Write an interesting problem.

2 as a Factor

How many sandpipers are there?

Each group has the same number, so we can multiply.

There are 4 groups of 2.

$$4 \times 2 = 8$$

factor   factor   product

$$\begin{array}{r} 2 \leftarrow \text{factor} \\ \times 4 \leftarrow \text{factor} \\ \hline 8 \leftarrow \text{product} \end{array}$$

There are 8 sandpipers.

CLASSWORK

Find each product.

1.

$$2 \times 2 = \square$$

2.

$$3 \times 2 = \square$$

3.

$$5 \times 2 = \square$$

4.
$$\begin{array}{r} 2 \\ \times 1 \\ \hline \end{array}$$
$$\begin{array}{r} 2 \\ \times 2 \\ \hline \end{array}$$
$$\begin{array}{r} 2 \\ \times 3 \\ \hline \end{array}$$
$$\begin{array}{r} 2 \\ \times 4 \\ \hline \end{array}$$
$$\begin{array}{r} 2 \\ \times 5 \\ \hline \end{array}$$
$$\begin{array}{r} 2 \\ \times 6 \\ \hline \end{array}$$
$$\begin{array}{r} 2 \\ \times 7 \\ \hline \end{array}$$
$$\begin{array}{r} 2 \\ \times 8 \\ \hline \end{array}$$
$$\begin{array}{r} 2 \\ \times 9 \\ \hline \end{array}$$

5.
$$\begin{array}{r} 2 \\ \times 4 \\ \hline \end{array}$$
6.
$$\begin{array}{r} 2 \\ \times 1 \\ \hline \end{array}$$
7.
$$\begin{array}{r} 2 \\ \times 7 \\ \hline \end{array}$$
8.
$$\begin{array}{r} 2 \\ \times 3 \\ \hline \end{array}$$
9.
$$\begin{array}{r} 2 \\ \times 9 \\ \hline \end{array}$$
10.
$$\begin{array}{r} 2 \\ \times 6 \\ \hline \end{array}$$
11.
$$\begin{array}{r} 2 \\ \times 8 \\ \hline \end{array}$$

PRACTICE

Find each product.

1. 2
  ×3

2. 2
  ×5

3. 2
  ×2

4. 2
  ×6

5. 2
  ×4

6. 2
  ×8

7. 2
  ×7

8. 2
  ×1

9. 2
  ×9

10. 2
   ×8

11. 2
   ×6

12. 2
   ×5

13. 2
   ×7

14. 2
   ×4

15. 2
   ×3

16. 2
   ×8

17. 2
   ×4

18. 2
   ×7

19. 2
   ×6

20. 2
   ×9

21. 2
   ×5

22. $6 \times 2 = \square$

23. $3 \times 2 = \square$

24. $9 \times 2 = \square$

25. $2 \times 2 = \square$

26. $7 \times 2 = \square$

27. $5 \times 2 = \square$

28. $4 \times 2 = \square$

29. $8 \times 2 = \square$

30. $2 \times 2 = \square$

31. $9 \times 2 = \square$

32. $3 \times 2 = \square$

33. $1 \times 2 = \square$

Complete the table. Each boat has two oars.

★34.

	1	2	3	4	5	6	7	8	9
	2	4							

APPLICATION

35. There were 9 swimmers. Each swimmer wore 2 flippers. How many flippers were there?

★36. The ferryboat made 2 trips each day. How many trips did it make in 1 week?

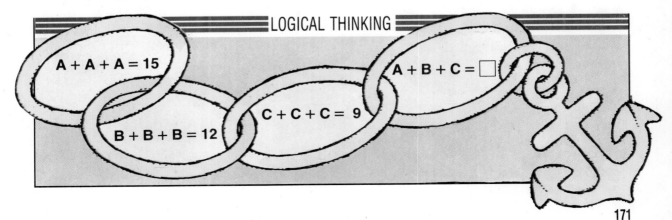

LOGICAL THINKING

A + A + A = 15

B + B + B = 12

C + C + C = 9

A + B + C = $\square$

171

3 as a Factor

Dolores and her friends caught fish.
There were 5 strings of 3 fish each.
How many fish did they catch in all?

5 groups of 3

$5 \times 3 = 15$

$$\begin{array}{r} 3 \\ \times 5 \\ \hline 15 \end{array}$$

They caught 15 fish in all.

CLASSWORK

Find each product.

1.

$4 \times 3 = \square$

2.

$7 \times 3 = \square$

3.

$8 \times 3 = \square$

4.
$\begin{array}{r} 3 \\ \times 1 \\ \hline \end{array}$
$\begin{array}{r} 3 \\ \times 2 \\ \hline \end{array}$
$\begin{array}{r} 3 \\ \times 3 \\ \hline \end{array}$
$\begin{array}{r} 3 \\ \times 4 \\ \hline \end{array}$
$\begin{array}{r} 3 \\ \times 5 \\ \hline \end{array}$
$\begin{array}{r} 3 \\ \times 6 \\ \hline \end{array}$
$\begin{array}{r} 3 \\ \times 7 \\ \hline \end{array}$
$\begin{array}{r} 3 \\ \times 8 \\ \hline \end{array}$
$\begin{array}{r} 3 \\ \times 9 \\ \hline \end{array}$

5. $\begin{array}{r} 3 \\ \times 3 \\ \hline \end{array}$
6. $\begin{array}{r} 3 \\ \times 6 \\ \hline \end{array}$
7. $\begin{array}{r} 3 \\ \times 8 \\ \hline \end{array}$
8. $\begin{array}{r} 3 \\ \times 5 \\ \hline \end{array}$
9. $\begin{array}{r} 3 \\ \times 2 \\ \hline \end{array}$
10. $\begin{array}{r} 3 \\ \times 9 \\ \hline \end{array}$
11. $\begin{array}{r} 3 \\ \times 1 \\ \hline \end{array}$

PRACTICE

Complete.

1. 3×1
2. 3×7
3. 3×2
4. 3×4

5. 3×6
6. 2×5
7. 3×8
8. 3×3

9. 2×7
10. 3×5
11. 2×2
12. 3×9

13. 2×4
14. 2×1
15. 3×2
16. 3×1

17. $7 \times 3 = \square$
18. $9 \times 2 = \square$

19. $9 \times 3 = \square$
20. $8 \times 2 = \square$

21. $6 \times 3 = \square$
22. $4 \times 3 = \square$

★23. $3 + 3 = \square \times 3$
★24. $\square \times \square = 2 + 2$

APPLICATION

25. There were 6 people on a fishing boat. Each person caught 3 tunas. How many tunas were caught in all?

26. Lobster pots held 23 lobsters. To the nearest ten, how many lobsters were there?

★27. Draw an underwater picture.

Show 3×2 snails.

Show 4×2 fish.

Show 3×3 shrimp.

Mixed Practice

1. $7 + 2$
2. $12 - 9$

3. $6 + 8$
4. $15 - 7$

5. $49 - 39$
6. $76 + 8$

7. $72 - 68$
8. $94 + 46$

9. $305 + 692$
10. $783 + 199$

11. $567 - 333$
12. $400 - 259$

13. $9,000 - 8,443$
14. $811 - 364$

Round to the nearest hundred.

15. 432
16. 381

17. 276
18. 647

19. 859
20. 773

21. 568
22. 924

23. 114
24. 883

173

4 as a Factor

Jason counted 3 groups of flags. Each group had 4 flags. How many flags were there in all?

3 groups of 4

$$3 \times 4 = 12 \qquad \begin{array}{r} 4 \\ \times 3 \\ \hline 12 \end{array}$$

There were 12 flags in all.

CLASSWORK

Multiply.

1.

4 × 4 = ☐

2.

6 × 4 = ☐

3.

7 × 4 = ☐

4. $\begin{array}{r} 4 \\ \times 1 \\ \hline \end{array}$ $\begin{array}{r} 4 \\ \times 2 \\ \hline \end{array}$ $\begin{array}{r} 4 \\ \times 3 \\ \hline \end{array}$ $\begin{array}{r} 4 \\ \times 4 \\ \hline \end{array}$ $\begin{array}{r} 4 \\ \times 5 \\ \hline \end{array}$ $\begin{array}{r} 4 \\ \times 6 \\ \hline \end{array}$ $\begin{array}{r} 4 \\ \times 7 \\ \hline \end{array}$ $\begin{array}{r} 4 \\ \times 8 \\ \hline \end{array}$ $\begin{array}{r} 4 \\ \times 9 \\ \hline \end{array}$

5. $\begin{array}{r} 4 \\ \times 5 \\ \hline \end{array}$ 6. $\begin{array}{r} 4 \\ \times 2 \\ \hline \end{array}$ 7. $\begin{array}{r} 4 \\ \times 8 \\ \hline \end{array}$ 8. $\begin{array}{r} 4 \\ \times 3 \\ \hline \end{array}$ 9. $\begin{array}{r} 4 \\ \times 9 \\ \hline \end{array}$ 10. $\begin{array}{r} 4 \\ \times 1 \\ \hline \end{array}$ 11. $\begin{array}{r} 4 \\ \times 6 \\ \hline \end{array}$

Multiply.

1. 4
    ×3

2. 4
    ×7

3. 4
    ×6

4. 4
    ×1

5. 4
    ×8

6. 4
    ×9

7. 4
    ×2

8. 4
    ×4

9. 4
    ×5

10. 2
     ×4

11. 3
     ×9

12. 4
     ×7

13. 4
     ×3

14. 3
     ×8

15. 2
     ×6

16. 3
     ×5

17. 4
     ×2

18. 2
     ×2

19. 3
     ×3

20. 4
     ×8

21. 4
     ×9

22. $1 \times 4 = \square$ 23. $7 \times 3 = \square$ 24. $4 \times 4 = \square$ 25. $5 \times 3 = \square$

26. $5 \times 2 = \square$ 27. $5 \times 4 = \square$ 28. $9 \times 3 = \square$ 29. $8 \times 2 = \square$

30. $4 \times 3 = \square$ 31. $9 \times 4 = \square$ 32. $3 \times 2 = \square$ 33. $6 \times 3 = \square$

Compare. Use >, <, or = for ●.

34. 6×4 ● 25 35. 9×4 ● 30 36. 3×4 ● 36

★37. 5×4 ● 9×3 ★38. 9×2 ● 7×3 ★39. 8×2 ● 4×4

APPLICATION

=== CALCULATOR ===

Have a friend time you as you find these products.

Do these without a calculator.   Do these with a calculator.

1. $1 \times 4 = \square$ $7 \times 4 = \square$
   $7 \times 3 = \square$ $6 \times 3 = \square$
   $4 \times 4 = \square$ $9 \times 2 = \square$
   $5 \times 3 = \square$ $3 \times 3 = \square$
   $6 \times 2 = \square$ $8 \times 3 = \square$

2. $9 \times 3 = \square$ $5 \times 2 = \square$
   $8 \times 4 = \square$ $4 \times 3 = \square$
   $6 \times 4 = \square$ $8 \times 3 = \square$
   $2 \times 2 = \square$ $5 \times 4 = \square$
   $3 \times 4 = \square$ $4 \times 2 = \square$

Time _____   Time _____

Is a calculator *always* faster?

5 as a Factor

Rhetta counted the arms on each starfish.
How many arms were there in all?

2 groups of 5

$2 \times 5 = 10$

$$\begin{array}{r} 5 \\ \times 2 \\ \hline 10 \end{array}$$

There were 10 arms in all.

CLASSWORK

Multiply.

1.
★ ★ ★ ★ ★
★ ★ ★ ★ ★
★ ★ ★ ★ ★

$3 \times 5 = \square$

2.
★ ★ ★ ★ ★
★ ★ ★ ★ ★
★ ★ ★ ★ ★
★ ★ ★ ★ ★

$4 \times 5 = \square$

3.
★ ★ ★ ★ ★
★ ★ ★ ★ ★
★ ★ ★ ★ ★
★ ★ ★ ★ ★
★ ★ ★ ★ ★

$5 \times 5 = \square$

4.
$\begin{array}{r} 5 \\ \times 1 \\ \hline \end{array}$
$\begin{array}{r} 5 \\ \times 2 \\ \hline \end{array}$
$\begin{array}{r} 5 \\ \times 3 \\ \hline \end{array}$
$\begin{array}{r} 5 \\ \times 4 \\ \hline \end{array}$
$\begin{array}{r} 5 \\ \times 5 \\ \hline \end{array}$
$\begin{array}{r} 5 \\ \times 6 \\ \hline \end{array}$
$\begin{array}{r} 5 \\ \times 7 \\ \hline \end{array}$
$\begin{array}{r} 5 \\ \times 8 \\ \hline \end{array}$
$\begin{array}{r} 5 \\ \times 9 \\ \hline \end{array}$

5.
$\begin{array}{r} 5 \\ \times 6 \\ \hline \end{array}$
6.
$\begin{array}{r} 5 \\ \times 8 \\ \hline \end{array}$
7.
$\begin{array}{r} 5 \\ \times 2 \\ \hline \end{array}$
8.
$\begin{array}{r} 5 \\ \times 9 \\ \hline \end{array}$
9.
$\begin{array}{r} 5 \\ \times 7 \\ \hline \end{array}$
10.
$\begin{array}{r} 5 \\ \times 1 \\ \hline \end{array}$
11.
$\begin{array}{r} 5 \\ \times 4 \\ \hline \end{array}$

Multiply.

1. 5
   ×6

2. 5
   ×3

3. 5
   ×5

4. 5
   ×8

5. 5
   ×2

6. 5
   ×9

7. 5
   ×7

8. 5
   ×4

9. 5
   ×1

10. 4
    ×8

11. 3
    ×7

12. 5
    ×9

13. 4
    ×5

14. 3
    ×5

15. 4
    ×2

16. 3
    ×9

17. 5
    ×6

18. 2
    ×7

19. 3
    ×8

20. 4
    ×6

21. 2
    ×9

22. $9 \times 5 = \square$ 23. $1 \times 5 = \square$ 24. $7 \times 5 = \square$ 25. $4 \times 3 = \square$

26. $9 \times 4 = \square$ 27. $8 \times 5 = \square$ 28. $7 \times 4 = \square$ 29. $8 \times 4 = \square$

30. $3 \times 5 = \square$ 31. $6 \times 5 = \square$ 32. $8 \times 2 = \square$ 33. $6 \times 3 = \square$

34. $4 \times 5 = \square$ 35. $3 \times 4 = \square$ 36. $5 \times 5 = \square$ 37. $4 \times 4 = \square$

Multiply across and down.

38.

2	1	
2	4	

★ 39.

2		8
	1	3
6	4	

★ 40.

	1	3
3		9
9	3	

APPLICATION

41. Each starfish has 5 points. How many points do 9 starfish have? Complete the table to find out.

starfish	5	6	7	8	9
points	25	30			

★ 42. Rhetta collected 36 shells at the seashore. She gave 12 to her sister and some to her brother. She had 10 shells left for herself. How many shells did Rhetta give to her brother?

Problem Solving

USING PATTERNS

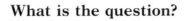

You can solve some problems by using a pattern.

Lisa practiced her swimming. She swam 10 minutes on Monday, 14 minutes on Tuesday, and 18 minutes on Wednesday. If she continues this pattern, how many minutes will Lisa swim on Friday?

What is the question?

How many minutes will Lisa swim on Friday?

What are the facts?

Lisa swam 10 minutes on Monday, 14 minutes on Tuesday, and 18 minutes on Wednesday.

How can you find the answer?

Look for a pattern. Make a table.

Do the work and solve the problem.

Each number is greater than the number before it.

$$10 + \square = 14 \qquad 14 + \square = 18$$

Each number is 4 greater than the number before it.

$$10 + 4 = 14 \qquad 14 + 4 = 18$$
So $\quad 18 + 4 = 22 \quad$ and $\quad 22 + 4 = 26$

Day	Minutes
Monday	10
Tuesday	14
Wednesday	18
Thursday	
Friday	

The next two numbers are 22 and 26.
Lisa will swim 26 minutes on Friday.

Check your answer. Does it make sense?

Each day, Lisa swims 4 minutes more than the day before. She will swim 26 minutes on Friday. That is 8 minutes more than she swam on Wednesday.

The answer makes sense.

Read and solve each problem.

1. Wally the porpoise jumps through a hoop. The hoop is raised 1 foot after each jump. Wally jumps 6 feet the first time. How high will he jump the fourth time?

2. The water-skiing show is held every 2 hours. The first show begins at 1:30 P.M. Laura and her family want to see the third show. What time will it begin?

3. Gina bought shells to make a bracelet. So far, she has used this pattern. If she continues the pattern, what will the next 2 colors be?

4. Gina now wants to make a necklace instead. She uses the same pattern and 15 shells. What is the color of the thirteenth shell?

5. Red shells cost 20¢ each. Green and yellow shells cost 10¢ each. How much did the shells in the picture cost?

★ 6. Gina made her sister a bracelet in the pattern shown. The shells she used cost $1.20. How many shells did Gina use?

★ 7. Beryl wants a necklace with 12 shells. The pattern she wants is red, yellow, red, yellow. How much will the shells cost?

CREATE YOUR OWN PROBLEM

These are the feeding times for some of the fish at the park. Find a pattern. Make up a problem about the pattern.

| Sharks | Rays | Turtles | Eels |

1 and 0 as Factors

How many sails are there in all?

$$5 \times 1 = 5$$
boats   sail   sails
on each   in all
boat

There are 5 sails in all.

▶ The product of any number and 1 is that number.

1	1	1	1	1	1	1	1	1
×1	×2	×3	×4	×5	×6	×7	×8	×9
1	2	3	4	5	6	7	8	9

How many sails are there now?

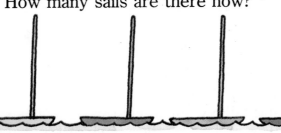

$$5 \times 0 = 0$$
boats   sails   sails
on each   in all
boat

There are no sails now.

▶ The product of any number and 0 is 0.

0	0	0	0	0	0	0	0	0	0
×0	×1	×2	×3	×4	×5	×6	×7	×8	×9
0	0	0	0	0	0	0	0	0	0

CLASSWORK

Find each product.

1. $\begin{array}{r} 1 \\ \times 7 \\ \hline \end{array}$
2. $\begin{array}{r} 0 \\ \times 2 \\ \hline \end{array}$
3. $\begin{array}{r} 1 \\ \times 8 \\ \hline \end{array}$
4. $\begin{array}{r} 0 \\ \times 3 \\ \hline \end{array}$
5. $\begin{array}{r} 0 \\ \times 0 \\ \hline \end{array}$
6. $\begin{array}{r} 1 \\ \times 9 \\ \hline \end{array}$
7. $\begin{array}{r} 1 \\ \times 0 \\ \hline \end{array}$

8. $6 \times 0 = \square$ 9. $1 \times 1 = \square$ 10. $0 \times 4 = \square$ 11. $6 \times 1 = \square$

PRACTICE

Find each product.

1.	2.	3.	4.	5.	6.	7.
1 $\times 3$	0 $\times 8$	1 $\times 2$	1 $\times 4$	0 $\times 7$	0 $\times 3$	5 $\times 6$

8.	9.	10.	11.	12.	13.	14.
1 $\times 9$	0 $\times 2$	4 $\times 7$	2 $\times 8$	0 $\times 1$	5 $\times 0$	4 $\times 3$

15.	16.	17.	18.	19.	20.	21.
3 $\times 6$	7 $\times 0$	5 $\times 8$	4 $\times 1$	2 $\times 9$	3 $\times 5$	5 $\times 1$

22. $9 \times 5 = \square$ 23. $8 \times 1 = \square$ 24. $4 \times 5 = \square$ 25. $9 \times 0 = \square$

26. $7 \times 3 = \square$ 27. $6 \times 2 = \square$ 28. $4 \times 0 = \square$ 29. $7 \times 5 = \square$

30. $9 \times 4 = \square$ 31. $0 \times 9 = \square$ 32. $7 \times 2 = \square$ 33. $0 \times 3 = \square$

Use a calculator to find each product.

34. $2 \times 1 \times 4 \times 3 \times 5 = \square$ 35. $3 \times 6 \times 4 \times 1 \times 5 = \square$

36. $4 \times 4 \times 7 \times 1 \times 2 = \square$ 37. $6 \times 5 \times 1 \times 1 \times 1 = \square$

Find each missing number.

★38. $5 \times 4 - \square = 1$ ★39. $7 \times 3 - \square = 1$ ★40. $8 \times 5 - \square = 1$

APPLICATION

Write a number sentence for each.

41. Craig Jensen saw 5 surfers in the ocean. Each surfer was on a surfboard. How many surfboards were there?

★42. There are 6 pairs of water skis on the dock. There are no water skiers. How many water skiers are there in all?

EVEN AND ODD NUMBERS

Even numbers end in 0, 2, 4, 6, or 8.

Odd numbers end in 1, 3, 5, 7, or 9.

Tell whether each number is even or odd.

1. 23   2. 4   3. 18

4. 56   5. 35   6. 41

Order in Multiplying

How many seahorses are there in each picture?

3 groups of 4
3 × 4 = 12

4 groups of 3
4 × 3 = 12

There are 12 seahorses in each picture.

► The order in which numbers are multiplied does not change the product.

6 × 3 = 18
3 × 6 = 18

5	7	4	6
×7	×5	×6	×4
35	35	24	24

CLASSWORK

Find each product.

Facts we know   New facts

1. 6 × 5 = ☐   2. 5 × 6 = ☐

3. 7 × 1 = ☐   4. 1 × 7 = ☐

5. 8 × 2 = ☐   6. 2 × 8 = ☐

7. 9 × 4 = ☐   8. 4 × 9 = ☐

9. 8 × 5 = ☐   10. 5 × 8 = ☐

11. 9 × 2 = ☐   12. 2 × 9 = ☐

13. 7 × 3 = ☐   14. 3 × 7 = ☐

When we
know one fact,
we know
another
fact.

PRACTICE

Complete.

1. $\begin{array}{r} 4 \\ \times 7 \end{array}$ $\begin{array}{r} 7 \\ \times 4 \end{array}$
2. $\begin{array}{r} 5 \\ \times 3 \end{array}$ $\begin{array}{r} 3 \\ \times 5 \end{array}$
3. $\begin{array}{r} 2 \\ \times 6 \end{array}$ $\begin{array}{r} 6 \\ \times 2 \end{array}$
4. $\begin{array}{r} 1 \\ \times 9 \end{array}$ $\begin{array}{r} 9 \\ \times 1 \end{array}$

5. $\begin{array}{r} 2 \\ \times 5 \end{array}$
6. $\begin{array}{r} 4 \\ \times 8 \end{array}$
7. $\begin{array}{r} 3 \\ \times 2 \end{array}$
8. $\begin{array}{r} 0 \\ \times 5 \end{array}$
9. $\begin{array}{r} 5 \\ \times 4 \end{array}$
10. $\begin{array}{r} 3 \\ \times 9 \end{array}$
11. $\begin{array}{r} 4 \\ \times 1 \end{array}$

12. $\begin{array}{r} 4 \\ \times 4 \end{array}$
13. $\begin{array}{r} 1 \\ \times 8 \end{array}$
14. $\begin{array}{r} 4 \\ \times 5 \end{array}$
15. $\begin{array}{r} 5 \\ \times 2 \end{array}$
16. $\begin{array}{r} 2 \\ \times 4 \end{array}$
17. $\begin{array}{r} 3 \\ \times 3 \end{array}$
18. $\begin{array}{r} 5 \\ \times 5 \end{array}$

19. $4 \times 0 = \square$
    $0 \times 4 = \square$
20. $7 \times 2 = \square$
    $2 \times 7 = \square$
21. $9 \times 5 = \square$
    $5 \times 9 = \square$
22. $8 \times 3 = \square$
    $3 \times 8 = \square$

★ 23. $8 \times 4 = 4 \times \square$ ★ 24. $6 \times 3 = \square \times 6$ ★ 25. $7 \times 1 = 1 \times \square$

Complete. Follow the rule, if given.

Rule:
Multiply by 4.

	Input	Output
26.	7	
27.	5	
28.	9	

Rule:
Multiply by 5.

	Input	Output
29.	6	
30.	8	
31.	3	

Find the rule.

★ 32.

Input	Output
4	12
3	9
6	18

APPLICATION

33. Draw a picture to show that
    $3 \times 5 = 5 \times 3$.

34. Draw a picture to show that
    $6 \times 4 = 4 \times 6$.

★ 35. There are 18 seashells. Find
    6 ways to arrange them into rows.

6 as a Factor

A costume maker is sewing 5 sailor costumes. Each costume needs 6 buttons. How many buttons will he use?

　　5 groups of 6

$$\begin{array}{cccc} 5 & \times & 6 & = & 30 \\ \text{costumes} & \text{on each} & \text{buttons} \\ & \text{costume} & \text{in all} \end{array}$$

The costume maker will use 30 buttons.

| We already know these facts. | $\begin{array}{r}0\\ \times 6\\ \hline 0\end{array}$ | $\begin{array}{r}1\\ \times 6\\ \hline 6\end{array}$ | $\begin{array}{r}2\\ \times 6\\ \hline 12\end{array}$ | $\begin{array}{r}3\\ \times 6\\ \hline 18\end{array}$ | $\begin{array}{r}4\\ \times 6\\ \hline 24\end{array}$ | $\begin{array}{r}5\\ \times 6\\ \hline 30\end{array}$ |

| We know these facts, too. | $\begin{array}{r}6\\ \times 0\\ \hline 0\end{array}$ | $\begin{array}{r}6\\ \times 1\\ \hline 6\end{array}$ | $\begin{array}{r}6\\ \times 2\\ \hline 12\end{array}$ | $\begin{array}{r}6\\ \times 3\\ \hline 18\end{array}$ | $\begin{array}{r}6\\ \times 4\\ \hline 24\end{array}$ | $\begin{array}{r}6\\ \times 5\\ \hline 30\end{array}$ |

| Here are the new facts. | $\begin{array}{r}6\\ \times 6\\ \hline 36\end{array}$ | $\begin{array}{r}6\\ \times 7\\ \hline 42\end{array}$ | $\begin{array}{r}6\\ \times 8\\ \hline 48\end{array}$ | $\begin{array}{r}6\\ \times 9\\ \hline 54\end{array}$ |

CLASSWORK

Find each product.

1.

　　3 × 6 = ☐

2.

　　4 × 6 = ☐

3.
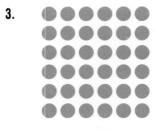

　　6 × 6 = ☐

4.　$\begin{array}{r}6\\ \times 0\\ \hline\end{array}$　　5.　$\begin{array}{r}6\\ \times 2\\ \hline\end{array}$　　6.　$\begin{array}{r}6\\ \times 1\\ \hline\end{array}$　　7.　$\begin{array}{r}6\\ \times 5\\ \hline\end{array}$　　8.　$\begin{array}{r}6\\ \times 9\\ \hline\end{array}$　　9.　$\begin{array}{r}6\\ \times 7\\ \hline\end{array}$　　10.　$\begin{array}{r}6\\ \times 8\\ \hline\end{array}$

Find each product.

| 1. 6 ×8 | 2. 6 ×3 | 3. 6 ×1 | 4. 6 ×7 | 5. 4 ×9 | 6. 6 ×2 | 7. 5 ×5 |

| 8. 6 ×9 | 9. 6 ×4 | 10. 5 ×7 | 11. 8 ×0 | 12. 5 ×9 | 13. 2 ×7 | 14. 3 ×8 |

| 15. 5 ×8 | 16. 0 ×6 | 17. 5 ×4 | 18. 6 ×5 | 19. 4 ×8 | 20. 3 ×6 | 21. 0 ×4 |

22. $9 \times 3 = \square$ 23. $5 \times 7 = \square$ 24. $4 \times 3 = \square$ 25. $6 \times 6 = \square$

26. $6 \times 4 = \square$ 27. $6 \times 5 = \square$ 28. $2 \times 6 = \square$ 29. $7 \times 3 = \square$

Choose the correct number sentence. Then solve.

30. The costume maker needs ribbons for 7 costumes. He has enough ribbons for 6 costumes. How many costumes still need ribbons?

a. $7 + 6 = \square$ b. $7 - 6 = \square$

c. $7 \times 6 = \square$ d. $7 \div 6 = \square$

Compare. Use >, <, or = for ●.

31. 3×6 ● 20

32. 0×6 ● 0

33. 9×5 ● 45

34. 8×5 ● 13

★35. 8×6 ● 9×5

★36. 7×5 ● 6×6

★37. 6×1 ● 1×6

APPLICATION

CALCULATOR

Multiplying a number is like adding it over and over.

Start with 0.
Add 6's until you get to 54.
How many 6's did you add?
$9 \times 6 = 54$

How many do you add?
1. Add 4's until you get to 28.
2. Add 3's until you get to 18.
3. Add 5's until you get to 40.

7 as a Factor

In *Gulliver's Travels,* Gulliver was shipwrecked on an island. Little people made him seem like a giant. He was so much bigger that he could pull their ships! How many ships were there?

3 groups of 7

$3 \times 7 = 21$

There were 21 ships.

We know these facts.

$$\begin{array}{ccccccc} 7 & 7 & 7 & 7 & 7 & 7 & 7 \\ \underline{\times 0} & \underline{\times 1} & \underline{\times 2} & \underline{\times 3} & \underline{\times 4} & \underline{\times 5} & \underline{\times 6} \\ 0 & 7 & 14 & 21 & 28 & 35 & 42 \end{array}$$

Here are the new facts.

$$\begin{array}{ccc} 7 & 7 & 7 \\ \underline{\times 7} & \underline{\times 8} & \underline{\times 9} \\ 49 & 56 & 63 \end{array}$$

CLASSWORK

Multiply.

1.

▲▲▲▲▲▲▲
▲▲▲▲▲▲▲

$2 \times 7 = \square$

2.

▲▲▲▲▲▲▲
▲▲▲▲▲▲▲
▲▲▲▲▲▲▲
▲▲▲▲▲▲▲

$4 \times 7 = \square$

3.

▲▲▲▲▲▲▲
▲▲▲▲▲▲▲
▲▲▲▲▲▲▲
▲▲▲▲▲▲▲
▲▲▲▲▲▲▲

$5 \times 7 = \square$

4.
$$\begin{array}{c} 7 \\ \underline{\times 1} \end{array}$$

5.
$$\begin{array}{c} 7 \\ \underline{\times 0} \end{array}$$

6.
$$\begin{array}{c} 7 \\ \underline{\times 9} \end{array}$$

7.
$$\begin{array}{c} 7 \\ \underline{\times 7} \end{array}$$

8.
$$\begin{array}{c} 7 \\ \underline{\times 8} \end{array}$$

9.
$$\begin{array}{c} 7 \\ \underline{\times 6} \end{array}$$

10.
$$\begin{array}{c} 7 \\ \underline{\times 3} \end{array}$$

Multiply.

1.	2.	3.	4.	5.	6.	7.
7 $\times 2$	7 $\times 8$	7 $\times 6$	7 $\times 7$	7 $\times 1$	7 $\times 3$	6 $\times 7$

8.	9.	10.	11.	12.	13.	14.
7 $\times 4$	7 $\times 5$	7 $\times 0$	7 $\times 9$	5 $\times 8$	3 $\times 6$	5 $\times 9$

15.	16.	17.	18.	19.	20.	21.
6 $\times 8$	7 $\times 2$	7 $\times 7$	7 $\times 6$	7 $\times 4$	6 $\times 5$	4 $\times 8$

22. $8 \times 7 = \square$ 23. $9 \times 7 = \square$ 24. $9 \times 6 = \square$ 25. $3 \times 6 = \square$

26. $7 \times 3 = \square$ 27. $9 \times 3 = \square$ 28. $7 \times 7 = \square$ 29. $6 \times 4 = \square$

Write a multiplication fact for each.

30. ✳ ✳ ✳ ✳ ✳ ✳ ✳   31. ✳ ✳   32. ✳ ✳ ✳ ✳ ✳ ✳ ✳
    ✳ ✳ ✳ ✳ ✳ ✳ ✳   ✳ ✳   ✳ ✳ ✳ ✳ ✳ ✳ ✳
                                      ✳ ✳ ✳ ✳ ✳ ✳ ✳

Complete.

33. 1 week = $\square$ days   34. 2 weeks = $\square$ days

★35. 6 weeks = $\square$ days   ★36. 9 weeks = $\square$ days

APPLICATION

MENTAL ARITHMETIC

Solve each mentally. Use patterns you have learned.
Remember to move from left to right, doing one
operation at a time.

1. $1 \times 7 \times 1 \times 7 \times 1 = \square$ 2. $0 \times 7 \times 7 \times 7 \times 7 = \square$

3. $7 \times 7 + 0 - 49 = \square$ 4. $7 \times 7 \times 1 \times 0 + 7 = \square$

8 as a Factor

In *Gulliver's Travels*, little people lived in little houses. How many houses were there?

2 groups of 8

$2 \times 8 = 16$

There were 16 houses.

We know these facts.

$$\begin{array}{cccccccc} 8 & 8 & 8 & 8 & 8 & 8 & 8 & 8 \\ \times 0 & \times 1 & \times 2 & \times 3 & \times 4 & \times 5 & \times 6 & \times 7 \\ \hline 0 & 8 & 16 & 24 & 32 & 40 & 48 & 56 \end{array}$$

Here are the new facts.

$$\begin{array}{cc} 8 & 8 \\ \times 8 & \times 9 \\ \hline 64 & 72 \end{array}$$

We can show multiplication on a number line.

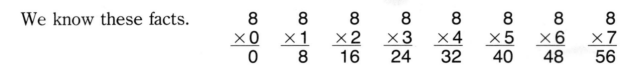

$$7 \times 8 = 56$$

CLASSWORK

Find each product.

1.  $\qquad 3 \times 8 = \square$

2. 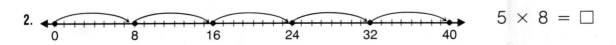 $\qquad 5 \times 8 = \square$

3. $\begin{array}{r} 8 \\ \times 8 \\ \hline \end{array}$
4. $\begin{array}{r} 8 \\ \times 6 \\ \hline \end{array}$
5. $\begin{array}{r} 8 \\ \times 9 \\ \hline \end{array}$
6. $\begin{array}{r} 8 \\ \times 2 \\ \hline \end{array}$
7. $\begin{array}{r} 8 \\ \times 7 \\ \hline \end{array}$
8. $\begin{array}{r} 8 \\ \times 4 \\ \hline \end{array}$
9. $\begin{array}{r} 8 \\ \times 0 \\ \hline \end{array}$

Find each product.

1. 8
    ×0

2. 5
    ×6

3. 4
    ×9

4. 8
    ×2

5. 0
    ×8

6. 5
    ×7

7. 8
    ×4

8. 5
    ×9

9. 8
    ×1

10. 7
    ×8

11. 8
    ×6

12. 8
    ×3

13. 3
    ×7

14. 8
    ×7

15. 6
    ×9

16. 8
    ×5

17. 6
    ×8

18. 8
    ×8

19. 1
    ×9

20. 8
    ×9

21. 4
    ×7

22. $6 \times 8 = \square$ 23. $9 \times 7 = \square$ 24. $7 \times 8 = \square$ 25. $6 \times 7 = \square$

26. $8 \times 8 = \square$ 27. $9 \times 8 = \square$ 28. $4 \times 6 = \square$ 29. $5 \times 8 = \square$

Follow the rule to complete.

Rule:
Multiply by 8.

	Input	Output
30.	5	
31.	2	
32.	3	

Rule:
Multiply by 6.

	Input	Output
33.	6	
34.	7	
35.	9	

Rule:
Multiply by 7.

	Input	Output
36.	8	
37.	4	
38.	7	

Compare. Use >, <, or = for ●.

39. 7×8 ● 50

40. 0×8 ● 8

41. 5×8 ● 40

★ 42. 4×8 ● $30 - 5$

★ 43. $9 + 4$ ● 6×8

★ 44. 3×8 ● $72 - 48$

APPLICATION

45. Gulliver saw 3 groups of
    little men. There were 8 men in
    each group. How many men
    were there in all?

★ 46. Each day Gulliver ate 8 tiny
    fishcakes. How many did he eat
    in 7 days? Make a table to show
    a pattern.

9 as a Factor

Allyson sells beach hats. She puts them in 4 piles of 9 each. How many beach hats are there?

$4 \times 9 = \square$

We know that $9 \times 4 = 36$, so $4 \times 9 = 36$.

There are 36 beach hats.

We know these facts.

| $\begin{array}{r}9\\ \times 0\\ \hline 0\end{array}$ | $\begin{array}{r}9\\ \times 1\\ \hline 9\end{array}$ | $\begin{array}{r}9\\ \times 2\\ \hline 18\end{array}$ | $\begin{array}{r}9\\ \times 3\\ \hline 27\end{array}$ | $\begin{array}{r}9\\ \times 4\\ \hline 36\end{array}$ | $\begin{array}{r}9\\ \times 5\\ \hline 45\end{array}$ | $\begin{array}{r}9\\ \times 6\\ \hline 54\end{array}$ | $\begin{array}{r}9\\ \times 7\\ \hline 63\end{array}$ | $\begin{array}{r}9\\ \times 8\\ \hline 72\end{array}$ |

Here is the new fact.
$\begin{array}{r}9\\ \times 9\\ \hline 81\end{array}$

CLASSWORK

Multiply.

1. $3 \times 9 = \square$ 2. $5 \times 9 = \square$ 3. $2 \times 9 = \square$ 4. $0 \times 9 = \square$

5. $7 \times 9 = \square$ 6. $8 \times 9 = \square$ 7. $6 \times 9 = \square$ 8. $9 \times 9 = \square$

9. $\begin{array}{r}9\\ \times 6\end{array}$ 10. $\begin{array}{r}9\\ \times 1\end{array}$ 11. $\begin{array}{r}9\\ \times 4\end{array}$ 12. $\begin{array}{r}9\\ \times 8\end{array}$ 13. $\begin{array}{r}9\\ \times 5\end{array}$ 14. $\begin{array}{r}9\\ \times 3\end{array}$ 15. $\begin{array}{r}9\\ \times 7\end{array}$

PRACTICE

Multiply.

1. 9×1 2. 9×6 3. 9×4 4. 9×2 5. 9×5 6. 9×3 7. 7×6

8. 9×8 9. 4×6 10. 9×9 11. 6×8 12. 9×4 13. 9×6 14. 8×9

15. 3×8 16. 9×3 17. 9×8 18. 6×9 19. 8×4 20. 9×5 21. 9×0

22. 8×3 23. 9×7 24. 7×8 25. 4×9 26. 9×3 27. 8×8 28. 9×9

29. $0 \times 9 = \square$ 30. $4 \times 3 = \square$ 31. $8 \times 9 = \square$ 32. $7 \times 9 = \square$

33. $4 \times 9 = \square$ 34. $1 \times 9 = \square$ 35. $9 \times 9 = \square$ 36. $2 \times 9 = \square$

Use a calculator to multiply.

37. $1 \times 9 \times 2 \times 3 \times 5 = \square$ 38. $9 \times 9 \times 1 \times 1 \times 1 = \square$

39. $1 \times 9 \times 9 \times 9 \times 0 = \square$ 40. $8 \times 1 \times 2 \times 9 \times 1 = \square$

Solve.

★41. $9 \times 9 - \square = 1$ ★42. $9 \times 8 + \square = 100$

APPLICATION

VISUAL THINKING

Find two designs that are exactly the same.

1.
2.
3.
4.

Fast Facts

Multiply as fast as you can.

1. 4
    ×1

2. 7
    ×4

3. 2
    ×2

4. 5
    ×3

5. 1
    ×1

6. 3
    ×8

7. 3
    ×2

8. 4
    ×4

9. 0
    ×5

10. 6
     ×6

11. 2
     ×9

12. 8
     ×1

13. 8
     ×7

14. 7
     ×0

15. 2
     ×5

16. 7
     ×9

17. 6
     ×2

18. 5
     ×5

19. 1
     ×0

20. 5
     ×7

21. 6
     ×3

22. 1
     ×4

23. 6
     ×8

24. 5
     ×2

25. 1
     ×6

26. 4
     ×8

27. 5
     ×0

28. 7
     ×7

29. 9
     ×3

30. 3
     ×0

31. 3
     ×4

32. 8
     ×8

33. 2
     ×7

34. 2
     ×3

35. 7
     ×5

36. 9
     ×9

37. 0
     ×4

38. 3
     ×6

39. 8
     ×2

40. 5
     ×4

41. 0
     ×9

42. 7
     ×8

43. 2
     ×1

44. 9
     ×4

45. 2
     ×8

46. 0
     ×7

47. 5
     ×6

48. 3
     ×9

49. 5
     ×9

50. 8
     ×0

51. 4
×7

52. 6
×0

53. 8
×9

54. 6
×7

55. 9
×1

56. 1
×5

57. 9
×2

58. 7
×6

59. 0
×8

60. 5
×8

61. 6
×4

62. 5
×1

63. 0
×3

64. 8
×6

65. 7
×2

66. 8
×4

67. 1
×9

68. 4
×5

69. 4
×9

70. 2
×6

71. 7
×1

72. 9
×5

73. 0
×1

74. 3
×7

75. 6
×1

76. 2
×4

77. 9
×6

78. 1
×8

79. 0
×2

80. 4
×3

81. 4
×0

82. 6
×9

83. 1
×7

84. 8
×5

85. 7
×3

86. 1
×2

87. 8
×3

88. 6
×5

89. 0
×6

90. 3
×1

91. 9
×7

92. 4
×2

93. 9
×0

94. 3
×5

95. 4
×6

96. 1
×3

97. 0
×0

98. 9
×8

99. 3
×3

100. 2
×0

FAST FACTS

Problem Solving

SKILLS AND STRATEGIES REVIEW At the Seashore

Docking Rates

Full Day - $9

Half Day - $6

Solve each problem. Make up a fact if one is missing.

1. Mike, Lucy, and Dana collected seashells. They each collected 9 shells. How many shells did they collect in all?

2. The children made 2 belts with the seashells. They used 19 shells to make both belts. How many shells were left?

3. Mike had 257 shells at the end of the week. Lucy had 262 shells and Dana had 213 shells. How many shells did Mike and Lucy have?

4. Maria and her father went on a fishing trip for 5 hours. They left at 11:30 A.M. What time did they return?

5. There are 8 docks at the marina. Four boats are tied at each dock. How many boats are tied in all?

6. Five boats stay tied at the dock for a full day. How much does each boat's owner pay?

7. What is the total amount of money collected by the marina for all 5 boats?

8. Four boats dock for half a day each. How much is paid in all?

9. A sailboat leaves dock 3 at 9:00 A.M. It heads for a port 250 miles away. What time does it arrive?

10. Two big marlins were caught. One weighed 1,090 pounds. How much did the second marlin weigh?

Look at the graph. It shows the distance in miles between a sailboat and a lighthouse at different times.

Answer each question. Use the graph.

11. How far is the boat from the lighthouse at 1:00?

12. What time is it when the boat is 18 miles from the lighthouse?

★ 13. What time should the boat reach the lighthouse?

★ 14. How far will the boat be from the lighthouse at 2:30 if the pattern continues?

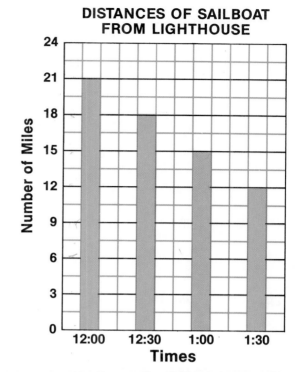

DISTANCES OF SAILBOAT FROM LIGHTHOUSE

THEN AND NOW

In 1880 the population of Boston was 362,535. The population of Providence was 104,760.† How much greater was the population of Boston than that of Providence?

In 1980 the population of Boston was 618,300. The population of Providence was 165,000. How much greater was the population of Boston than that of Providence?

†Henry B. Maglathin, *The Complete Arithmetic,* Boston and New York: Leach, Shewell, and Sanborn, 1881.

Find each product. pages 168–177, 180–181, 184–193

1. $3 \times 8 = \square$ 2. $7 \times 0 = \square$ 3. $6 \times 5 = \square$ 4. $4 \times 8 = \square$

5. $2 \times 9 = \square$ 6. $3 \times 6 = \square$ 7. $7 \times 7 = \square$ 8. $0 \times 5 = \square$

9. $6 \times 1 = \square$ 10. $3 \times 7 = \square$ 11. $8 \times 3 = \square$ 12. $5 \times 0 = \square$

13. $7 \times 9 = \square$ 14. $1 \times 8 = \square$ 15. $1 \times 4 = \square$ 16. $6 \times 7 = \square$

17. $\begin{array}{r} 2 \\ \times 6 \\ \hline \end{array}$
18. $\begin{array}{r} 7 \\ \times 9 \\ \hline \end{array}$
19. $\begin{array}{r} 3 \\ \times 3 \\ \hline \end{array}$
20. $\begin{array}{r} 7 \\ \times 6 \\ \hline \end{array}$
21. $\begin{array}{r} 8 \\ \times 2 \\ \hline \end{array}$
22. $\begin{array}{r} 9 \\ \times 9 \\ \hline \end{array}$
23. $\begin{array}{r} 4 \\ \times 5 \\ \hline \end{array}$

24. $\begin{array}{r} 5 \\ \times 5 \\ \hline \end{array}$
25. $\begin{array}{r} 0 \\ \times 2 \\ \hline \end{array}$
26. $\begin{array}{r} 6 \\ \times 1 \\ \hline \end{array}$
27. $\begin{array}{r} 8 \\ \times 7 \\ \hline \end{array}$
28. $\begin{array}{r} 2 \\ \times 5 \\ \hline \end{array}$
29. $\begin{array}{r} 7 \\ \times 5 \\ \hline \end{array}$
30. $\begin{array}{r} 6 \\ \times 2 \\ \hline \end{array}$

31. $\begin{array}{r} 5 \\ \times 1 \\ \hline \end{array}$
32. $\begin{array}{r} 6 \\ \times 8 \\ \hline \end{array}$
33. $\begin{array}{r} 3 \\ \times 9 \\ \hline \end{array}$
34. $\begin{array}{r} 0 \\ \times 6 \\ \hline \end{array}$
35. $\begin{array}{r} 2 \\ \times 2 \\ \hline \end{array}$
36. $\begin{array}{r} 7 \\ \times 8 \\ \hline \end{array}$
37. $\begin{array}{r} 5 \\ \times 9 \\ \hline \end{array}$

38. $\begin{array}{r} 9 \\ \times 8 \\ \hline \end{array}$
39. $\begin{array}{r} 3 \\ \times 6 \\ \hline \end{array}$
40. $\begin{array}{r} 2 \\ \times 9 \\ \hline \end{array}$
41. $\begin{array}{r} 4 \\ \times 8 \\ \hline \end{array}$
42. $\begin{array}{r} 9 \\ \times 6 \\ \hline \end{array}$
43. $\begin{array}{r} 6 \\ \times 5 \\ \hline \end{array}$
44. $\begin{array}{r} 9 \\ \times 3 \\ \hline \end{array}$

Multiply. pages 182–183

45. $5 \times 8 = \square$ 46. $6 \times 4 = \square$ 47. $3 \times 2 = \square$ 48. $7 \times 1 = \square$

   $8 \times 5 = \square$ $4 \times 6 = \square$ $2 \times 3 = \square$ $1 \times 7 = \square$

Use a pattern to make a table for each problem.
Then answer each question. pages 178–179, 194–195

49. There are 3 schools of fish. Each school has 6 fish. How many fish are there in all?

50. Susan uses 4 shells for each pin she makes. How many shells does she need for 8 pins?

Multiply.

1. 9
   ×1

2. 5
   ×4

3. 6
   ×6

4. 4
   ×9

5. 2
   ×4

6. 8
   ×6

7. 6
   ×9

8. 2
   ×7

9. 5
   ×2

10. 1
    ×4

11. 8
    ×9

12. 3
    ×7

13. 8
    ×8

14. 3
    ×4

15. 6
    ×7

16. 0
    ×8

17. 4
    ×2

18. 5
    ×7

19. 5
    ×6

20. 2
    ×8

21. 9
    ×4

22. 3
    ×0

23. 1
    ×5

24. 7
    ×2

25. $4 \times 3 = \square$ 26. $0 \times 9 = \square$ 27. $3 \times 4 = \square$ 28. $4 \times 4 = \square$

Find each product.

29. $1 \times 2 = \square$

   $2 \times 1 = \square$

30. $5 \times 3 = \square$

   $3 \times 5 = \square$

31. $4 \times 7 = \square$

   $7 \times 4 = \square$

Use a pattern to make a table for 32–33.
Then answer each question.

32. Divers brought up 7 bags of coral. Each bag had 9 pieces of coral. How many pieces of coral did the divers bring up?

33. Seven people went fishing for sea bass. Each person caught 6 bass. How many bass were caught?

A fishing trip lasted two days. On the first day, 3 boats pulled in 4 fish apiece. On the second day, each of 5 boats pulled in 2 fish. On which day were more fish caught?

EGG CARTON ARRAYS

You will need:

- · an egg carton
- · 45 beads
- · masking tape

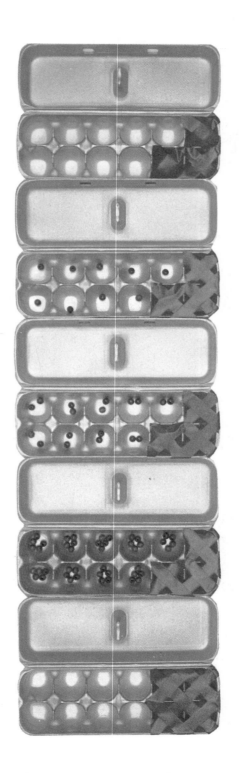

1. Tape over three sections. How many sections are left?

2. Put 1 bead into each section. How many beads are there in all?

$$9 \times 1 = \square$$

3. Put 1 more bead into each section. How many beads are there in all?

$$9 \times 2 = \square$$

4. Now use the rest of the beads. Put the same number of beads into each section. How many beads are there in each section?

$$9 \times \square = 45$$

5. Tape over one more section.

Use 48 beads.

Try some arrays of your own.

WHAT NUMBER AM I?

Read the clues. Write the number.

1. What number am I?

I am an even number.
I am less than the
product of 2 and 3.
I am not 2.

2. What number am I?

If you multiply me by 2,
your answer is less than 3.
If you multiply me by 5,
your answer is greater than 4.
If you multiply me by 3,
your answer is 3.

3. What number am I?

I am an odd number.
If you multiply me by 1,
your answer is less than 5.
If you multiply me by 3,
your answer is greater than 8.

4. What number am I?

If you multiply me by myself,
you get an even number.
If you add me to myself,
you get the same even number.

CUMULATIVE REVIEW

Choose the correct answer. Write A, B, C, or D.

1. $7 + \square = 16$

A 9   C 7

B 5   D not given

2. $18 - 9 = \square$

A 10   C 9

B 8   D not given

3. What is another fact in the family? $6 + 8 = 14$

A $7 + 7 = \square$ C $8 - 6 = \square$

B $14 - 8 = 6$ D not given

4. Choose the number for two hundred four.

A 2,004   C 244

B 204   D not given

5. Compare. 196 ● 264

A <   C =

B >   D not given

6. Choose the next 3 numbers.

1, 3, 5, 7, —, —, —

A 71, 72, 73   C 9, 11, 13

B 10, 12, 15   D not given

7. $36 + 41 = \square$

A 77   C 75

B 79   D not given

8. $57 + 21 + 43 = \square$

A 112   C 101

B 121   D not given

9.   1,481
        $+2,799$

A 3,170   C 4,280

B 3,270   D not given

10. $\$80.62 + \$13.72 = \square$

A $93.10   C $90.34

B $66.90   D not given

11. $140 - 25 = \square$

A 125   C 115

B 15   D not given

12.   4,579
        $-1,288$

A 3,291   C 3,297

B 3,391   D not given

Choose the correct answer. Write A, B, C, or D.

13. $10.95 - $2.80 = □

A $8.20   C $12.75

B $8.15   D not given

19. 5 × 4 = □

A 15   C 2

B 20   D not given

14. Estimate. 6,407 − 2,315 = □

A 3,000   C 5,000

B 4,000   D not given

20. 1 × 0 = □

A 0   C 10

B 1   D not given

15. What is the time?

A 5:47   C 3:15

B 4:35   D not given

21.
$$\begin{array}{r} 6 \\ \times 3 \\ \hline \end{array}$$

A 12   C 18

B 20   D not given

16. About how long does it take to feed a pet?

A 2 hours   C 15 minutes

B 60 minutes   D not given

22.
$$\begin{array}{r} 7 \\ \times 7 \\ \hline \end{array}$$

A 35   C 42

B 49   D not given

17. What month is October?

A seventh   C third

B sixth   D not given

23. 5 × 8 = □

A 35   C 40

B 48   D not given

18. Compare. $8.20 ● $8.02

A >   C =

B <   D not given

24. 2 × 9 = □

A 18   C 21

B 11   D not given

Choose the correct answer. Write A, B, C, or D.

Tell whether you would add or subtract. Then solve 25 and 26.

25. Mr. Ky sold 25 boards on Tuesday and 35 on Wednesday. How many boards did he sell on those two days?

   A subtract; 50   C add; 60

   B add; 10   D not given

26. Ana spent 35¢ on tacks and 48¢ on tape. How much more did she spend on tape than on tacks?

   A subtract; 13¢   C add; 63¢

   B add; 13¢   D not given

Which fact is missing?

27. Sal spent 45¢ on nails and 35¢ on tacks. What was his change?

   A amount paid   C name of store

   B 45¢   D not given

Which fact is extra?

28. Joe bought 7 feet of wire at 9¢ a foot. Another kind of wire cost 13¢ a foot. How much did Joe pay for the wire?

   A 7 feet of wire   C Another kind cost 13¢ a foot.

   B Joe bought some wire.   D not given

Use the graph for 29 and 30.

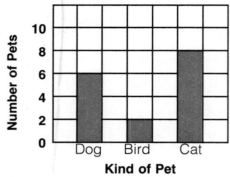

Pets Owned by Students

29. How many more dogs than birds do students own?

   A 4   C 2

   B 12   D not given

30. How many more cats than dogs do students own?

   A 4   C 2

   B 12   D not given

What comes next in each pattern?

31. 27, 37, 47, —, —, —

   A 48, 49, 50   C 5, 6, 7

   B 57, 67, 77   D not given

32. □, △, ○, ○, ▽, □, △, —, —

   A ○, ▽   C ○, ○

   B ○, □   D not given

Theme: Mountains

Understanding Division

There are 6 skiers going on the chair lift. Each chair takes 2 skiers. How many chairs do the skiers need?

6 skiers in all   2 on each chair

How many groups of 2?

There are 3 groups of 2.

We divide to find how many groups.

$$6 \div 2 = 3$$
in all   in each   groups
      group

We say, "Six divided by two equals three."

The skiers need 3 chairs.

CLASSWORK

1. How many groups of 2?

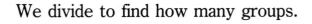

$4 \div 2 = \square$

2. How many groups of 2?

$8 \div 2 = \square$

3. How many groups of 4?

$8 \div 4 = \square$

4. How many groups of 3?

$9 \div 3 = \square$

1. How many groups of 3?

▲▲▲ ▲▲▲

6 ÷ 3 = ☐

2. How many groups of 2?

▲▲ ▲▲ ▲▲

6 ÷ 2 = ☐

3. How many groups of 4?

▲▲▲▲
▲▲▲▲
▲▲▲▲

12 ÷ 4 = ☐

4. How many groups of 5?

▲▲▲▲▲
▲▲▲▲▲

10 ÷ 5 = ☐

Divide.

5. 12 ÷ 3 = ☐

6. 10 ÷ 2 = ☐

7. 15 ÷ 5 = ☐

8. 16 ÷ 2 = ☐

9. 15 ÷ 3 = ☐

10. 14 ÷ 2 = ☐

11. 12 ÷ 6 = ☐

12. 16 ÷ 4 = ☐

13. 18 ÷ 9 = ☐

Write a division fact for each.

★14.
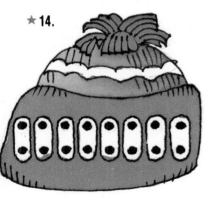

★15.
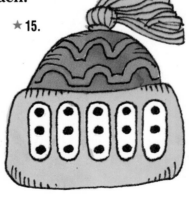

★16.

17. There were 12 racers in the Beech Mountain race. They raced 2 at a time. How many groups of 2 raced?

★18. Write a story about skiing. Use the fact 14 ÷ 2 = 7.

205

Dividing by 2

The Hikers' Club arranged to have 8 members picked up by floatplane. The pilot can take 2 hikers on each trip. How many trips will he make?

8 hikers in all   2 on each trip

How many trips?

$$8 \div 2 = 4$$
dividend   divisor   quotient

The pilot will make 4 trips.

CLASSWORK

Find each quotient.

1.

    $10 \div 2 = \square$

2.

    $14 \div 2 = \square$

3.

    $12 \div 2 = \square$

4. $4 \div 2 = \square$ 5. $8 \div 2 = \square$ 6. $6 \div 2 = \square$ 7. $2 \div 2 = \square$

8. $16 \div 2 = \square$ 9. $12 \div 2 = \square$ 10. $18 \div 2 = \square$ 11. $10 \div 2 = \square$

Find each quotient.

1. $8 \div 2 = \square$ 2. $12 \div 2 = \square$ 3. $6 \div 2 = \square$ 4. $4 \div 2 = \square$

5. $10 \div 2 = \square$ 6. $4 \div 2 = \square$ 7. $16 \div 2 = \square$ 8. $18 \div 2 = \square$

9. $2 \div 2 = \square$ 10. $14 \div 2 = \square$ 11. $12 \div 2 = \square$ 12. $8 \div 2 = \square$

13. $6 \div 2 = \square$ 14. $16 \div 2 = \square$ 15. $2 \div 2 = \square$ 16. $10 \div 2 = \square$

Complete each table.

17. Divide by 2.

2	4	6	8	10	12	14	16	18

18. Multiply by 2.

1	2	3	4	5	6	7	8	9

Write a division fact for each.

★ 19. Divide 18 by 2.   ★ 20. Divide 14 by 2.   ★ 21. Divide 16 by 2.

APPLICATION

22. Mr. Cole had 12 students in his mountain-climbing class. He divided the class into groups of 2. Find a pattern. Tell how many groups there were.

★ 23. Draw a picture that shows 10 mountain peaks in groups of 2. Write a division fact and a multiplication fact for this picture.

LOGICAL THINKING

1. Write the number 5. Multiply it by 2. Divide the answer by 2. What number do you get?

2. Write any number from 1 to 9. Multiply it by 2. Divide the answer by 2. What happens?

Dividing by 3

Sam and his friends gathered 18 cactus flowers into 3 baskets. They put the same number of flowers into each basket. How many are in each basket?

18 flowers   3 baskets

How many in each basket?

We divide to find how many in each group.

$$18 \div 3 = 6$$
in all   groups   in each
group

There are 6 in each group.

There are 6 flowers in each basket.

CLASSWORK

1. How many in each group?

$12 \div 3 = \square$

2. How many in each group?

$9 \div 3 = \square$

Find each quotient.

3. $21 \div 3 = \square$ 4. $15 \div 3 = \square$ 5. $3 \div 3 = \square$ 6. $18 \div 3 = \square$

7. $24 \div 3 = \square$ 8. $27 \div 3 = \square$ 9. $6 \div 3 = \square$ 10. $12 \div 3 = \square$

1. How many in each group?

$6 \div 3 = \square$

2. How many in each group?

$21 \div 3 = \square$

Find each quotient.

3. $12 \div 3 = \square$ 4. $9 \div 3 = \square$ 5. $15 \div 3 = \square$ 6. $18 \div 2 = \square$

7. $3 \div 3 = \square$ 8. $18 \div 3 = \square$ 9. $14 \div 2 = \square$ 10. $21 \div 3 = \square$

11. $27 \div 3 = \square$ 12. $16 \div 2 = \square$ 13. $12 \div 3 = \square$ 14. $24 \div 3 = \square$

Compare. Use >, <, or = for ●.

15. $18 \div 3 \; ● \; 7$ 16. $24 \div 3 \; ● \; 8$ 17. $15 \div 3 \; ● \; 3$ 18. $21 \div 3 \; ● \; 8$

Write a division fact for each.

★19. 12 cactus plants
3 equal groups
How many in each group?

★20. 10 Mexican blankets
2 equal groups
How many in each group?

APPLICATION

21. How many flowers must you add or subtract to make equal groups of 3?

★22. Think how these flowers can be placed in 3 equal groups. Write a division fact.

===== CALCULATOR =====

For each exercise, display the first number. Then press 3 keys over and over to get the other numbers. What 3 keys will you press?

1. 3, 6, 9, 12, 15, 18, 21, 24, 27

2. 27, 24, 21, 18, 15, 12, 9, 6, 3

3. 27, 9, 3, 1

4. 1, 3, 9, 27

Dividing by 4

In *Heidi*, by Johanna Spyri, Peter took his goats up the mountain to graze. Suppose he had 16 goats and divided them into 4 equal groups. How many were there in each group?

16 goats   4 equal groups

How many in each group?

16 ÷ 4 = 4

There were 4 goats in each group.

CLASSWORK

Divide.

1.

8 ÷ 4 = ☐

2.

20 ÷ 4 = ☐

3.

16 ÷ 4 = ☐

4. 24 ÷ 4 = ☐   5. 28 ÷ 4 = ☐   6. 12 ÷ 4 = ☐   7. 36 ÷ 4 = ☐

8. 32 ÷ 4 = ☐   9. 8 ÷ 4 = ☐   10. 4 ÷ 4 = ☐   11. 20 ÷ 4 = ☐

Divide.

1. $12 \div 4 = \square$ 2. $24 \div 4 = \square$ 3. $8 \div 4 = \square$ 4. $16 \div 2 = \square$

5. $32 \div 4 = \square$ 6. $4 \div 4 = \square$ 7. $28 \div 4 = \square$ 8. $20 \div 4 = \square$

9. $16 \div 4 = \square$ 10. $36 \div 4 = \square$ 11. $27 \div 3 = \square$ 12. $18 \div 2 = \square$

13. $24 \div 4 = \square$ 14. $15 \div 3 = \square$ 15. $20 \div 4 = \square$ 16. $28 \div 4 = \square$

17. $32 \div 4 = \square$ 18. $16 \div 4 = \square$ 19. $9 \div 3 = \square$ 20. $18 \div 3 = \square$

21. $4 \div 4 = \square$ 22. $12 \div 2 = \square$ 23. $28 \div 4 = \square$ 24. $24 \div 4 = \square$

Complete each table.

25. Multiply by 4.

1	2	3	4	5	6	7	8	9

26. Divide by 4.

4	8	12	16	20	24	28	32	36

Compare. Use >, <, or = for ●.

★27. $6 \times 4 \; ● \; 24 \div 4$

★28. $36 \div 4 \; ● \; 27 \div 3$

APPLICATION

29. Heidi brought 12 rolls home to Granny. Suppose Granny set them out in 4 equal groups. How many rolls would there be in each group?

★30. Use counters as "rolls." Show other ways to divide 12 rolls into equal groups.

211

Dividing by 5

Dr. Lia Lakis is a botanist. She studied 20 plants on Mount Washington in New Hampshire. There were 5 plants of each kind. How many different kinds of plants did Dr. Lakis study?

20 plants   5 of each kind

How many different kinds?

20 ÷ 5 = 4

Dr. Lakis studied 4 different kinds of plants.

CLASSWORK

Divide.

1.

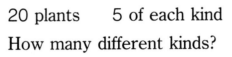

$$10 \div 5 = \square$$

2.

$$15 \div 5 = \square$$

3.

$$5 \div 5 = \square$$

4. $25 \div 5 = \square$ 5. $30 \div 5 = \square$ 6. $20 \div 5 = \square$ 7. $35 \div 5 = \square$

8. $40 \div 5 = \square$ 9. $45 \div 5 = \square$ 10. $15 \div 5 = \square$ 11. $10 \div 5 = \square$

Divide.

1. $15 \div 5 = \square$ 2. $5 \div 5 = \square$ 3. $30 \div 5 = \square$ 4. $25 \div 5 = \square$

5. $28 \div 4 = \square$ 6. $10 \div 5 = \square$ 7. $18 \div 2 = \square$ 8. $45 \div 5 = \square$

9. $36 \div 4 = \square$ 10. $40 \div 5 = \square$ 11. $35 \div 5 = \square$ 12. $27 \div 3 = \square$

13. $5 \div 5 = \square$ 14. $20 \div 5 = \square$ 15. $18 \div 3 = \square$ 16. $32 \div 4 = \square$

17. $30 \div 5 = \square$ 18. $21 \div 3 = \square$ 19. $40 \div 5 = \square$ 20. $35 \div 5 = \square$

Complete the table.

★ 21.

Number of nickels	1	2			5	6			9
Amount of money	5¢	10¢	15¢	20¢			35¢	40¢	

Choose the correct number sentence.

22. Dr. Lakis looked at 7 tiny flowers under a microscope. Each flower had 5 petals. How many petals were there?

    a. $7 + 5 = 12$ b. $7 \times 5 = 35$

    c. $7 - 5 = 2$ d. $5 + 7 = 12$

23. Dr. Lakis divided her 40 plant slides into 5 equal groups. How many were there in each group?

    a. $40 - 5 = 35$ b. $40 + 5 = 45$

    c. $40 \div 5 = 8$ d. $5 + 40 = 45$

APPLICATION

===== LOGICAL THINKING =====

Find each pair of numbers.

1. Our sum is 12.
   Our quotient is 5.
   What numbers are we?

2. Our difference is 30.
   Our quotient is 7.
   What numbers are we?

3. Our product is 12.
   Our quotient is 3.
   What numbers are we?

4. Our sum is 10.
   Our quotient is 1.
   What numbers are we?

Division with 1 and 0

Some mountain streams provide the water for big cities.

3 deer in all
1 group
3 ÷ 1 = 3
There are 3 deer in the group.

3 dogs in all
3 groups
3 ÷ 3 = 1
There is 1 dog in each group.

0 fish in all
3 groups
0 ÷ 3 = 0
There are 0 fish in each group.

▶Facts to remember:

Any number divided by 1 is that number.
Any number (except 0) divided by itself is 1.
0 divided by any number (except 0) is 0.
Never divide by 0.

CLASSWORK

Find each quotient.

1. 8 ÷ 1 = ☐   2. 6 ÷ 6 = ☐   3. 0 ÷ 2 = ☐   4. 4 ÷ 1 = ☐

5. 0 ÷ 5 = ☐   6. 9 ÷ 1 = ☐   7. 7 ÷ 7 = ☐   8. 1 ÷ 1 = ☐

9. 6 ÷ 1 = ☐   10. 5 ÷ 5 = ☐   11. 0 ÷ 8 = ☐   12. 9 ÷ 9 = ☐

214

Find each quotient.

1. $4 \div 1 = \square$ 2. $3 \div 1 = \square$

3. $5 \div 5 = \square$ 4. $8 \div 8 = \square$

5. $0 \div 8 = \square$ 6. $0 \div 1 = \square$

7. $7 \div 1 = \square$ 8. $2 \div 2 = \square$

9. $9 \div 9 = \square$ 10. $12 \div 3 = \square$

11. $0 \div 3 = \square$ 12. $45 \div 5 = \square$

13. $9 \div 1 = \square$ 14. $7 \div 7 = \square$

15. $0 \div 4 = \square$ 16. $0 \div 7 = \square$

17. $16 \div 4 = \square$ 18. $32 \div 4 = \square$

Compare. Use >, <, or = for ●.

19. $7 \div 7$ ● 1 20. $5 \div 1$ ● 6

21. $0 \div 2$ ● 2 22. $4 \div 4$ ● 4

23. $0 \div 1$ ● 1 24. $0 \div 9$ ● 0

★ 25. $6 \div 1$ ● 6×0 ★ 26. 9×1 ● $9 \div 1$

APPLICATION

MENTAL ARITHMETIC

Solve these mentally by using patterns you have just learned.

1. $10 \div 1 = \square$ 2. $37 \div 1 = \square$

3. $18 \div 18 = \square$ 4. $76 \div 76 = \square$

5. $0 \div 15 = \square$ 6. $0 \div 63 = \square$

1. $\begin{array}{r} 6 \\ \times 4 \\ \hline \end{array}$ 2. $\begin{array}{r} 9 \\ -0 \\ \hline \end{array}$

3. $\begin{array}{r} 5 \\ +0 \\ \hline \end{array}$ 4. $\begin{array}{r} 12 \\ -\ 9 \\ \hline \end{array}$

5. $\begin{array}{r} 9 \\ +4 \\ \hline \end{array}$ 6. $\begin{array}{r} 4 \\ \times 7 \\ \hline \end{array}$

7. $\begin{array}{r} 6 \\ \times 9 \\ \hline \end{array}$ 8. $\begin{array}{r} 15 \\ -\ 6 \\ \hline \end{array}$

9. $\begin{array}{r} 18 \\ -\ 9 \\ \hline \end{array}$ 10. $\begin{array}{r} 8 \\ \times 6 \\ \hline \end{array}$

11. $\begin{array}{r} 5 \\ +9 \\ \hline \end{array}$ 12. $\begin{array}{r} 11 \\ -\ 8 \\ \hline \end{array}$

13. $8 \times 9 = \square$

14. $1 + 9 = \square$

15. $7 - 2 = \square$

16. $5 \times 9 = \square$

17. $4 + 8 = \square$

18. $16 - 9 = \square$

19. $3 \times 9 = \square$

20. $6 \times 7 = \square$

Fact Families

A cog railway took 15 passengers to the top of Pikes Peak. There were 3 cars with the same number of passengers in each car. How many were in each car?

$$15 \div 3 = \square$$

Think $3 \times \square = 15$

The missing factor is 5.

$$3 \times 5 = 15$$

So $15 \div 3 = 5$.

There were 5 passengers in each car.

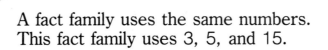

A fact family uses the same numbers. This fact family uses 3, 5, and 15.

$3 \times 5 = 15$	$15 \div 5 = 3$
$5 \times 3 = 15$	$15 \div 3 = 5$

Fact families help us remember our multiplication and division facts.

CLASSWORK

Give the other facts in each family.

1. $2 \times 4 = 8$ 2. $6 \times 4 = 24$ 3. $5 \times 1 = 5$ 4. $4 \times 4 = 16$

Find each missing factor.

5. $\square \times 3 = 18$ 6. $4 \times \square = 4$ 7. $\square \times 3 = 27$ 8. $8 \times \square = 32$

9. $1 \times \square = 7$ 10. $\square \times 4 = 20$ 11. $4 \times \square = 28$ 12. $\square \times 5 = 40$

Complete.

1. $4 \times \square = 8$ 2. $6 \times 3 = \square$ 3. $3 \times 5 = \square$ 4. $1 \times 3 = \square$

$\square \times 4 = 8$ $3 \times 6 = \square$ $5 \times 3 = \square$ $3 \times 1 = \square$

$8 \div \square = 4$ $\square \div 3 = 6$ $\square \div 5 = 3$ $3 \div \square = 1$

$8 \div 4 = \square$ $\square \div 6 = 3$ $\square \div 3 = 5$ $3 \div 1 = \square$

Give the other facts in each family.

5. $2 \times 3 = 6$ 6. $8 \times 3 = 24$ 7. $7 \times 2 = 14$ 8. $9 \times 2 = 18$

Find each missing factor.

9. $8 \times \square = 24$ 10. $6 \times \square = 30$ 11. $\square \times 4 = 28$ 12. $\square \times 5 = 45$

13. $4 \times \square = 0$ 14. $\square \times 2 = 18$ 15. $3 \times \square = 15$ 16. $\square \times 2 = 14$

Complete. Follow the rule, if given.

Rule:
Divide by 5.

	Input	Output
17.	20	
18.	30	
19.	45	
20.	15	
21.	40	
22.	35	

Rule:
Multiply by 4.

	Input	Output
23.	9	
24.	6	
25.	4	
26.	2	
27.	5	
28.	8	

Find the rule.

	Input	Output
★ 29.	27	9
	18	6
	12	4
	6	2
	15	5
	9	3

APPLICATION

30. A railway car had 24 passengers. They were divided equally into 4 rows. How many passengers were there in each row?

★ 31. Draw a picture that shows 16 railway cars in equal groups. Write as many multiplication and division facts as you can.

Problem Solving

TWO-STEP PROBLEMS

Sometimes you must answer more than one question to solve a problem. You must look for a "hidden question."

The feed-store workers need 20 sacks of grain. They have 8 sacks in stock. The grain comes in containers of 4 sacks each. How many containers must they order?

They need 20 sacks. They have 8.

Answer the hidden question first.

How many more sacks do they need?

$20 - 8 = \square$
$$\begin{array}{r} 20 \\ -\ 8 \\ \hline 12 \end{array}$$

They need 12 more sacks.

Answer the main question next.

How many containers must they order?

Divide the number of sacks they still need by the number of sacks in each container.

$12 \div 4 = \square \qquad 12 \div 4 = 3$

They must order 3 containers.

Check the answer. Does it make sense?

$$\begin{array}{r} 12 \\ +\ 8 \\ \hline 20 \end{array} \qquad \begin{array}{r} 4 \\ \times 3 \\ \hline 12 \end{array}$$

The answer makes sense.

PRACTICE

Read each problem. Tell which is the hidden question.

1. Mr. Lonegan bought 4 bandanas for his daughter. Each bandana cost $1.50. How much change did he get from a ten-dollar bill?

   a. How many bandanas did he buy?

   b. How much did he pay?

   c. How much change did he get?

   d. What is the cost of 4 bandanas?

2. Mrs. Kahn used 40 feet of string to tie 8 boxes. String costs 2¢ a foot. How much did it cost to tie each box?

   a. How much string was used per box?

   b. How many boxes were tied?

   c. How much does string cost?

   d. How many feet of string were used?

Solve.

3. Four rodeo riders bought rope and saddle soap. They paid $12 for the rope and $4 for the soap. They shared the cost equally. How much did each one pay?

4. Janet bought 2 hats for $12.50 each. Her sister bought a handmade belt for $8.00. How much money did Janet and her sister spend in all?

★5. The 4 rodeo riders shared their prize money equally. Howard had won $8. Donna had won $5. Lori had won $5. Alan had won $2. How much did each person get?

★6. The county horse race began at 9:30 A.M. The first horse finished in 2 hours. The last horse finished 1 hour later. What time did the last horse finish?

CREATE YOUR OWN PROBLEM

Here are two number sentences.

$$3 + 8 = 11 \qquad 20 - 11 = 9$$

1. Write a problem for each number sentence.

2. Write one problem that uses both number sentences.

219

Another Sign for Division

Winter is coming. Elk come down the mountains to avoid the cold, snowy weather. There are 20 elk in 4 equal groups. How many are there in each group?

We can show division in two ways.

dividend   quotient
$$20 \div 4 = 5$$
divisor

$$\begin{array}{r} 5 \leftarrow \text{quotient} \\ 4\overline{)20} \leftarrow \text{dividend} \end{array}$$
divisor

There are 5 elk in each group.

More Examples

a. $35 \div 5 = 7$ $5\overline{)35}^{\,7}$

b. $27 \div 3 = 9$ $3\overline{)27}^{\,9}$

c. $32 \div 4 = 8$ $4\overline{)32}^{\,8}$

CLASSWORK

Find each quotient.

1. $2\overline{)14}$ 2. $3\overline{)21}$ 3. $4\overline{)36}$ 4. $5\overline{)25}$ 5. $4\overline{)8}$ 6. $5\overline{)15}$

7. $3\overline{)24}$ 8. $5\overline{)45}$ 9. $2\overline{)18}$ 10. $4\overline{)24}$ 11. $3\overline{)18}$ 12. $2\overline{)4}$

PRACTICE

Find each quotient.

1. $5\overline{)5}$ 　　2. $4\overline{)12}$ 　　3. $2\overline{)12}$ 　　4. $4\overline{)16}$ 　　5. $1\overline{)7}$ 　　6. $9\overline{)0}$

7. $5\overline{)30}$ 　　8. $2\overline{)16}$ 　　9. $5\overline{)40}$ 　　10. $4\overline{)28}$ 　　11. $3\overline{)12}$ 　　12. $4\overline{)20}$

13. $5\overline{)10}$ 　　14. $2\overline{)0}$ 　　15. $1\overline{)9}$ 　　16. $2\overline{)8}$ 　　17. $4\overline{)28}$ 　　18. $3\overline{)6}$

19. $4\overline{)4}$ 　　20. $2\overline{)6}$ 　　21. $3\overline{)21}$ 　　22. $1\overline{)5}$ 　　23. $3\overline{)15}$ 　　24. $5\overline{)20}$

25. $1\overline{)2}$ 　　26. $3\overline{)9}$ 　　27. $4\overline{)16}$ 　　28. $5\overline{)40}$ 　　29. $7\overline{)7}$ 　　30. $3\overline{)12}$

31. $10 \div 5 = \square$ 　　32. $15 \div 3 = \square$ 　　33. $16 \div 2 = \square$ 　　34. $18 \div 2 = \square$

35. $35 \div 5 = \square$ 　　36. $27 \div 3 = \square$ 　　37. $6 \div 3 = \square$ 　　38. $32 \div 4 = \square$

39. $12 \div 4 = \square$ 　　40. $5 \div 5 = \square$ 　　41. $10 \div 2 = \square$ 　　42. $9 \div 9 = \square$

Find each missing number.

★ 43. $5\overline{)\square}$ with quotient 4 　　★ 44. $\square\overline{)4}$ with quotient 2 　　★ 45. $\square\overline{)28}$ with quotient 7 　　★ 46. $\square\overline{)35}$ with quotient 7 　　★ 47. $\square\overline{)16}$ with quotient 4 　　★ 48. $1\overline{)\square}$ with quotient 3

APPLICATION

49. A male elk had 6 points on each of its 2 antlers. How many points did the elk have in all?

50. Saul counted deer in groups of 5. How many groups are there in a herd of 45 deer? Use the pattern to make a table.

★ 51. Three boys each bring 5 apples to feed the deer. There are 5 deer. How many apples will each deer get?

Dividing by 6

Climbers of Mount McKinley need 6 stoves for each camp they make. They have 42 stoves. How many camps can they make?

42 stoves in all
6 for each camp

$$42 \div 6 = \square$$

Think $\square \times 6 = 42$

The missing factor is 7.

$$7 \times 6 = 42$$

So $42 \div 6 = 7$.

$$\begin{array}{r} 7 \leftarrow \text{quotient} \\ 6\overline{)42} \leftarrow \text{dividend} \\ \uparrow \\ \text{divisor} \end{array}$$

They can make 7 camps.

CLASSWORK

Divide.

1. $12 \div 6 = \square$ 2. $30 \div 6 = \square$ 3. $42 \div 6 = \square$ 4. $54 \div 6 = \square$

5. $6 \div 6 = \square$ 6. $36 \div 6 = \square$ 7. $48 \div 6 = \square$ 8. $18 \div 6 = \square$

9. $6\overline{)24}$ 10. $6\overline{)42}$ 11. $6\overline{)12}$ 12. $6\overline{)54}$ 13. $6\overline{)6}$ 14. $6\overline{)30}$

Divide.

1. $6\overline{)36}$
2. $6\overline{)48}$
3. $6\overline{)30}$
4. $6\overline{)18}$
5. $6\overline{)24}$
6. $1\overline{)6}$

7. $6\overline{)12}$
8. $6\overline{)6}$
9. $2\overline{)14}$
10. $6\overline{)42}$
11. $4\overline{)36}$
12. $6\overline{)54}$

13. $18 \div 6 = \square$
14. $45 \div 5 = \square$
15. $12 \div 6 = \square$
16. $48 \div 6 = \square$

17. $42 \div 6 = \square$
18. $54 \div 6 = \square$
19. $30 \div 6 = \square$
20. $6 \div 6 = \square$

Find each missing number.

21. $3 \times 6 = \square$
22. $\square \times 6 = 54$
23. $\square \times 6 = 48$
24. $5 \times \square = 30$

$6 \times 3 = \square$
$6 \times \square = 54$
$6 \times \square = 48$
$\square \times 5 = 30$

$\square \div 6 = 3$
$54 \div 6 = \square$
$48 \div \square = 6$
$30 \div \square = 5$

$\square \div 3 = 6$
$54 \div \square = 6$
$48 \div 6 = \square$
$30 \div 5 = \square$

Use a calculator to find each quotient.

25. $36 \div 4 \div 3 \div 1 = \square$
26. $72 \div 9 \div 2 \div 2 \div 1 = \square$

27. $54 \div 9 \div 2 \div 3 = \square$
28. $63 \div 7 \div 1 \div 3 = \square$

Solve.

★29. $6 \times 6 = \square \times 4$
★30. $30 \div 6 = 10 - \square$
★31. $0 \div 6 = 6 \times \square$

APPLICATION

32. Mrs. Kohlman packed 18 bags of rye crackers for the trip. She put 6 bags into each knapsack. How many knapsacks were there?

★33. Write a funny story about how George helped his father pack for the trip. Use some of these facts.

| 36 raisins | 48 nuts |
| 24 socks | 6 blankets |

223

Dividing by 7

Jeffrey attends a work-training program each summer.
It is near the Coast Mountains in British Columbia. He
worked 56 days last summer. How many weeks did
Jeffrey work?

$56 \div 7 = \square$

Think $\square \times 7 = 56$

The missing factor is 8.

$8 \times 7 = 56$

So $56 \div 7 = 8.$ $\quad 7\overline{)56}^{\,8}$

Jeffrey worked 8 weeks.

CLASSWORK

Divide.

1. $14 \div 7 = \square$ 2. $21 \div 7 = \square$ 3. $7 \div 7 = \square$ 4. $0 \div 7 = \square$

5. $42 \div 7 = \square$ 6. $28 \div 7 = \square$ 7. $35 \div 7 = \square$ 8. $49 \div 7 = \square$

9. $7\overline{)56}$ 10. $7\overline{)63}$ 11. $7\overline{)42}$ 12. $7\overline{)21}$ 13. $7\overline{)14}$ 14. $7\overline{)35}$

Divide.

1. $7\overline{)49}$ 2. $7\overline{)35}$ 3. $7\overline{)7}$ 4. $7\overline{)42}$ 5. $7\overline{)56}$ 6. $4\overline{)28}$

7. $7\overline{)28}$ 8. $7\overline{)0}$ 9. $7\overline{)14}$ 10. $7\overline{)21}$ 11. $2\overline{)18}$ 12. $7\overline{)63}$

13. $7\overline{)7}$ 14. $7\overline{)35}$ 15. $7\overline{)49}$ 16. $7\overline{)56}$ 17. $7\overline{)42}$ 18. $1\overline{)6}$

19. $7\overline{)63}$ 20. $5\overline{)20}$ 21. $7\overline{)21}$ 22. $3\overline{)0}$ 23. $6\overline{)54}$ 24. $7\overline{)14}$

25. $49 \div 7 = \square$ 26. $63 \div 7 = \square$ 27. $48 \div 6 = \square$ 28. $28 \div 7 = \square$

Find each missing number.

29. $4 \times 7 = \square$ 30. $\square \times 7 = 42$ 31. $7 \times \square = 35$ 32. $\square \times 8 = 56$

$7 \times 4 = \square$ $7 \times \square = 42$ $\square \times 7 = 35$ $8 \times \square = 56$

$\square \div 7 = 4$ $42 \div 7 = \square$ $35 \div 7 = \square$ $56 \div 8 = \square$

$\square \div 4 = 7$ $42 \div \square = 7$ $35 \div \square = 7$ $56 \div \square = 8$

★ 33. $32 \div 4 \div 2 + 8 - 3 = \square$ ★ 34. $6 \times 7 \times 0 + 14 - 8 = \square$

APPLICATION

35. A busload of 42 teenagers arrived at the park. The instructor divided them into 7 equal groups. How many were there in each group?

★ 36. Rosita took 16 photographs. She has 3 pages left in her album. Each page holds 6 photographs. How many more photographs will she need to fill the last page?

▆▆▆ CALCULATOR ▆▆▆

For each exercise, display the first number. Then press 3 keys over and over to get the other numbers. What 3 keys will you press?

1. 7, 14, 21, 28, 35, 42, 49, 56, 63

2. 63, 56, 49, 42, 35, 28, 21, 14, 7

3. 49, 7, 1

4. 1, 7, 49

Dividing by 8

The dog owner has 24 dogs. He hitches 8 dogs to a sled. How many sleds does he need?

$24 \div 8 = \square$

Think $\square \times 8 = 24$

The missing factor is 3.

$3 \times 8 = 24$

So $24 \div 8 = 3$.

$$8\overline{)24} \qquad \begin{array}{c} 3 \end{array}$$

He needs 3 sleds.

CLASSWORK

Find each quotient.

1. $8 \div 8 = \square$ 2. $16 \div 8 = \square$ 3. $32 \div 8 = \square$ 4. $64 \div 8 = \square$

5. $40 \div 8 = \square$ 6. $56 \div 8 = \square$ 7. $48 \div 8 = \square$ 8. $72 \div 8 = \square$

9. $8\overline{)24}$ 10. $8\overline{)48}$ 11. $8\overline{)16}$ 12. $8\overline{)64}$ 13. $8\overline{)0}$ 14. $8\overline{)8}$

Find each quotient.

1. $8\overline{)32}$ 2. $8\overline{)40}$ 3. $8\overline{)24}$ 4. $8\overline{)48}$ 5. $6\overline{)36}$ 6. $8\overline{)56}$

7. $8\overline{)8}$ 8. $5\overline{)40}$ 9. $8\overline{)72}$ 10. $8\overline{)0}$ 11. $8\overline{)16}$ 12. $4\overline{)32}$

13. $7\overline{)63}$ 14. $8\overline{)56}$ 15. $3\overline{)15}$ 16. $8\overline{)64}$ 17. $7\overline{)21}$ 18. $8\overline{)40}$

19. $8\overline{)48}$ 20. $8\overline{)32}$ 21. $8\overline{)16}$ 22. $6\overline{)48}$ 23. $8\overline{)72}$ 24. $8\overline{)24}$

25. $40 \div 8 = \square$ 26. $56 \div 8 = \square$ 27. $8 \div 8 = \square$ 28. $0 \div 3 = \square$

29. $16 \div 8 = \square$ 30. $25 \div 5 = \square$ 31. $49 \div 7 = \square$ 32. $64 \div 8 = \square$

Complete the table. Each sled has 8 dogs.

33.

	1	2	3	4	5	6	7	8	9
	8	16							

Choose the correct number sentence. Then solve it.

34. Eight first-aid stations were set up along a race course. There were 3 volunteers for each station. How many volunteers were there?

a. $3 + 8 = \square$ b. $8 \div 3 = \square$

c. $8 \times 3 = \square$ d. $8 - 2 = \square$

Find the answer.

★ 35. Divide 72 by 8. Add 21.   ★ 36. Divide 0 by 4. Add 4.

APPLICATION

37. Some sled drivers shared 32 packages of fruit. They each got 4 packages. How many drivers were there?

★ 38. Draw a picture that shows 16 snowshoes in pairs. Write a division fact for the picture you drew.

227

Dividing by 9

Each year Mindy and Steve Logan clear
a 9-mile stretch of the Appalachian Trail.
They have cleared 36 miles. How many
years have they been working?

$$36 \div 9 = \square$$

Think $\square \times 9 = 36$

The missing factor is 4.

$$4 \times 9 = 36$$

So $36 \div 9 = 4.$ $9\overline{)36}$ with 4 above

They have been working 4 years.

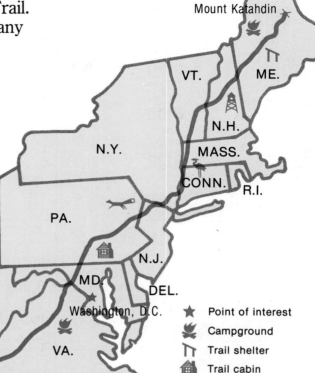

Point of interest ★
Campground 🔥
Trail shelter ⛺
Trail cabin 🏠
Wildlife refuge 🦢
Fire tower 🗼
Deer in vicinity 🦌
Foxes in vicinity 🦊

CLASSWORK

Divide.

1. $27 \div 9 = \square$ 2. $9 \div 9 = \square$ 3. $18 \div 9 = \square$ 4. $36 \div 9 = \square$

5. $81 \div 9 = \square$ 6. $72 \div 9 = \square$ 7. $54 \div 9 = \square$ 8. $63 \div 9 = \square$

9. $9\overline{)45}$ 10. $9\overline{)0}$ 11. $9\overline{)27}$ 12. $9\overline{)72}$ 13. $9\overline{)81}$ 14. $9\overline{)54}$

Divide.

1. $9\overline{)45}$ 2. $9\overline{)18}$ 3. $9\overline{)36}$ 4. $9\overline{)9}$ 5. $9\overline{)72}$ 6. $9\overline{)0}$

7. $4\overline{)20}$ 8. $9\overline{)27}$ 9. $9\overline{)54}$ 10. $5\overline{)45}$ 11. $9\overline{)63}$ 12. $7\overline{)49}$

13. $9\overline{)9}$ 14. $9\overline{)81}$ 15. $8\overline{)64}$ 16. $9\overline{)72}$ 17. $6\overline{)12}$ 18. $9\overline{)36}$

19. $7\overline{)21}$ 20. $9\overline{)45}$ 21. $9\overline{)63}$ 22. $8\overline{)56}$ 23. $1\overline{)9}$ 24. $9\overline{)18}$

Find each missing number.

25. $\square \times 9 = 54$ 26. $9 \times \square = 9$ 27. $\square \times 9 = 36$ 28. $\square \times 5 = 45$
    $54 \div 9 = \square$ $9 \div \square = 9$ $36 \div 9 = \square$ $45 \div 5 = \square$

29. $9 \times \square = 63$ 30. $\square \times 8 = 56$ 31. $2 \times \square = 18$ 32. $\square \times 9 = 81$
    $63 \div \square = 9$ $56 \div 8 = \square$ $18 \div \square = 2$ $81 \div 9 = \square$

Use $+$, $-$, $\times$, or $\div$ for ●.

33. $9 ● 9 = 1$ 34. $9 ● 7 = 63$ 35. $9 ● 9 = 18$

36. $9 ● 4 = 5$ 37. $27 ● 9 = 3$ 38. $9 ● 6 = 15$

★ 39. $9 ● 5 ● 5 = 40$ ★ 40. $3 ● 9 ● 3 = 30$ ★ 41. $36 ● 9 ● 5 = 9$

42. Frank Zeretski walks 9 hours each day along the Appalachian Trail. He has walked 72 hours. How many days has he walked?

★ 43. Write a mystery story or fairy tale about a mountain. Use animals or birds in your story. Use a division fact.

Fact Table

Josiah Purdy makes pottery in the Great Smoky Mountains. How many pots has he made?

$3 \times 6 = \square$

We can find products in the fact table.

- Find 3 in the row.
- Find 6 in the column.
- Find the product, 18, where the 3 row and the 6 column meet.

$3 \times 6 = 18$

He has made 18 pots.

We can find quotients in the fact table.

$40 \div 5 = \square$

- Find 40 in the 5 row. Follow that column from 40 up to the top to find the quotient, 8.

$40 \div 5 = 8$

column ↓

×	0	1	2	3	4	5	6	7	8	9
0	0	0	0	0	0	0	0	0	0	0
1	0	1	2	3	4	5	6	7	8	9
2	0	2	4	6	8	10	12	14	16	18
3	0	3	6	9	12	15	18	21	24	27
4	0	4	8	12	16	20	24	28	32	36
5	0	5	10	15	20	25	30	35	40	45
6	0	6	12	18	24	30	36	42	48	54
7	0	7	14	21	28	35	42	49	56	63
8	0	8	16	24	32	40	48	56	64	72
9	0	9	18	27	36	45	54	63	72	81

row →

CLASSWORK

Use the table to complete each fact.

1. $\begin{array}{r} 8 \\ \times 7 \\ \hline \end{array}$
2. $\begin{array}{r} 9 \\ \times 3 \\ \hline \end{array}$
3. $\begin{array}{r} 4 \\ \times 6 \\ \hline \end{array}$
4. $\begin{array}{r} 2 \\ \times 5 \\ \hline \end{array}$
5. $\begin{array}{r} 8 \\ \times 1 \\ \hline \end{array}$
6. $\begin{array}{r} 3 \\ \times 7 \\ \hline \end{array}$
7. $\begin{array}{r} 4 \\ \times 9 \\ \hline \end{array}$

8. $6\overline{)36}$
9. $4\overline{)32}$
10. $8\overline{)40}$
11. $5\overline{)20}$
12. $9\overline{)81}$
13. $7\overline{)28}$

PRACTICE

Complete each fact.

1. 5
×3

2. 7
×5

3. 0
×6

4. 3
×2

5. 6
×6

6. 2
×4

7. 9
×6

8. 7
×9

9. 4
×5

10. 6
×8

11. 2
×7

12. 4
×0

13. 2
×2

14. 8
×4

15. 5
×8

16. 7
×6

17. 3
×8

18. 7
×3

19. 0
×8

20. 1
×5

21. 6
×7

22. 2
×6

23. 4
×8

24. 6
×2

25. 4
×4

26. 9
×8

27. 5
×5

28. 0
×2

29. 7)14

30. 5)35

31. 8)64

32. 7)0

33. 3)12

34. 7)21

35. 2)6

36. 4)20

37. 8)56

38. 6)24

39. 5)45

40. 7)42

41. 8)24

42. 3)18

43. 2)16

44. 1)9

45. 5)15

46. 8)32

47. 9)63

48. 4)0

49. 4)16

50. 4)12

51. 8)48

52. 3)21

53. 6)18

54. 5)40

55. 8)72

56. 4)8

57. 9)0

58. 3)9

59. 9)45

60. 5)25

61. 2)10

62. 7)49

63. 9)72

64. 8)16

Complete the table.

★ 65.

×	6	7	8	9
4				
5				
6				
7				

APPLICATION

VISUAL THINKING

Find 5 squares in this drawing.

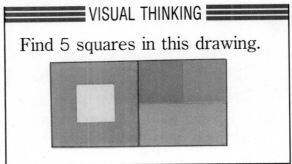

Problem Solving

Solve each problem, if possible.

1. It takes 8 logs to make a section of fence. How many sections can be made from 56 logs?

2. One of the ranch hands made 6 sections of fence. How many logs did he use?

3. Logs are 20 feet long. Each fence post is 5 feet long. How many fence posts can be cut from 1 log?

4. The ranchers need 35 fence posts to complete their fence. How many logs do they need?

5. Mr. Brown is the blacksmith on the ranch. Today he put shoes on 6 horses. He put 4 shoes on each of 4 horses. He put 3 shoes on each of 2 horses. How many horseshoes did he use?

6. The blacksmith charges $2 for each horseshoe. He put 4 horseshoes on Star. Star's owner gave him a ten-dollar bill. How much change will the blacksmith give back to the owner?

7. Each horseshoe takes 6 nails. How many nails will 4 horseshoes take?

8. Mr. Antonelli wants new shoes for his horses. How much will he pay?

NAILS

1 for	4¢
2 for	8¢
3 for	___ ¢
___ for	16¢
___ for	20¢

9. Mr. Brown made a sign showing how much nails cost. Copy the sign and complete it.

10. Mrs. Logan paid 25¢ and received 9¢ change. How many nails did she buy?

11. Tony feeds his 4 ducks. He gives them 16 ounces of grain. Each duck eats the same amount. How much grain does each duck eat?

12. There are 140 sheep, 257 cows, 23 horses, and 85 pigs on the ranch. How many animals are there in all?

13. There are 103 brown-and-white cows on the ranch. How many of the cows are not brown-and-white?

★ 14. There are 156 chickens and 84 ducks. How many more four-legged animals are there than two-legged animals?

Mrs. Santos is making a patchwork quilt.

Use the picture to answer each question.

15. How many patches will there be in all?

16. Tell whether a triangle, a circle, or a square goes with each letter, a–l.

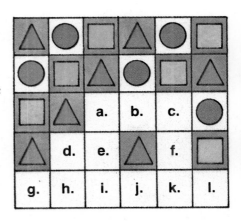

17. Will there be more circles than squares?

18. Will there be more triangles than circles?

★ 19. There will be 3 quilts like this one. How many triangles will be used in 3 quilts?

★ 20. Mrs. Santos plans to make a fourth quilt. She will use a circle in place of each triangle in the original pattern. How many circles will there be on her fourth quilt?

Find each quotient. pages 204–215

1. $12 \div 2 = \square$

2. $42 \div 6 = \square$

3. $36 \div 9 = \square$

4. $24 \div 4 = \square$

5. $56 \div 7 = \square$

6. $15 \div 3 = \square$

7. $27 \div 9 = \square$

8. $10 \div 5 = \square$

9. $24 \div 3 = \square$

10. $36 \div 4 = \square$

11. $28 \div 7 = \square$

12. $3 \div 3 = \square$

13. $18 \div 9 = \square$

14. $35 \div 7 = \square$

15. $28 \div 4 = \square$

Find the missing numbers. pages 216–217

16. $5 \times 4 = \square$
    $4 \times 5 = \square$
    $\square \div 4 = 5$
    $\square \div 5 = 4$

17. $2 \times 8 = \square$
    $8 \times 2 = \square$
    $\square \div 8 = 2$
    $\square \div 2 = 8$

18. $\square \times 6 = 42$
    $6 \times \square = 42$
    $42 \div 6 = \square$
    $42 \div \square = 6$

Divide. pages 220–231

19. $7\overline{)63}$

20. $9\overline{)54}$

21. $5\overline{)30}$

22. $6\overline{)12}$

23. $6\overline{)54}$

24. $2\overline{)8}$

25. $6\overline{)30}$

26. $8\overline{)16}$

27. $2\overline{)14}$

28. $3\overline{)27}$

29. $6\overline{)48}$

30. $3\overline{)6}$

31. $8\overline{)48}$

32. $8\overline{)56}$

33. $9\overline{)81}$

34. $5\overline{)35}$

35. $4\overline{)16}$

36. $3\overline{)18}$

37. $8\overline{)64}$

38. $8\overline{)32}$

39. $3\overline{)12}$

40. $7\overline{)49}$

41. $4\overline{)20}$

42. $7\overline{)21}$

43. $6\overline{)36}$

Solve. pages 218–219, 232–233

44. A ski club entered 15 racers in the downhill race at Loon Mountain. There are 5 racers on a team. How many teams are there?

45. There are 8 oranges and 6 apples to be shared among 7 campers. How many pieces of fruit will each camper get?

CHAPTER TEST

Find each quotient.

1. $25 \div 5 = \square$

2. $9 \div 9 = \square$

3. $42 \div 7 = \square$

4. $24 \div 6 = \square$

5. $40 \div 8 = \square$

6. $63 \div 9 = \square$

7. $45 \div 9 = \square$

8. $15 \div 3 = \square$

9. $20 \div 5 = \square$

10. $10 \div 2 = \square$

11. $5 \div 1 = \square$

12. $5 \div 5 = \square$

Find the missing numbers.

13. $6 \times 9 = \square$
    $9 \times 6 = \square$
    $\square \div 9 = 6$
    $\square \div 6 = 9$

14. $8 \times \square = 72$
    $\square \times 8 = 72$
    $72 \div \square = 8$
    $72 \div 8 = \square$

15. $8 \times 7 = \square$
    $7 \times 8 = \square$
    $\square \div 7 = 8$
    $\square \div 8 = 7$

Divide.

16. $4\overline{)32}$

17. $8\overline{)72}$

18. $5\overline{)25}$

19. $8\overline{)24}$

20. $4\overline{)12}$

21. $4\overline{)4}$

22. $5\overline{)40}$

23. $7\overline{)7}$

24. $3\overline{)21}$

25. $9\overline{)72}$

26. $7\overline{)14}$

27. $3\overline{)9}$

28. $6\overline{)18}$

29. $5\overline{)45}$

30. $8\overline{)8}$

31. $2\overline{)18}$

Solve.

32. Hikers found 6 bird nests. Each nest had an equal number of eggs. There were 30 eggs in all. How many eggs were there in each nest?

33. On their trip, 9 scouts each found 4 rocks. They put the rocks into bags. There were 6 rocks in each bag. How many bags did they use?

 Students found 24 mountain flowers while on a hike. There were 8 possible ways to group the flowers in equal groups. Draw pictures to show the ways the flowers could have been grouped.

DIVIDING A REGION

You will need:
- large-grid graph paper
- crayons

Mark off a region like this one.

1. How many small squares are there?

Here are two ways to divide this region into 2 equal parts. Now mark and color squares until you find another way. Use two crayons to do this.

2. How many other ways can you find? How many small squares are there in each equal part?

Mark off a region like this one.

3. How many small squares are there?

Here are two ways to divide this region into 3 equal parts. Now mark and color squares until you find another way. Use three crayons to do this. The squares in each part must touch.

4. How many other ways can you find? How many small squares are there in each equal part?

DIVISION LOGIC

1. Dave had fewer than 10 baseball cards. When he put them into piles of 4, he had 1 card left over. When he put them into piles of 3, he had none left over. How many cards did he have?

2. Rosa and Mike are setting up chairs for the show. They can make even rows of 4 or 5 chairs. They have fewer than 40 chairs. How many chairs do they have?

3. Diane has a sheet of paper 12 inches long by 12 inches wide. She wants to cut it into 4-inch squares. How many squares can she cut?

4. Andy, Bev, and Cass want to share Bev's marbles. Bev says, "If I give you each 3 marbles, and you each give me 1 back, we will be even." How many marbles are there?

USING BASIC IN PROGRAMS

To use computer programs,
we must understand instructions
written in BASIC.

In BASIC, we use *
for multiplication.

4 * 6 means 4 *times* 6.

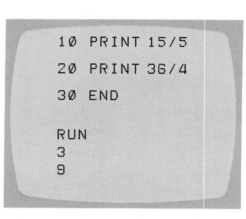

```
10  PRINT 4 * 6
20  PRINT 7 * 8
30  END

RUN
24
56
```

In BASIC, we use /
for division.

15/5 means 15 *divided by* 5.

```
10  PRINT 15/5
20  PRINT 36/4
30  END

RUN
3
9
```

For each program, tell what the output will be.

1.
```
10  PRINT 3 * 9
20  PRINT 8 * 2
30  PRINT 21/7
40  END
```

2.
```
10  PRINT 18/2
20  PRINT 6 * 5
30  PRINT 7 * 4
40  END
```

3.
```
10  PRINT 857 + 975
20  PRINT 232 - 48
30  PRINT 2 * 6
40  PRINT 14/2
50  END
```

4.
```
10  PRINT 13 + 14 + 15
20  PRINT 116 - 75
30  PRINT 9 * 7
40  PRINT 45/5
50  END
```

We can use quotation marks in a PRINT statement.
The computer will display *exactly* what is typed
inside the quotation marks.

These lines tell the computer
to print what is inside the
quotation marks.

```
10  PRINT "HELLO"
20  PRINT "LET'S MULTIPLY"
30  PRINT "3 TIMES 6"
40  PRINT 3 * 6
50  END
```

The computer will compute 3 × 6.

```
RUN
HELLO
LET'S MULTIPLY
3 TIMES 6
18
```

For each program, tell what the output will be.

5.
```
10  PRINT "HELLO STUDENT"
20  PRINT "LET'S DIVIDE"
30  PRINT "10 DIVIDED BY 2"
40  PRINT 10/2
50  PRINT "IS THIS CORRECT?"
60  END
```

6.
```
10  PRINT "SOME MATH FACTS"
20  PRINT "9 + 7 ="
30  PRINT 9 + 7
40  PRINT "6 - 5 ="
50  PRINT 6 - 5
60  END
```

=== AT THE COMPUTER ===

1. Enter and RUN each program in **1-4**, page 238.

2. Compare each output with your answer.

3. Enter and RUN each program on this page.

★ **4.** On Your Own: Write a program that will display
your name and telephone number.
Try your program on a computer.

MAINTAINING SKILLS

Choose the correct answer. Write A, B, C, or D.

1. Round 680 to the nearest hundred.

    A 600   **C** 700

    B 800   **D** not given

2. $\$16.43 + \$65.72 = \square$

    A $82.05   **C** $82.15

    B $71.15   **D** not given

3. $\begin{array}{r} 5,210 \\ -1,934 \\ \hline \end{array}$

    A 3,176   **C** 4,176

    B 3,276   **D** not given

4. Compare. $\$8.55 \bullet \$7.96$

    A >   **C** =

    B <   **D** not given

5. $1 \times 0 = \square$

    A 1   **C** 2

    B 0   **D** not given

6. $9 \times 9 = \square$

    A 72   **C** 1

    B 18   **D** not given

7. $27 \div 3 = \square$

    A 30   **C** 9

    B 7   **D** not given

8. $40 \div 5 = \square$

    A 8   **C** 9

    B 35   **D** not given

9. What is another fact in the family? $14 \div 7 = 2$

    A $14 - 7 = 7$ **C** $2 + 7 = 9$

    B $7 \times 2 = 14$ **D** not given

Find a pattern. Make a table to solve **10** and **11**.

10. Nick worked 2 hours every other day. He worked 2 hours on Tuesday. How many hours did he work on the next Tuesday?

    A 8   **C** 0

    B 2   **D** not given

11. Jo planted flowers. The pattern she used was a row of 5, a row of 3, a row of 5, a row of 3. How many flowers are in the next two rows?

    A 3, 5   **C** 3, 2

    B 5, 3   **D** not given

Metric Measurement 8

Theme: The Zoo

Centimeter

Naomi sketches animals at the zoo. Her pencil is about 4 paper clips long. It is about 2 erasers long. We can measure lengths with any unit.

▶We use the **centimeter** as a standard unit to measure short lengths. We write **cm** for centimeter.

The length of the pencil is between 11 and 12 centimeters. It is nearer to 12 centimeters. The length of the pencil is 12 centimeters to the nearest centimeter.

CLASSWORK

Measure each length to the nearest centimeter.

1.

2.

3.

Guess how long each is. Then measure to the nearest centimeter.

4. length of your longest finger

5. width of your desk

242

PRACTICE

Measure each length to the nearest centimeter.

1.

2.

3.   4.

Draw a bar of each length.

5. 2 centimeters   6. 8 centimeters

7. 3 centimeters   8. 1 centimeter

9. 9 centimeters   10. 10 centimeters

Guess how long each is. Then measure to the nearest centimeter.

11. width of this book   12. length of this book

13. length of your pencil   14. width of your hand

Measure 3 objects in your classroom that are

★ 15. longer than 10 centimeters.   ★ 16. shorter than 10 centimeters.

APPLICATION

Read each problem. Look for the hidden question. Then solve.

17. Val bought 8 cm of ribbon for 5¢ a cm. Her mother bought 8 cm for 4¢ a cm. How much did Val and her mother spend in all?

★ 18. The zookeeper needs 60 cm of chain. He has 15 cm. The chain comes in 5 cm pieces. How many pieces will he buy?

▀▀▀▀ CALCULATOR ▀▀▀▀

Sol, the chimpanzee, grows 9 centimeters each month. Sol was 25 centimeters long when he was born. What was his length when he was one year old?

Meter and Kilometer

A lion measures about 1 meter from its shoulder to the ground.

1 meter

▶We use the **meter** to measure lengths much longer than a centimeter. We write **m** for meter.

1 meter = 100 centimeters

The doorknob is about 1 meter from the floor.

▶We use the **kilometer** to measure longer lengths. We write **km** for kilometer.

1 kilometer = 1,000 meters

A fast walker can walk a distance of 1 kilometer in about 12 minutes.

1 meter

CLASSWORK

Choose centimeters, meters, or kilometers to measure each.

1. your height

2. length of your arm

3. length of a river

4. height of a giraffe

5. distance from home plate to first base

Complete.

6. 1 km = _____ m

7. 1,000 m = _____ km

8. 1 m = _____ cm

Guess how long each is. Then measure to the nearest meter.

9. length of the classroom

10. width of the classroom

Choose centimeters, meters, or kilometers to measure each.

1. height of a gorilla
2. length of a barge
3. distance a pigeon can fly
4. length of a car
5. length of a bus ticket
6. distance a bus travels
7. height of a telephone pole
8. length of a fish
9. length of a toothbrush
10. width of a TV screen

Complete.

11. 3,000 m = _____ km   12. 2,000 m = _____ km   13. 2 m = _____ cm

Guess how long each is. Then measure to the nearest meter.

14. height of your desk
15. width of the window
16. length of the chalkboard
17. height of the chalkboard

Measure 3 objects in your classroom

★ 18. that are longer than a meter.
★ 19. that are shorter than a meter.

APPLICATION

20. Ramon walked from the elephant yard to the giraffe area and back. How far did he walk?

★ 21. How long is the shortest path from the elephant yard to the deer park?

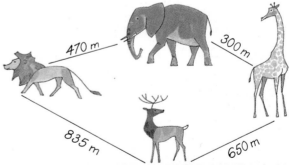

470 m   300 m   835 m   650 m

═══ LOGICAL THINKING ═══

In a race the cheetah was 50 meters ahead of the lion. The tiger was 10 meters behind the leopard. The lion was 30 meters ahead of the tiger. Who won the race? Who was second? third? last?

Problem Solving

EXPERIMENT

Sometimes a problem can best be solved by doing an experiment. Instead of drawing a picture, it is better to do the action.

1. A kangaroo covers 3 meters in one jump. How many jumps do you take to cover 3 meters?

THINK   How many jumps do I take?

PLAN   Measure 3 meters, and mark the distance on the ground.

SOLVE   Do an experiment. Jump and then count the number of jumps you made to cover 3 meters.

LOOK BACK   Do the experiment again. See if you get the same answer.

You probably take more than 2 jumps to cover 3 meters.

2. An owl can see a fly from 30 meters away. Can you see the difference between a nickel and a dime from 30 meters away?

Measure 30 meters between you and the coins.

Do an experiment. Look at the coins from a distance of 30 meters. Can you see the difference?

Do the experiment again. Stand 30 meters away in another direction. Can you see the difference?

You probably cannot see the difference between a nickel and a dime from 30 meters away.

PRACTICE

Do an experiment to solve each problem.

1. A giraffe is 4 meters tall. How many chalkboard erasers end to end does it take to reach 4 meters?

2. A brown bear is 2 meters tall. Can the bear fit through the door of your classroom?

3. Five elephants walked in a line. Each elephant was 4 meters long. How many classmates holding hands would reach as far as the line of elephants?

4. At the zoo lions and tigers are kept in fenced-in areas. These areas are 30 meters apart. How many cars could fit side by side between the areas?

5. The monkey ate 1 kilogram of bananas. How many things in your classroom weigh 1 kilogram?

6. An ostrich egg can be 20 centimeters long. How much longer is this than a chicken egg?

7. There is a big tree at the zoo. It took 6 children holding hands to reach around it. How many meters around might the tree be?

8. The zoo has an area with red bats. A red bat weighs only about 10 grams. How many standard-size paper clips are there in 10 grams?

=== CREATE YOUR OWN PROBLEM ===

Choose one of the facts below. Write a problem that can be solved by doing an experiment.

1. A grizzly bear cub weighs about 400 grams at birth.

2. A raccoon weighs about 9 kilograms.

3. A moose may have antlers that weigh 30 kilograms.

4. A mouse weighs about 30 grams.

Gram and Kilogram

Some zoo animals eat pellets of
food. Three pellets of grain
weigh about 1 gram.

▶We use the **gram** to measure the
weight of light objects.
We write **g** for gram.

A nickel weighs
about 5 grams.

▶We use the **kilogram** to measure
the weight of heavier objects.
We write **kg** for kilogram.

This book weighs about 1 kilogram.

1 kilogram = 1,000 grams

CLASSWORK

Choose grams or kilograms to measure each.

1. an apple

2. a dime

3. a truck

4. a tomato

5. a ski boot

6. a penny

Choose the correct measurement for each.

7. an orange
   a. 200 g   b. 200 kg

8. a dictionary
   a. 1 kg   b. 1 g

9. two raisins
   a. 1 kg   b. 1 g

10. a box of crayons
    a. 20 g   b. 20 kg

Choose grams or kilograms to measure each.

1. an alligator

2. a peach

3. a piece of paper

4. a motorcycle

5. a nail

6. a typewriter

7. a butterfly

8. an elephant

9. a cat

Choose the correct measurement for each.

10. a vitamin pill
  a. 1 kg   b. 1 g

11. the family car
  a. 900 kg   b. 900 g

12. a chimpanzee
  a. 50 kg   b. 50 g

13. a lion
  a. 225 g   b. 225 kg

14. a loaf of bread
  a. 500 g   b. 500 kg

15. a can of soup
  a. 300 g   b. 300 kg

Compare. Use >, <, or = for ●.

16. 1 gram ● 1 kilogram

17. 1,000 grams ● 1 kilogram

★18. 2 kilograms ● 3,000 grams

★19. 5,000 grams ● 4 kilograms

APPLICATION

20. The zookeeper puts sand around the seesaw. He has 8 pails. He puts 2 kilograms of sand in each pail. How many kilograms of sand does he use?

★21. Bo-Bo the orangutan weighs 47 kilograms. Find your weight in kilograms. Do you weigh more or less than Bo-Bo?

MENTAL ARITHMETIC

Two African elephants each eat 300 kilograms of grain a day. The zookeeper can carry 200 kilograms of grain in his truck. How many trips will he make each day to feed the two elephants?

Milliliter and Liter

Snookie gets a teaspoon of vitamins every day. A teaspoon holds about 5 milliliters of liquid.

▶ We use the **milliliter** to measure small amounts of liquid. We write **mL** for milliliter.

1 mL   250 mL

▶ We use the **liter** to measure large amounts of liquid. We write **L** for liter.

1 L   5 L

1 liter = 1,000 milliliters

CLASSWORK

Choose milliliters or liters to measure each.

1. water in a glass
2. gasoline in a car
3. paint in a bucket
4. water in a bathtub
5. medicine in a spoon
6. milk in a baby's bottle
7. juice in a small can
8. perfume in a bottle
9. water in a swimming pool
10. oil in a tanker

Choose the correct measurement for each.

11. a watering can
    a. 10 mL   b. 1 L

12. a water tank
    a. 150 L   b. 150 mL

PRACTICE

Choose milliliters or liters to measure each.

1. tea in a teacup
2. milk in a glass
3. water in a pitcher
4. a spoonful of soup
5. cider in a jug
6. fruit punch for the class

Write possible or not possible for each.

7. My brother drank 50 liters of water.
8. Dorothea made 3 liters of soup for dinner.
9. A small glass will hold 900 liters of milk.
10. The thirsty boy drank 200 milliliters of water.
11. Megan filled the pitcher with 50 liters of juice.
12. The cat drank 25 liters of water.

Choose the correct measurement for each.

13. a carton of milk
    a. 2 L   b. 2 mL

14. a glass
    a. 200 L   b. 200 mL

15. a pitcher
    a. 3 mL   b. 3 L

16. a soup bowl
    a. 250 L   b. 250 mL

Compare. Use >, <, or = for ●.

17. 1 milliliter ● 1 liter

18. 1 liter ● 1,000 milliliters

★ 19. 900 milliliters ● 1 liter

★ 20. 2 liters ● 3,000 milliliters

APPLICATION

21. Two elephants each drink 75 liters of water a day. About how much water should the zookeeper put in their pool each day?

★ 22. Snookie gets 5 milliliters of vitamins every day. About how many milliliters of vitamins does Snookie get in one month?

▰▰▰▰▰ CALCULATOR ▰▰▰▰▰

The zookeeper buys 1 liter of vitamins a week. A liter costs $3.45. How much money does he spend on vitamins in 3 weeks? in 6 weeks?

251

Degree Celsius

When it is 0 degrees Celsius, the fur keeps the polar bear warm.

We write 0°C.

When it is 30 degrees Celsius, the fur keeps the polar bear cool.

We write 30°C.

▶We use the **degree Celsius** as a unit to measure temperature. We write **°C** for degree Celsius. Temperature shows how hot or cold something is.

The thermometer shows 22°C. That is a comfortable room temperature.

CLASSWORK

Use the thermometer to answer the questions.

1. At what temperature does water boil?

2. At what temperature does water freeze?

3. What is the normal body temperature?

4. Is it a hot or cold day when the temperature is 35°C?

5. Is it a hot or cold day when the temperature is 0°C?

°C

Water boils → 100

90

80

70

60

50

Normal body temperature 37° → 40

30

20

10

Water freezes → 0

252

PRACTICE

Read the Celsius temperature on each.

1.

10
5
0
−5
−10

2.

30
25
20
15
10

3.

10
5
0
−5
−10

Choose the most likely temperature.

4.

a. 5°C   b. 35°C

5.

a. 0°C   b. 50°C

Match. Choose the most likely temperature.

6. cold day   a. 0°C

7. freezing point of water   b. 19°C

8. boiling water   c. 5°C

9. hot summer day   d. 40°C

10. autumn day   e. 100°C

Write true or false.

11. The temperature on a cold day could be 5°C.

12. The temperature on a hot day could be 30°C.

APPLICATION

13. The overnight temperature will be 10°C. Will the bears' wading pool freeze?

★ 14. The temperature was 30°C. It fell 6°. Then it fell 5°. What was the temperature then?

Mixed Practice

1. $58 + 472 = \square$

2. $\begin{array}{r} \$10.00 \\ -1.73 \\ \hline \end{array}$

3. $\begin{array}{r} 3{,}890 \\ +1{,}927 \\ \hline \end{array}$

4. $\begin{array}{r} 5{,}235 \\ -2{,}982 \\ \hline \end{array}$

5. $\begin{array}{r} 8{,}263 \\ +1{,}057 \\ \hline \end{array}$

6. $\begin{array}{r} 9{,}768 \\ -4{,}685 \\ \hline \end{array}$

7. $2 \times 7 = \square$

8. $9 \div 3 = \square$

9. $4 \times \square = 24$

10. $0 \times 7 = \square$

11. $7 \times 8 = \square$

12. $64 \div 8 = \square$

13. $9 \times 9 = \square$

14. $4\overline{)36}$

15. $5\overline{)25}$

16. $3\overline{)27}$

17. $8\overline{)40}$

18. $7\overline{)63}$

19. $9\overline{)54}$

20. $6\overline{)48}$

253

Problem Solving

SKILLS AND STRATEGIES REVIEW The Petting Zoo

1. The school is setting up a petting zoo. George spent $36 for 9 meters of wire fencing for the rabbit pen. How much did 1 meter of fencing cost?

2. Barry is making birdhouses for the zoo. He cut a 42-centimeter rod for perches. Each perch was 6 centimeters long. How many perches did he make?

Use the table for 3–4.

Animal	Cost of Feed (per kilogram)
Bird	$3.75
Reptile	$4.20
Rabbit	$1.00

3. Jamie bought food for the zoo. She bought 1 kilogram of birdseed and 1 kilogram of reptile food. How much did she spend?

4. The following week, Jamie bought 3 kilograms of rabbit food and 1 kilogram of birdseed. How much did she spend?

5. A newborn chick weighed 2 grams. After one week it weighed 5 grams. After two weeks it weighed 8 grams. If this pattern continues, what will it weigh after 5 weeks?

6. The students will keep the reptiles at 16°C inside. The temperature outside is 7 degrees colder. What is the outside temperature?

Use the table for 7–9.

7. How much more than a wren does an owl weigh?

8. What is the difference in weight between the lightest bird and the heaviest bird?

9. Which two birds are closest in weight?

Bird	Weight (in grams)
Goose	5,662
Duck	4,664
Crow	552
Owl	505
Swallow	27
Wren	11

Problem Solving

WHAT WOULD YOU DO . . .?

After their trip to the zoo, the children in Mr. Kwan's class wanted to set up an aquarium. They decided to have only goldfish. The charts show the items the students priced at a pet store. They had $25.00 to spend.

Aquarium Supplies	
Tank	$8.00 each
Colored pebbles	$1.50 a bag
Plants	$ .50 each
Food	$2.50 a box
Heater	$7.25 each
Castle	$2.45 each

Goldfish	
Black Moor	$2.50
Gold Moor	$2.25
Calico	$1.85
Orange and white	$2.00
Common gold	$ .50

Answer each question and explain.

1. What items are needed to set up an aquarium?

2. What is the total cost of these items?

3. How much money is left to buy fish?

4. What fish can be bought with the money that is left?

What would you do?

5. If you had $10.00 more to spend, what would you buy?

6. If you could choose any 3 goldfish, which ones would you choose?

7. If you could spend any amount, what would you buy?

8. If you bought a tank and a heater, how much money would you spend?

255

CHAPTER REVIEW

Measure to the nearest centimeter. pages 242–243

1. [   ]
2. [   ]

Choose centimeters, meters, or kilometers to measure each. pages 242–245

3. height of a tree

4. length of a shoe

5. distance across your state

6. height of a building

7. length of the school yard

8. distance around the earth

9. height of a soup can

10. length of a dollar bill

Choose grams or kilograms to measure each. pages 248–249

11. a bag of potatoes

12. a zebra

13. a leaf

14. a safety pin

Choose liters or milliliters to measure each. pages 250–251

15. a few raindrops

16. a bowl of soup

17. a large fish tank

18. a can of paint

Write each Celsius temperature. pages 252-253

19.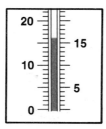

20.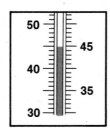

21.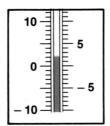

Solve. pages 246–247, 254–255

22. Elise rode her bicycle 457 meters to the pool. Then she rode 325 meters to the store. How far did she ride in all?

23. There is 1 L of water in a jar. Choose the best way to find how many glasses of water the jar holds.

a. Pour water into same size glasses and count.

b. Pour water into another jar and measure it.

Measure each to the nearest centimeter.

1. ▬▬▬▬▬▬▬▬▬▬   2. ▬▬▬▬▬▬▬▬▬▬▬▬▬

Complete. Choose centimeters, meters, or kilometers.

3. A shoelace is 30_____ long.

4. The distance between Boston and Los Angeles is less than 5,000_____ .

5. A baseball bat is 1 _____ long.   6. The flagpole is 30 _____ high.

7. A car is 6 _____ long.   8. A child's finger is about 1 _____ wide.

Choose grams or kilograms to measure each.

9. elephant   10. orange   11. TV set   12. tennis ball

Choose the correct measurement for each.

13. a juice glass
   a. 250 mL   b. 250 L

14. a birdbath
   a. 1 L   b. 1 mL

15. a washing machine
   a. 600 L   b. 600 mL

16. a flower vase
   a. 500 L   b. 500 mL

Write the Celsius temperature.

17.

18.

Solve.

19. Mr. Rooney cut some beach grass that was 90 centimeters high. He cut it down to 24 centimeters. How much was cut off?

20. The garden hose was 16 meters long. Was that longer or shorter than your classroom?

The temperature dropped 2 degrees each hour before a storm. The temperature was 12°C at 8 P.M. What was the temperature at 2 A.M.?

READING A MAP

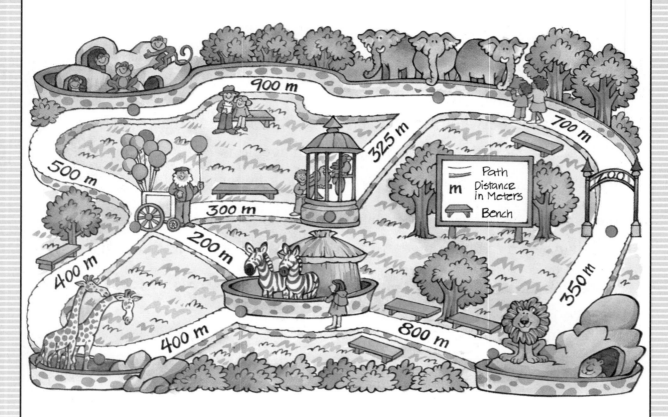

Use the map to answer each question.

1. How far is it from the Balloon Stand to the Bird House?

2. How far is it from the Zebra Den to the Bird House?

3. Is it farther from the Lion House to the Zebra Den or from the Lion House to the Entrance?

4. Which two paths on the map are the same length?

5. Carl is at the Bird House. What is the shortest path back to the Entrance?

6. Lynn is at the Zebra Den. What is the shortest path back to the Entrance?

Draw a map of your school.

7. Show the classrooms, the principal's office, the library, the gym, and the water fountains.

8. Estimate the distances. Then make up three questions about your map.

READING A TABLE

The blue whale is the biggest animal that has ever lived on earth.

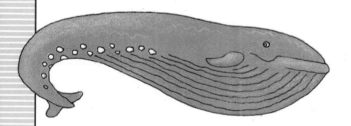

One blue whale weighs about the same as 30 elephants.

This table gives some facts about whales.

Kind of Whale	Length in Meters	Weight in Metric Tons*	Type of Food Eaten	Lifetime in Years	Minutes It Can Hold a Breath
blue	30	152	plankton	100	30
sei	18	25	plankton	70	15
killer	9	8	seal/dolphin	40	30
fin	24	71	plankton	100	20
sperm	18	61	octopus/shark	75	60

*1 metric ton = 1,000 kilograms

Baleen whales have no teeth. They have thin plates called baleen. The edges of the plates strain their food, or plankton.

Use the table.

1. Which whales have teeth?

2. Which kind of whale weighs the least?

3. Which whale holds its breath the longest?

4. How often does a sei whale have to come out of the water to breathe?

5. How much longer is a blue whale than a sei whale? than a fin whale?

MAINTAINING SKILLS

Choose the correct answer. Write A, B, C, or D.

1. $405 + 918 = \square$

  A 1,303   C 1,323

  B 1,333   D not given

2. $\begin{array}{r} 9,835 \\ -3,471 \\ \hline \end{array}$

  A 6,364   C 634

  B 6,634   D not given

3. Compare. $\$12.75 \bullet \$17.25$

  A $>$ C $=$

  B $<$ D not given

4. $12 \div 4 = \square$

  A 4   C 8

  B 1   D not given

5. $27 \div 3 = \square$

  A 8   C 7

  B 9   D not given

6. $56 \div 8 = \square$

  A 6   C 7

  B 9   D not given

7. _____ cm = 1 m

  A 100   C 1,000

  B 200   D not given

8. 2,000 g = _____ kg

  A 3   C 2

  B 1   D not given

9. _____ km = 1,000 m

  A 10   C 0

  B 100   D not given

10. 1 L = _____ mL

  A 100   C 10

  B 1,000   D not given

Find the hidden question. Solve.

11. Mrs. Hill divided the 24 third graders into 3 equal groups. Each child in one of the groups bought a sticker for 8¢. How much money did the group spend?

  A 16¢   C 64¢

  B 24¢   D not given

Theme: City Life

Parts of Regions

Peter's vegetable stand has 4 equal parts. He filled one fourth of the stand with tomatoes.

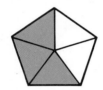

$\dfrac{1}{4}$ green part
equal parts

- write $\dfrac{1}{4}$
- read   one fourth

One fourth is green.

More Examples

          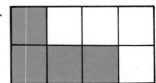

$\dfrac{3}{5}$ green parts
equal parts

$\dfrac{1}{2}$ green part
equal parts

$\dfrac{5}{8}$ green parts
equal parts

Three fifths are green.   One half is green.   Five eighths are green.

▶ A fraction can name part of a whole. $\dfrac{1}{4}, \dfrac{3}{5}, \dfrac{1}{2},$ and $\dfrac{5}{8}$ are fractions.

CLASSWORK

**Write a fraction for the part that is green.
Then read the fraction.**

1.   2.   3.

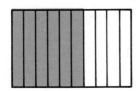   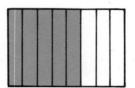

4.   5.   6.

     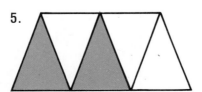   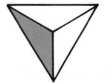

PRACTICE

Write a fraction for the part that is green.

1.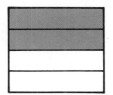

2.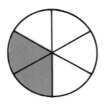

3.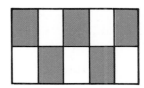

4.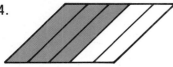

5.

6.

7.

★8.

★9.

Match each fraction with its word name.

10. $\frac{7}{8}$ a. three fifths

11. $\frac{2}{7}$ b. two sevenths

12. $\frac{3}{5}$ c. seven eighths

13. $\frac{2}{4}$ d. one half

14. $\frac{1}{8}$ e. two fourths

15. $\frac{1}{2}$ f. one eighth

APPLICATION

16. Peter's fruit stand has 3 bins of equal size. One bin has apples. What fraction names this part of the whole stand?

★17. Myra cut the peach into 6 equal pieces. She ate 5 of the pieces. What fraction names the part she ate? What fraction names the part that is not eaten?

LOGICAL THINKING

Four quarters equal one dollar.

One quarter is one fourth of a dollar.

What part of a dollar is

two quarters?

three quarters?

four quarters?

Parts of Groups

There are 5 players on the basketball court. What part of the group are girls?

▶We can use a fraction to name part of a group.

Three out of 5 players are girls.

$\frac{3}{5}$ girls
  players in all

● write $\frac{3}{5}$

● read three fifths

Three fifths of the group are girls.

More Examples

$\frac{3}{4}$ are brown.

$\frac{6}{8}$ are green.

CLASSWORK

Write a fraction for the part that is green.
Then read the fraction.

1.
☐ green pompoms
5 pompoms in all

2.
☐ green pennants
4 pennants in all

3. ○○○○○
   ○○○○○

4.

5.

Write a fraction for the part that is green.

1. 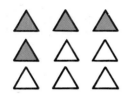 ☐ green squares
10 squares in all

2. 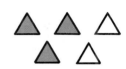 ☐ green circles
6 circles in all

3.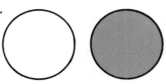

4.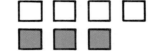

5.

6.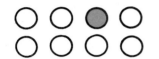

7.

8.

Write a fraction for each.

9. Two out of 5 players scored points.

10. Four out of 5 players wear knee pads.

11. Five out of 7 cheerleaders have pompoms.

12. Six out of 12 teams played on Saturday.

13. Seven out of 10 players made foul shots.

14. One out of 9 games goes into overtime.

★15. Five out of 5 players wear team shirts.

★16. Zero out of 12 teams lost all games.

APPLICATION

Write the fractions to complete the table.

	THE GROUP	Blue Part	Red Part	Green Part
17.	★ ★ ★ ★ ★			
18.	★ ★ ★ ★ ★ ★			
19.	★ ★ ★ ★ ★ ★ ★			
★20.	★ ★ ★ ★ ★ ★			

Equivalent Fractions

What part of each
building is painted?

$\frac{1}{2}$ is painted. $\frac{2}{4}$ are painted.

The same amount of each building
is painted. $\frac{1}{2} = \frac{2}{4}$

▶Fractions that name the same amount $\frac{1}{2}$ and $\frac{2}{4}$ are
  are **equivalent fractions.**   equivalent fractions.

More Examples

a.
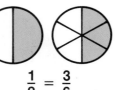

$\frac{1}{2} = \frac{3}{6}$

b.
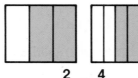

$\frac{2}{3} = \frac{4}{6}$

CLASSWORK

Complete.

1.
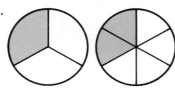

$\frac{1}{3} = \frac{\square}{6}$

2.
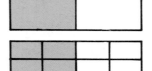

$\frac{1}{2} = \frac{\square}{8}$

3.
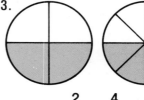

$\frac{2}{4} = \frac{4}{\square}$

4.
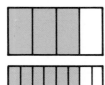

$\frac{3}{4} = \frac{6}{\square}$

5.
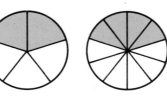

$\frac{2}{5} = \frac{\square}{10}$

6.
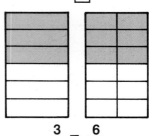

$\frac{3}{6} = \frac{6}{\square}$

PRACTICE

Complete.

1.
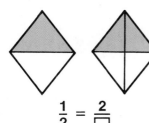

$$\frac{1}{2} = \frac{2}{\square}$$

2.
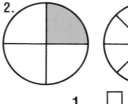

$$\frac{1}{4} = \frac{\square}{8}$$

3.
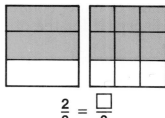

$$\frac{2}{3} = \frac{\square}{9}$$

Write two fractions for the part that is shaded.

4.
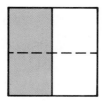

5.
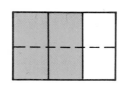

6.
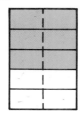

★7.
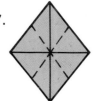

APPLICATION

8. The apartment house is divided into 6 equal parts. One half of the parts were painted last week. How many parts still need to be painted?

★ 9. Two thirds of the windows were washed on Monday. One third were washed on Tuesday. How many windows were washed on both days?

In case you wondered
How I spend my day,
I will show you
In this clever way.

Make your own table.
Estimate the time.
Write the fractions.

	Activity	Estimate the hours spent.	Write a fraction.	$\dfrac{\square \text{ hours spent}}{24 \text{ hours in a day}}$
10.	Sleep			
11.	School	6		$\dfrac{6}{24}$
12.	Eat			
13.	Play			

Comparing Fractions

During the Olympics in Los Angeles, flags of many countries were displayed for the athletes.

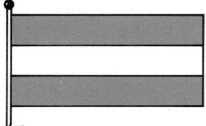

$\frac{2}{3}$ of this flag is green. $\frac{1}{3}$ of this flag is green.

Compare $\frac{2}{3}$ and $\frac{1}{3}$.

$\frac{2}{3}$ is greater than $\frac{1}{3}$. $\frac{2}{3} > \frac{1}{3}$

The first flag has more green.

More Examples

a.
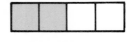
$\frac{2}{4} < \frac{3}{4}$

b.
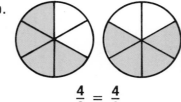
$\frac{4}{6} = \frac{4}{6}$

CLASSWORK

Compare. Use >, <, or = for ●.

1.
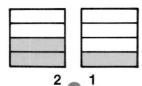
$\frac{2}{4}$ ● $\frac{1}{4}$

2.
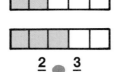
$\frac{2}{5}$ ● $\frac{3}{5}$

3.
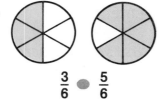
$\frac{3}{6}$ ● $\frac{5}{6}$

4.
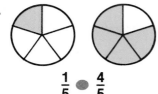
$\frac{1}{5}$ ● $\frac{4}{5}$

5.
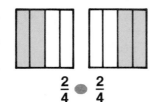
$\frac{2}{4}$ ● $\frac{2}{4}$

6.
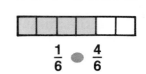
$\frac{1}{6}$ ● $\frac{4}{6}$

Compare. Use >, <, or = for ●.

1.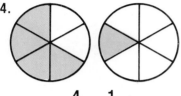

$$\frac{1}{3} \bullet \frac{2}{3}$$

2.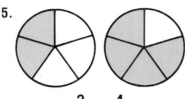

$$\frac{6}{7} \bullet \frac{5}{7}$$

3.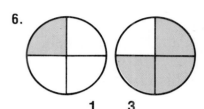

$$\frac{3}{8} \bullet \frac{3}{8}$$

4.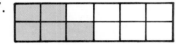

$$\frac{4}{6} \bullet \frac{1}{6}$$

5.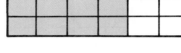

$$\frac{2}{5} \bullet \frac{4}{5}$$

6.

$$\frac{1}{4} \bullet \frac{3}{4}$$

7.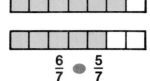

$$\frac{5}{12} \bullet \frac{8}{12}$$

★8. $\frac{6}{10} \bullet \frac{2}{10}$ ★9. $\frac{8}{10} \bullet \frac{10}{10}$ ★10. $\frac{5}{10} \bullet \frac{2}{10}$ ★11. $\frac{1}{10} \bullet \frac{1}{10}$

APPLICATION

12. Glen ate $\frac{2}{4}$ of an apple. Maria ate $\frac{1}{4}$ of an apple the same size. Who ate more, Glen or Maria?

★13. Six people went to San Antonio. One half of them rode boats. One third of them walked on the river walk. Did more people ride or walk?

─── VISUAL THINKING ───

Tell whether there is more green or more white in each figure.

A.

B.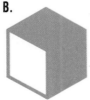

C.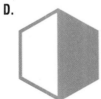

D.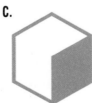

E.

Comparing Unlike Fractions

Cam and Lee sell fish in San Francisco. Who has more fish?

Cam's stand is $\frac{1}{3}$ full. Lee's stand is $\frac{1}{4}$ full.

Compare $\frac{1}{3}$ and $\frac{1}{4}$.

$\frac{1}{3}$ is greater than $\frac{1}{4}$. $\frac{1}{3} > \frac{1}{4}$

Cam has more fish.

This chart will help you compare fractions.

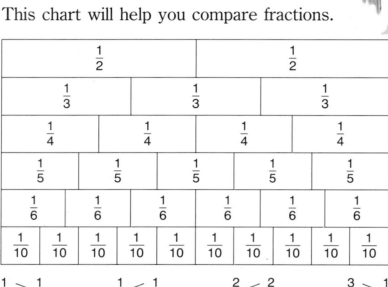

$\frac{1}{2} > \frac{1}{3}$ $\frac{1}{5} < \frac{1}{3}$ $\frac{2}{6} < \frac{2}{3}$ $\frac{3}{4} > \frac{1}{2}$

CLASSWORK

Compare. Use >, <, or = for ⬤.

1.
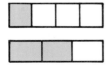

$\frac{1}{4}$ ⬤ $\frac{2}{3}$

2.

$\frac{1}{5}$ ⬤ $\frac{2}{10}$

3.
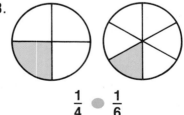

$\frac{1}{4}$ ⬤ $\frac{1}{6}$

Compare. Use >, <, or = for ⬤. Use the chart above.

4. $\frac{1}{6}$ ⬤ $\frac{1}{5}$ 5. $\frac{1}{10}$ ⬤ $\frac{2}{5}$ 6. $\frac{1}{2}$ ⬤ $\frac{3}{4}$ 7. $\frac{2}{3}$ ⬤ $\frac{1}{6}$

PRACTICE

Compare. Use >, <, or = for ●.

1.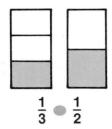

$\dfrac{1}{3}$ ● $\dfrac{1}{2}$

2.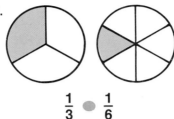

$\dfrac{1}{3}$ ● $\dfrac{1}{6}$

3.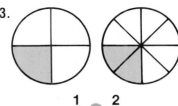

$\dfrac{1}{4}$ ● $\dfrac{2}{8}$

Compare. Use >, <, or = for ●. Use the chart on page 270.

4. $\dfrac{2}{6}$ ● $\dfrac{2}{10}$

5. $\dfrac{1}{4}$ ● $\dfrac{2}{6}$

6. $\dfrac{1}{3}$ ● $\dfrac{1}{5}$

7. $\dfrac{3}{6}$ ● $\dfrac{1}{2}$

8. $\dfrac{1}{3}$ ● $\dfrac{2}{5}$

9. $\dfrac{5}{10}$ ● $\dfrac{1}{2}$

10. $\dfrac{1}{2}$ ● $\dfrac{2}{4}$

11. $\dfrac{2}{4}$ ● $\dfrac{3}{5}$

**Choose the sentence that answers the question.
Then answer the question.**

12. Ling has $\dfrac{1}{2}$ of a basket of fish.
Sue has $\dfrac{1}{3}$ of a basket of fish.
Who has more fish?

a. $\dfrac{1}{3} > \dfrac{1}{2}$ b. $\dfrac{1}{2} > \dfrac{1}{3}$

c. $\dfrac{1}{3} = \dfrac{1}{2}$ d. $\dfrac{1}{2} < \dfrac{1}{3}$

13. Jay ran $\dfrac{1}{4}$ of the way home from
the market. Jan ran $\dfrac{1}{5}$ of the way.
Who ran farther?

a. $\dfrac{1}{4} = \dfrac{1}{5}$ b. $\dfrac{1}{5} > \dfrac{1}{4}$

c. $\dfrac{1}{4} > \dfrac{1}{5}$ d. $\dfrac{1}{4} < \dfrac{1}{5}$

APPLICATION

14. Experiment and fold a square
piece of paper into 16 sections.
How many times did you fold it?

15. Cam filled 1 fish stand in $\dfrac{1}{2}$ hour.
Lee filled 1 stand in $\dfrac{1}{3}$ hour. Who
filled a stand in less time?

★16. Jane read $\dfrac{1}{3}$ of a story on
Monday. She read $\dfrac{1}{5}$ on Tuesday.
On Thursday she read $\dfrac{1}{6}$ of the
story. When did she read most of
the story?

★17. Kim sold $\dfrac{1}{3}$ of her fish by 8 A.M.
Paul sold $\dfrac{1}{4}$ of his fish. Eddie sold
$\dfrac{2}{3}$ of his fish. Who had sold the
most fish?

Problem Solving

MAKING AND USING DRAWINGS

A drawing can help to make a problem clear. You can make a drawing to show the facts in a problem.

The Quinns have just put a new television antenna on the roof. The new antenna is 13 feet high. The old antenna was 8 feet high. How much higher is the new antenna than the old antenna?

What is the question?

How much higher is the new antenna than the old antenna?

What are the facts?

New antenna = 13 feet
Old antenna = 8 feet

How can you find the answer?

Make a drawing to show the facts.

Carry out the plan. Do the work and find the answer.

Show that the new antenna is higher than the old antenna.
Subtract to find the difference in height.

$$13 - 8 = 5$$

The new antenna is 5 feet higher than the old antenna.

Is your arithmetic correct? Does the answer make sense?

Check by adding.

$$8 + 5 = 13$$

The answer is correct.
Look at the drawing. The answer makes sense.

272

For each problem, make a drawing to show the facts. Use your drawing to solve the problem.

1. A grasshopper jumps 7 inches with each jump. How many inches does a grasshopper jump in 4 jumps?

2. Larry threw a ball 28 feet. Jerry threw it 32 feet. How much farther did Jerry throw the ball?

3. Celeste, Billy, and Betty are counting cars. Celeste counted 9 blue cars. Betty counted 7 red cars. Billy counted 6 white cars. How many cars did they count in all?

4. Four children took bottle caps to school for a project. They each took in the same number of caps. There were 24 caps in all. How many bottle caps did each child take?

5. Janet had 2 bunches of grapes in her lunchbox. Each bunch had 8 grapes. She gave 5 grapes away. How many grapes did she have left?

6. There are 3 trees in the yard. The elm is 3 feet taller than the spruce. The maple is 2 feet shorter than the elm. Which is the shortest tree?

★7. The children had a broad-jump contest. Lucy jumped $\frac{1}{2}$ of a yard. Dan jumped $\frac{5}{8}$ of a yard. Millie jumped $\frac{3}{4}$ of a yard. Who jumped the farthest?

★8. Ben is 2 feet ahead of Cal in the sack race. Cal is 1 foot behind Dot. Dot is $1\frac{1}{2}$ feet behind Ethel. Who is winning?

=== CREATE YOUR OWN PROBLEM ===

Here is a picture of balloons. Make up a problem about the picture.

Fractional Parts

Each year Indianapolis has an exciting parade. One school has 8 marchers in the parade. One half of the marchers have red hats. How many have red hats?

$\frac{1}{2}$ of **8** = □

Think 8 marchers, 2 equal groups

Divide by 2. **8 ÷ 2 = 4**

$\frac{1}{2}$ of **8** = **4**

There are 4 marchers in each group. So 4 marchers have red hats.

Another Example

$\frac{1}{3}$ of **6** = □

Think Divide by 3.

6 ÷ 3 = 2

$\frac{1}{3}$ of **6** = **2**

CLASSWORK

Complete.

1. ★ ★ ★
    ★ ★ ★

   $\frac{1}{2}$ of 6 = □

2. ★ ★ ★
    ★ ★ ★
    ★ ★ ★

   $\frac{1}{3}$ of 9 = □

3. ★ ★ ★ ★ ★
    ★ ★ ★ ★ ★

   $\frac{1}{5}$ of 10 = □

4. $\frac{1}{3}$ of 12 = □

5. $\frac{1}{4}$ of 16 = □

6. $\frac{1}{2}$ of 14 = □

7. $\frac{1}{6}$ of 30 = □

8. $\frac{1}{3}$ of 18 = □

9. $\frac{1}{5}$ of 20 = □

PRACTICE

Complete.

1.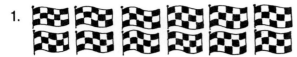

$\frac{1}{2}$ of 12 = □

2. $\frac{1}{3}$ of 6 = □

3. $\frac{1}{2}$ of 10 = □

4. $\frac{1}{7}$ of 21 = □

5. $\frac{1}{9}$ of 54 = □

6. $\frac{1}{8}$ of 72 = □

7. $\frac{1}{5}$ of 40 = □

Rule: Find $\frac{1}{4}$ of Input.

	Input	Output
8.	8	
9.	12	
10.	16	
11.	20	

Rule: Find $\frac{1}{8}$ of Input.

	Input	Output
12.	16	
13.	24	
14.	32	
15.	40	

Compare. Use >, <, or = for ●.

16. $\frac{1}{3}$ of 15 ● 9

17. $\frac{1}{2}$ of 14 ● 5

★18. $\frac{1}{9}$ of 36 ● $\frac{1}{3}$ of 12

★19. $\frac{1}{4}$ of 36 ● $\frac{1}{4}$ of 12

★20. $\frac{1}{5}$ of 20 ● $\frac{1}{3}$ of 27

★21. $\frac{1}{6}$ of 42 ● $\frac{1}{9}$ of 63

APPLICATION

22. There are 27 twirlers in the parade. One third of them have silver tassels. How many have silver tassels?

★23. There are 54 marchers in the parade. One sixth of them are wearing red. One ninth of them are wearing blue. How many are wearing either red or blue?

1. 7
    +4

2. 11
    − 3

3. 2
    +0

4. 5
    +8

5. 4)36

6. 17
    − 8

7. 8
    +2

8. 6)30

9. 7
    +7

10. 3
    ×9

11. 9
    −8

12. 7)42

13. 53 + 35 = □

14. $5.00 − $1.53 = □

15. 72 ÷ 9 = □

16. 2 × 6 = □

17. 3 × 0 = □

18. 9 + 1 = □

19. 48 ÷ 6 = □

20. 95 − 47 = □

Mixed Numbers

Students at P.S. 87 painted pictures on store windows. They completed 1 large window and $\frac{3}{4}$ of another window.

They completed 1 and $\frac{3}{4}$ pictures. $1\frac{3}{4}$ is a **mixed number.** It has a whole number and a fraction.

- write $1\frac{3}{4}$
- read   one and three fourths

More Examples

a.

1 and $\frac{2}{3}$ are green.
$1\frac{2}{3}$
one and two thirds

b.

3 and $\frac{1}{5}$ are green.
$3\frac{1}{5}$
three and one fifth

CLASSWORK

**Write the mixed number for the part that is green.
Then read the mixed number.**

1.
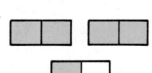

2.
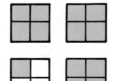

3.
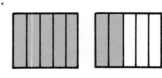

4.
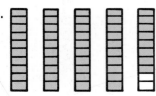

5.
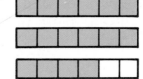

6.
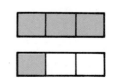

Write the mixed number for the part that is green.

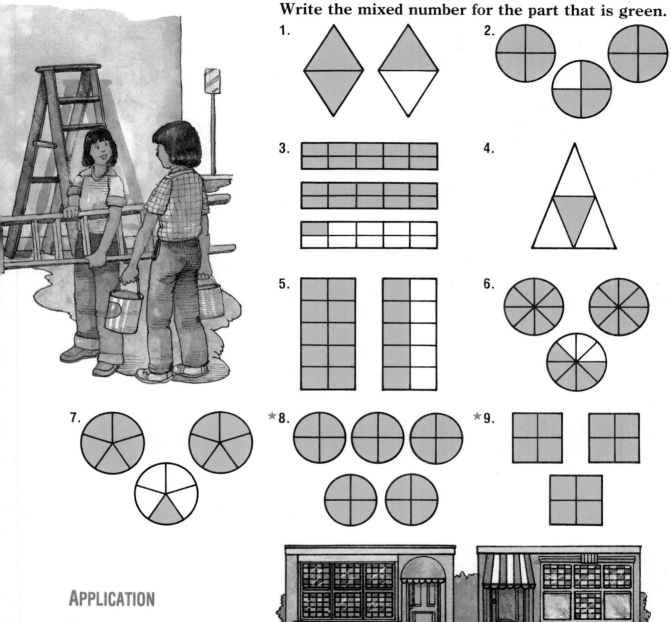

1.

2.

3.

4.

5.

6.

7.

★8.

★9.

APPLICATION

Use the picture to solve.

10. Write a mixed number for the parts with stained glass.

11. Write the fraction for the parts without stained glass.

★12. Make a drawing of some fences to show that four and two thirds of the fences have been painted.

★13. Make a drawing to show the fraction seven fourths. Write the mixed number.

Decimals Less Than 1

There are 10 buildings in one city block. People planted roof gardens on 3 rooftops. Three tenths of the buildings have roof gardens.

We can write $\frac{3}{10}$ as a decimal.

- **write** 0.3

- **read** three tenths

▶A decimal is a number with places to the right of the decimal point.

More Examples

a.

$\frac{1}{10} = 0.1$

one tenth

b.

$\frac{5}{10} = 0.5$

five tenths

c.

$\frac{9}{10} = 0.9$

nine tenths

CLASSWORK

Write a decimal for the part that is green.

1.

2.

3.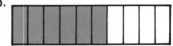

Write a decimal.

4. eight tenths

5. three tenths

6. seven tenths

7. $\frac{2}{10}$

8. $\frac{9}{10}$

9. $\frac{1}{10}$

10. $\frac{6}{10}$

11. $\frac{4}{10}$

PRACTICE

Write a decimal for the part that is green.

1.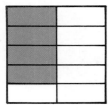
2.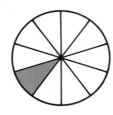
3.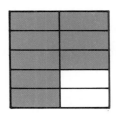

Write a decimal for each.

4. five tenths

5. two tenths

6. six tenths

7. $\frac{3}{10}$

8. $\frac{1}{10}$

9. $\frac{7}{10}$

10. $\frac{9}{10}$

11. $\frac{4}{10}$

Use the number line. Write a decimal for each point.

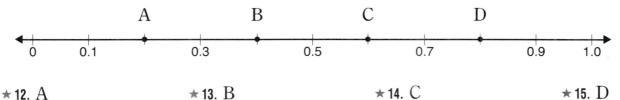

★ 12. A

★ 13. B

★ 14. C

★ 15. D

APPLICATION

16. Ruth has 10 plants. Four are geraniums. Write the decimal for the part that is geraniums and the part that is not geraniums.

17. Harry planted an herb garden. Four tenths of the plants were parsley. Write a decimal for the plants that were not parsley.

★ 18. Ten tenths of David's garden were tomato plants. What part of his garden was beans?

CALCULATOR

How can $\frac{7}{10}$ be entered on a calculator?

Think $\frac{7}{10} = 0.7$

Press ⬜0 ⬜• ⬜7

Enter these fractions by thinking of the decimal.

1. $\frac{2}{10}$

2. $\frac{9}{10}$

3. $\frac{6}{10}$

4. $\frac{3}{10}$

5. $\frac{1}{10}$

6. $\frac{4}{10}$

Decimals Greater Than 1

Each row in the parking lot has 10 spaces. Two rows are filled. One row is $\frac{7}{10}$ filled. So $2\frac{7}{10}$ rows of parking spaces are filled.

We can write $2\frac{7}{10}$ as a decimal.

- **write** 2.7
- **read**   two and seven tenths

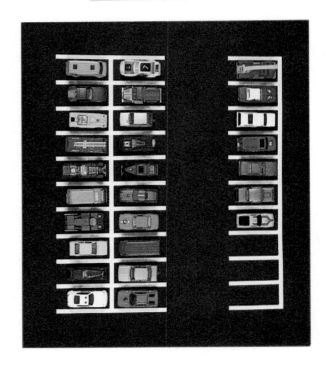

We can show decimals in a place-value table.

tens	ones	tenths	read
	4.	3	four and three tenths
	3.	5	three and five tenths
1	0.	6	ten and six tenths

CLASSWORK

Write the decimal for the part that is green.

1.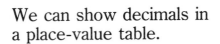

2.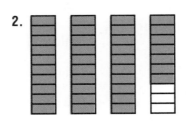

3.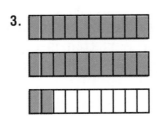

Write the decimal for each.

4. four and three tenths

5. six and two tenths

6. one and nine tenths

7. $3\frac{1}{10}$

8. $7\frac{6}{10}$

9. $\frac{8}{10}$

10. $5\frac{4}{10}$

11. $8\frac{5}{10}$

PRACTICE

Write a decimal for the part that is green.

1.   2.   3.

4.

Write a decimal for each.

5. three and two tenths

6. six and seven tenths

7. five and four tenths

8. one and five tenths

9. $2\frac{9}{10}$ 10. $\frac{3}{10}$ 11. $5\frac{8}{10}$ 12. $4\frac{7}{10}$ 13. $6\frac{4}{10}$ 14. $3\frac{1}{10}$

15.
tens	ones	tenths
	6.	5

16.
tens	ones	tenths
	5.	9

17.
tens	ones	tenths
	3.	3

★ 18.
tens	ones	tenths
1	8.	6

★ 19.
tens	ones	tenths
	4.	0

★ 20.
tens	ones	tenths
7	9.	0

APPLICATION

Solve.

21. In one parking row, 6 of the 10 cars are blue. Write the fraction and decimal for the part of the row that has blue cars.

★ 22. In 3 rows, all 10 cars were small cars. In the next filled row, only 2 cars were small. Write a decimal to show the number of cars that were not small.

281

Adding and Subtracting Decimals

Each year runners compete in the New York City Marathon.

What is the distance from the starting line to the hospital?

$1.3 + 2.9 = \square$

We add decimals the same way we add other numbers.

Step 1 Line up the decimal points.	Step 2 Add tenths. Regroup.	Step 3 Add ones. Place the decimal point in the answer.

$$\begin{array}{r} 1.3 \\ +2.9 \\ \hline \end{array}$$

$$\begin{array}{r} \overset{1}{1}.3 \\ +2.9 \\ \hline 2 \end{array}$$ 12 tenths = 1 one 2 tenths

$$\begin{array}{r} \overset{1}{1}.3 \\ +2.9 \\ \hline 4.2 \end{array}$$

The distance is 4.2 kilometers.

We subtract decimals the way we subtract other numbers.

Step 1 Line up the decimal points.	Step 2 Regroup ones. Subtract tenths.	Step 3 Subtract ones. Place the decimal point in the answer.

$$\begin{array}{r} 6.3 \\ -2.6 \\ \hline \end{array}$$

$$\begin{array}{r} \overset{5\ 13}{\cancel{6}.\cancel{3}} \\ -2.6 \\ \hline 7 \end{array}$$ 6 tens 3 ones = 5 tens 13 ones

$$\begin{array}{r} \overset{5\ 13}{\cancel{6}.\cancel{3}} \\ -2.6 \\ \hline 3.7 \end{array}$$

CLASSWORK

Add or subtract.

1. $\begin{array}{r} 3.6 \\ +4.2 \\ \hline \end{array}$

2. $\begin{array}{r} 8.5 \\ -2.1 \\ \hline \end{array}$

3. $\begin{array}{r} 7.9 \\ -3.7 \\ \hline \end{array}$

4. $\begin{array}{r} 6.4 \\ +7.8 \\ \hline \end{array}$

5. $\begin{array}{r} 11.3 \\ -10.5 \\ \hline \end{array}$

6. $7.6 + 1.8 = \square$

7. $29.3 - 8.4 = \square$

8. $72.6 + 9.1 = \square$

1.3 km

2.9 km

EMERGENCY

PRACTICE

Add or subtract.

1. 1.8
   +7.1

2. 1.4
   +6.2

3. 0.5
   +1.3

4. 6.5
   +7.6

5. 2.6
   +7.2

6. 1.2
   +5.0

7. 7.8
   −3.9

8. 8.6
   −3.7

9. 8.7
   −3.9

10. 16.3
    − 6.8

11. 6.2
    −5.4

12. 10.0
    − 3.3

13. $9.5 + 0.3 = \square$

14. $4.6 - 0.9 = \square$

15. $2.9 + 7.9 = \square$

16. $7.4 - 6.4 = \square$

17. $68.5 - 14.2 = \square$

18. $8.3 + 5.8 = \square$

Compare. Use >, <, or = for ●.

★19. $15.8 - 7.3$ ● 8.5

★20. $0.4 + 13.2$ ● 1.6

★21. $4.5 + 2.4$ ● $9.1 - 2.2$

★22. $9.8 - 5.5$ ● $4.3 + 1.0$

APPLICATION

23. Mary Kotch ran 9.8 kilometers. Hank Kotch ran 6.3 kilometers. How much farther did Mary run?

★24. Beth Ely ran 7.7 kilometers. After a 2-minute rest, she ran 2.9 more kilometers. John Kelly ran 10.8 kilometers. Who ran farther? How much farther?

=== CALCULATOR ===

Remember to enter decimal points when they are needed. $35.2 + 6.7 = \square$

Press   = 41.9

What answer would you get without the decimal points?

Place the decimal points so that each answer is correct.

1. $35 + 62 = 9.7$

2. $966 - 41 = 92.5$

3. $100 + 98 = 19.8$

Problem Solving

SKILLS AND STRATEGIES REVIEW

Herb, Debbie, Bruce, and Lauren are spending the day in the city.

1. The children walked past a toy store. The owner had removed one car. Each car costs $1.79. What color is the missing car?

2. The children stopped for lunch. Herb folded his napkin in half. He folded it in half again. Then he folded it in half again. When he opened it up, how many sections were there?

3. The children ordered 2 sandwiches and 2 salads for lunch. The salads cost $1.75 each. The sandwiches cost $1.25 each. Will a five-dollar bill cover the cost of the lunch?

The children took a bus ride around the city.

4. They counted 12 passengers and 24 seats when they got on the bus. What fractional part of the seats was taken before they sat down?

5. The children counted 10 steps between telephone poles. How many steps were there between the first and the fourth poles?

The children started home at 3:30 P.M.

Use the table to answer the following questions.

CHILDREN'S TRIP HOME		
	Number of Minutes to Each Home	Time of Arrival at Each Home
Herb	45	4:15 P.M.
Debbie	25	3:55 P.M.
Bruce	35	4:05 P.M.
Lauren	30	4:00 P.M.

6. How long did it take Herb to arrive home?

7. At what time did Debbie arrive home?

8. Who arrived home at 4:00 P.M.?

9. Who was the first to arrive home?

10. Who was the last to arrive home?

★11. Who took $1\frac{1}{2}$ hours to get home?

Lauren visited a museum. She saw antique toys.

Use the pictograph to answer 12–17.

VISITORS TO ANTIQUE TOY EXHIBIT	
First week	𝕩 𝕩 𝕩 𝕩
Second week	𝕩 𝕩 𝕩 𝕩 𝕩
Third week	𝕩 𝕩 𝕩
Fourth week	𝕩 𝕩 𝕩 𝕩

𝕩 = 100 people

12. How many people visited the exhibit during the second week?

13. During what week did the least number of people visit?

14. How many people visited the exhibit in four weeks?

15. How many more people came during the fourth week than the third week?

16. How many more people came during the second week than the third week?

17. During what two weeks did the same number of people visit the exhibit?

===== SOMETHING EXTRA =====

H-Three-in-a-Row

This is a game for two players. Here are the rules.

1. The first player puts an *X* in any empty space.

2. The second player puts an *O* in any empty space.

3. Players take turns putting their marks in empty spaces.

4. The first player to get three in a row wins the game.

Here are the ways *X* can win.

Make a copy of this game board.
Play the game with a friend.

CHAPTER REVIEW

Write a fraction for the part that is green. pages 262–265

1.

2.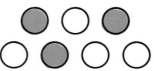

3.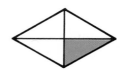

Write two fractions for the part that is green. pages 266–267

4.

5.

6.

Compare. Use >, <, or = for ●. pages 268–271

7.

$\frac{1}{2}$ ● $\frac{2}{4}$

8.

$\frac{1}{5}$ ● $\frac{1}{3}$

9.

$\frac{4}{6}$ ● $\frac{5}{6}$

Complete. pages 274–275

10. $\frac{1}{5}$ of 20 = □

11. $\frac{1}{2}$ of 14 = □

12. $\frac{1}{6}$ of 42 = □

Write a mixed number for the part that is green. pages 276–277

13.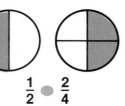

14.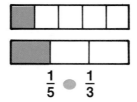

15.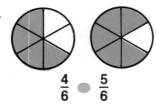

Write a decimal for each. pages 278–281

16. one and six tenths

17. $8\frac{9}{10}$

18. $3\frac{5}{10}$

19. two tenths

Add or subtract. pages 282–283

20. $\begin{array}{r} 6.7 \\ +8.1 \\ \hline \end{array}$

21. $\begin{array}{r} 19.6 \\ -\ 2.5 \\ \hline \end{array}$

22. $\begin{array}{r} 25.5 \\ -12.6 \\ \hline \end{array}$

23. $\begin{array}{r} 60.9 \\ +37.3 \\ \hline \end{array}$

24. $\begin{array}{r} 75.0 \\ -42.4 \\ \hline \end{array}$

Solve. pages 272–273, 284–285

25. Toni jogged 2.5 km from home. She turned around and jogged 1.7 km back. Make a drawing to see how far from home she was.

26. To prepare for the marathon, Richard jogs 3.5 km on each of 2 days a week. How many km does he jog each week?

Write a fraction for each.

1.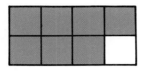

2.

3.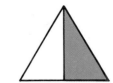

Compare. Use >, <, or = for ●.

4.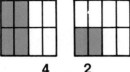

$$\frac{4}{8} \ ● \ \frac{2}{8}$$

5.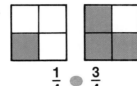

$$\frac{1}{4} \ ● \ \frac{3}{4}$$

6.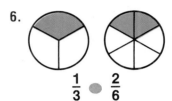

$$\frac{1}{3} \ ● \ \frac{2}{6}$$

Complete.

7. $\frac{1}{4}$ of 16 = ☐

8. $\frac{1}{5}$ of 25 = ☐

9. $\frac{1}{2}$ of 12 = ☐

Write a mixed number for the part that is green.

10.

11.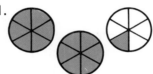

12.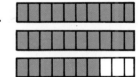

Write a decimal for the part that is green.

13.

14.

15.

Add or subtract.

16. 4.4 + 6.2 = ☐

17. 3.9 − 1.8 = ☐

18. 7.2 − 5.3 = ☐

Solve.

19. There are 24 painters working. One fourth of them are on ladders. How many painters are on ladders?

20. Alan rode $1\frac{3}{4}$ km. Maria rode $2\frac{1}{4}$ km. Make a drawing to show how much farther Maria rode.

Lee and Julie were in a race. Lee finished in 10.2 seconds and Julie finished in 12.1 seconds. Who won the race? How much faster was the winning time?

FRACTION PIES

You will need:
- tracing paper
- construction paper of different colors
- scissors
- marking pen
- envelope for holding pieces of fraction pies

Trace the circles below on tracing paper. Use the circles as models on construction paper. Mark the pieces as shown.

Cut out each circle carefully. Cut along the lines and keep the pieces of fraction pies in an envelope.

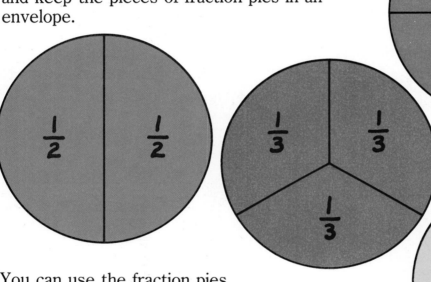

You can use the fraction pies to show that $\frac{3}{4} > \frac{1}{2}$.

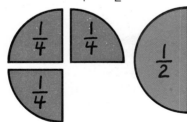

Compare with the fraction pies. Use >, <, or = for ●.

1. $\frac{1}{2}$ ● $\frac{1}{4}$

2. $\frac{1}{3}$ ● $\frac{1}{2}$

3. $\frac{4}{4}$ ● 1

4. $\frac{1}{3}$ ● $\frac{1}{4}$

COMPARING FRACTIONS AND DECIMALS

You can compare a fraction to a
decimal by drawing a picture.

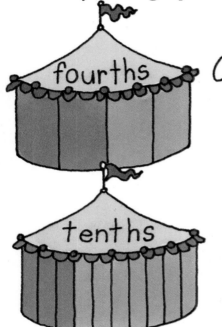

fraction	read	decimal
$\frac{1}{10}$	one tenth	0.1
$\frac{2}{10}$	two tenths	0.2
$\frac{3}{10}$	three tenths	0.3
$\frac{4}{10}$	four tenths	0.4
$\frac{5}{10}$	five tenths	0.5
$\frac{6}{10}$	six tenths	0.6
$\frac{7}{10}$	seven tenths	0.7
$\frac{8}{10}$	eight tenths	0.8
$\frac{9}{10}$	nine tenths	0.9

Compare $\frac{2}{4}$ and 0.3.

You can see from the picture
that $\frac{2}{4}$ > 0.3.

Compare each of these by drawing a picture.
Use >, <, or = for ●.

1. 0.2 ● $\frac{1}{2}$ 2. $\frac{1}{3}$ ● 0.5   3. $\frac{1}{4}$ ● 0.4   4. $\frac{1}{3}$ ● 0.1

5. $\frac{1}{4}$ ● 0.6   6. 0.5 ● $\frac{1}{2}$ 7. 0.8 ● $\frac{1}{5}$ 8. 0.9 ● $\frac{3}{4}$

9. 0.4 ● $\frac{2}{3}$ 10. 0.6 ● $\frac{3}{5}$ 11. 0.7 ● $\frac{2}{5}$ 12. $\frac{5}{6}$ ● 0.6

LET STATEMENTS

A computer can store numbers in its memory. A computer memory has many places (locations) to store numbers.

In BASIC, we use a LET statement to name a location and put a number in it.

```
10 LET A = 8.5
```

Line 10 tells the computer to store the number 8.5 in a location named A.

A		
8.5		

```
10 LET A = 8.5
20 LET B = 2.3
```

Line 20 tells the computer to store the number 2.3 in a location named B.

A	B	
8.5	2.3	

Use the program to tell what number is stored at each location.

```
10 LET R = 20.9
20 LET S = 6.3
30 LET T = 48
40 LET U = 117
```

1. R
2. S
3. T
4. U

Write a LET statement to store these numbers.

5. 9 in location D
6. 2.7 in location E
7. 3.6 in location F
8. 128 in location G

COMPUTER

Once the numbers are stored in the memory, they can be found and used in a program.

8.5 is stored in A.
2.3 is stored in B.

The computer finds the numbers in A and in B, and prints them.

The computer finds the numbers and prints their sum and difference.

```
10 LET A = 8.5
20 LET B = 2.3
30 PRINT A
40 PRINT B
50 PRINT A + B
60 PRINT A - B
70 END
RUN
8.5
2.3
10.8
6.2
```

For each program, tell what the output will be.

9.
```
10 LET X = 27.9
20 LET Y = 60.2
30 PRINT X
40 PRINT Y
50 END
```

10.
```
10 LET P = 12.1
20 LET Q = 76.5
30 PRINT "THE SUM IS"
40 PRINT P + Q
50 END
```

11.
```
10 LET M = 63.9
20 LET N = 14.7
30 PRINT M - N
40 END
```

12.
```
10 LET A = 2.4
20 LET B = 18.9
30 LET S = A + B
40 PRINT "THE SUM IS"
50 PRINT S
60 END
```

AT THE COMPUTER

1. Enter and RUN each program on this page.

2. Compare each output with your answer.

★3. On Your Own: Write a program using LET statements that will add three decimals. Try your program on a computer.

CUMULATIVE REVIEW

Choose the correct answer. Write A, B, C, or D.

1. $24 + 39 + 8 = \square$

A 62　　　　　C 85

B 71　　　　　D not given

2.　759
　$+646$

A 956　　　　　C 1,405

B 1,395　　　　D not given

3.　600
　-259

A 351　　　　　C 341

B 460　　　　　D not given

4. $37.17 - \$19.08 = \square$

A $18.09　　　C $22.11

B $7.67　　　　D not given

5. What is the value of 2 five-dollar bills, 3 dimes, 1 penny?

A $5.31　　　　C $2.31

B $10.31　　　D not given

6. What time will it be in 3 hours?

A 3:45　　　　　C 5:45

B 6:30　　　　　D not given

7. $6 \times 4 = \square$

A 24　　　　　C 18

B 10　　　　　D not given

8.　9
　$\times 8$

A 64　　　　　C 56

B 72　　　　　D not given

9. $5 \times 2 = \square \times 5$

A 5　　　　　C 2

B 10　　　　　D not given

10. $8 \times 7 = \square$

A 49　　　　　C 56

B 15　　　　　D not given

11. $12 \div 6 = \square$

A 2　　　　　C 3

B 6　　　　　D not given

12. Name another fact in the family.　$7 \times 3 = 21$

A $49 \div 7 = 7$　　C $7 \div 3 = 21$

B $21 \div 3 = 7$　　D not given

Choose the correct answer. Write A, B, C, or D.

13. $4\overline{)36}$

    A 9   **C** 6

    B 8   **D** not given

18. What is a fraction for the green part?

    A $\frac{4}{8}$ **C** $\frac{3}{6}$

    B $\frac{3}{8}$ **D** not given

14. $7 \div 1 = \square$

    A 1   **C** 5

    B 11   **D** not given

19. Complete.
$\frac{1}{3} = \frac{\square}{9}$

    A 6   **C** 1

    B 3   **D** not given

15. Measure to the nearest centimeter.

    A 3 cm   **C** 4 cm

    B 2 cm   **D** not given

20. $\frac{1}{4}$ of $16 = \square$

    A 8   **C** 4

    B 2   **D** not given

16. How much does your math book weigh?

    A 1 gram   **C** 1 kilogram

    B 10 kilograms   **D** not given

21. What is a decimal for five and seven tenths?

    A 57   **C** 5.7

    B .57   **D** not given

17. What is the most likely temperature if you are flying a kite?

    A 0°C   **C** 18°C

    B 10°C   **D** not given

22. $26.4 + 17.8 = \square$

    A 34.2   **C** 8.6

    B 44.2   **D** not given

Choose the correct answer. Write A, B, C, or D.

Tell whether you would add or subtract. Then solve **23** and **24**.

23. Leeann sold 46 boxes of cards. Bryan sold 39 boxes. How many did they sell in all?

- **A** add; 85 boxes
- **C** add; 75 boxes
- **B** subtract; 7 boxes
- **D** not given

24. The third-grade class raised $43.25. The fourth-grade class raised $26.00. How much more did the third grade raise?

- **A** subtract; $27.25
- **C** subtract; $17.25
- **B** add; $69.25
- **D** not given

Solve.

27. The pony rides leave every half hour. The first ride leaves at 12:00 P.M. What time does the sixth ride leave?

- **A** 2:30 P.M.
- **C** 4:00 P.M.
- **B** 3:30 P.M.
- **D** not given

28. Doug has 6 stickers on the first page of his book, 9 on the second page, and 12 on the third page. If he continues this pattern, how many stickers will be on page 7?

- **A** 27
- **C** 21
- **B** 24
- **D** not given

Use the graph for **25** and **26**.

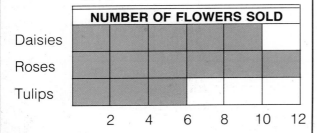

NUMBER OF FLOWERS SOLD

Daisies / Roses / Tulips

2 4 6 8 10 12

25. How many more daisies than tulips were sold?

- **A** 2
- **C** 6
- **B** 4
- **D** not given

26. How many flowers were sold in all?

- **A** 30
- **C** 28
- **B** 22
- **D** not given

Solve.

Dana bought a tennis racket for $28.95. She bought 9 tennis balls for $.80 each. How much did she spend in all?

29. What is the hidden question?

- **A** How much change did she get?
- **B** How much did she give the clerk?
- **C** What is the cost of 9 tennis balls?
- **D** not given

30. How much did Dana spend in all?

- **A** $36.15
- **C** $22.55
- **B** $29.75
- **D** not given

Theme: The Farm

Reviewing Basic Facts

Sheila Gibson helps farmers solve problems. Last week Sheila worked 5 days. She visited 2 farms each day. How many farms did she visit?

$$5 \times 2 = 10$$
↑   ↑   ↑
factor   factor   product

$$
\begin{array}{r}
2 \leftarrow \text{factor} \\
\times 5 \leftarrow \text{factor} \\
\hline
10 \leftarrow \text{product}
\end{array}
$$

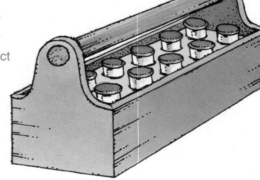

She visited 10 farms.

CLASSWORK

Find each product.

1. $\begin{array}{r} 9 \\ \times 3 \\ \hline \end{array}$
2. $\begin{array}{r} 4 \\ \times 7 \\ \hline \end{array}$
3. $\begin{array}{r} 8 \\ \times 6 \\ \hline \end{array}$
4. $\begin{array}{r} 6 \\ \times 5 \\ \hline \end{array}$
5. $\begin{array}{r} 1 \\ \times 8 \\ \hline \end{array}$
6. $\begin{array}{r} 4 \\ \times 9 \\ \hline \end{array}$
7. $\begin{array}{r} 2 \\ \times 7 \\ \hline \end{array}$

8. $6 \times 3 = \square$
9. $8 \times 7 = \square$
10. $3 \times 7 = \square$
11. $9 \times 0 = \square$

PRACTICE

Find each product.

1. 9×1
2. 8×3
3. 7×5
4. 6×2

5. 4×3
6. 2×9
7. 8×8
8. 0×7

9. 6×9
10. 5×7
11. 3×5
12. 7×2

13. $6 \times 7 = \square$

14. $9 \times 8 = \square$

15. $8 \times 0 = \square$

16. $3 \times 1 = \square$

Find each missing factor.

17. $6 \times 8 = \square \times 6$

18. $8 \times 9 = 9 \times \square$

19. $\square \times 1 = 1 \times 4$

20. $5 \times 2 = \square \times 5$

Find the greatest number for each $\square$.

★ 21. $\square \times 6 < 25$

★ 22. $\square \times 8 < 33$

★ 23. $\square \times 9 < 49$

★ 24. $\square \times 3 < 17$

APPLICATION

For each problem, make a drawing to show the facts. Use your drawing to solve the problem.

25. Sheila visited 6 farms. She collected 4 soil samples from each farm. How many samples did she collect?

★ 26. Six centimeters of rain fell in one week. Twice as much rain fell in another week. How much rain fell in both weeks?

Mixed Practice

1. $9 - 5$
2. $5 + 6$

3. 7×9
4. $9\overline{)36}$

5. $9 + 3$
6. 6×7

7. $2 + 4$
8. $7\overline{)28}$

9. $8\overline{)64}$
10. $17 - 9$

11. $3 + 6$
12. $7\overline{)56}$

13. 6×4
14. $2\overline{)10}$

15. $0 + 4 = \square$

16. $72 \div 9 = \square$

17. $7 - 3 = \square$

18. $7 + 6 = \square$

19. $5 \times 6 = \square$

20. $54 \div 6 = \square$

Multiplying Tens and Hundreds

Wade Johnson planted 6 rows of beans. There are 10 plants in each row. How many plants are there?

$6 \times 10 = \square$

Multiplying with 10 is like counting by 10's.

| $\begin{array}{r} 10 \\ \times\ 1 \\ \hline 10 \end{array}$ | $\begin{array}{r} 10 \\ \times\ 2 \\ \hline 20 \end{array}$ | $\begin{array}{r} 10 \\ \times\ 3 \\ \hline 30 \end{array}$ | $\begin{array}{r} 10 \\ \times\ 4 \\ \hline 40 \end{array}$ | $\begin{array}{r} 10 \\ \times\ 5 \\ \hline 50 \end{array}$ | $\begin{array}{r} 10 \\ \times\ 6 \\ \hline 60 \end{array}$ | $\begin{array}{r} 10 \\ \times\ 7 \\ \hline 70 \end{array}$ | $\begin{array}{r} 10 \\ \times\ 8 \\ \hline 80 \end{array}$ | $\begin{array}{r} 10 \\ \times\ 9 \\ \hline 90 \end{array}$ |

There are 60 plants.

Multiplying with 100 is like counting by 100's.

| $\begin{array}{r} 100 \\ \times\ 1 \\ \hline 100 \end{array}$ | $\begin{array}{r} 100 \\ \times\ 2 \\ \hline 200 \end{array}$ | $\begin{array}{r} 100 \\ \times\ 3 \\ \hline 300 \end{array}$ | $\begin{array}{r} 100 \\ \times\ 4 \\ \hline 400 \end{array}$ | $\begin{array}{r} 100 \\ \times\ 5 \\ \hline 500 \end{array}$ | $\begin{array}{r} 100 \\ \times\ 6 \\ \hline 600 \end{array}$ | $\begin{array}{r} 100 \\ \times\ 7 \\ \hline 700 \end{array}$ | $\begin{array}{r} 100 \\ \times\ 8 \\ \hline 800 \end{array}$ | $\begin{array}{r} 100 \\ \times\ 9 \\ \hline 900 \end{array}$ |

Knowing basic facts can help us multiply tens and hundreds.

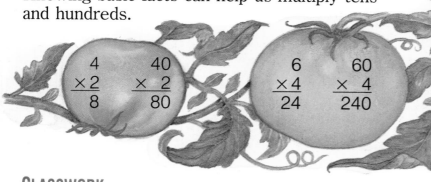

$\begin{array}{r} 4 \\ \times 2 \\ \hline 8 \end{array}$ $\qquad$ $\begin{array}{r} 40 \\ \times\ 2 \\ \hline 80 \end{array}$

$\begin{array}{r} 6 \\ \times 4 \\ \hline 24 \end{array}$ $\qquad$ $\begin{array}{r} 60 \\ \times\ 4 \\ \hline 240 \end{array}$

$\begin{array}{r} 7 \\ \times 3 \\ \hline 21 \end{array}$ $\qquad$ $\begin{array}{r} 700 \\ \times\ \ 3 \\ \hline 2,100 \end{array}$

CLASSWORK

Multiply.

1. $\begin{array}{r} 1 \\ \times 8 \\ \hline \end{array}$ $\begin{array}{r} 10 \\ \times\ 8 \\ \hline \end{array}$

2. $\begin{array}{r} 6 \\ \times 7 \\ \hline \end{array}$ $\begin{array}{r} 60 \\ \times\ 7 \\ \hline \end{array}$

3. $\begin{array}{r} 2 \\ \times 3 \\ \hline \end{array}$ $\begin{array}{r} 200 \\ \times\ \ 3 \\ \hline \end{array}$

4. $\begin{array}{r} 7 \\ \times 5 \\ \hline \end{array}$ $\begin{array}{r} 700 \\ \times\ \ 5 \\ \hline \end{array}$

5. $2 \times 90 = \square$

6. $4 \times 100 = \square$

7. $6 \times 80 = \square$

8. $3 \times 800 = \square$

9. $9 \times 300 = \square$

10. $7 \times 90 = \square$

PRACTICE

Multiply.

1. $\begin{array}{r} 1 \\ \times 7 \end{array}$ $\begin{array}{r} 10 \\ \times\ 7 \end{array}$

2. $\begin{array}{r} 8 \\ \times 2 \end{array}$ $\begin{array}{r} 80 \\ \times\ 2 \end{array}$

3. $\begin{array}{r} 3 \\ \times 6 \end{array}$ $\begin{array}{r} 300 \\ \times\ 6 \end{array}$

4. $\begin{array}{r} 1 \\ \times 1 \end{array}$ $\begin{array}{r} 100 \\ \times\ 1 \end{array}$

5. $\begin{array}{r} 10 \\ \times\ 3 \end{array}$

6. $\begin{array}{r} 10 \\ \times\ 0 \end{array}$

7. $\begin{array}{r} 100 \\ \times\ 9 \end{array}$

8. $\begin{array}{r} 100 \\ \times\ 6 \end{array}$

9. $\begin{array}{r} 10 \\ \times\ 8 \end{array}$

10. $\begin{array}{r} 100 \\ \times\ 4 \end{array}$

11. $\begin{array}{r} 30 \\ \times\ 4 \end{array}$

12. $\begin{array}{r} 400 \\ \times\ 5 \end{array}$

13. $\begin{array}{r} 20 \\ \times\ 6 \end{array}$

14. $\begin{array}{r} 300 \\ \times\ 8 \end{array}$

15. $\begin{array}{r} 50 \\ \times\ 7 \end{array}$

16. $\begin{array}{r} 700 \\ \times\ 9 \end{array}$

17. $\begin{array}{r} 800 \\ \times\ 2 \end{array}$

18. $\begin{array}{r} 60 \\ \times\ 4 \end{array}$

19. $\begin{array}{r} 700 \\ \times\ 8 \end{array}$

20. $\begin{array}{r} 50 \\ \times\ 2 \end{array}$

21. $\begin{array}{r} 600 \\ \times\ 9 \end{array}$

22. $\begin{array}{r} 100 \\ \times\ 5 \end{array}$

23. $5 \times 20 = \square$

24. $5 \times 10 = \square$

25. $7 \times 100 = \square$

26. $7 \times 300 = \square$

27. $3 \times 30 = \square$

28. $9 \times 400 = \square$

29. $8 \times 500 = \square$

30. $6 \times 600 = \square$

31. $9 \times 80 = \square$

★32. $4 \times 2 \times 10 = \square$

★33. $3 \times 1 \times 30 = \square$

★34. $2 \times 2 \times 20 = \square$

APPLICATION

Use the graph to answer each question.

35. How many seeds did Mary plant?

36. How many did Jacob plant?

37. How many did Peter plant?

38. How many seeds were planted in all?

★39. What would this symbol stand for?

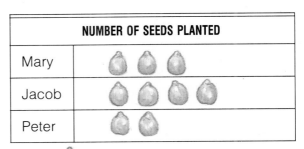

NUMBER OF SEEDS PLANTED	
Mary	🌰 🌰 🌰
Jacob	🌰 🌰 🌰 🌰
Peter	🌰 🌰

Each 🌰 stands for 10 seeds.

★40. What is the difference between the least number and the greatest number of seeds that were planted?

299

Multiplying Two-Digit Numbers

In *Strawberry Girl* by Lois Lenski, children picked strawberries. Each wooden carrier held 12 boxes of strawberries. How many boxes did the children pick to fill 3 carriers?

$3 \times 12 = \square$

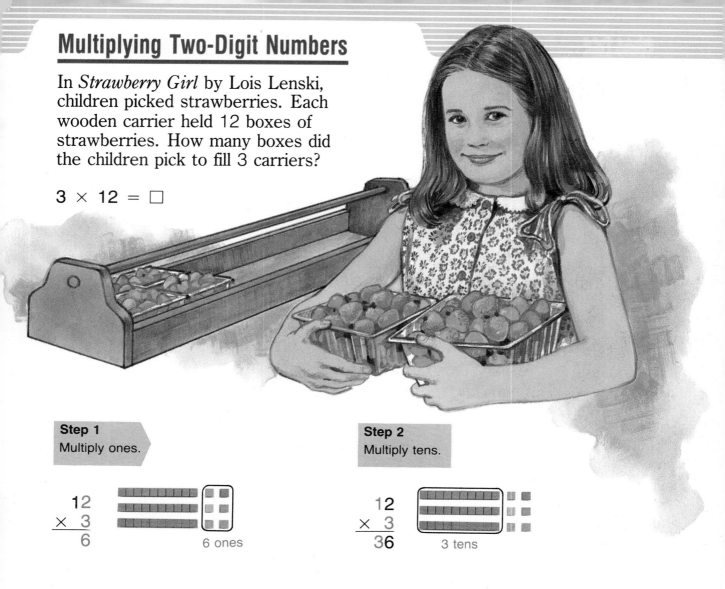

Step 1
Multiply ones.

$$\begin{array}{r} 12 \\ \times\ 3 \\ \hline 6 \end{array}$$

6 ones

Step 2
Multiply tens.

$$\begin{array}{r} 12 \\ \times\ 3 \\ \hline 36 \end{array}$$

3 tens

The children picked 36 boxes of strawberries.

CLASSWORK

Multiply.

1. $\begin{array}{r} 32 \\ \times\ 3 \\ \hline \end{array}$
   2. $\begin{array}{r} 11 \\ \times\ 8 \\ \hline \end{array}$
   3. $\begin{array}{r} 12 \\ \times\ 4 \\ \hline \end{array}$
   4. $\begin{array}{r} 43 \\ \times\ 2 \\ \hline \end{array}$
   5. $\begin{array}{r} 21 \\ \times\ 3 \\ \hline \end{array}$
   6. $\begin{array}{r} 75 \\ \times\ 1 \\ \hline \end{array}$

7. $2 \times 14 = \square$ 8. $9 \times 11 = \square$ 9. $3 \times 13 = \square$ 10. $2 \times 44 = \square$

Find each product.

1. 23
    × 2

2. 21
    × 4

3. 13
    × 3

4. 89
    × 1

5. 11
    × 7

6. 14
    × 2

7. 97
    × 0

8. 12
    × 3

9. 68
    × 1

10. 41
    × 2

11. 22
    × 3

12. 20
    × 4

13. 10
    × 5

14. 79
    × 1

15. 12
    × 2

16. 32
    × 3

17. 14
    × 1

18. 31
    × 2

19. 6 × 11 = ☐   20. 3 × 20 = ☐   21. 2 × 13 = ☐   22. 2 × 33 = ☐

23. 2 × 24 = ☐   24. 0 × 67 = ☐   25. 1 × 60 = ☐   26. 9 × 10 = ☐

Find the missing numbers.

27.   1▮
    × 2
    ────
     22

28.   4▮
    × 2
    ────
     84

29.   3▮
    × 3
    ────
    ▮3

★ 30.   ▮▮
     × 2
    ────
     68

★ 31.   ▮4
     × 1
    ────
     7▮

★ 32.   ▮▮
     × 3
    ────
     99

APPLICATION

33. A farmer placed 11 strawberries into each of 9 baskets. How many strawberries did she use? Complete the table to find out.

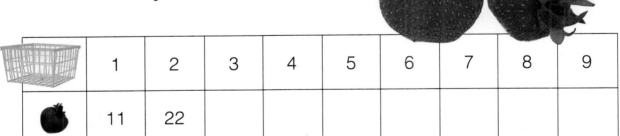

	1	2	3	4	5	6	7	8	9
	11	22							

★ 34. Look at the products of 11. What pattern do you see?

★ 35. Find the sum of the 2 digits in each lower box. What pattern do you see?

Problem Solving

FINDING ANOTHER WAY

Sometimes you can solve a problem in more than one way. No matter how you solve it, your answer should be the same.

Inez and Elena are planting a small garden. They plant 2 rows of peppers, with 7 plants in each row. They plant 3 rows of tomatoes, with 9 plants in each row. How many plants are there altogether?

We can solve this problem in two ways.

First way

Make a drawing of the garden.

Draw 2 rows of pepper plants, with 7 plants in each row.

Draw 3 rows of tomato plants, with 9 plants in each row.

```
P P P P P P P          T T T T T T T T T
P P P P P P P          T T T T T T T T T
                       T T T T T T T T T
```

Count the plants. There are 41 plants altogether.

Second way

Each row of pepper plants has the same number of plants. Multiply to find how many pepper plants there are.

2 × 7 = 14   There are 14 pepper plants.

Each row of tomato plants has the same number of plants. Multiply to find how many tomato plants there are.

3 × 9 = 27   There are 27 tomato plants.

Add the number of pepper plants and the number of tomato plants.

```
  14
+27
  41
```
There are 41 plants altogether.

The answer is the same either way you solve the problem.

PRACTICE

Solve each problem, using any way you like.

1. Ralph and Miriam are putting a fence around the garden. The fence is in the shape of a rectangle. It is 14 feet long and 10 feet wide. What is the distance around the garden?

2. Miriam is planting rosebushes on all 4 sides of the garden. She will plant a bush in each corner. When she finishes, there will be 4 bushes on each side. How many bushes will there be in all?

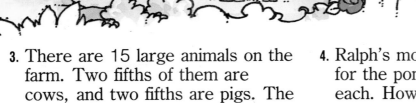

3. There are 15 large animals on the farm. Two fifths of them are cows, and two fifths are pigs. The rest are horses. Are there more horses or cows?

4. Ralph's mother bought 6 lily pads for the pond. She paid $.50 for each. How much did she spend for the 6 lily pads?

5. Ralph bought 12 baby ducklings. He bought 2 times as many yellow ducklings as black ducklings. How many black ducklings did he buy?

6. Miriam started her homework at 6:30 P.M. She spent 1 hour and 15 minutes on her homework. Then she spent 20 minutes doing chores. Finally, she spent 30 minutes reading a book. What time was it then?

CREATE YOUR OWN PROBLEM

Write a problem about the farm.
Solve your problem in two different ways.

Look back to see that your answers are the same.

Regrouping Ones

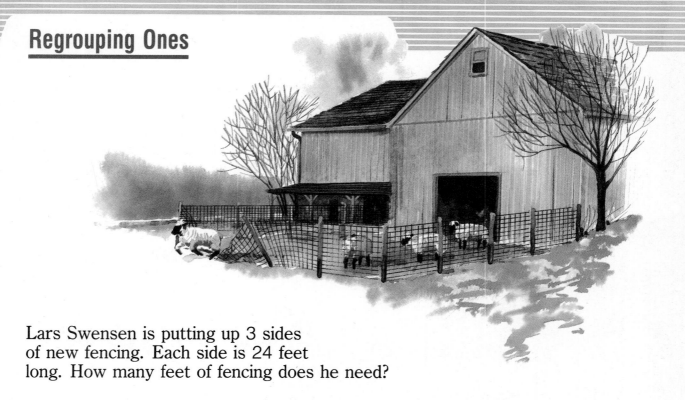

Lars Swensen is putting up 3 sides of new fencing. Each side is 24 feet long. How many feet of fencing does he need?

3 × 24 = □

Step 1
Multiply ones.
Regroup.

$$\begin{array}{r} 1 \\ 24 \\ \times\ 3 \\ \hline 2 \end{array}$$

12 ones = 1 ten 2 ones

Step 2
Multiply tens.
Add 1 ten.

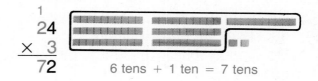

$$\begin{array}{r} 1 \\ 24 \\ \times\ 3 \\ \hline 72 \end{array}$$

6 tens + 1 ten = 7 tens

Lars needs 72 feet of fencing.

CLASSWORK

Multiply.

1. $\begin{array}{r} 18 \\ \times\ 4 \\ \hline \end{array}$
2. $\begin{array}{r} 16 \\ \times\ 6 \\ \hline \end{array}$
3. $\begin{array}{r} 45 \\ \times\ 2 \\ \hline \end{array}$
4. $\begin{array}{r} 15 \\ \times\ 5 \\ \hline \end{array}$
5. $\begin{array}{r} 26 \\ \times\ 3 \\ \hline \end{array}$
6. $\begin{array}{r} 15 \\ \times\ 4 \\ \hline \end{array}$

7. $\begin{array}{r} 14 \\ \times\ 7 \\ \hline \end{array}$
8. $\begin{array}{r} 25 \\ \times\ 3 \\ \hline \end{array}$
9. $\begin{array}{r} 13 \\ \times\ 6 \\ \hline \end{array}$
10. $\begin{array}{r} 14 \\ \times\ 3 \\ \hline \end{array}$
11. $\begin{array}{r} 48 \\ \times\ 2 \\ \hline \end{array}$
12. $\begin{array}{r} 12 \\ \times\ 5 \\ \hline \end{array}$

Multiply.

1. $\begin{array}{r}36\\ \times\ 2\\ \hline\end{array}$	2. $\begin{array}{r}13\\ \times\ 7\\ \hline\end{array}$	3. $\begin{array}{r}16\\ \times\ 5\\ \hline\end{array}$	4. $\begin{array}{r}12\\ \times\ 8\\ \hline\end{array}$	5. $\begin{array}{r}27\\ \times\ 3\\ \hline\end{array}$	6. $\begin{array}{r}25\\ \times\ 2\\ \hline\end{array}$
7. $\begin{array}{r}12\\ \times\ 7\\ \hline\end{array}$	8. $\begin{array}{r}62\\ \times\ 1\\ \hline\end{array}$	9. $\begin{array}{r}17\\ \times\ 5\\ \hline\end{array}$	10. $\begin{array}{r}28\\ \times\ 3\\ \hline\end{array}$	11. $\begin{array}{r}17\\ \times\ 4\\ \hline\end{array}$	12. $\begin{array}{r}26\\ \times\ 2\\ \hline\end{array}$
13. $\begin{array}{r}21\\ \times\ 4\\ \hline\end{array}$	14. $\begin{array}{r}16\\ \times\ 3\\ \hline\end{array}$	15. $\begin{array}{r}19\\ \times\ 5\\ \hline\end{array}$	16. $\begin{array}{r}15\\ \times\ 1\\ \hline\end{array}$	17. $\begin{array}{r}24\\ \times\ 4\\ \hline\end{array}$	18. $\begin{array}{r}12\\ \times\ 6\\ \hline\end{array}$

19. $9 \times 10 = \square$ 20. $4 \times 23 = \square$ 21. $4 \times 13 = \square$ 22. $5 \times 18 = \square$

23. $5 \times 14 = \square$ 24. $2 \times 32 = \square$ 25. $2 \times 17 = \square$ 26. $3 \times 15 = \square$

Find the product of each.

27. two and nineteen

28. five and thirteen

29. six and seventy

30. three and twenty-four

Find each missing number.

★ 31. $2 \times 45 + \square = 100$

★ 32. $3 \times 27 - \square = 50$

APPLICATION

33. Lars needs 16 rails for each side of a corral. How many rails does he need for all 4 sides?

★ 34. A truck brought 5 bundles of rails. There are 10 rails in each bundle. Three rails are broken. How many are not broken?

CALCULATOR

Arrange the numbers 1, 2, and 3 in any way to fill each $\square$.

1. Multiply. The product is _____. Arrange the numbers another way.

2. Multiply. The product is _____. Continue doing this.

3. What arrangement gives the greatest product?

4. What arrangement gives the least product?

Regrouping Ones and Tens

The Hayward farm has a prize-winning cow. It produces 54 quarts of milk a day. How many quarts does it produce in 7 days?

$7 \times 54 = \square$

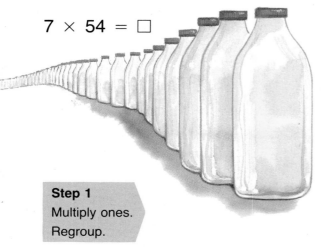

Step 1
Multiply ones.
Regroup.

$$\begin{array}{r} \overset{2}{} \\ 54 \\ \times\ 7 \\ \hline 8 \end{array}$$ 28 ones = 2 tens 8 ones

Step 2
Multiply tens.
Add 2 tens. Regroup.

$$\begin{array}{r} \overset{2}{} \\ 54 \\ \times\ 7 \\ \hline 378 \end{array}$$ 35 tens + 2 tens = 37 tens, or 3 hundreds 7 tens

It produces 378 quarts in 7 days.

Find 3×46.

$$\begin{array}{r} \overset{1}{} \\ 46 \\ \times\ 3 \\ \hline 8 \end{array}$$ 18 ones = 1 ten 8 ones

$$\begin{array}{r} \overset{1}{} \\ 46 \\ \times\ 3 \\ \hline 138 \end{array}$$ 12 tens + 1 ten = 13 tens, or 1 hundred 3 tens

CLASSWORK

Multiply.

1. $\begin{array}{r} 76 \\ \times\ 2 \\ \hline \end{array}$
2. $\begin{array}{r} 63 \\ \times\ 4 \\ \hline \end{array}$
3. $\begin{array}{r} 45 \\ \times\ 3 \\ \hline \end{array}$
4. $\begin{array}{r} 52 \\ \times\ 5 \\ \hline \end{array}$
5. $\begin{array}{r} 24 \\ \times\ 6 \\ \hline \end{array}$
6. $\begin{array}{r} 50 \\ \times\ 9 \\ \hline \end{array}$

7. $4 \times 49 = \square$
8. $7 \times 25 = \square$
9. $8 \times 26 = \square$
10. $3 \times 29 = \square$

PRACTICE

Multiply.

1. $\begin{array}{r} 23 \\ \times\ 6 \end{array}$
2. $\begin{array}{r} 22 \\ \times\ 9 \end{array}$
3. $\begin{array}{r} 43 \\ \times\ 4 \end{array}$
4. $\begin{array}{r} 64 \\ \times\ 3 \end{array}$
5. $\begin{array}{r} 78 \\ \times\ 2 \end{array}$
6. $\begin{array}{r} 32 \\ \times\ 5 \end{array}$

7. $\begin{array}{r} 33 \\ \times\ 8 \end{array}$
8. $\begin{array}{r} 13 \\ \times\ 7 \end{array}$
9. $\begin{array}{r} 32 \\ \times\ 4 \end{array}$
10. $\begin{array}{r} 25 \\ \times\ 8 \end{array}$
11. $\begin{array}{r} 15 \\ \times\ 9 \end{array}$
12. $\begin{array}{r} 47 \\ \times\ 6 \end{array}$

13. $\begin{array}{r} 91 \\ \times\ 9 \end{array}$
14. $\begin{array}{r} 67 \\ \times\ 4 \end{array}$
15. $\begin{array}{r} 97 \\ \times\ 3 \end{array}$
16. $\begin{array}{r} 45 \\ \times\ 7 \end{array}$
17. $\begin{array}{r} 51 \\ \times\ 8 \end{array}$
18. $\begin{array}{r} 53 \\ \times\ 9 \end{array}$

19. $3 \times 99 = \square$
20. $0 \times 86 = \square$
21. $5 \times 50 = \square$
22. $8 \times 73 = \square$

Find each missing number.

23. $\begin{array}{r} 3\blacksquare \\ \times\ 2 \\ \hline 70 \end{array}$
24. $\begin{array}{r} \blacksquare 2 \\ \times\ 6 \\ \hline 132 \end{array}$
25. $\begin{array}{r} \blacksquare 4 \\ \times\ 6 \\ \hline 204 \end{array}$
★ 26. $\begin{array}{r} 76 \\ \times\ \blacksquare \\ \hline 152 \end{array}$
★ 27. $\begin{array}{r} 62 \\ \times\ \blacksquare \\ \hline 372 \end{array}$
★ 28. $\begin{array}{r} 55 \\ \times\ \blacksquare \\ \hline 275 \end{array}$

Choose the correct answer.

29. What is the product of 8 and 11 rounded to the nearest ten?

a. 90　　b. 100
c. 20　　d. 80

30. What is the product of 2 and 77 rounded to the nearest hundred?

a. 150　　b. 100
c. 200　　d. 250

APPLICATION

LOGICAL THINKING

Another way to multiply:

$\begin{array}{r} 29 \\ \times\ 3 \end{array}$　Since $29 = 20 + 9$, we can multiply 20 by 3 and 9 by 3, and then add.

$\begin{array}{r} 20 \\ \times\ 3 \\ \hline 60 \end{array}$ $\begin{array}{r} 9 \\ \times\ 3 \\ \hline 27 \end{array}$ $= 87$　$\begin{array}{r} 29 \\ \times\ 3 \\ \hline 87 \end{array}$

Try these.

1. $4 \times 65 = \square$　2. $7 \times 42 = \square$　3. $6 \times 81 = \square$　4. $5 \times 73 = \square$

Multiplying Three-Digit Numbers

Workers at Mayfair Orchards picked 210 baskets of apples every day for 6 days. How many baskets of apples did they pick?

$6 \times 210 = \square$

Step 1	**Step 2**	**Step 3**
Multiply ones.	Multiply tens.	Multiply hundreds. Regroup.

$$\begin{array}{r} 210 \\ \times\quad 6 \\ \hline 0 \end{array} \qquad \begin{array}{r} 210 \\ \times\quad 6 \\ \hline 60 \end{array} \qquad \begin{array}{r} 210 \\ \times\quad 6 \\ \hline 1{,}260 \end{array}$$

12 hundreds = 1 thousand 2 hundreds

They picked 1,260 baskets of apples.

More Examples

$$\begin{array}{r} \overset{2}{2}15 \\ \times\quad 4 \\ \hline 860 \end{array}$$

$$\begin{array}{r} \overset{1}{4}26 \\ \times\quad 3 \\ \hline 1{,}278 \end{array}$$

$$\begin{array}{r} \overset{3}{1}51 \\ \times\quad 7 \\ \hline 1{,}057 \end{array}$$

$$\begin{array}{r} \overset{1}{7}20 \\ \times\quad 8 \\ \hline 5{,}760 \end{array}$$

CLASSWORK

Find each product.

1. $\begin{array}{r} 136 \\ \times\quad 2 \\ \hline \end{array}$
2. $\begin{array}{r} 162 \\ \times\quad 4 \\ \hline \end{array}$
3. $\begin{array}{r} 310 \\ \times\quad 9 \\ \hline \end{array}$
4. $\begin{array}{r} 105 \\ \times\quad 6 \\ \hline \end{array}$
5. $\begin{array}{r} 471 \\ \times\quad 5 \\ \hline \end{array}$

6. $3 \times 224 = \square$ 7. $2 \times 345 = \square$ 8. $7 \times 811 = \square$ 9. $8 \times 120 = \square$

308

Find each product.

1. 215
   × 3

2. 103
   × 8

3. 248
   × 2

4. 141
   × 7

5. 151
   × 5

6. 121
   × 6

7. 242
   × 4

8. 233
   × 3

9. 284
   × 2

10. 601
    × 9

11. 411
    × 8

12. 225
    × 4

13. 283
    × 3

14. 274
    × 2

15. 108
    × 7

16. $5 \times 170 = \square$ 17. $9 \times 700 = \square$ 18. $7 \times 60 = \square$ 19. $8 \times 76 = \square$

20. $4 \times 209 = \square$ 21. $2 \times 844 = \square$ 22. $3 \times 291 = \square$ 23. $6 \times 200 = \square$

Follow the rule to complete.

Rule:
Multiply by 4.

	Input	Output
24.	20	
25.	200	
26.	220	
27.	222	

Rule:
Multiply by 5.

	Input	Output
28.	5	
29.	50	
30.	500	
31.	550	

Rule:
Multiply by 6.

	Input	Output
★ 32.	40	
★ 33.	400	
★ 34.	440	
★ 35.	444	

APPLICATION

36. A machine can pack 240 cans of fruit into boxes each hour. How many cans of fruit can it pack in 3 hours?

37. There are 400 baskets of green grapes and 275 baskets of purple grapes. How many more baskets of green grapes are there?

38. The south orchard has 172 fruit trees. The west orchard has 268. How many fruit trees are there in both orchards?

★ 39. Kurt packed jars of applesauce in 9 boxes. Every box had 2 layers of 12 jars each. How many jars did Kurt pack?

Problem Solving

Kole and Emily sold fruits and vegetables at a stand. They had 4 boxes of peppers, 3 boxes of blueberries, 5 boxes of tomatoes, 4 boxes of peaches, and 7 boxes of plums.

1. They sold 3 boxes of blueberries first. How many different kinds of fruits and vegetables were left?

2. How many boxes of fruits and vegetables were left after their first sale?

3. Emily sold half of the boxes of peaches. How many boxes of peaches were left?

4. Plums cost $.50 per box. How much do all of the boxes of plums cost?

5. Kole sold half of the boxes of peppers. Then he sold half of what was left. How many boxes of peppers were left then?

6. Tomatoes sold for $1.25 per box. Mrs. Green bought 1 box of tomatoes and 2 boxes of plums. How much did she spend?

7. Each box of peppers sold for $.80. How much did Kole make on the first two boxes of peppers?

8. Mr. Bell bought plums. He paid $2.00. He received $.50 change. How many boxes did he buy?

★9. Mrs. Long bought apples at $3.00 a basket. She paid with a twenty-dollar bill and received $2.00 change. How many baskets of apples did Mrs. Long buy?

★10. Artie opened a produce stand. The first day he earned $2.00. The second day he earned $5.00. The third day he earned $9.00. The fourth day he earned $14.00. If the pattern continues, how much will he earn on the sixth day?

Problem Solving

WHAT WOULD YOU DO . . .?

You are putting up a fence along the
edge of your dad's farm. You must put
the posts into the ground. The tops
of the posts must be 4 feet above
the ground. You have 2 posts that are
each 5 feet tall. You have 2 posts
that are each 6 feet tall. You have
2 posts that are each 7 feet tall.

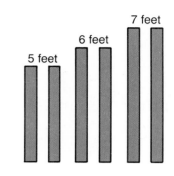

Answer each question and explain.

1. Could you just hammer each post into the ground?

2. Could you mark 4 feet on each post and then
   hammer the posts into the ground?

3. Do you have a better way?

What would you do?

If you chose **2**, how would you find
the 4-foot mark?

Your grandfather is buying 13 farm
animals. He has a list of sheep,
chickens, pigs, horses, and goats.
You would like to choose 7 of the
farm animals.

Answer each question and explain.

4. Could you choose 2 sheep and 4 chickens?

5. Could you choose 3 pigs, 1 horse, and 3 goats?

What would you do?

6. Which 7 animals would you choose?
   Why?

311

Find each product. pages 296–297

1. 6
×5

2. 9
×8

3. 7
×6

4. 5
×9

5. 7
×7

Multiply. pages 298–299

6. 30
× 5

7. 70
× 9

8. 80
× 7

9. 60
× 7

10. 50
× 8

11. 700
× 3

12. 800
× 6

13. 900
× 4

14. 600
× 5

15. 300
× 2

Find each product. pages 300–301, 304–309

16. 23
× 3

17. 61
× 8

18. 38
× 3

19. 57
× 2

20. 62
× 9

21. 83
× 2

22. 25
× 8

23. 87
× 2

24. 31
× 7

25. 73
× 5

26. 14
× 6

27. 43
× 7

28. 51
× 9

29. 12
× 3

30. 23
× 4

31. 107
× 3

32. 211
× 7

33. 790
× 7

34. 891
× 9

35. 909
× 9

36. 8 × 406 = ☐

37. 4 × 622 = ☐

38. 5 × 117 = ☐

Solve. pages 302–303, 310–311

39. Phil Hardy took 9 baskets of pears to the farmers' market. Each basket had 35 pears. How many pears were there in all?

40. A shelf has 6 rows of canned tomatoes and 8 rows of canned peaches. Each row has 5 cans. How many cans are there in all?

Find each product.

1. $9 \times 6 = \square$ 2. $8 \times 7 = \square$ 3. $7 \times 9 = \square$ 4. $8 \times 8 = \square$

Multiply.

5.	80 $\times\ 2$	6.	50 $\times\ 7$	7.	60 $\times\ 5$	8.	30 $\times\ 6$	9.	70 $\times\ 0$

10.	200 $\times\ \ 4$	11.	800 $\times\ \ 3$	12.	300 $\times\ \ 5$	13.	900 $\times\ \ 7$	14.	700 $\times\ \ 6$

Find each product.

15.	20 $\times\ 4$	16.	34 $\times\ 2$	17.	12 $\times\ 7$	18.	91 $\times\ 5$	19.	43 $\times\ 3$

20.	56 $\times\ 5$	21.	46 $\times\ 2$	22.	29 $\times\ 7$	23.	36 $\times\ 9$	24.	65 $\times\ 8$

25.	145 $\times\ \ 2$	26.	173 $\times\ \ 3$	27.	451 $\times\ \ 8$	28.	612 $\times\ \ 8$	29.	130 $\times\ \ 6$

30. $4 \times 207 = \square$ 31. $5 \times 861 = \square$

Solve.

Mrs. Kelly gave every neighbor 3 baskets with
29 tomatoes in each. She has 4 neighbors.

32. How many tomatoes were in 3
baskets?

33. How many tomatoes did she give
away in all?

Lou has 20 rabbits, some brown and some white.
He has 3 times as many brown rabbits as white
rabbits. How many of each does he have?

ESTIMATION

How long will it take you to read a book?

Estimate the time it will take
before you read the whole book.
Follow these steps.

1. Count the pages in the book and
   write down the number.

32 pages

2. Choose a page that does not have
   too many pictures. Time yourself
   to see how many minutes it takes
   to read this page. Suppose it
   takes 4 minutes.

4 minutes per page

3. Multiply the number of pages by
   the minutes per page. The answer
   is an estimate of the time it
   will take to read the whole book.

```
    32 pages
×    4 minutes per page
  128 minutes to read
       the whole book
```

It will take you 128 minutes to read the whole book.
That is a little more than 2 hours.

MULTIPLYING THREE NUMBERS

4 rows of 2 plants
3 gardens of plants
How many plants?

$4 \times 2 \times 3 = \square$

Multiply the first two numbers.	$(4 \times 2) \times 3 = \square$
Multiply that product by the third number.	$8 \quad \times 3 = 24$
or	
Multiply the second two numbers.	$4 \times (2 \times 3) = \square$
Multiply the first number by that product.	$4 \times \quad 6 \quad = 24$

Either way, $4 \times 2 \times 3 = 24$. There are 24 plants.

Find each product.

1. $4 \times 1 \times 5 = \square$ 2. $4 \times 2 \times 1 = \square$ 3. $2 \times 4 \times 2 = \square$

4. $6 \times 0 \times 7 = \square$ 5. $3 \times 3 \times 2 = \square$ 6. $6 \times 1 \times 3 = \square$

7. $3 \times 1 \times 3 = \square$ 8. $9 \times 1 \times 4 = \square$ 9. $3 \times 2 \times 2 = \square$

Choose the correct answer. Write A, B, C, or D.

1. $6 \times 9 = \square$

  A 64   **C** 15

  B 54   **D** not given

2. $8\overline{)48}$

  A 8   **C** 6

  B 4   **D** not given

3. How long is the bar?

  A 5 cm   **C** 3 cm

  B 4 cm   **D** not given

4. Choose the correct unit of measure for a glass of juice.

  A mL   **C** either

  B L   **D** not given

5. What part is red?

  A $\frac{2}{6}$ **C** $\frac{5}{8}$

  B $\frac{6}{8}$ **D** not given

6. Compare. $\frac{1}{2} \bullet \frac{1}{6}$

  A $=$ **C** $>$

  B $<$ **D** not given

7. $7 \times 700 = \square$

  A 49   **C** 4,900

  B 420   **D** not given

8. $5 \times 14 = \square$

  A 50   **C** 19

  B 70   **D** not given

9.
$$\begin{array}{r} 716 \\ \times\ \ \ 6 \\ \hline \end{array}$$

  A 1,372   **C** 4,296

  B 4,266   **D** not given

Use a drawing to solve **10** and **11**.

10. Jill ate $\frac{5}{8}$ of a pizza. Todd ate $\frac{3}{4}$ of a pizza. Who ate more?

  A Jill   **C** They ate the same amount.

  B Todd   **D** not given

11. Ed's desk is 63 cm long. His bookshelf is 70 cm long. How much longer is his bookshelf than his desk?

  A 7 cm   **C** 133 cm

  B 17 cm   **D** not given

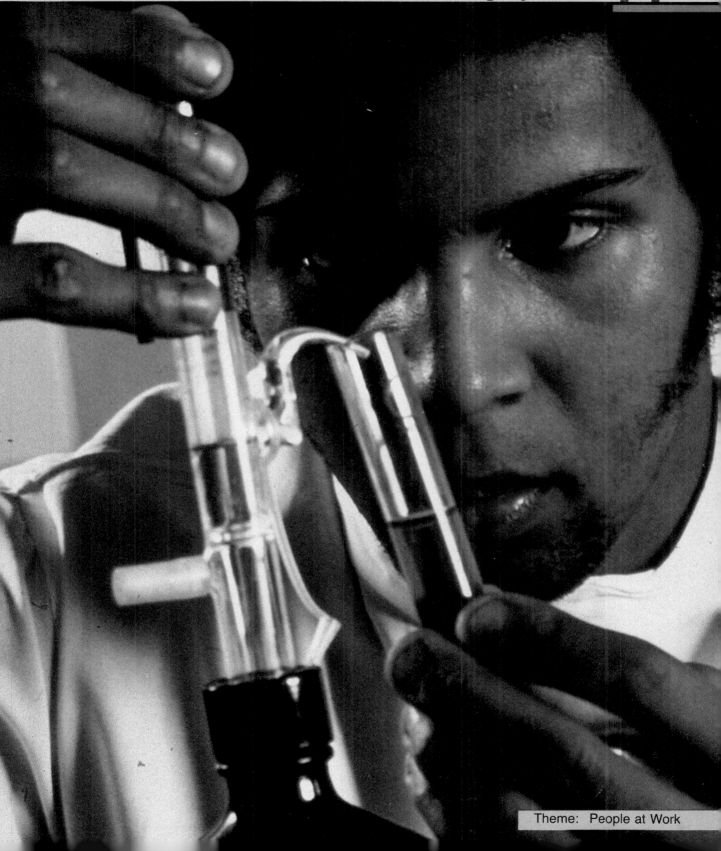

Theme: People at Work

Reviewing Basic Facts

Kate Jordan, an author, worked 45 hours on her new mystery book. She wrote 5 hours each day. On how many days did Kate Jordan write?

$$45 \div 5 = \square$$

Think $\quad 9 \times 5 = 45$

So $\quad 45 \div 5 = 9.$

$$\overset{\text{quotient}}{\underset{\text{divisor}}{5)\overset{9}{45}}} \leftarrow \text{dividend}$$

$$\underset{\text{dividend}}{45} \div \underset{\text{quotient}}{5} = \underset{\text{divisor}}{9}.$$

Kate Jordan wrote on 9 days.

CLASSWORK

Find each quotient.

1. $3)\overline{18}$
2. $9)\overline{36}$
3. $8)\overline{56}$
4. $9)\overline{9}$
5. $3)\overline{6}$
6. $4)\overline{32}$

7. $21 \div 7 = \square$
8. $42 \div 7 = \square$
9. $30 \div 6 = \square$
10. $8 \div 1 = \square$

318

Find each quotient.

1. $5\overline{)15}$
2. $8\overline{)64}$
3. $9\overline{)72}$
4. $7\overline{)63}$
5. $3\overline{)9}$
6. $7\overline{)14}$

7. $8\overline{)24}$
8. $5\overline{)25}$
9. $8\overline{)48}$
10. $6\overline{)42}$
11. $2\overline{)16}$
12. $6\overline{)36}$

13. $8\overline{)40}$
14. $4\overline{)12}$
15. $4\overline{)20}$
16. $9\overline{)54}$
17. $2\overline{)8}$
18. $9\overline{)81}$

19. $28 \div 4 = \square$
20. $54 \div 6 = \square$
21. $27 \div 9 = \square$
22. $36 \div 4 = \square$

23. $32 \div 8 = \square$
24. $48 \div 6 = \square$
25. $56 \div 7 = \square$
26. $40 \div 5 = \square$

27. $49 \div 7 = \square$
28. $63 \div 9 = \square$
29. $35 \div 7 = \square$
30. $72 \div 8 = \square$

Complete. Follow the rule, if given.

Rule:
Divide by 6.

	Input	Output
31.	36	
32.	42	
33.	48	
34.	54	

Rule:
Divide by $\square$.

★ 35.

Input	Output
42	6
49	7
56	8
63	9

Rule:
Divide by $\square$.

★ 36.

Input	Output
54	6
63	7
72	8
81	9

APPLICATION

37. There are 21 people waiting to get Kate Jordan's autograph. They are standing in 3 equal lines. How many people are in each line?

38. In her mystery story, 4 boys found 24 old coins in the attic. They divided them equally. How many coins did each one get?

★ 39 Last week, 40 copies of Kate Jordan's new book were sold. An equal number of books was sold each day. How many books were sold each day?

Bookstore

Closed
Sunday and
Monday

Dividing by 1 Through 6

The pet store owner has 7 puppies. He put 2 in each window box. How many boxes are there with 2 puppies? How many puppies are there left over?

$7 \div 2 = \square$

$$\overset{3}{2\overline{)7}} \quad \text{remainder } 1$$

There are 3 window boxes with 2 puppies. There is 1 puppy left over.

Find $17 \div 3$.

$17 \div 3 = 5 \text{ R2}$ $\qquad \overset{5 \text{ R2}}{3\overline{)17}}$ $\qquad$ The remainder must be less than the divisor.

CLASSWORK

Find each quotient and remainder.

1. $3\overline{)10}$
2. $4\overline{)15}$
3. $5\overline{)32}$
4. $6\overline{)44}$
5. $5\overline{)48}$
6. $4\overline{)21}$

7. $9 \div 2 = \square$
8. $19 \div 5 = \square$
9. $37 \div 6 = \square$
10. $59 \div 6 = \square$

PRACTICE

Divide.

1. $4\overline{)30}$ 2. $2\overline{)5}$ 3. $3\overline{)11}$ 4. $6\overline{)28}$

5. $5\overline{)23}$ 6. $3\overline{)28}$ 7. $4\overline{)19}$ 8. $2\overline{)15}$

9. $6\overline{)48}$ 10. $5\overline{)37}$ 11. $4\overline{)24}$ 12. $3\overline{)23}$

13. $2\overline{)19}$ 14. $4\overline{)21}$ 15. $5\overline{)35}$ 16. $6\overline{)17}$

17. $3\overline{)17}$ 18. $3\overline{)24}$ 19. $6\overline{)53}$ 20. $4\overline{)14}$

21. $5\overline{)15}$ 22. $2\overline{)7}$ 23. $4\overline{)31}$ 24. $6\overline{)46}$

25. $29 \div 6 = \square$ 26. $46 \div 5 = \square$

27. $35 \div 4 = \square$ 28. $54 \div 6 = \square$

29. $28 \div 5 = \square$ 30. $12 \div 3 = \square$

31. $39 \div 6 = \square$ 32. $33 \div 4 = \square$

★33. Divide 24 by 5.   ★34. Divide 56 by 6.

★35. Divide 38 by 4.   ★36. Divide 22 by 3.

APPLICATION

37. Miss Nicholas wants to put 45 hamsters into 8 cages. Can she put an equal number into each cage?

★38. There are 9 rabbits at the pet store. The same number are in each cage and 1 is hopping on the floor. How many cages are there? How many are in each cage?

Mixed Practice

1. $\begin{array}{r} 643 \\ -245 \end{array}$ 2. $\begin{array}{r} 2.8 \\ +1.3 \end{array}$

3. $\begin{array}{r} 26 \\ \times\ 4 \end{array}$ 4. $\begin{array}{r} 572 \\ +419 \end{array}$

5. $\begin{array}{r} 113 \\ \times\ 6 \end{array}$ 6. $\begin{array}{r} 77 \\ \times\ 5 \end{array}$

7. $\begin{array}{r} 94 \\ -37 \end{array}$ 8. $\begin{array}{r} 25.8 \\ -\ 7.6 \end{array}$

9. $\begin{array}{r} 46.3 \\ +\ 8.9 \end{array}$ 10. $\begin{array}{r} 72 \\ \times\ 4 \end{array}$

11. $\begin{array}{r} 8.4 \\ -2.1 \end{array}$ 12. $\begin{array}{r} 63 \\ +49 \end{array}$

13. $\begin{array}{r} 976 \\ +736 \end{array}$ 14. $\begin{array}{r} 46 \\ \times\ 5 \end{array}$

15. $\begin{array}{r} 33 \\ \times\ 6 \end{array}$ 16. $\begin{array}{r} 582 \\ -273 \end{array}$

17. $\begin{array}{r} 76.7 \\ +14.8 \end{array}$ 18. $\begin{array}{r} 3.1 \\ -1.7 \end{array}$

19. $\begin{array}{r} 830 \\ \times\ 7 \end{array}$ 20. $\begin{array}{r} 45 \\ \times\ 9 \end{array}$

321

Dividing by 7 Through 9

At Galaxy Toy Factory, 34 robots came down the assembly line. Mel Jackson packed 8 robots to a box. How many boxes of 8 robots were there? How many robots were there left over?

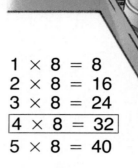

$34 \div 8 = \square$

How many eights are in 34?   **Think**

$$1 \times 8 = 8$$
$$2 \times 8 = 16$$
$$3 \times 8 = 24$$
$$\boxed{4 \times 8 = 32}$$
$$5 \times 8 = 40$$

There are 4 eights in 34.

Write 4 in the quotient.

Multiply. $4 \times 8 = 32$
Subtract. $34 - 32 = 2$
Compare. $2 < 8$
Write the remainder in the quotient.

$$\begin{array}{r} 4 \text{ R2} \\ 8\overline{)34} \\ -32 \\ \hline 2 \end{array}$$

There were 4 boxes of 8 robots.
There were 2 robots left over.

Find $25 \div 7$.

$$\begin{array}{r} 3 \text{ R4} \\ 7\overline{)25} \\ -21 \\ \hline 4 \end{array}$$

Check

Multiply.

$$\begin{array}{r} 7 \\ \times 3 \\ \hline 21 \end{array}$$

Add the remainder.

$$\begin{array}{r} 21 \\ + 4 \\ \hline 25 \end{array}$$

These numbers should match.

CLASSWORK

Divide. Check by multiplying.

1. $8\overline{)27}$ 2. $7\overline{)24}$ 3. $9\overline{)23}$ 4. $7\overline{)19}$ 5. $8\overline{)46}$ 6. $8\overline{)60}$

7. $39 \div 9 = \square$ 8. $43 \div 7 = \square$ 9. $58 \div 8 = \square$ 10. $65 \div 9 = \square$

Divide. Check by multiplying.

1. $7\overline{)30}$ 2. $9\overline{)12}$ 3. $8\overline{)26}$ 4. $6\overline{)43}$ 5. $7\overline{)38}$ 6. $8\overline{)13}$

7. $5\overline{)42}$ 8. $7\overline{)52}$ 9. $9\overline{)31}$ 10. $4\overline{)31}$ 11. $8\overline{)42}$ 12. $8\overline{)17}$

13. $3\overline{)25}$ 14. $9\overline{)40}$ 15. $7\overline{)57}$ 16. $8\overline{)35}$ 17. $7\overline{)41}$ 18. $9\overline{)52}$

19. $20 \div 6 = \square$ 20. $14 \div 3 = \square$ 21. $32 \div 7 = \square$ 22. $50 \div 8 = \square$

23. $16 \div 9 = \square$ 24. $43 \div 5 = \square$ 25. $33 \div 4 = \square$ 26. $26 \div 9 = \square$

27. $44 \div 8 = \square$ 28. $60 \div 7 = \square$ 29. $51 \div 6 = \square$ 30. $58 \div 7 = \square$

Find each missing number.

31.
$$
\begin{array}{r}
8\ R\,\blacksquare \\
3\overline{)26} \\
-\,\blacksquare\blacksquare \\
\hline
\blacksquare
\end{array}
$$

32.
$$
\begin{array}{r}
\blacksquare\ R\,\blacksquare \\
4\overline{)39} \\
-\,36 \\
\hline
\blacksquare
\end{array}
$$

33.
$$
\begin{array}{r}
\blacksquare\ R\,\blacksquare \\
8\overline{)65} \\
-\,\blacksquare\blacksquare \\
\hline
\blacksquare
\end{array}
$$

34.
$$
\begin{array}{r}
\blacksquare\ R\,\blacksquare \\
5\overline{)48} \\
-\,\blacksquare\blacksquare \\
\hline
\blacksquare
\end{array}
$$

★35.
$$
\begin{array}{r}
7\ R\,\blacksquare \\
6\overline{)\blacksquare\blacksquare} \\
-\,42 \\
\hline
3
\end{array}
$$

★36.
$$
\begin{array}{r}
4\ R\,\blacksquare \\
7\overline{)\blacksquare 4} \\
-\,28 \\
\hline
\blacksquare
\end{array}
$$

★37.
$$
\begin{array}{r}
\blacksquare\ R\,\blacksquare \\
9\overline{)\blacksquare\blacksquare} \\
-\,54 \\
\hline
3
\end{array}
$$

★38.
$$
\begin{array}{r}
9\ R\,\blacksquare \\
2\overline{)\blacksquare\blacksquare} \\
-\,\blacksquare\blacksquare \\
\hline
1
\end{array}
$$

APPLICATION

39. Yoki assembled 58 moon racers at the factory. She sent an equal number to 7 toy stores. How many did she send to each toy store? How many were left over?

★40. Andy had 5 trays of 6 space bugs. He had 2 trays of 9 space bugs. He packed 6 space bugs to a box. How many boxes did Andy pack?

Problem Solving

MAKING AND USING TABLES

Sometimes there are many facts in a word problem. Putting the facts in a table can help to solve the problem. A table makes the facts easier to think about.

Mr. and Mrs. Garvey own the Village Party Center. They sell party supplies. One morning Mr. Garvey sold 50 balloons and 32 prizes. That afternoon Mrs. Garvey sold 46 favors and 25 decorations. Which item sold the most?

You can make a table to organize the information.

PARTY SUPPLIES				
Item	Balloons	Prizes	Favors	Decorations
Number sold	50	32	46	25

The table lists the kinds of party supplies sold.
It lists the number of each kind sold.
The table makes it easy to see that balloons sold the most.

You can get other information from the table.
You can find out how many items were sold in all.
You can find out how many more of one item than of another were sold.
You can find out which item sold the least.

Galaxy Toy Factory makes piñatas of different kinds. The factory has 200 fish, 345 donkeys, 250 bulls, 85 roosters, and 172 parrots.

Complete the table. Then answer each question.

1. How many donkeys are there?

2. How many parrots are there?

3. Which kind of piñata do they have the most of?

4. How many more fish are there than roosters?

5. How many more donkeys than roosters are there?

PIÑATAS	
Kind	Number
Fish	200
Donkeys	
	250
Roosters	85

The toy factory has part-time workers who pack toys.

Complete the table. Then answer each question.

PART-TIME WORK SCHEDULE			
Packer	Number of Days Worked per Week ×	Number of Hours Worked per Day =	Total Hours Worked per Week
Lina Barbieri	3	6	
Ivan Jones		5	15
Bertha Moore	5	4	

6. Who works the least number of hours per week?

7. How many fewer hours per week does Ivan Jones work than Bertha Moore works?

8. How many more days per week does Bertha Moore work than Lina Barbieri works?

CREATE YOUR OWN PROBLEM

Workers at Galaxy Toy Factory use rings, jacks, whistles, balls, and other small toys to fill the piñatas. Create a problem that could be easily solved by using a table. Then make the table.

Dividing Tens and Hundreds

Carl Martorana baked 80 bagels. He placed them into 4 baskets. Each basket had the same number of bagels. How many bagels were there in each basket?

$$80 \div 4 = \square$$

Knowing basic facts can help us to divide tens.

$$\begin{array}{c} 2 \\ 4\overline{)8} \end{array} \qquad \begin{array}{c} 20 \\ 4\overline{)80} \end{array}$$

There were 20 bagels in each basket.

Knowing basic facts can help us to divide hundreds.

$$\begin{array}{c} 2 \\ 4\overline{)8} \end{array} \qquad \begin{array}{c} 20 \\ 4\overline{)80} \end{array} \qquad \begin{array}{c} 200 \\ 4\overline{)800} \end{array}$$

More Examples

a. $\begin{array}{c} 1 \\ 2\overline{)2} \end{array} \qquad \begin{array}{c} 10 \\ 2\overline{)20} \end{array} \qquad \begin{array}{c} 100 \\ 2\overline{)200} \end{array}$

b. $\begin{array}{c} 5 \\ 3\overline{)15} \end{array} \qquad \begin{array}{c} 50 \\ 3\overline{)150} \end{array} \qquad \begin{array}{c} 500 \\ 3\overline{)1,500} \end{array}$

c. $\begin{array}{c} 4 \\ 6\overline{)24} \end{array} \qquad \begin{array}{c} 40 \\ 6\overline{)240} \end{array} \qquad \begin{array}{c} 400 \\ 6\overline{)2,400} \end{array}$

CLASSWORK

Divide.

1. $2\overline{)8}$ $2\overline{)80}$ $2\overline{)800}$ 2. $3\overline{)3}$ $3\overline{)30}$ $3\overline{)300}$

3. $5\overline{)15}$ $5\overline{)150}$ $5\overline{)1,500}$ 4. $4\overline{)12}$ $4\overline{)120}$ $4\overline{)1,200}$

5. $3\overline{)24}$ $3\overline{)240}$ $3\overline{)2,400}$ 6. $5\overline{)30}$ $5\overline{)300}$ $5\overline{)3,000}$

7. $60 \div 2 = \square$ 8. $900 \div 3 = \square$ 9. $2,800 \div 4 = \square$

PRACTICE

Divide.

1. $4\overline{)4}$ $4\overline{)40}$ $4\overline{)400}$ 2. $3\overline{)6}$ $3\overline{)60}$ $3\overline{)600}$

3. $2\overline{)4}$ $2\overline{)40}$ $2\overline{)400}$ 4. $5\overline{)5}$ $5\overline{)50}$ $5\overline{)500}$

5. $3\overline{)12}$ $3\overline{)120}$ $3\overline{)1,200}$ 6. $2\overline{)16}$ $2\overline{)160}$ $2\overline{)1,600}$

7. $5\overline{)35}$ $5\overline{)350}$ $5\overline{)3,500}$ 8. $4\overline{)20}$ $4\overline{)200}$ $4\overline{)2,000}$

9. $6\overline{)36}$ $6\overline{)360}$ $6\overline{)3,600}$ 10. $3\overline{)27}$ $3\overline{)270}$ $3\overline{)2,700}$

11. $120 \div 2 = \square$ 12. $100 \div 5 = \square$ 13. $160 \div 4 = \square$

14. $250 \div 5 = \square$ 15. $320 \div 4 = \square$ 16. $180 \div 3 = \square$

17. $1,200 \div 6 = \square$ 18. $1,800 \div 2 = \square$ 19. $3,200 \div 4 = \square$

★20. $420 \div 7 = \square$ ★21. $5,400 \div 9 = \square$ ★22. $720 \div 8 = \square$

APPLICATION

MENTAL ARITHMETIC

We can use patterns we know to find quotients for greater numbers.

$$3\overline{)6,000} = 2,000 \qquad 3\overline{)60,000} = 20,000$$

Try dividing mentally.

1. $2\overline{)8,000}$ $2\overline{)80,000}$ 2. $4\overline{)4,000}$ $4\overline{)40,000}$

3. $5\overline{)25,000}$ $5\overline{)250,000}$ 4. $7\overline{)56,000}$ $7\overline{)560,000}$

Two-Digit Quotients

Mr. Roth, an architect, is drawing a blueprint of 48 townhouses. There are 4 in each cluster. How many clusters of townhouses are there?

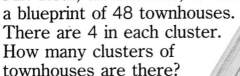

$48 \div 4 = \square$

Step 1

```
   1
4)48
  -4
   0
```

Divide tens. 4)4
Multiply. 1 × 4 = 4
Subtract. 4 − 4 = 0
Compare. 0 < 4

Step 2

```
   12
4)48
  -4↓
   08
  - 8
    0
```

Bring down 8 ones.

Divide ones. 4)8
Multiply. 2 × 4 = 8
Subtract. 8 − 8 = 0
Compare. 0 < 4

There are 12 clusters of townhouses.

When the remainder is 0, do not write 0 in the quotient.

Find 34 ÷ 2.

Step 1

```
   1
2)34
  -2
   1
```

Divide tens. 2)3
Multiply. 1 × 2 = 2
Subtract. 3 − 2 = 1
Compare. 1 < 2

Step 2

```
   17
2)34
  -2↓
   14
  -14
    0
```

Bring down 4 ones.

Divide ones. 2)14
Multiply. 7 × 2 = 14
Subtract. 14 − 14 = 0
Compare. 0 < 2

CLASSWORK

Divide.

1. 2)64
2. 3)96
3. 6)72
4. 4)56
5. 6)90
6. 5)85

7. $75 \div 3 = \square$
8. $84 \div 4 = \square$
9. $50 \div 2 = \square$
10. $68 \div 4 = \square$

Divide.

1. 3)33   2. 2)52   3. 6)24   4. 5)75   5. 3)69   6. 4)52

7. 5)95   8. 2)76   9. 3)45   10. 4)17   11. 2)92   12. 5)50

13. 5)39   14. 4)88   15. 3)51   16. 7)30   17. 5)65   18. 6)96

19. $60 \div 6 = \square$ 20. $22 \div 3 = \square$ 21. $78 \div 6 = \square$ 22. $81 \div 3 = \square$

Follow the rule to complete.

Rule:
Divide by 8.

	Input	Output
23.	72	
24.	80	
25.	88	

Rule:
Divide by 7.

	Input	Output
26.	77	
27.	84	
28.	91	

Rule:
Divide by 9.

	Input	Output
29.	72	
30.	81	
31.	90	

Complete.

32. $100 \div 5 = \square \times 4 = \square \div 5 = \square \times 4 = 64$

33. $60 \times 3 = \square \div 6 = \square \times 3 = \square \div 6 = 15$

Compare. Use >, <, or = for ●.

★ 34. $50 \div 2 \bullet 78 \div 3$ ★ 35. $96 \div 4 \bullet 84 \div 3$ ★ 36. $80 \div 5 \bullet 32 \div 2$

APPLICATION

37. Mr. Roth's blueprint shows 64 windows for 4 townhouses. If each townhouse has the same number of windows, how many does each have?

38. Twelve doors are needed for each townhouse. There are 70 doors on order. How many townhouses will have 12 doors? How many doors will be left over? Make a table to solve.

★ 39. The outdoor plan shows 54 shrubs in equal groups. Name the possible groups.

Two-Digit Quotients with Remainders

The hotel manager ordered 74 floral pieces. She wanted 6 pieces on each tray. How many trays had 6 pieces? How many pieces were left over?

$74 \div 6 = \square$

Step 1
Divide tens.
Multiply.
Subtract and compare.

$$\begin{array}{r} 1 \\ 6\overline{)74} \\ -6 \\ \hline 1 \end{array}$$

Think
$6\overline{)7}$
$1 \times 6 = 6$
$7 - 6 = 1$
$1 < 6$

Step 2
Bring down ones.
Divide ones.
Multiply.
Subtract and compare.

$$\begin{array}{r} 12 \text{ R2} \\ 6\overline{)74} \\ -6\downarrow \\ \hline 14 \\ -12 \\ \hline 2 \end{array}$$

Think
$6\overline{)14}$
$2 \times 6 = 12$
$14 - 12 = 2$
$2 < 6$

Write the remainder in the quotient.

There were 12 trays with 6 pieces. There were 2 pieces left over.

Find $59 \div 5$.

$$\begin{array}{r} 11 \text{ R4} \\ 5\overline{)59} \\ -5\downarrow \\ \hline 09 \\ -5 \\ \hline 4 \end{array}$$

Find $91 \div 3$.

$$\begin{array}{r} 30 \text{ R1} \\ 3\overline{)91} \\ -9\downarrow \\ \hline 01 \\ -0 \\ \hline 1 \end{array}$$

CLASSWORK

Divide.

1. $4\overline{)57}$
2. $6\overline{)64}$
3. $3\overline{)79}$
4. $4\overline{)47}$
5. $2\overline{)63}$
6. $5\overline{)82}$

7. $93 \div 6 = \square$
8. $95 \div 4 = \square$
9. $46 \div 3 = \square$
10. $74 \div 3 = \square$

Divide.

1. 2)35   2. 3)47   3. 4)59   4. 5)68   5. 2)79   6. 6)83

7. 5)65   8. 4)93   9. 3)96   10. 4)75   11. 6)87   12. 5)57

13. 3)92   14. 5)83   15. 8)27   16. 4)98   17. 4)72   18. 3)43

19. 4)50   20. 2)55   21. 6)98   22. 5)63   23. 3)97   24. 6)28

25. $33 \div 4 = \square$ 26. $95 \div 3 = \square$ 27. $54 \div 7 = \square$ 28. $73 \div 5 = \square$

29. $57 \div 2 = \square$ 30. $75 \div 2 = \square$ 31. $93 \div 5 = \square$ 32. $83 \div 3 = \square$

Which sentence does not fit the picture?

33. a. $6 + 6 + 6 + 6 = 24$
    b. $4 \times 6 = 24$
    c. $6 \times 6 = 36$
    d. $24 \div 6 = 4$

★34. a. $6 + 6 + 1 + 1 + 1 = 15$
    b. $15 \div 6 = 2 \text{ R}3$
    c. $2 \times 6 + 3 = 15$
    d. $30 \div 2 = 15$

APPLICATION

=== LOGICAL THINKING ===

There is a pattern in the remainders when we divide the numbers below by 3. What is the pattern?

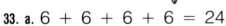

$$\begin{array}{r} 1 \\ 3\overline{)3} \\ -3 \\ \hline 0 \end{array} \quad \begin{array}{r} 1 \\ 3\overline{)4} \\ -3 \\ \hline 1 \end{array} \quad \begin{array}{r} 1 \\ 3\overline{)5} \\ -3 \\ \hline 2 \end{array} \quad \begin{array}{r} 2 \\ 3\overline{)6} \\ -6 \\ \hline 0 \end{array} \quad \begin{array}{r} 2 \\ 3\overline{)7} \\ -6 \\ \hline 1 \end{array} \quad \begin{array}{r} 2 \\ 3\overline{)8} \\ -6 \\ \hline 2 \end{array}$$

Divide. What pattern do you get in the remainders?

4)4   4)5   4)6   4)7   4)8   4)9   4)10   4)11

Three-Digit Quotients

Luke Horvath raises chickens. He has 334 chickens divided equally between 2 coops. How many chickens are there in each coop?

$334 \div 2 = \square$

Step 1
Divide hundreds.
Multiply.
Subtract and compare.

```
   1        Think
2)334       2)3
 -2         1 × 2 = 2
  1         3 − 2 = 1
            1 < 2
```

Step 2
Bring down tens.
Divide tens.
Multiply.
Subtract and compare.

```
  16
2)334
 -2↓
  13        Think
 -12        2)13
   1        6 × 2 = 12
            13 − 12 = 1
            1 < 2
```

Step 3
Bring down ones.
Divide ones.
Multiply.
Subtract and compare.

```
 167
2)334
 -2
  13
 -12↓
   14       Think
  -14       2)14
    0       7 × 2 = 14
            14 − 14 = 0
            0 < 2
```

There are 167 chickens in each coop.

Find $398 \div 3$.

Divide hundreds.

```
   1
3)398
 -3
  0
```

Divide tens.

```
  13
3)398
 -3↓
  09
 - 9
   0
```

Divide ones.

```
 132 R2
3)398
 -3
  09
 - 9↓
   08
  - 6
    2
```

CLASSWORK

Divide.

1. 3)456   2. 6)819   3. 5)675   4. 3)758   5. 4)565

6. $372 \div 2 = \square$ 7. $724 \div 4 = \square$ 8. $939 \div 5 = \square$

332

Divide.

1. 2)558 2. 3)791 3. 5)813 4. 3)749 5. 4)865

6. 5)895 7. 5)46 8. 4)672 9. 7)65 10. 6)696

11. 3)814 12. 2)725 13. 3)891 14. 6)78 15. 5)588

16. 4)792 17. 8)37 18. 3)384 19. 6)940 20. 4)647

21. 894 ÷ 6 = □ 22. 475 ÷ 5 = □ 23. 985 ÷ 3 = □

Choose the correct answer for each.

24. 675 ÷ 6 = □
    a. 121 R2 b. 12 R3
    c. 112 R3 d. 115

25. 280 ÷ 2 = □
    a. 14 b. 144
    c. 104 d. 140

26. 647 ÷ 4 = □
    a. 161 b. 161 R3
    c. 16 R3 d. 16

Find each missing number.

★ 27.

726   ÷6   +4   ×5   ÷4

APPLICATION

═══ CALCULATOR ═══

62   2

Here are two numbers. Add them. Subtract them. Multiply them. Divide them. Make a table to show the answers.

Add, subtract, multiply, and divide these pairs of numbers. Show the answers in your table.

Numbers	+	−	×	÷
62, 2	64	60		

1. 75 3

2. 234 2

3. 408 4

Problem Solving

SKILLS AND STRATEGIES REVIEW

Use the picture to answer 1–3.

1. What is the name of the store?

2. How long has the store been in business?

3. Stan Malik made a window display. He put 36 boxes of earphones in groups of 6. How many groups did he make?

Burton's is having a sale Monday through Friday on records, tapes, and video games.

Use the table to answer each question.

SALES MADE DURING SALE DAYS					
Item	Monday	Tuesday	Wednesday	Thursday	Friday
Records	150	121	127	145	111
Tapes	213	172	146	260	227
Video games	87	84	77	95	62

4. How many tapes were sold on Wednesday?

5. How many records were sold on Friday?

6. How many more video games were sold on Thursday than on Monday?

7. How many fewer tapes were sold on Tuesday than on Monday?

8. How many records and video games in all were sold on Friday?

9. How many records and tapes in all were sold on Wednesday?

10. About how many items were sold on Tuesday? Round to the nearest hundred.

11. About how many items were sold on Monday? Round to the nearest hundred.

★ 12. How many tapes in all were sold on Tuesday and Friday?

★ 13. Which item sold the most during the sale?

334

Patricia Gray is making bouquets of dried flowers. She puts 7 flowers in each bouquet. She has a box of 96 dried flowers.

Read and solve each problem.

14. How many bouquets can she make?

15. How many more flowers does she need to make the last bouquet?

16. How many bouquets can Patricia make if she uses 6 flowers in each bouquet?

17. How many flowers will Patricia have left over?

Ben Kotch works at Ticket Center. Tickets for a special concert for children are selling at $5 each.

Read and solve each problem.

18. Ben sold 12 tickets as soon as Ticket Center opened. What was the cost of the tickets?

19. By noon, Ben had taken in $500 for the children's concert. How many tickets had he sold?

20. By the end of the work day, Ben had sold 350 tickets. How many tickets had he sold that afternoon?

21. How much money had Ben taken in that day for the children's concert?

Find each quotient. pages 318–319

1. $42 \div 6 = \square$ 2. $56 \div 7 = \square$ 3. $54 \div 9 = \square$ 4. $63 \div 7 = \square$

Find each quotient and remainder. pages 320–323

5. $4\overline{)27}$ 6. $2\overline{)15}$ 7. $3\overline{)23}$ 8. $5\overline{)42}$ 9. $6\overline{)39}$

10. $9\overline{)19}$ 11. $7\overline{)24}$ 12. $8\overline{)34}$ 13. $7\overline{)50}$ 14. $8\overline{)44}$

15. $39 \div 9 = \square$ 16. $22 \div 7 = \square$ 17. $18 \div 8 = \square$

Divide. pages 326–333

18. $4\overline{)80}$ 19. $3\overline{)60}$ 20. $5\overline{)250}$ 21. $2\overline{)400}$ 22. $4\overline{)3,200}$

23. $6\overline{)72}$ 24. $6\overline{)84}$ 25. $4\overline{)92}$ 26. $3\overline{)93}$ 27. $5\overline{)55}$

28. $3\overline{)47}$ 29. $4\overline{)61}$ 30. $4\overline{)58}$ 31. $5\overline{)59}$ 32. $3\overline{)76}$

33. $2\overline{)656}$ 34. $3\overline{)718}$ 35. $6\overline{)953}$ 36. $4\overline{)872}$ 37. $5\overline{)667}$

38. $4\overline{)463}$ 39. $2\overline{)317}$ 40. $5\overline{)735}$ 41. $3\overline{)524}$ 42. $6\overline{)798}$

Solve. pages 324–325, 334–335

43. Mr. Jules, the baker, set out 144 hot rolls on 6 baking pans. Each pan had the same number of rolls. How many rolls were on each baking pan?

44. The hotel maid chose 38 new towels from the linen closet. She placed 4 in each room. How many rooms have 4 towels? How many towels are left over?

45. Miss Jordan has 78 pages of her new book to be typed. The typist can do 6 pages an hour. How many hours will it take him to type all the pages?

46. Ethel Bloom was packing toys in boxes of 15. She had 70 toys. How many boxes did she fill? How many toys were left over? Make a table to solve the problem.

CHAPTER TEST

Find each quotient.

1. $36 \div 4 = \square$ 2. $42 \div 6 = \square$ 3. $64 \div 8 = \square$

Find each quotient and remainder.

4. $3\overline{)17}$ 5. $3\overline{)29}$ 6. $4\overline{)33}$ 7. $5\overline{)26}$ 8. $4\overline{)19}$

9. $7\overline{)18}$ 10. $9\overline{)47}$ 11. $7\overline{)31}$ 12. $8\overline{)25}$ 13. $8\overline{)19}$

Divide.

14. $90 \div 3 = \square$ 15. $800 \div 2 = \square$ 16. $1,500 \div 5 = \square$

17. $3\overline{)78}$ 18. $6\overline{)96}$ 19. $5\overline{)65}$ 20. $4\overline{)84}$ 21. $2\overline{)62}$

22. $2\overline{)67}$ 23. $5\overline{)72}$ 24. $6\overline{)83}$ 25. $4\overline{)55}$ 26. $3\overline{)49}$

27. $5\overline{)813}$ 28. $2\overline{)247}$ 29. $4\overline{)536}$ 30. $3\overline{)642}$ 31. $6\overline{)752}$

Solve.

32. The school nurse teaches first aid to 72 adults. They are divided into 4 equal classes. How many adults are in each class?

33. Curt tied flowers in bunches of 12. He had 80 flowers. How many bunches did he make? How many flowers were left over? Make a table to solve the problem.

 Ned Beal has 172 cartons of eggs. He packs them equally into 8 crates. How many cartons are in each crate? How many cartons are left over?

ACTION DIVISION

You will need:
- a meterstick
- a ball of cord
- a pair of scissors

Find 110 ÷ 8.

1. Measure and cut a piece of cord 110 cm long.

2. Start at one end of the cord and cut pieces that are 8 cm long. Cut as many pieces as possible. Measure carefully.

3. Count the number of 8-cm pieces you have cut.

4. Measure the piece that is left over.

110 ÷ 8 = 13 R6

Show other division sentences. Make and complete a table like this one.

DIVIDING CORD				
Length of single piece of cord	Length of pieces to be cut from single piece	Number of exact-size pieces that can be cut from single piece	Size of left-over piece	Division sentence
57 cm	7 cm	8	1 cm	57 ÷ 7 = 8 R1
32 cm	5 cm			
115 cm	9 cm			
75 cm	8 cm			

DIVISIBILITY BY 3

The number 12 can be divided by 3, leaving a remainder of 0. We say that 12 is *divisible* by 3.

$$3\overline{)12}^{\,4}$$

Are these numbers divisible by 3?

$1 \times 3 = 3$
$2 \times 3 = 6$
$3 \times 3 = 9$
$4 \times 3 = 12$
$5 \times 3 = 15$
$6 \times 3 = 18$
$7 \times 3 = 21$
$8 \times 3 = 24$
$9 \times 3 = 27$

33   120   78   1,692

Use a calculator to divide each number by 3.

If the remainder is 0, the number is divisible by 3.

$$33 \div 3 = 11$$
$$120 \div 3 = 40$$
$$78 \div 3 = 26$$
$$1,692 \div 3 = 564$$

Each number is divisible by 3.

There is another way to tell whether the numbers above are divisible by 3.

1. Add the digits in 33. $3 + 3 = 6$ 6 is divisible by 3.

2. Add the digits in 120. $1 + 2 + 0 = 3$ 3 is divisible by 3.

3. Add the digits in 78. $7 + 8 = 15$

   Continue to add until there is only one digit in the sum. $1 + 5 = 6$ 6 is divisible by 3.

4. Add the digits in 1,692. $1 + 6 + 9 + 2 = 18$

   Continue to add until there is only one digit in the sum. $1 + 8 = 9$ 9 is divisible by 3.

▶If the sum of the digits in a number is divisible by 3, the number is divisible by 3.

Which of these numbers is divisible by 3?
Add the digits. Check, using a calculator.

1. 360   2. 168   3. 689   4. 1,920   5. 2,367

COMPUTERS IN INDUSTRY

Computers are used in many different ways by companies that make products.

Computers help engineers to make new products. The engineers are able to look at new designs on the computer screen.

For example, the airline industry uses computers to make airplanes safer. The computer can "act out" the conditions under which airplanes fly. This tells the engineers how the airplane will fly even before it is built. When the airplane is built, computers can test it.

At airports, computers help to direct air traffic. Computers handle schedules and reservations for flights all over the world.

Many companies use robots. Computers are used to tell robots what to do. Robots sort nuts and bolts. Robots help build cars. Other robots make clocks or knit sweaters.

Many people in industry like robots. Robots can work long hours. They can do the same job over and over. They never get tired or bored. They can even work with dangerous chemicals. Some robots can "see" shapes and tell how far away they are. They can "feel" heat and tell how tightly they are holding an object.

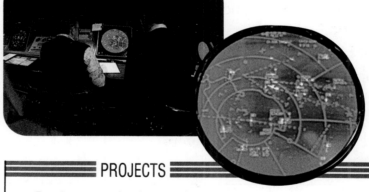

PROJECTS

1. Invite an airplane pilot to talk to the class. Ask the pilot how computers are used in an airplane.

2. Collect pictures of robots at work. Display your pictures on a bulletin board in class.

3. Some people do not like robots. Give 2 reasons why robots might not be wanted in industry.

MAINTAINING SKILLS

Choose the correct answers. Write A, B, C, or D.

1. $372 - 196 = \square$

   A 176   C 568

   B 286   D not given

2. $45 \div 5 = \square$

   A 8   C 7

   B 9   D not given

3. Which is the best unit to measure the distance from the earth to the moon?

   A cm   C km

   B m   D not given

4. Compare. $\frac{3}{8} \bullet \frac{4}{8}$

   A >   C =

   B <   D not given

5. $3 \times 26 = \square$

   A 29   C 78

   B 68   D not given

6. $7 \times 541 = \square$

   A 3,787   C 4,897

   B 3,827   D not given

7. $6\overline{)420}$

   A 60   C 7

   B 76   D not given

8. $87 \div 2 = \square$

   A 43 R1   C 430 R2

   B 44 R2   D not given

9. $643 \div 4 = \square$

   A 160 R3   C 16 R2

   B 120 R3   D not given

10. $5\overline{)605}$

    A 110   C 101

    B 120   D not given

Solve.

11. A parking lot has 7 rows of cars and 5 rows of trucks. If each row has 10 cars or trucks, how many cars and trucks are there in all?

    A 22   C 120

    B 1,200   D not given

342 CHAPTER RESOURCE

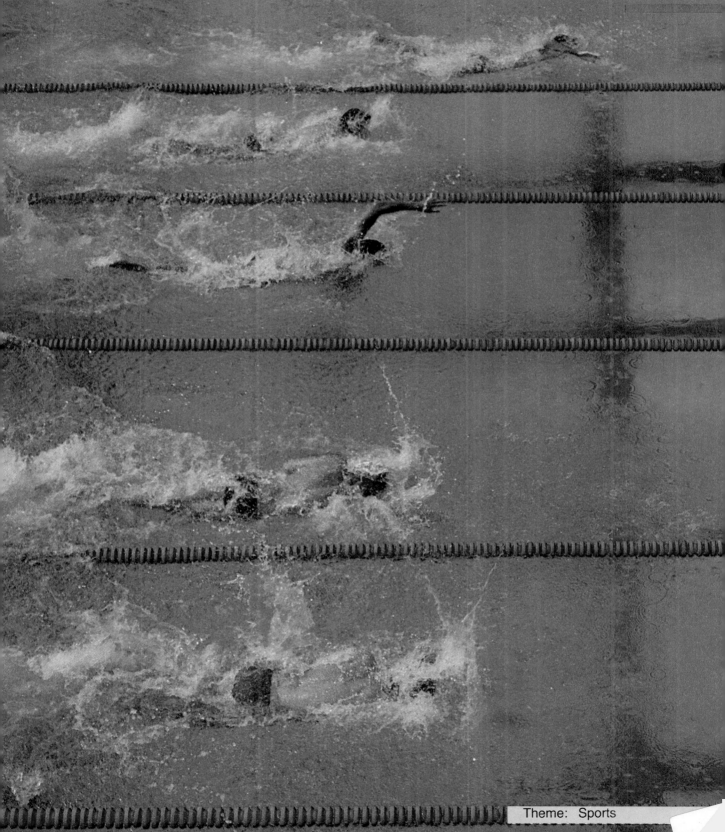

Theme: Sports

Fractions of an Inch

Eve won a ribbon for tumbling. How long was the ribbon?

▶We use the **inch** to measure short lengths in the customary system. We write **in.** for inch.

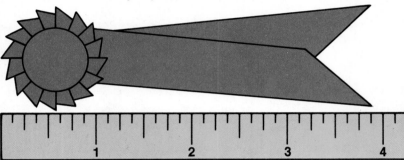

The ribbon is between 3 inches and 4 inches long. It is closer to 4 inches. It is 4 inches long to the nearest inch.

▶We also use the **half inch ($\frac{1}{2}$ in.)** and the **fourth inch ($\frac{1}{4}$ in.)** to measure length.

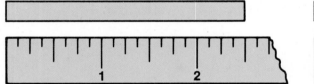
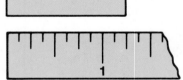

This bar is about $2\frac{1}{2}$ inches long. This bar is about $1\frac{1}{4}$ inches long.

CLASSWORK

Measure each bar to the nearest inch.

1. 2.

Measure each bar to the nearest $\frac{1}{2}$ inch.

3. 4.

Measure each bar to the nearest $\frac{1}{4}$ inch.

5. 6.

PRACTICE

Measure each bar to the nearest inch.

1.

2.

3.

Measure each bar to the nearest $\frac{1}{2}$ inch.

4.

5.

6.

7.

Measure each bar to the nearest $\frac{1}{4}$ inch.

8.

9.

Guess how long each is. Then measure to the nearest inch.

10.

11.

Draw a bar of each length.

12. $5\frac{1}{4}$ in.

★ 13. $2\frac{3}{4}$ in.

★ 14. $4\frac{3}{4}$ in.

Measure the distance between

★ 15. A and B

A •

B •

★ 16. B and C

C •

APPLICATION

The teacher measured the heights of 4 children. Use the table to answer 17–18.

17. Which student is the tallest?

18. How much taller is Ted than Barry?

★ 19. Measure the height of several classmates. Record the measurements, in inches, in a table.

Student	Height
Barry	50 inches
Elsa	47 inches
Jodi	54 inches
Ted	53 inches

345

Foot, Yard, Mile

In a track and field meet, we use other customary units to measure length.

▶We use the **foot** to measure length. We write **ft** for foot.

12 inches = 1 foot

▶We use the **yard** to measure longer lengths. We write **yd** for yard.

36 inches = 1 yard
3 feet = 1 yard

▶We use the **mile** to measure very long distances. We write **mi** for mile.

5,280 feet = 1 mile
1,760 yards = 1 mile

CLASSWORK

Choose foot, yard, or mile to measure each.

1. width of a Ping-Pong table

2. a pass in a football game

3. distance in a marathon race

4. fabric for a dress

Complete.

5. 36 in. = _____ yd

6. 5,280 ft = _____ mi

7. 1 ft = _____ in.

Guess how long each is. Then measure to the nearest foot.

8. length of the chalkboard

9. length of your left arm

PRACTICE

Choose foot, yard, or mile to measure each.

1. height of a tree
2. distance a jogger runs
3. length of a football field
4. length of a bicycle race
5. length of a river
6. width of a volleyball net

Complete.

7. 12 in. = _____ ft
8. 3 ft = _____ yd
9. 24 in. = _____ ft

Guess how long each is. Then measure to the nearest foot.

10. length of the classroom door
11. length of your desk

Complete. Choose foot, yard, or mile.

12. Max jogged 5 ___.
13. Cathy's long jump was 5 ___ long.
14. Al threw the football 15 ___.
15. The Ping-Pong table is 9 ___ long.

Name 3 objects in the classroom that are

★16. longer than 6 feet.
★17. shorter than 6 feet.

APPLICATION

18. Tom ran 365 yd from home to school and 220 yd beyond school. Then he ran 275 yd to the store and 900 yd back home. How far did he run in all?

★19. Tara ran the 100-yard dash. How many feet did she run?

═══ LOGICAL THINKING ═══
In the main race Dennis was 70 ft ahead of Max. Stan was 40 ft behind Gene. Max was 30 ft ahead of Stan. Who won the race? Who placed second? third? last?

Ounce and Pound

Andrew's baseball cap weighs about 2 ounces.
The baseball weighs about 6 ounces.

▶We use the **ounce** to measure the weight of
light objects. We write **oz** for ounce.

▶We use the **pound** to measure the weight of
heavier objects. We write **lb** for pound.

16 ounces = 1 pound

6 ounces

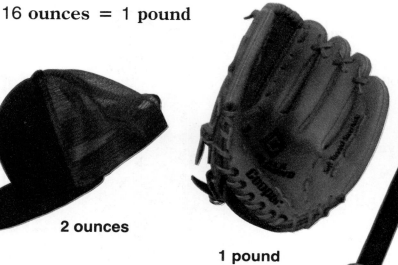

2 pounds

2 ounces

1 pound

8 ounces

CLASSWORK

Choose ounce or pound to measure the weight of each.

1. a baseball player

2. a pair of socks

3. a catcher's mask

4. shoelaces

5. a baseball

6. a bicycle

7. a table

8. a letter

Choose the better estimate for each weight.

9. a box of baseballs
   a. 4 lb   b. 4 oz

10. a box of cereal
    a. 12 lb   b. 12 oz

11. a 10-year-old boy
    a. 5 lb   b. 50 lb

12. an egg
    a. 4 oz   b. 4 lb

Choose ounce or pound to measure the weight of each.

7 ounces

1. a football team   2. a horse

3. a score book   4. a full water jug

5. the coach's pencil   6. an apple

7. a pair of skates   8. a pair of skis

Choose the better estimate for each weight.

9. a football   10. an orange

  a. 1 oz   b. 1 lb   a. 8 oz   b. 8 lb

11. a bicycle   12. a ruler

  a. 25 oz   b. 25 lb   a. 3 oz   b. 3 lb

Compare. Use >, <, or = for ●.

13. 1 lb ● 1 oz   14. 16 oz ● 1 lb

★ 15. 20 oz ● 1 lb   ★ 16. 1 lb ● 26 oz

APPLICATION

Copy and complete the table. Each box of baseballs weighs 4 lb.

Boxes of Baseballs	1	2	3	4	5	6
Pounds	4	8				
Cost	$16	$32				

17. What is the weight of 6 boxes?   ★ 18. What is the cost of 6 boxes?

MENTAL ARITHMETIC

How much less than 1 pound is 7 ounces?

Think   16 ounces = 1 pound
  So   16 − 7 = 9.   The answer is 9 ounces.

How much less than 1 pound is each of these?

1. 12 oz   2. 6 oz   3. 9 oz   4. 3 oz

5. 10 oz   6. 2 oz   7. 4 oz   8. 5 oz

Problem Solving

USING A MODEL

You can solve some problems by using a model. You can use a pencil and paper, or objects to show the action and solve the problem.

Ana, Ben, and Cindy are kicking a ball. Each child kicks the ball to the other 2 children. How many times is the ball kicked?

What is the question?

How many times is the ball kicked?

What are the facts?

There are 3 children. Each child kicks to the other 2 children.

How can you find the answer?

Make a model or a drawing.

Carry out the plan. Do the work and find the answer.

Show that Ana kicks to Ben and Cindy. Show that Ben kicks to Ana and Cindy. Show that Cindy kicks to Ana and Ben. Count the number of times the ball is kicked.

The ball is kicked 6 times.

Check your answer. Does it make sense?

3 × 2 = 6

Your answer makes sense.

Read each problem. Use paper and pencil to make a model.

1. Alice finished the 50-yard race 5 yards ahead of Olga.

2. The catcher stood 2 yards behind the plate.

3. Wyatt and Millie started in the same place. They ran in opposite directions. Millie ran 110 yards. Wyatt ran 130 yards.

4. Ross and Ada started in the same place. They ran in the same direction. Ross ran 110 yards. Ada ran 130 yards.

5. Matt and Dawn were scuba diving. Matt dove 68 feet. Dawn dove 60 feet.

6. Helga and Cora are running a 200-foot race. Helga has run 122 feet. Cora is 72 feet from the finish line.

Solve each problem by using a model.

7. Roy is making a triangle of pennies. He starts with 1 penny. In the second row he puts 2 pennies. In each of the next rows he puts 1 more penny than in the row before. How many pennies will there be in the seventh row? How many pennies will there be in 7 rows?

★8. Scott had a long rod of wood. He cut it in half. He cut each piece in half again. Then he cut each of these pieces in half. How many pieces does he now have?

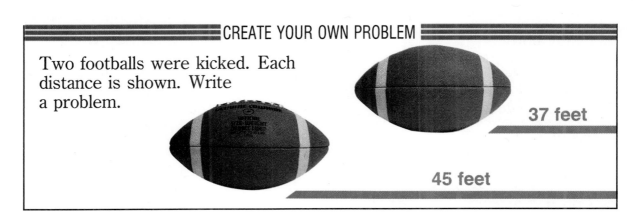

CREATE YOUR OWN PROBLEM

Two footballs were kicked. Each distance is shown. Write a problem.

37 feet

45 feet

Cup, Pint, Quart, Gallon

Amy sold juice at the game. She used a cup to measure the juice.

▶ We use the **cup, pint, quart,** and **gallon** to measure liquids. We write **c** for cup, **pt** for pint, **qt** for quart, and **gal** for gallon.

cup

2 cups = 1 pint

2 pints = 1 quart

4 quarts = 1 gallon

pint

quart

CLASSWORK

Choose cup, pint, quart, or gallon to measure each amount.

1. milk in a school lunch

2. gasoline needed to fill the school bus tank

3. soup in a bowl

4. water in a bathtub

5. juice in a pitcher

gallon

Choose the better measurement for each.

6. a baby bottle

   a. 1 qt   **b.** 1 c

7. a teakettle

   a. 1 c   **b.** 1 qt

8. a small flower vase

   a. 1 pt   **b.** 1 gal

9. a can of paint

   a. 1 c   **b.** 1 gal

Complete.

10. 2 pt = _____ qt

11. 4 qt = _____ gal

12. 2 c = _____ pt

PRACTICE

Choose cup, pint, quart, or gallon to measure each amount.

1. juice squeezed from 4 oranges

2. large bottle of milk

3. 2-cup jar of oil

4. water in a bucket

Write *possible* or *not possible* for each.

5. A child drank 3 gallons of water at the game.

6. A baseball player drank a pint of juice.

7. Each cup held 1 quart of water.

8. The coach drank 2 cups of water.

9. Amy sold 10 gallons of juice at the game.

Complete.

10. 1 gal = _____ qt

11. 1 pt = _____ c

12. 1 qt = _____ pt

★13. 4 c = _____ pt

★14. 2 gal = _____ qt

★15. 4 pt = _____ qt

APPLICATION

Amy and Rory used this recipe to make a fruit drink.

6 cups orange juice
6 cups pineapple juice
1 cup lemon juice
3 cups grape juice

16. How many cups of fruit drink does the recipe make?

17. Double the recipe. Now how many cups are made?

★18. How many gallons of fruit drink are there after the recipe is doubled?

★19. Some cans of juice were stacked in a pyramid at the refreshment stand. There were 8 in the bottom row. Use a model to arrange 21 cans.

CALCULATOR

Milk is delivered to Maple Glen School. Each of 7 classes gets 25 pints a day. How many pints of milk are delivered in 1 day? in 5 days?

Degree Fahrenheit

The temperature on the dock is 85°F.

The temperature at the pond is 30°F.

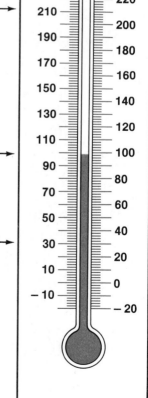

°F

▶ We use the **degree Fahrenheit** as a unit to measure temperature. We write **°F** for degree Fahrenheit. To read the temperature, look at the number beside the top of the red column.

Water boils 212°

The thermometer shows 98.6°F. This is normal body temperature.

Normal body temperature 98.6°

CLASSWORK

Read the Fahrenheit thermometer to answer these.

Water freezes 32°

1. At what temperature does water freeze?

2. At what temperature does water boil?

3. What is normal body temperature?

4. What kind of day is it at 100°F?

5. What kind of day is it at 0°F?

PRACTICE

Read the Fahrenheit temperature shown on each.

1.
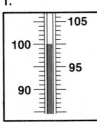

2.
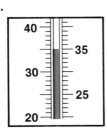

3.
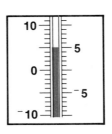

Choose the most likely temperature.

4. a. 42°F   b. 78°F   5. a. 20°F   b. 50°F

Match. Choose the most likely temperature.

6. a very hot summer day   a. 70°F

7. the freezing point of water   b. 212°F

8. room temperature   c. 95°F

9. the boiling point of water   d. 5°F

10. a very cold winter day   e. 32°F

APPLICATION

11. Joan's temperature was 99.8°F. How much above normal body temperature was that?

★ 12. The temperature was 18°F at 4 P.M. It fell 2° an hour. What temperature was it at 8 P.M.?

Mixed Practice

1. $\begin{array}{r} 4 \\ 2 \\ +8 \\ \hline \end{array}$ 2. $\begin{array}{r} 33 \\ 3 \\ +43 \\ \hline \end{array}$

3. $\begin{array}{r} 116 \\ -\ 72 \\ \hline \end{array}$ 4. $\begin{array}{r} 97 \\ -25 \\ \hline \end{array}$

5. $\begin{array}{r} 405 \\ +306 \\ \hline \end{array}$ 6. $\begin{array}{r} \$1.85 \\ -\ \ .86 \\ \hline \end{array}$

7. $\$1.63 - \$.84 = \Box$

8. $\$3.32 + \$4.96 = \Box$

9. $6 \times 8 = \Box$

10. $25 \div 5 = \Box$

11. $3\overline{)30}$

12. $9\overline{)54}$

13. $\begin{array}{r} 5 \\ \times 6 \\ \hline \end{array}$ 14. $\begin{array}{r} 6 \\ \times 4 \\ \hline \end{array}$

15. $\begin{array}{r} 8 \\ \times 2 \\ \hline \end{array}$ 16. $\begin{array}{r} 7 \\ \times 7 \\ \hline \end{array}$

17. $9\overline{)72}$

18. $6\overline{)48}$

19. $8 \times 8 = \Box$

20. $18 \div 3 = \Box$

Experiments and Outcomes

Sometimes we toss a coin to decide which team will bat first. Tossing a coin is an **experiment**.

When we toss a coin, there are 2 possible **outcomes:** heads or tails. Rene chose heads. The chance of heads coming up is 1 chance out of 2 chances. The coin landed heads up. Rene won the toss.

What are the possible outcomes of spinning this spinner? The possible outcomes are red, blue, or green. The chance of one color coming up is 1 out of 3.

CLASSWORK

Use the spinner at the right to answer each question.

1. How many different colors can the pointer stop on?

2. What are the possible outcomes of a spin?

3. What is the chance of the pointer stopping on red?

4. What is the chance of the pointer stopping on green?

5. What is the chance of the pointer stopping on blue?

Use the spinner to answer each question.

1. How many different colors can the pointer stop on?

2. What are the possible outcomes of a spin?

3. What is the chance of the pointer stopping on blue?

4. What is the chance of the pointer stopping on orange or green?

What are the chances of picking a black marble? Choose the correct answer.

5.   ★ 6.   ★ 7.

| a. 1 out of 2 | a. 2 out of 5 | a. 2 out of 5 |
| b. 1 out of 3 | b. 2 out of 3 | b. 3 out of 5 |

APPLICATION

8. Andrew Barton has 11 marbles in a bag. One marble is purple. If Andrew is blindfolded, what is the chance of his drawing the purple marble from the bag?

★ 9. There are 1 blue, 3 green, 3 yellow, and 3 red marbles in a bag. Without looking, one marble is drawn. What is the chance that it is green? yellow? red? blue?

★ 10. There are 1 white and 2 green tennis balls in a bag. Three persons draw a ball out of the bag and replace it. Would you expect the number of green balls picked to be greater than, less than, or the same as the white ball?

Frequency Tables

Twenty runs were scored in the kickball game.

The Bears scored 7 out of 20 runs.
The Bobcats scored 13 out of 20 runs.
You can keep a record of these runs
in a table.

The scorekeeper uses tally marks to keep a
record. One run is shown like this: | .
Five runs are shown like this: ⑷⑷ .

Runs Scored

Team A	Team B
⑷⑷ ||	⑷⑷ ⑷⑷ ||

Team A scored 7 runs.
Team B scored 12 runs.

CLASSWORK

Danny tossed a coin 20 times. His results
are recorded in the table below.

Heads	Tails
⑷⑷ ||||	⑷⑷ ⑷⑷	

Use the table to answer each question.

1. How many times did heads show?

2. How many times did tails show?

3. Is the number of heads close to the number
   of tails?

4. Why is the number of heads about the same
   as the number of tails?

PRACTICE

Rachel picked a tennis ball out of a box 30 times. She replaced the ball each time. Paul recorded the number of times each color was drawn.

Green	Orange
⊁⊁⊁ ⊁⊁⊁ ⊁⊁⊁ I	⊁⊁⊁ ⊁⊁⊁ IIII

Look at the picture. Read the table. Then answer each question.

1. How many balls are in the box?

2. What color are the balls?

3. How many times did Rachel pick out the orange ball?

4. How many times did Rachel pick out the green ball?

★ 5. Explain why the number of green balls drawn is about the same as the number of orange balls drawn.

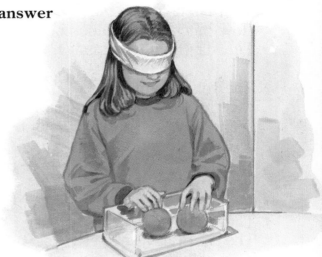

Choose the correct answer.

6. Rachel's chance of picking out the green ball is

   a. 1 out of 2.　　　b. 2 out of 2.　　　c. 1 out of 3.

7. Rachel's chance of picking out the orange ball is

   a. 2 out of 3.　　　b. 1 out of 2.　　　c. 3 out of 4.

8. Is the number of tallies for green close to the number of tallies for orange?

   a. yes　　　b. sometimes　　　c. no

APPLICATION

9. Do the experiment that Rachel did. Use 2 marbles or balls of different colors. Close your eyes or use a blindfold. Work with a friend who will record the results in a table.

10. Compare your results with Rachel's results.

★ 11. Do Rachel's experiment with 3 balls of different colors. Record your results in a table.

Problem Solving

SKILLS AND STRATEGIES REVIEW Sports

Solve each problem.

home   5.9 mi   store

4.1 mi   3.9 mi

school

1. Adam is training for the track meet. He runs from his home to school on Monday. He runs from his home to the store on Tuesday. How much farther does he run on Tuesday than on Monday?

2. The relay team runs 3 laps in each race. Judy ran her lap in 7.3 seconds. Mitch ran his lap in 8.1 seconds. Jerry ran his lap in 6.0 seconds. How long did it take the team to run the race?

3. Leta rode her bike 2.3 miles on Monday, the first day of her training program. She plans to add 1.0 miles each day. She rode 3.3 miles on Tuesday. How far should she ride on Thursday?

4. There are 4 bases in baseball. The Mets have player A on first base and player B on third base. If player C hits a single, and each player moves one base, where will each player be?

★5. Someone once said that Wilt Chamberlain, the famous basketball player, was "only 6 feet 14 inches tall." How tall is that?

★6. In 1985, Pete Rose broke Ty Cobb's record for the number of hits in a career. Suppose he had 200 hits every year for 20 years, plus 192 more hits. Figure the new record.

Problem Solving

WHAT IF . . .?

Rhoda plays a game with her friends. They throw balls that stick to a target. They earn points according to where the balls stick on the target.

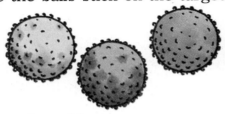

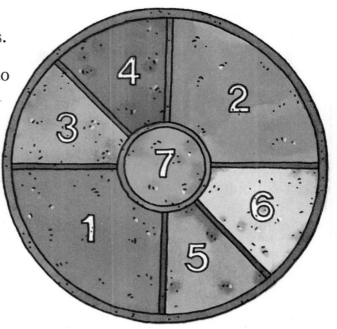

Solve each problem.

1. Rhoda's first ball landed on 3. Her second ball landed on 3. Her third ball landed in the center. What was Rhoda's score?

What if Rhoda's first ball had missed the board?

2. What would her score be if this had happened?

3. What would be the difference between the two scores?

4. Jason scored 15. All 3 balls landed in the same space. Where did they land?

What if each ball that Jason threw landed in a different space?

5. Where could each ball have landed for a score of 15?

6. Where could each ball have landed for a score of 13?

7. Miriam said, "I hit the target with all three balls. Two balls landed in the same space. My score was 7." Where could the balls have landed?

What if Miriam's score had been 2?

8. Could she have hit the board with all three balls?

9. How could Miriam have made a score of 2?

361

CHAPTER REVIEW

Guess how long each bar is. Then measure each to the nearest inch. pages 344–345

1. 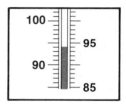 2.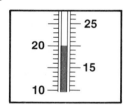

Choose foot, yard, or mile to measure each. pages 346–347

3. your height   4. a river   5. a curtain

Choose ounce or pound to measure each. pages 348–349

6. a softball   7. a telephone   8. a baby's shoe

Complete. pages 352–353

9. 2 c = _____ pt   10. 4 qt = _____ gal   11. 1 qt = _____ pt

Write each Fahrenheit temperature. pages 354–355

12.   13.   14.

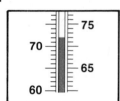

	Red	Green	White
	‖‖‖	‖‖‖ ‖‖‖	‖‖‖ ‖‖‖ ‖‖

Use the table to answer each question. pages 356–359

15. What are the possible outcomes?
16. What are the chances of green coming up?
17. How many times did the spinner stop on white?
18. How many spins were there in all?

Solve. pages 350–351, 360–361

19. Tim drinks 1 pt of milk in the morning and 1 qt in the evening. How many pints does Tim drink in 1 day?

20. Bryan tossed a nickel and dime together. The dime fell 5 times on heads; 1 on tails. The nickel fell 3 times on heads; 3 on tails. How many times did Bryan toss the nickel and dime?

Measure each bar to the nearest $\frac{1}{4}$ inch.

1. [bar] 2. [bar]

Complete. Choose feet, yards, or miles.

3. A football field is 100 _____ long.

4. The length of the canoe is 15 _____.

5. The swimming pool is 4 _____ deep.

6. The distance of the bike road race is 50 _____.

Choose the better measurement for each.

7. a whistle
   a. 2 lb   b. 2 oz

8. an apple
   a. 3 oz   b. 3 lb

9. a helmet
   a. 8 lb   b. 8 oz

10. a teapot
    a. 4 c   b. 4 gal

11. a pail
    a. 1 qt   b. 1 gal

12. a pitcher
    a. 1 qt   b. 1 c

Black	Yellow	Blue	Orange
IIII	⊮⊮ II	⊮⊮ ⊮⊮ I	III

Use the table to answer each question.

13. What are the possible outcomes?

14. What are the chances of the spinner stopping on blue?

15. What are the chances of the spinner stopping on yellow?

16. How many times did the spinner stop on black?

17. How many times did the spinner stop on blue?

18. How many spins were there in all?

Solve.

19. Matt bought 3 boxes of Ping-Pong balls. There were 6 balls in each box. The 3 boxes weigh 27 oz. What does 1 box weigh?

20. The temperature was 11°F at 6 A.M. It had risen 5° by 12 noon and had fallen 2° by 4 P.M. Use a model to show the temperature at 4 P.M.

Alice used 3 yd of fabric. Mrs. Larson used 10 ft of fabric. Who used more fabric? How much more?

CRAYON EXPERIMENT

You will need: · 4 crayons: 2 black, 1 red, 1 green
· a paper bag
· pencil and paper

Copy this table and record your results.

Black	Red

Put 1 black crayon and 1 red crayon into a bag. Close your eyes. Pick a crayon from the bag and record the color picked. Do this 10 times. Remember to return the crayon to the bag after each draw.

1. What are the chances you will pick red?

   a. 1 out of 4   b. 1 out of 3   c. 1 out of 2

2. What are the chances you will pick black?

   a. 1 out of 2   b. 2 out of 3   c. 1 out of 3

3. How many times out of 10 did you pick red? black?

Add the green crayon to the bag. Repeat the experiment 10 times.

Black	Green	Red

4. What are the chances you will pick green?

   a. 1 out of 2   b. 2 out of 3   c. 1 out of 3

5. What are the chances you will pick red?

   a. 1 out of 4   b. 1 out of 3   c. 1 out of 2

Add the other black crayon to the bag. Repeat the experiment 10 times.

6. What are the chances you will pick black?

   a. 1 out of 4   b. 2 out of 4   c. 1 out of 2

7. What are the chances you will pick green?

   a. 1 out of 3   b. 1 out of 4   c. 2 out of 3

A DIFFERENT RULER

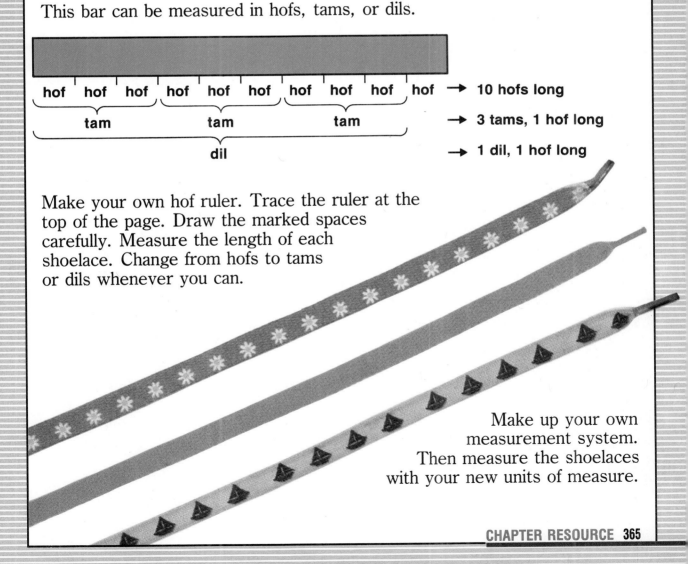

hof ruler

This ruler is marked in hof units. How many hofs long is the ruler?

In this measurement system:

$$3 \text{ hofs} = 1 \text{ tam}$$
$$3 \text{ tams} = 1 \text{ dil}$$

This bar can be measured in hofs, tams, or dils.

| hof | hof | hof | hof | hof | hof | hof | hof | hof | hof | → 10 hofs long |

tam   tam   tam   → 3 tams, 1 hof long

dil   → 1 dil, 1 hof long

Make your own hof ruler. Trace the ruler at the top of the page. Draw the marked spaces carefully. Measure the length of each shoelace. Change from hofs to tams or dils whenever you can.

Make up your own measurement system. Then measure the shoelaces with your new units of measure.

Choose the correct answer. Write A, B, C, or D.

1. $93.59
    − 46.55

    A $47.04   C $57.04

    B $140.14   D not given

7. Measure to the nearest $\frac{1}{4}$ inch.

    A 3 in.   C $2\frac{1}{2}$ in.

    B $2\frac{1}{4}$ in.   D not given

2. Write a decimal for the red part.

    A 0.17   C 1.7

    B 1.8   D not given

8. Choose the unit to measure your height.

    A ft   C mi

    B yd   D not given

3. 2 × 43 = ☐

    A 16   C 41

    B 76   D not given

9. Choose the unit to measure the water in a swimming pool.

    A c   C gal

    B qt   D not given

4. 5 × 962 = ☐

    A 4,500   C 1,517

    B 4,810   D not given

Use the table for **10** and **11**.

BAGELS SOLD		
May	**June**	**July**
1,547	1,530	1,564

5. 6)32

    A 5 R2   C 6 R2

    B 7 R2   D not given

10. How many bagels were sold in May and June?

    A 3,077   C 3,094

    B 2,077   D not given

6. 752 ÷ 4 = ☐

    A 173   C 188

    B 153   D not given

11. How many more were sold in July than in May?

    A 13   C 17

    B 51   D not given

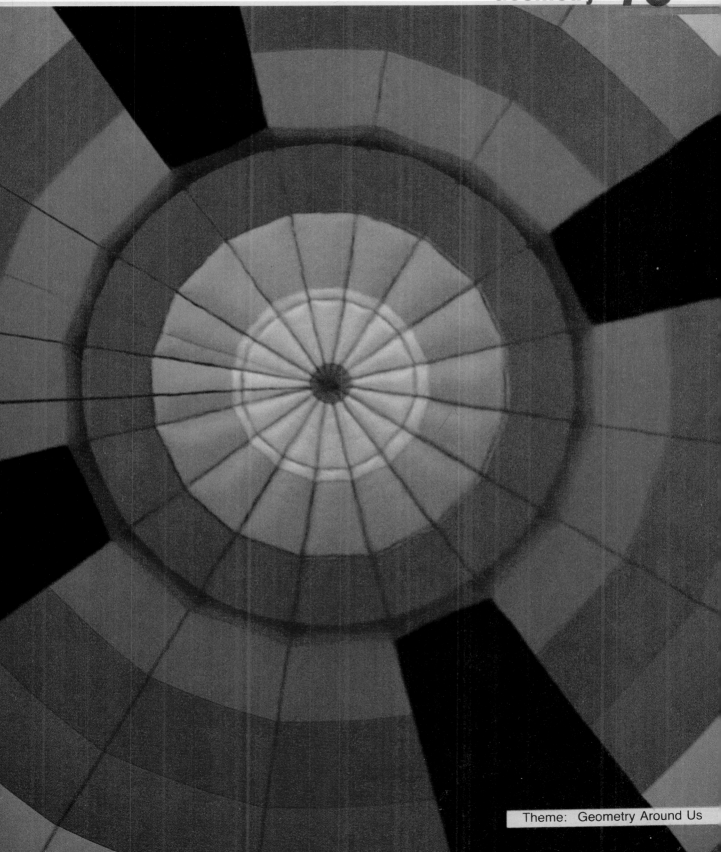

Theme: Geometry Around Us

Space Figures

Bonnie was given a puppet for her birthday. The puppet was made of objects shaped like **space figures**.

cone

sphere

rectangular prism

cylinder

Some space figures have faces, edges, and corners.

edge
corner
face

cube   pyramid

CLASSWORK

Name the space figure suggested by each object.

1.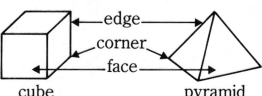

2.

3.

4.

5.

6.

Name the part shown by the arrow.

7.

8.

9.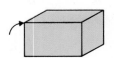

Name the space figure suggested by each object.

1.

2.
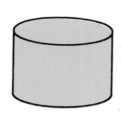

3.
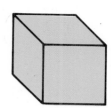

4.

5.
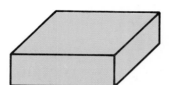

6.
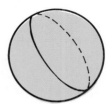

Name the part shown by the arrow.

7.
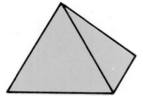

★8.

★9.

10. Bonnie got a beach ball for her birthday. What space figure does it look like?

★11. Take a piece of paper. Glue the opposite ends together. What space figure does it look like?

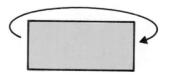

===== LOGICAL THINKING =====

Stuart had 7 checkers and 3 cubes. He stacked each group. What space figure did each stack look like?

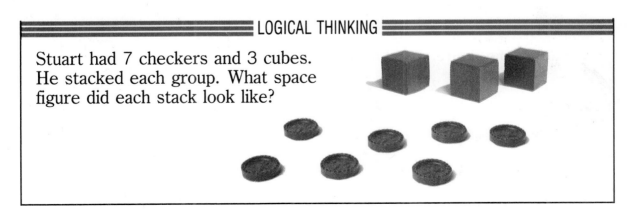

Triangles, Rectangles, Squares, Circles

Leah painted one face of each block. She pressed
the wet face on paper to make these shapes.
The outline of each shape is a **plane figure.**

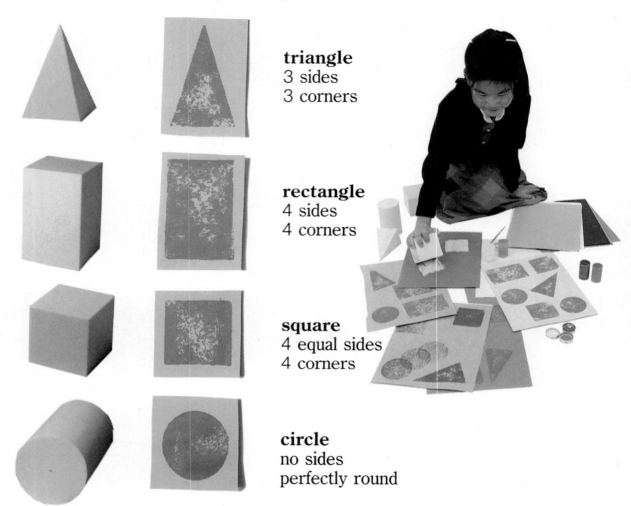

triangle
3 sides
3 corners

rectangle
4 sides
4 corners

square
4 equal sides
4 corners

circle
no sides
perfectly round

CLASSWORK

Name each plane figure. Tell how many sides it has.

1.

2.

3.

4.

370

Name each plane figure. Tell how many sides it has.

1.
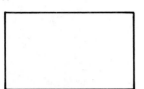

2.
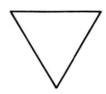

3.

4.

5.
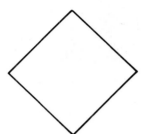

6.
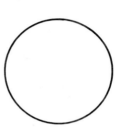

7.
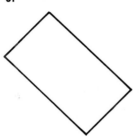

8.
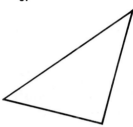

Draw each plane figure.

9. a square   10. a rectangle   11. a triangle   ★ 12. a circle

APPLICATION

Answer each question about the picture.

13. How many ◯ are there?

14. How many ☐ are there?

★ 15. How many ☐ are there?

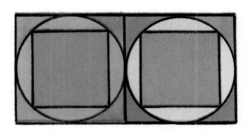

=== VISUAL THINKING ===

1. How many triangles are there?

2. How many squares are there?

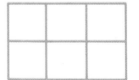

Lines, Line Segments, Rays, Angles

Sonja can make a pinwheel with this pattern. The pattern shows some figures.

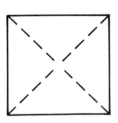

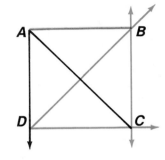

A **line** is straight. It has no endpoints. A line goes on and on in both directions.

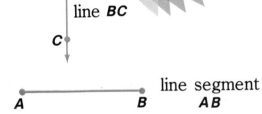

line **BC**

A **line segment** is part of a line. It has two endpoints.

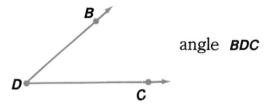

line segment **AB**

A **ray** is part of a line. It has one endpoint. A ray goes on and on in one direction.

ray **DC**

Two rays that have the same endpoint form an **angle.**

angle **BDC**

CLASSWORK

Name each figure.

1.

2.

3.

4.

5.

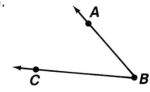

6.

Name each figure.

1.

2.

3.

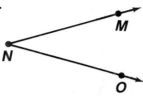

4.

5.

6.

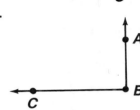

How many endpoints does each figure have?

7.

8.

9.

How many line segments are there?

★**10.**

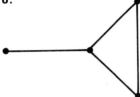

★**11.**

APPLICATION

Name the figures in the drawing.

12. the red figures

13. the blue figure

14. the green figure

**Make a drawing of one of the following.
Label the figures you use.**

★ **15.** the classroom clock ★ **16.** your classroom ★ **17.** your house

Congruent Figures

Todd is making a kite. He needs
two rectangles of the same size and shape.

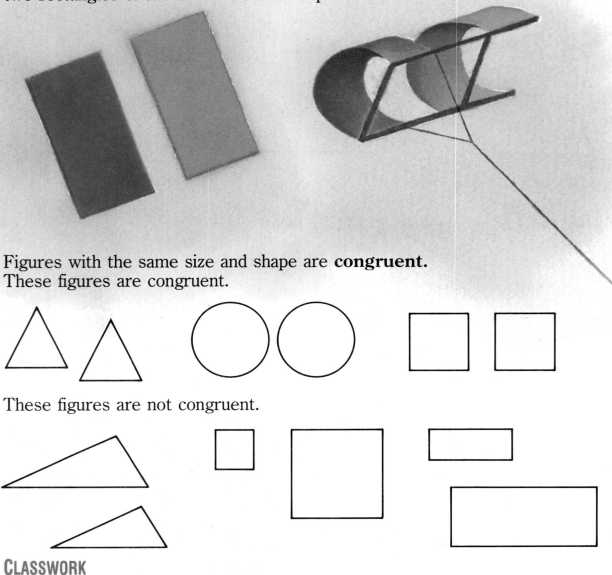

Figures with the same size and shape are **congruent**.
These figures are congruent.

These figures are not congruent.

CLASSWORK

Tell if the figures are congruent.

1. 2. 3.

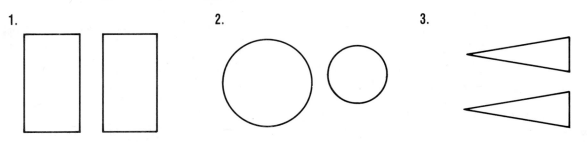

Tell if the figures are congruent.

1.

2.

3.

4.

Tell which figure is congruent to the first.

5.

   a.

   b.

   c.

6.

   a.

   b.

   c.

7.

   a.

   b.

   c.

★8.

   a.

   b.

   c.

APPLICATION

VISUAL THINKING

How many △ are there?

How many ☐ are there?
Are the ⬡ congruent?

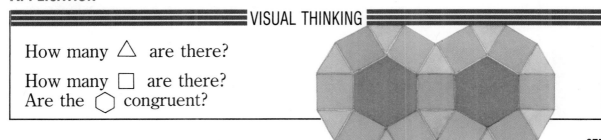

Line of Symmetry

Ronda made decorations for Valentine's day.

If each shape is folded along the dashed line, the two parts will match. Each shape has **symmetry.** The dashed line is a **line of symmetry.**

These shapes do not have symmetry.

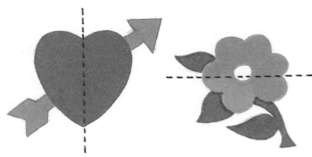

If each shape is folded along the dashed line, the two parts will not match.

CLASSWORK

Tell if each dashed line is a line of symmetry.

1.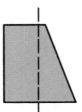

2.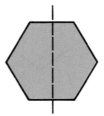

3.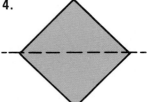

4.

5.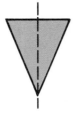

6.

7.

8.

Tell if each dashed line is a line of symmetry.

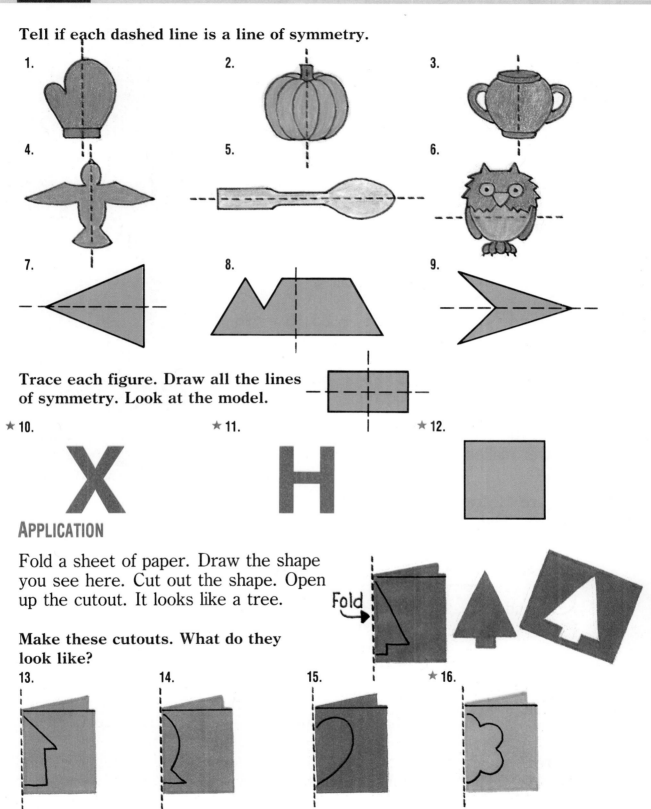

1.

2.

3.

4.

5.

6.

7.

8.

9.

Trace each figure. Draw all the lines of symmetry. Look at the model.

★ 10.

★ 11.

★ 12.

X

H

Fold a sheet of paper. Draw the shape you see here. Cut out the shape. Open up the cutout. It looks like a tree.

Fold

Make these cutouts. What do they look like?

13.

14.

15.

★ 16.

Problem Solving

GUESS AND TEST

At times you can guess an answer. Then you can test your guess. If you are wrong, you can change your guess and do another test.

1. Jay bought 2 frames. He spent $6.20. Which 2 frames did Jay buy?

Make a guess. Then test your guess.

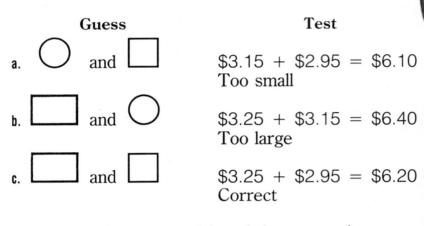

	Guess		Test
a.	◯ and ▢		$3.15 + $2.95 = $6.10 Too small
b.	▢ and ◯		$3.25 + $3.15 = $6.40 Too large
c.	▢ and ▢		$3.25 + $2.95 = $6.20 Correct

Jay bought the rectangular and the square frames. The answer makes sense. Together the frames cost $6.20.

2. There are 12 frames left, all circular or square. There are 2 more square than circular frames. How many square frames are there?

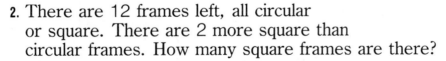

	Guess		Test
a.	6 ◯ and 6 ▢		6 + 6 = 12 The sum is correct, but the number of each is equal. Guess again.
b.	5 ◯ and 7 ▢		5 + 7 = 12 The sum is correct; there are 2 more square than circular frames. The guess is correct.

There are 7 square frames.
7 − 5 = 2   The answer makes sense.

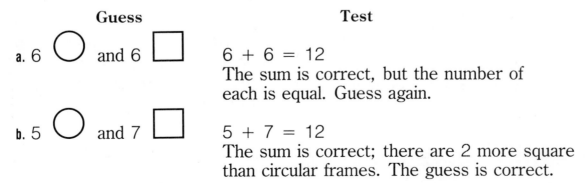

Guess; then test your guess to solve each problem.

1. In Luigi's Restaurant a circular table seats 4 people. A table that is rectangular seats 6 people. Luigi wants to seat 18 people. How can he do it?

2. Twenty-eight people are waiting for tables. Luigi wants to seat them at 5 tables. How can he seat them?

3. Luigi has 8 new tablecloths. All the tablecloths are circular or rectangular. He has 4 more circular than rectangular tablecloths. How many circular tablecloths does he have?

★ 4. Luigi's Restaurant has 15 rows of tables. All of the tables are rectangular or circular. There are 3 more rows of rectangular than circular tables. How many rows of rectangular tables are there?

CREATE YOUR OWN PROBLEM

Use the picture to write a guess-and-test problem.

Perimeter

Dora's father is making a pen for her dog, Chester. How much fencing will he use?

The **perimeter** is the distance around a figure.

▶ To find the perimeter, add the lengths of the sides.

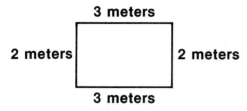

2 + 3 + 2 + 3 = 10

The perimeter of Chester's pen is 10 meters. Dora's father will use 10 meters of fencing.

Find the perimeter.

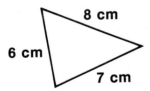

6 + 8 + 7 = 21
The perimeter is 21 centimeters.

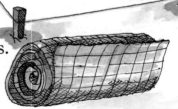

CLASSWORK

Find the perimeter of each figure.

1.
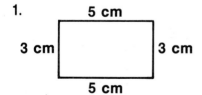

2.
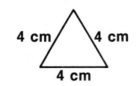

3.
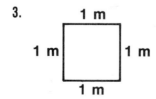

4.
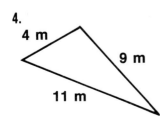

5.
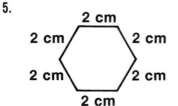

6.
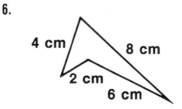

PRACTICE

Find the perimeter of each figure.

1.
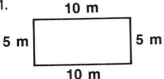

2.
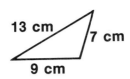

3.
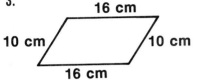

4.
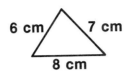

Use your centimeter ruler to measure each side. Then find the perimeter of each figure.

5.

6.
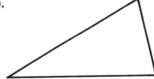

Find the length of the fourth side.

★7. The perimeter is 34 centimeters.

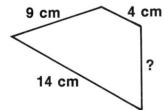

★8. The perimeter is 75 meters.

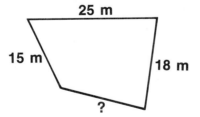

APPLICATION

MENTAL ARITHMETIC

Find the perimeter of a square with the following sides.

1. 5 meters
2. 10 meters
3. 12 meters
4. 8 meters
5. 40 centimeters
6. 100 centimeters

1. $643 + 179$

2. $805 - 276$

3. $21 + 9 + 17 = \square$

4. $85 - 39 = \square$

5. $9 \times 6 = \square$

6. $3 \times 8 = \square$

7. $15 \div 5 = \square$

8. $42 \div 6 = \square$

9. 7×8

10. 4×9

11. $8)\overline{72}$

12. $7)\overline{35}$

13. $\frac{1}{2}$ of $16 = \square$

14. $\frac{1}{4}$ of $20 = \square$

15. $\frac{1}{3}$ of $6 = \square$

16. $2 \times 40 = \square$

17. $3 \times 12 = \square$

18. $2 \times 26 = \square$

19. $14 \div 5 = \square$

20. $25 \div 8 = \square$

21. $527 \div 4 = \square$

Area

Tracy is using squares of carpeting to cover a floor. Each square is a **square unit.** How many squares of carpeting does Tracy need to cover the floor?

The **area** of a figure is the number of square units that cover the figure.

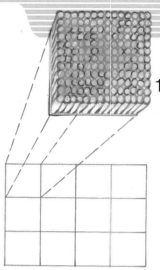
1 square unit

▶ To find the area, count the number of square units.

The area of Tracy's floor is 12 square units. Tracy needs 12 squares of carpeting to cover the floor.

More Examples

a.

b.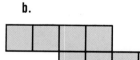

The area is
6 square units.

The area is
8 square units.

Find the area of each figure.

1.

2.

3.

4.

5.

6.

Find the area of each figure.

1.
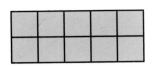

2.

3.
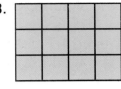

4.

5.

6.
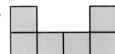

7.

8.
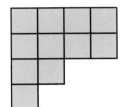

★9.
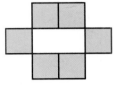

★10.

★11.

★12.
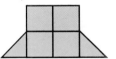

APPLICATION

13. A rectangular garden is 16 meters all around. No side is less than 3 meters. What are the lengths of the sides? Guess and test.

14. Find the area of the yard in the drawing.

15. Find the area of the garden.

★ 16. Find the area of the shed.

YARD

Shed ➡

Garden

Volume

Susan keeps a toy box under her bed. What is the volume of the toy box?

The unit used to measure volume is a cube. It is called a **cubic unit.**

The **volume** of a space figure is the number of cubic units that fit inside it.

▶ To find the volume, count the number of cubic units that fit inside a space figure.

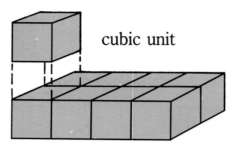

cubic unit

The volume of the toy box is 8 cubic units.

More Examples

a.

The volume is 4 cubic units.

b.

The volume is 10 cubic units.

CLASSWORK

Find the volume of each figure.

1.

2.

3.

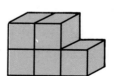

4.

5.

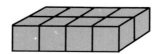

6.

Find the volume of each figure.

1.
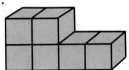

2.
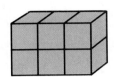

3.
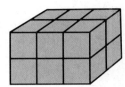

4.

5.
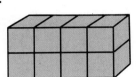

6.
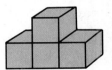

7.
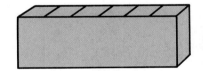

8.
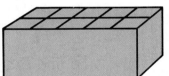

9.
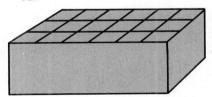

Find the volume. Each box has two layers.

★10.
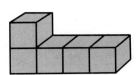

★11.
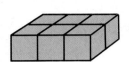

★12.
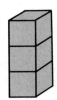

13. Randy uses these crayons. What is the volume of the box?

★14. Alicia keeps her pens in a box. She keeps her art paper in another box. Which box has the greater volume?

385

Ordered Pairs

This map shows Len's backyard. Where is Len's bicycle?

Start at 0.
Go 2 spaces to the right.

Go 5 spaces up.

Len's bicycle is at (2,5).

We call (2,5) an ordered pair of numbers.

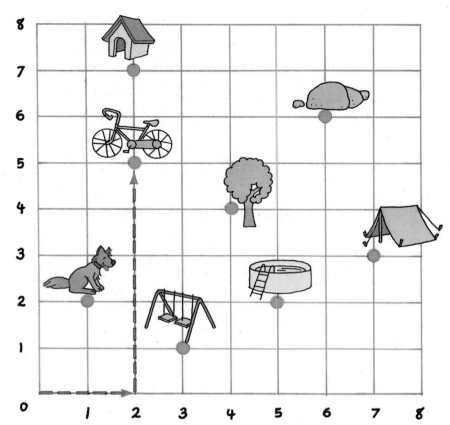

▶An **ordered pair** of numbers gives the location of a place on a map.

To find the tree:

    Start at 0.
    Go 4 spaces to the right.
    Go 4 spaces up.
    The tree is at (4,4).

To find Len's dog:

    Start at 0.
    Go 1 space to the right.
    Go 2 spaces up.
    Len's dog is at (1,2).

CLASSWORK

Use the map above to answer each question.

1. What ordered pair gives the location of the rock?

2. What ordered pair gives the location of the doghouse?

3. What ordered pair gives the location of the pool?

4. What is located at (3,1)?

5. What is located at (7,3)?

This map shows some of Brooke's favorite things.

Use the map to answer each question.

1. What ordered pair gives the location of the skateboard?

2. What ordered pair gives the location of the cat?

3. What ordered pair gives the location of the book?

4. What is located at (3,3)?

5. What is located at (4,5)?

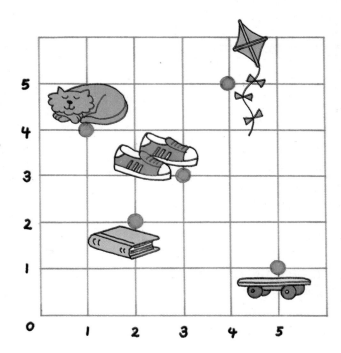

Trace the map. Locate each object at any point you choose. Then name the ordered pair.

★ 6. a beach ball   ★ 7. an apple   ★ 8. a flower

★ 9. a ring   ★ 10. a T-shirt

APPLICATION

Christine made a puzzle for her friend, Gerry. Find the letter for each ordered pair and read the hidden message.

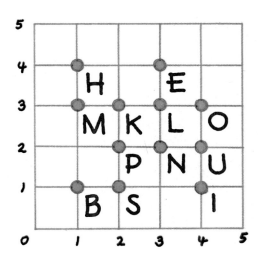

11. _____ _____ _____ _____ _____
    (2,1)   (1,3)   (4,1)   (3,3)   (3,4)

★ 12. Write the ordered pairs that spell LEMON.

★ 13. Write the ordered pairs that spell HELP US.

Problem Solving

SKILLS AND STRATEGIES REVIEW Using Shapes

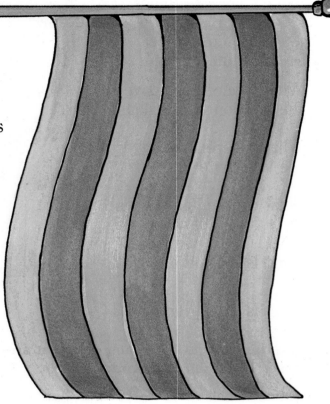

There was a contest in school for the best flag. Dena and Marvin won. Their flag has 4 yellow stripes and 3 blue stripes. Each stripe is 2 inches wide and 18 inches long.

1. How long is the flag?

2. How wide is the flag?

3. What shape is the flag?

Dena and Marvin made the stripes out of 2-inch-wide ribbon.

4. How many inches long was the yellow ribbon they used?

5. How many inches long was the blue ribbon they used?

6. The yellow ribbon sells for $1.00 per yard. Dena bought 2 yards. How much did she pay?

7. Dena and Marvin will make a flag twice as long as their first flag. How long will the new flag be?

Marcella's flag won a prize.

8. Marcella spent $5 on cloth for her flag. She spent $2 on blue cloth. She spent $1 on yellow cloth. How much did she spend on red cloth?

★9. What is the length of her flag?

★10. What is the width of her flag?

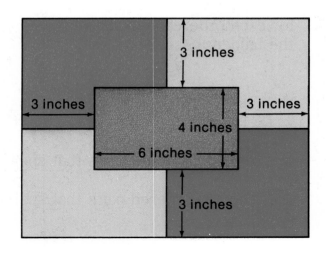

388

11. Mrs. Dahl bought 1 potholder. She spent $2.00. Which potholder did she buy?

12. Mr. Nolan has $1.50. What potholders can he buy with his money?

13. Jane bought 3 potholders of the same kind. She spent more than $1.00 but less than $2.00. Which kind did she buy?

★14. How many squares are there in the square potholder below?

★15. How many triangles are there in the triangular potholder below?

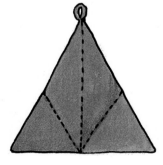

389

Name each figure. pages 368–373

1.

2.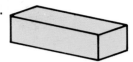

3.

4.

5.

6.

Tell if the figures are congruent. pages 374–375

7.

8.

9.

Tell if each dashed line is a line of symmetry. pages 376–377

10.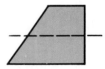

11.

12.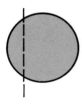

Find the perimeter.
pages 380–381

Find the area in square units.
pages 382–383

Find the volume in cubic units.
pages 384–385

13.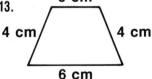
3 cm
4 cm / 4 cm
6 cm

14.

15.

Tell what the ordered pair means. pages 386–387

16. (5,2) Go _____ spaces to the right.
Go _____ spaces up.

Solve. pages 378–379, 388–389

17. A triangular banner in the Grant School cafeteria is 120 centimeters long on each side. What is the perimeter of the banner?

18. The perimeter of Ed's rectangular room is 12 meters. No side is less than 2 meters long. What are the lengths of the sides? Guess and test.

Name each figure.

1.

2.

3.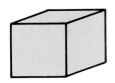

4.

5.

6.

Tell which figure is congruent to the first.

7.

a.

b.

c.

Tell if each dashed line is a line of symmetry.

8.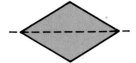

9.

10.

Find the perimeter.

11.
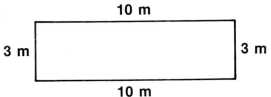
10 m
3 m   3 m
10 m

Find the area in square units.

12.

Find the volume in cubic units.

13.

Tell what the ordered pair means.

14. (7,3)
Go ___ spaces to the right.
Go ___ spaces up.

Solve.

15. A rectangle is 24 centimeters all around. No side is shorter than 5 centimeters. What are the lengths of the sides? Guess and test.

 Which pieces are congruent to A?

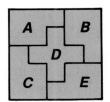

FLIPS, SLIDES, AND TURNS

We can move a geometric figure. The size and shape of the figure do not change.

One kind of move is a **flip.** Flip the figure over the dashed line. This gives a mirror image.

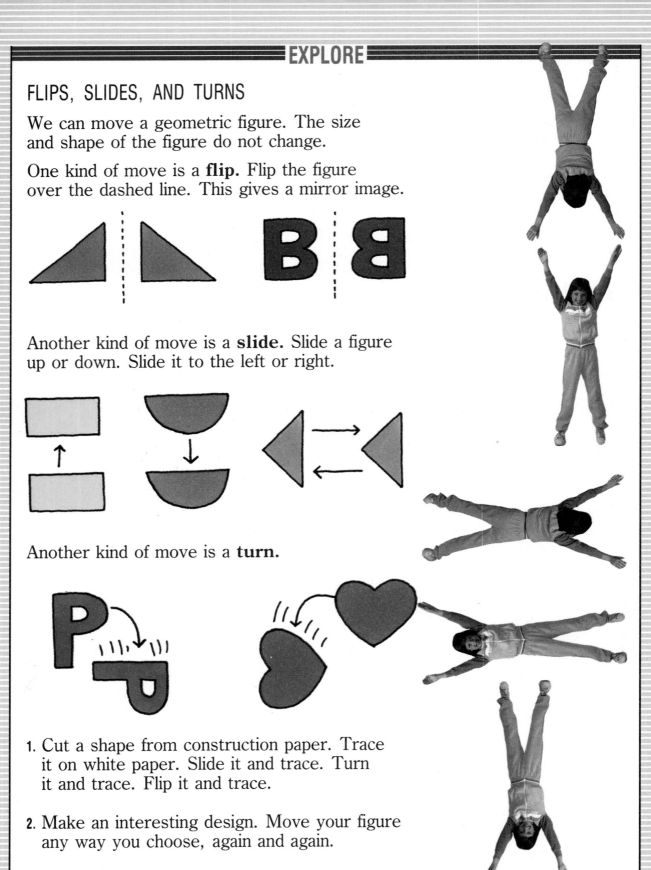

Another kind of move is a **slide.** Slide a figure up or down. Slide it to the left or right.

Another kind of move is a **turn.**

1. Cut a shape from construction paper. Trace it on white paper. Slide it and trace. Turn it and trace. Flip it and trace.

2. Make an interesting design. Move your figure any way you choose, again and again.

RIGHT ANGLES

A special kind of angle is a **right angle.**
A right angle is formed in any corner
of a square.

right
angle

We can find right angles in other figures, too.

right angle   right angle

Count the right angles in each figure.

4 right angles   1 right angle   1 right angle   2 right angles

Is the angle a right angle?

1.   2.   3.   4.

Count the right angles in each figure.

5.   6.   7.

8.   9.

INPUT STATEMENTS

In BASIC, we can use an INPUT statement to enter information while a program is running.

```
10 PRINT "PERIMETER OF A SQUARE"
20 PRINT "ENTER THE LENGTH OF A
SIDE"
30 INPUT S
40 LET P = S + S + S + S
50 PRINT "PERIMETER = "
60 PRINT P
70 END
```

The computer will display a question mark and wait for you to enter a number.

If we enter 7, the computer computes P and displays the output.

```
RUN
PERIMETER OF A SQUARE
ENTER THE LENGTH OF A SIDE
? 7
PERIMETER =
28
```

Use the program above. Tell what the output will be after entering each number.

1. 5   2. 13   3. 26   4. 30   5. 47

6. 3.1   7. 0.5   8. 19.2   9. 60   10. 20.4

Sometimes a program asks for two numbers.

The computer will display a question mark and wait for you to enter a number.

```
10 PRINT "PERIMETER OF A
   RECTANGLE"
20 PRINT "ENTER THE LENGTH"
30 INPUT L
40 PRINT "ENTER THE WIDTH"
50 INPUT W
60 LET P = L + W + L + W
70 PRINT "PERIMETER = "
80 PRINT P
90 END
```

When the program is RUN, a question mark is displayed, waiting for L.
When we enter 4, it continues.
When we enter 5, it computes P and displays the output.

```
RUN
PERIMETER OF A RECTANGLE
ENTER THE LENGTH
? 4
ENTER THE WIDTH
? 5
PERIMETER =
18
```

═ AT THE COMPUTER ═

1. Enter and RUN the program on page 394. Enter the numbers in 1–10.

2. Compare each output with your answers.

3. Enter and RUN the program on this page.

4. Compare the computer output with the one shown.

★5. On Your Own: Draw three rectangles. Measure the sides. Enter the measurements in the program above to find the perimeters.

===== FINAL REVIEW =====

Choose the correct answer. Write A, B, C, or D.

1. $4 + 3 + 2 = \square$

A 1   C 9

B 8   D not given

7. $6{,}992 - 6{,}354 = \square$

A 648   C 12,246

B 638   D not given

2. Choose the number for ninety-two thousand.

A 9,200   C 90,200

B 92,000   D not given

8. What time will it be in 25 minutes?

A 4:15   C 4:05

B 3:25   D not given

3. Compare. 874 ● 847

A >   C =

B <   D not given

9. What is the fourth month in the year?

A February   C March

B May   D not given

4. $765 + 847 = \square$

A 1,602   C 1,512

B 1,612   D not given

10. $4 \times 4 = \square$

A 8   C 0

B 16   D not given

5. Estimate. $412 + 167 = \square$

A 500   C 600

B 300   D not given

11. $0 \times 0 = \square$

A 1   C 2

B 10   D not given

6. $\$8.25 - \$2.49 = \square$

A $6.86   C $5.76

B $10.74   D not given

12. $8 \times 9 = \square$

A 64   C 72

B 17   D not given

Choose the correct answer. Write A, B, C, or D.

13. $45 \div 5 = \square$

  A 40   **C** 8

  B 9   **D** not given

19. $\frac{1}{3} = \frac{\square}{6}$

  A 1   **C** 3

  B 2   **D** not given

14. What is another fact in the family? $3 \times 5 = 15$

  A $3 + 5 = 8$ **C** $15 \div 3 = 5$

  B $15 - 3 = 12$ **D** not given

20. What is the mixed number?

  A $1\frac{1}{2}$ **C** $1\frac{1}{4}$

  B 2   **D** not given

15. $8\overline{)64}$

  A 8   **C** 7

  B 9   **D** not given

21. $2.6 + 1.7 = \square$

  A 4.3   **C** 3.3

  B 0.9   **D** not given

16. 1 kilometer = _____ meters

  A 10   **C** 100

  B 1,000   **D** not given

22. $4 \times 42 = \square$

  A 38   **C** 46

  B 168   **D** not given

17. 1,000 grams = _____ kilograms

  A 10   **C** 2

  B 100   **D** not given

23. $8 \times 17 = \square$

  A 96   **C** 136

  B 25   **D** not given

18. 1 liter = _____ milliliters

  A 100   **C** 1,000

  B 10   **D** not given

24. $5 \times 361 = \square$

  A 1,605   **C** 355

  B 1,805   **D** not given

Choose the correct answer. Write A, B, C, or D.

25. $49 \div 7 = \square$

A 42   C 7

B 8   D not given

26. $180 \div 3 = \square$

A 50   C 183

B 60   D not given

27. $84 \div 6 = \square$

A 14   C 78

B 8   D not given

28. $5\overline{)895}$

A 173   C 179

B 180   D not given

29. 1 yard = _____ inches

A 24   C 12

B 36   D not given

30. 1 pound = _____ ounces

A 16   C 4

B 12   D not given

31. 1 quart = _____ pints

A 2   C 4

B 1   D not given

32. At what temperature does water boil?

A 10°F   C 0°F

B 32°F   D not given

33. Name the figure.

A cone   C circle

B square   D not given

34. Are the figures congruent?

A yes   C no

B maybe   D not given

35. Find the perimeter.

5 cm / 2 cm / 2 cm / 5 cm

A 20 cm   C 12 cm

B 14 cm   D not given

Choose the correct answer. Write A, B, C, or D.

Use the picture for 36 and 37.

36. How much money does Dee have?

    A $1.15   C $1.10

    B $1.05   D not given

37. Dee spent 1 quarter, 1 dime, and 2 nickels. What coins does she have left?

    A 5 nickels   C 2 quarters, 2 nickels

    B 2 quarters, 1 dime, 2 nickels   D not given

Tell whether you would add or subtract in 38 and 39. Then solve.

38. Hal entered 3 calves, 6 piglets, and 2 lambs at the county fair. How many more piglets were there than lambs?

    A subtract; 1   C subtract; 4

    B add; 11   D not given

39. How many calves, piglets, and lambs were entered?

    A add; 11   C add; 9

    B subtract; 4   D not given

Which fact is missing in 40 and 41?

40. One half of the deer were along the edge of the lake. How many deer were there altogether near the edge of the lake?

    A one third of the deer   C one fourth of the deer

    B total number of deer   D not given

41. In a forest, there were 148 pine trees, 215 spruce trees, and some oak trees. How many trees were there altogether?

    A number of pine trees   C number of oak trees

    B number of spruce trees   D not given

Which fact is extra?

42. Asa wrote 3 postcards a day for 5 days. Then she went to the beach. How many postcards did she write in all?

    A Asa is on vacation.   C Then she went to the beach.

    B 8 postcards   D not given

Choose the correct answer. Write A, B, C, or D.

Solve.

43. Forty-seven people took a bus. Twelve got off. Then 9 got on. How many people are on the bus now?

A 44   C 34

B 24   D not given

44. Two sleeping bags cost $18.50 each. A tent costs $41.75. How much do all three things cost?

A $60.25   C $78.75

B $37.00   D not given

Make a drawing to solve **45** and **46.**

45. There are 3 buildings. Each building has 4 windows. Each window has 2 panes of glass. How many panes of glass are there altogether?

A 24   C 9

B 12   D not given

46. José lives farther from Bonnie than from Greg. Heather lives between Bonnie and Greg. Who lives farthest from José?

A Greg   C Bonnie

B Heather   D not given

Make a table to solve.

47. Jim was packing envelopes in boxes of 10. He had 60 envelopes. How many boxes did he fill?

A 70   C 50

B 6   D not given

Solve. Use guess and test.

I have 5 shapes, all squares or triangles. They have 17 sides in all.

48. How many squares do I have?

A 5   C 2

B 12   D not given

49. How many triangles do I have?

A 12   C 22

B 3   D not given

50. A ring cost $.75, a bracelet cost $1.30, and a barrette cost $1.75. Alice spent $2.05 for two items. Which two did she buy?

A ring and bracelet   C ring and barrette

B barrette and bracelet   D not given

SET 1   Find each sum.

pages 2–3

1. $6 + 2$	2. $0 + 8$	3. $6 + 1$	4. $1 + 4$	5. $3 + 4$	6. $5 + 5$	7. $1 + 6$
8. $5 + 1$	9. $1 + 2$	10. $0 + 5$	11. $8 + 0$	12. $2 + 1$	13. $2 + 6$	14. $4 + 5$

15. $4 + 4 = \square$ 16. $0 + 3 = \square$ 17. $3 + 3 = \square$ 18. $5 + 4 = \square$

19. $4 + 3 = \square$ 20. $4 + 1 = \square$ 21. $5 + 0 = \square$ 22. $1 + 9 = \square$

23. $9 + 1 = \square$ 24. $2 + 2 = \square$ 25. $1 + 5 = \square$ 26. $0 + 1 = \square$

SET 2   Find each sum.

pages 4–5

1. $3 + 2$ $2 + 3$	2. $6 + 0$ $0 + 6$	3. $1 + 3$ $3 + 1$	4. $2 + 7$ $7 + 2$
5. $1 + 7$ $7 + 1$	6. $2 + 8$ $8 + 2$	7. $0 + 9$ $9 + 0$	8. $2 + 5$ $5 + 2$
9. $7 + 3$ $3 + 7$	10. $2 + 4$ $4 + 2$	11. $5 + 3$ $3 + 5$	12. $6 + 3$ $3 + 6$

13. $6 + 4 = \square$ 14. $0 + 7 = \square$ 15. $8 + 1 = \square$ 16. $0 + 4 = \square$

$4 + 6 = \square$ $7 + 0 = \square$ $1 + 8 = \square$ $4 + 0 = \square$

SET 3   Add.

pages 6–7

1. $6 + 5$	2. $9 + 3$	3. $6 + 6$	4. $7 + 5$	5. $5 + 8$	6. $8 + 3$	7. $9 + 5$
8. $9 + 9$	9. $6 + 8$	10. $7 + 6$	11. $5 + 6$	12. $6 + 9$	13. $4 + 8$	14. $9 + 2$

15. $5 + 7 = \square$ 16. $8 + 4 = \square$ 17. $6 + 5 = \square$ 18. $7 + 7 = \square$

19. $9 + 7 = \square$ 20. $9 + 6 = \square$ 21. $7 + 8 = \square$ 22. $8 + 8 = \square$

23. $4 + 9 = \square$ 24. $7 + 4 = \square$ 25. $8 + 6 = \square$ 26. $9 + 8 = \square$

EXTRA PRACTICE

SET 1   Find each missing addend.

1. $\begin{array}{r} 6 \\ + \square \\ \hline 11 \end{array}$	2. $\begin{array}{r} \square \\ + 8 \\ \hline 17 \end{array}$	3. $\begin{array}{r} 8 \\ + \square \\ \hline 13 \end{array}$

1. $\begin{array}{r} 6 \\ +\ \square \\ \hline 11 \end{array}$
2. $\begin{array}{r} \square \\ +\ 8 \\ \hline 17 \end{array}$
3. $\begin{array}{r} 8 \\ +\ \square \\ \hline 13 \end{array}$
4. $\begin{array}{r} \square \\ +\ 9 \\ \hline 16 \end{array}$
5. $\begin{array}{r} 6 \\ +\ \square \\ \hline 14 \end{array}$
6. $\begin{array}{r} 9 \\ +\ \square \\ \hline 15 \end{array}$
7. $\begin{array}{r} 6 \\ +\ \square \\ \hline 15 \end{array}$

8. $\begin{array}{r} \square \\ +\ 6 \\ \hline 12 \end{array}$
9. $\begin{array}{r} 4 \\ +\ \square \\ \hline 9 \end{array}$
10. $\begin{array}{r} \square \\ +\ 2 \\ \hline 7 \end{array}$
11. $\begin{array}{r} 7 \\ +\ \square \\ \hline 10 \end{array}$
12. $\begin{array}{r} 3 \\ +\ \square \\ \hline 8 \end{array}$
13. $\begin{array}{r} \square \\ +\ 7 \\ \hline 16 \end{array}$
14. $\begin{array}{r} 9 \\ +\ \square \\ \hline 18 \end{array}$

15. $\begin{array}{r} 8 \\ +\ \square \\ \hline 17 \end{array}$
16. $\begin{array}{r} \square \\ +\ 4 \\ \hline 12 \end{array}$
17. $\begin{array}{r} \square \\ +\ 5 \\ \hline 14 \end{array}$
18. $\begin{array}{r} 8 \\ +\ \square \\ \hline 16 \end{array}$
19. $\begin{array}{r} 1 \\ +\ \square \\ \hline 7 \end{array}$
20. $\begin{array}{r} 4 \\ +\ \square \\ \hline 12 \end{array}$
21. $\begin{array}{r} \square \\ +\ 6 \\ \hline 13 \end{array}$

SET 2   Add.

1. $\begin{array}{r} 2 \\ 3 \\ +5 \\ \hline \end{array}$
2. $\begin{array}{r} 5 \\ 4 \\ +4 \\ \hline \end{array}$
3. $\begin{array}{r} 6 \\ 1 \\ +5 \\ \hline \end{array}$
4. $\begin{array}{r} 2 \\ 3 \\ +6 \\ \hline \end{array}$
5. $\begin{array}{r} 5 \\ 1 \\ +4 \\ \hline \end{array}$
6. $\begin{array}{r} 1 \\ 4 \\ +3 \\ \hline \end{array}$
7. $\begin{array}{r} 7 \\ 2 \\ +6 \\ \hline \end{array}$

8. $\begin{array}{r} 5 \\ 2 \\ +6 \\ \hline \end{array}$
9. $\begin{array}{r} 6 \\ 2 \\ +3 \\ \hline \end{array}$
10. $\begin{array}{r} 3 \\ 3 \\ +3 \\ \hline \end{array}$
11. $\begin{array}{r} 4 \\ 2 \\ +7 \\ \hline \end{array}$
12. $\begin{array}{r} 3 \\ 5 \\ +1 \\ \hline \end{array}$
13. $\begin{array}{r} 7 \\ 1 \\ +8 \\ \hline \end{array}$
14. $\begin{array}{r} 5 \\ 4 \\ +3 \\ \hline \end{array}$

15. $2 + 5 + 2 = \square$
16. $2 + 1 + 8 = \square$
17. $8 + 0 + 8 = \square$
18. $8 + 1 + 6 = \square$
19. $6 + 3 + 4 = \square$
20. $4 + 5 + 2 = \square$

SET 3   Find each difference.

1. $\begin{array}{r} 3 \\ -2 \\ \hline \end{array}$
2. $\begin{array}{r} 5 \\ -4 \\ \hline \end{array}$
3. $\begin{array}{r} 4 \\ -2 \\ \hline \end{array}$
4. $\begin{array}{r} 7 \\ -3 \\ \hline \end{array}$
5. $\begin{array}{r} 10 \\ -\ 4 \\ \hline \end{array}$
6. $\begin{array}{r} 8 \\ -3 \\ \hline \end{array}$
7. $\begin{array}{r} 9 \\ -5 \\ \hline \end{array}$

8. $\begin{array}{r} 7 \\ -5 \\ \hline \end{array}$
9. $\begin{array}{r} 6 \\ -3 \\ \hline \end{array}$
10. $\begin{array}{r} 5 \\ -2 \\ \hline \end{array}$
11. $\begin{array}{r} 8 \\ -6 \\ \hline \end{array}$
12. $\begin{array}{r} 9 \\ -3 \\ \hline \end{array}$
13. $\begin{array}{r} 10 \\ -\ 7 \\ \hline \end{array}$
14. $\begin{array}{r} 8 \\ -4 \\ \hline \end{array}$

15. $9 - 7 = \square$
16. $7 - 4 = \square$
17. $10 - 3 = \square$
18. $8 - 5 = \square$
19. $10 - 6 = \square$
20. $6 - 2 = \square$
21. $9 - 9 = \square$
22. $7 - 0 = \square$
23. $6 - 1 = \square$
24. $10 - 1 = \square$
25. $9 - 0 = \square$
26. $9 - 2 = \square$

SET 1 Subtract.
pages 16–17

1. $12 - 7$ 2. $13 - 5$ 3. $13 - 6$ 4. $11 - 2$ 5. $12 - 8$ 6. $11 - 6$

7. $11 - 7$ 8. $11 - 5$ 9. $13 - 8$ 10. $12 - 5$ 11. $13 - 9$ 12. $12 - 4$

13. $12 - 9 = \square$ 14. $11 - 8 = \square$ 15. $12 - 6 = \square$ 16. $13 - 9 = \square$

17. $12 - 3 = \square$ 18. $13 - 10 = \square$ 19. $12 - 0 = \square$ 20. $11 - 6 = \square$

21. $11 - 2 = \square$ 22. $11 - 9 = \square$ 23. $13 - 9 = \square$ 24. $13 - 4 = \square$

SET 2 Subtract.
pages 18–19

1. $14 - 7$ 2. $15 - 9$ 3. $14 - 5$ 4. $16 - 7$ 5. $15 - 8$ 6. $13 - 7$

7. $14 - 6$ 8. $15 - 7$ 9. $16 - 7$ 10. $14 - 9$ 11. $16 - 8$ 12. $17 - 9$

13. $15 - 6$ 14. $14 - 8$ 15. $17 - 8$ 16. $11 - 8$ 17. $12 - 5$ 18. $13 - 8$

19. $12 - 6 = \square$ 20. $11 - 7 = \square$ 21. $13 - 6 = \square$ 22. $12 - 8 = \square$

23. $17 - 9 = \square$ 24. $15 - 9 = \square$ 25. $16 - 9 = \square$ 26. $18 - 9 = \square$

SET 3 Add or subtract. Watch the signs.
pages 22–23

1. $9 + 3$ $3 + 9$ $12 - 9$ $12 - 3$ 2. $15 - 6$ $15 - 9$ $9 + 6$ $6 + 9$

3. $11 - 4$ $11 - 7$ $7 + 4$ $4 + 7$ 4. $8 + 5$ $5 + 8$ $13 - 5$ $13 - 8$

Give other facts in each family.

5. $8 + 6 = 14$ 6. $10 - 6 = 4$ 7. $6 + 3 = 9$ 8. $13 - 9 = 4$

9. $8 + 7 = 15$ 10. $14 - 9 = 5$ 11. $8 + 3 = 11$ 12. $10 - 3 = 7$

SET 1 Write the number. pages 34–35

1. 6 tens 7 ones   2. 2 tens 1 one   3. 1 ten 2 ones

4. 8 tens 4 ones   5. 9 tens 5 ones   6. 4 tens 3 ones

7. 3 tens 7 ones   8. 5 tens 1 one   9. 7 tens 5 ones

10. seventy-seven   11. nineteen   12. forty-eight

13. fifty-nine   14. thirty-six   15. sixty-three

16. ninety-four   17. seventy-eight   18. eighty-seven

SET 2 Write the number. pages 36–37

1. 3 hundreds 8 tens 5 ones   2. 7 hundreds 1 ten 8 ones

3. 500 + 10 + 5   4. 800 + 50 + 4

5. four hundred thirty-three   6. seven hundred eight

7. one hundred eleven   8. nine hundred eighteen

Give the value of the digit 2 in each number.

9. 258   10. 602   11. 12   12. 128   13. 25

Give the value of the digit 7 in each number.

14. 379   15. 647   16. 741   17. 173   18. 748

SET 3 Write the missing numbers. pages 38–39

1. 136, 137, ___, ___, ___   2. 90, ___, ___, 120, ___

3. ___, 300, ___, ___, 600   4. ___, ___, ___, 351, 352

Give the number that comes just before and the
number that comes just after.

5. 29   6. 199   7. 72   8. 235

SET 1   Compare. Write > or < for ●.   pages 40–41

1. 168 ● 165   2. 79 ● 81   3. 582 ● 528   4. 67 ● 76

5. 54 ● 45   6. 889 ● 898   7. 53 ● 39   8. 285 ● 258

9. 26 ● 29   10. 63 ● 61   11. 491 ● 419   12. 280 ● 208

13. 110 ● 101   14. 238 ● 229   15. 535 ● 543   16. 319 ● 321

SET 2   Write the amount. Use a dollar sign and decimal point.   pages 42–43

1. four dollars and eighty cents   2. six dollars and six cents

3. ninety-nine cents   4. eight dollars and nineteen cents

5. one dollar and sixty-one cents   6. fifty-eight cents

7. 6 dollars 7 dimes   8. 1 dollar 8 pennies

9. 4 dimes 5 pennies   10. 9 dollars 6 dimes

SET 3   Round to the nearest ten.   pages 46–47

1. 14   2. 27   3. 46   4. 81   5. 44   6. 36

7. 59   8. 87   9. 13   10. 66   11. 55   12. 24

13. 48   14. 91   15. 39   16. 68   17. 73   18. 67

19. 43   20. 64   21. 75   22. 34   23. 92   24. 19

SET 4   Round to the nearest hundred.   pages 48–49

1. 371   2. 249   3. 668   4. 490   5. 329

6. 770   7. 838   8. 674   9. 556   10. 932

11. 283   12. 410   13. 633   14. 875   15. 145

EXTRA PRACTICE

SET 1   Write the number. pages 50–51

1. 6 thousands 0 hundreds 5 tens 2 ones

2. 3,000 + 500 + 90 + 6

3. one thousand, six hundred two

4. 7,000 + 200 + 80

5. nine thousand, ninety-nine

6. one thousand, seven hundred

7. three thousand, five hundred forty-three

8. 4,000 + 900 + 40 + 7

9. four thousand, thirty

10. seven thousand, sixty-five

Give the value of the digit 6 in each number.

11. 561   12. 8,006   13. 2,677   14. 6,910   15. 699

SET 2   Write > or < for ●. pages 52–53

1. 3,209 ● 2,895   2. 1,546 ● 1,571   3. 7,366 ● 7,356

4. 9,952 ● 9,592   5. 8,767 ● 8,966   6. 988 ● 1,001

7. 3,343 ● 3,434   8. 2,878 ● 2,788   9. 5,005 ● 4,595

10. 8,169 ● 8,168   11. 2,076 ● 2,267   12. 4,530 ● 4,503

SET 3   Write the number. pages 54–55

1. seventy-seven thousand, seventy-seven

2. fifty thousand, nine hundred eleven

3. two hundred eighteen thousand, forty-nine

4. six hundred six thousand, one hundred twenty

5. three hundred forty thousand, fifty

Give the value of the digit 9 in each number.

6. 293,850   7. 966,248   8. 511,319   9. 489,702

SET 1 Add.
pages 64–65

1. 25
   +40

2. 14
   + 5

3. 68
   +21

4. 76
   +10

5. 25
   +30

6. 11
   +66

7. 13
   +51

8. 32
   +41

9. 51
   + 2

10. 52
   +23

11. 36
   + 1

12. 22
   + 6

13. 7 + 32 = ☐

14. 21 + 31 = ☐

15. 17 + 41 = ☐

16. 64 + 1 = ☐

17. 2 + 93 = ☐

18. 40 + 7 = ☐

19. 40 + 37 = ☐

20. 26 + 13 = ☐

21. 11 + 27 = ☐

SET 2 Add. Check by adding up.
pages 66–67

1. 43
   +28

2. 84
   + 6

3. 79
   +16

4. 17
   +29

5. 36
   +44

6. 25
   +28

7. 32
   +38

8. 56
   +26

9. 13
   +27

10. 9
   +32

11. 37
   +14

12. 24
   +36

13. 37 + 46 = ☐

14. 59 + 5 = ☐

15. 8 + 27 = ☐

16. 19 + 34 = ☐

17. 28 + 42 = ☐

18. 29 + 63 = ☐

19. 65 + 18 = ☐

20. 49 + 25 = ☐

21. 58 + 36 = ☐

SET 3 Add. Check by adding up.
pages 68–69

1. 46
   +92

2. 31
   +71

3. 82
   +73

4. 24
   +85

5. 93
   +50

6. 75
   +92

7. 62
   +62

8. 68
   +81

9. 62
   +47

10. 72
   +75

11. 90
   +99

12. 75
   +33

13. 30 + 82 = ☐

14. 58 + 61 = ☐

15. 91 + 73 = ☐

16. 98 + 61 = ☐

17. 94 + 82 = ☐

18. 76 + 63 = ☐

19. 71 + 87 = ☐

20. 84 + 93 = ☐

21. 67 + 72 = ☐

SET 1 **Add. Check by adding up.** pages 70–71

1. 86 +15	2. 65 +66	3. 89 +23	4. 96 +47	5. 65 +96	6. 78 +35
7. 46 +84	8. 52 +58	9. 89 +91	10. 48 +77	11. 69 +87	12. 29 +85

Add.

13. $35 + 79 = \Box$ 14. $23 + 98 = \Box$ 15. $98 + 52 = \Box$

16. $43 + 78 = \Box$ 17. $37 + 85 = \Box$ 18. $68 + 57 = \Box$

SET 2 **Add mentally. Then write the answer.** pages 72–73

1. 4 +3	14 + 3	24 + 3	34 + 3	2. 8 +5	18 + 5	28 + 5	38 + 5
3. 7 +6	17 + 6	27 + 6	37 + 6	4. 9 +3	19 + 3	29 + 3	39 + 3

5. $5 + 2 = \Box$ 6. $8 + 3 = \Box$ 7. $9 + 6 = \Box$
   $15 + 2 = \Box$ $18 + 3 = \Box$ $19 + 6 = \Box$
   $25 + 2 = \Box$ $28 + 3 = \Box$ $29 + 6 = \Box$
   $35 + 2 = \Box$ $38 + 3 = \Box$ $39 + 6 = \Box$

SET 3 **Add. Check by adding up.** pages 74–75

1. 21 6 +12	2. 34 20 +13	3. 15 22 +31	4. 7 14 +32	5. 40 26 +18	6. 21 63 + 8
7. 45 11 +42	8. 61 15 + 2	9. 34 20 +21	10. 77 50 + 2	11. 13 25 +10	12. 42 17 +81

13. $9 + 60 + 43 = \Box$ 14. $49 + 36 + 52 = \Box$ 15. $75 + 94 + 30 = \Box$

SET 1 Add. Check by adding up.   pages 78–79

1.	2.	3.	4.	5.
362 +133	158 +529	243 +506	802 +476	281 +223

6.	7.	8.	9.	10.
737 24 +100	128 47 +313	656 121 + 22	283 55 +620	741 234 +522

11. $409 + 213 = \square$ 12. $68 + 208 = \square$ 13. $573 + 204 = \square$

SET 2 Add. Check by adding up.   pages 80–81

1.	2.	3.	4.	5.
373 +287	367 +344	881 +274	572 +863	694 +542

6.	7.	8.	9.	10.
457 22 +253	848 506 + 32	906 46 +931	85 320 +813	591 94 +410

11.	12.	13.	14.	15.
245 46 +421	527 69 +703	301 475 + 82	53 304 +841	130 706 +563

16. $34 + 786 = \square$ 17. $369 + 365 = \square$ 18. $292 + 670 + 29 = \square$

SET 3 Add. Check by adding up.   pages 82–83

1.	2.	3.	4.	5.
755 +489	369 +638	491 +989	675 +526	207 +897

6.	7.	8.	9.	10.
29 652 +830	676 34 +975	183 292 +936	425 705 +895	687 710 +336

11.	12.	13.	14.	15.
7 344 +853	72 406 +535	9 43 +951	327 963 +833	648 763 +952

16. $226 + 795 = \square$ 17. $821 + 679 = \square$ 18. $379 + 782 = \square$

EXTRA PRACTICE

SET 1 Add. Check by adding up.

1. $3{,}552$
$+5{,}234$

2. $2{,}435$
$+6{,}401$

3. $4{,}301$
$+3{,}618$

4. $9{,}289$
$+2{,}610$

5. $4{,}534$
$+1{,}058$

6. $6{,}108$
$+4{,}593$

7. $5{,}082$
$+3{,}637$

8. $7{,}038$
$+9{,}404$

9. $2{,}067$
$+2{,}269$

10. $3{,}785$
$+9{,}547$

11. $9{,}475 + 324 = \square$

12. $902 + 6{,}321 = \square$

13. $3{,}781 + 5{,}050 = \square$

14. $603 + 3{,}598 = \square$

15. $6{,}493 + 807 = \square$

16. $2{,}468 + 7{,}532 = \square$

SET 2 Add. Check by adding up.

pages 86–87

1. $\$.42$
$+ \ .34$

2. $\$5.19$
$+ \ 2.77$

3. $\$8.07$
$+ \ 8.60$

4. $\$43.73$
$+ \ 29.46$

5. $\$27.93$
$+ \ 32.65$

6. $\$.30$
$.19$
$+ \ .31$

7. $\$7.05$
$.37$
$+ \ .92$

8. $\$7.68$
9.08
$+ \ 5.15$

9. $\$39.37$
30.21
$+ \ 6.00$

10. $\$53.00$
42.66
$+ \ 21.14$

11. $\$4.06 + \$1.72 = \square$

12. $\$3.48 + \$2.52 = \square$

13. $\$.89 + \$4.36 = \square$

14. $\$3.57 + \$9.48 = \square$

SET 3 Round to the nearest ten and estimate each sum.

pages 88–89

1. 57
$+32$

2. 46
$+91$

3. 48
$+68$

4. 31
$+15$

5. 28
$+34$

6. $42 + 15 = \square$

7. $22 + 56 = \square$

8. $46 + 73 = \square$

9. $57 + 14 = \square$

10. $25 + 66 = \square$

11. $66 + 74 = \square$

Round to the nearest hundred and estimate each sum.

12. 383
$+165$

13. 180
$+271$

14. 297
$+561$

15. 783
$+605$

16. 932
$+532$

17. $504 + 285 = \square$

18. $110 + 733 = \square$

19. $761 + 679 = \square$

20. $749 + 255 = \square$

21. $309 + 337 = \square$

22. $467 + 443 = \square$

SET 1 Subtract.

pages 102–103

1. $\begin{array}{r}28\\-7\\\hline\end{array}$
2. $\begin{array}{r}45\\-23\\\hline\end{array}$
3. $\begin{array}{r}36\\-25\\\hline\end{array}$
4. $\begin{array}{r}73\\-12\\\hline\end{array}$
5. $\begin{array}{r}96\\-80\\\hline\end{array}$
6. $\begin{array}{r}29\\-17\\\hline\end{array}$

7. $\begin{array}{r}47\\-21\\\hline\end{array}$
8. $\begin{array}{r}68\\-36\\\hline\end{array}$
9. $\begin{array}{r}26\\-4\\\hline\end{array}$
10. $\begin{array}{r}65\\-30\\\hline\end{array}$
11. $\begin{array}{r}79\\-53\\\hline\end{array}$
12. $\begin{array}{r}97\\-32\\\hline\end{array}$

13. $\begin{array}{r}35\\-13\\\hline\end{array}$
14. $\begin{array}{r}76\\-34\\\hline\end{array}$
15. $\begin{array}{r}89\\-5\\\hline\end{array}$
16. $\begin{array}{r}41\\-20\\\hline\end{array}$
17. $\begin{array}{r}59\\-38\\\hline\end{array}$
18. $\begin{array}{r}99\\-26\\\hline\end{array}$

19. $69 - 3 = \square$
20. $81 - 20 = \square$
21. $95 - 62 = \square$

SET 2 Subtract.

pages 104–105

1. $\begin{array}{r}31\\-8\\\hline\end{array}$
2. $\begin{array}{r}53\\-16\\\hline\end{array}$
3. $\begin{array}{r}26\\-19\\\hline\end{array}$
4. $\begin{array}{r}95\\-89\\\hline\end{array}$
5. $\begin{array}{r}51\\-32\\\hline\end{array}$
6. $\begin{array}{r}80\\-42\\\hline\end{array}$

7. $\begin{array}{r}57\\-38\\\hline\end{array}$
8. $\begin{array}{r}78\\-29\\\hline\end{array}$
9. $\begin{array}{r}62\\-3\\\hline\end{array}$
10. $\begin{array}{r}80\\-67\\\hline\end{array}$
11. $\begin{array}{r}73\\-56\\\hline\end{array}$
12. $\begin{array}{r}46\\-38\\\hline\end{array}$

13. $\begin{array}{r}47\\-29\\\hline\end{array}$
14. $\begin{array}{r}52\\-24\\\hline\end{array}$
15. $\begin{array}{r}83\\-9\\\hline\end{array}$
16. $\begin{array}{r}60\\-18\\\hline\end{array}$
17. $\begin{array}{r}74\\-28\\\hline\end{array}$
18. $\begin{array}{r}32\\-17\\\hline\end{array}$

19. $84 - 55 = \square$
20. $63 - 47 = \square$
21. $71 - 38 = \square$

22. $34 - 16 = \square$
23. $61 - 25 = \square$
24. $50 - 13 = \square$

SET 3 Subtract. Check by adding.

pages 106–107

1. $\begin{array}{r}547\\-136\\\hline\end{array}$
2. $\begin{array}{r}838\\-426\\\hline\end{array}$
3. $\begin{array}{r}592\\-81\\\hline\end{array}$
4. $\begin{array}{r}760\\-350\\\hline\end{array}$
5. $\begin{array}{r}944\\-643\\\hline\end{array}$

6. $\begin{array}{r}138\\-27\\\hline\end{array}$
7. $\begin{array}{r}809\\-308\\\hline\end{array}$
8. $\begin{array}{r}361\\-141\\\hline\end{array}$
9. $\begin{array}{r}727\\-314\\\hline\end{array}$
10. $\begin{array}{r}638\\-405\\\hline\end{array}$

11. $248 - 126 = \square$
12. $749 - 225 = \square$
13. $791 - 460 = \square$

14. $438 - 227 = \square$
15. $644 - 331 = \square$
16. $871 - 520 = \square$

17. $943 - 610 = \square$
18. $749 - 407 = \square$
19. $588 - 571 = \square$

EXTRA PRACTICE

SET 1   Subtract. Check by adding.   pages 108–109

1.	741 − 27	2.	564 − 392	3.	328 − 219	4.	949 − 258	5.	291 − 73
6.	351 − 146	7.	488 − 369	8.	626 − 242	9.	582 − 367	10.	859 − 476

11. $146 - 76 = \square$ 12. $713 - 221 = \square$ 13. $425 - 132 = \square$

SET 2   Subtract.   pages 110–111

1.	428 − 79	2.	243 − 175	3.	956 − 379	4.	684 − 187	5.	573 − 284
6.	360 − 275	7.	512 − 476	8.	971 − 683	9.	391 − 97	10.	471 − 282

11. $462 - 85 = \square$ 12. $746 - 558 = \square$ 13. $632 - 368 = \square$

SET 3   Subtract.   pages 112–113

1.	300 − 83	2.	501 − 124	3.	700 − 437	4.	530 − 182	5.	908 − 671
6.	800 − 458	7.	706 − 53	8.	600 − 225	9.	400 − 276	10.	900 − 858

11. $200 - 71 = \square$ 12. $807 - 468 = \square$ 13. $990 - 326 = \square$

SET 4   Subtract.   pages 116–117

1.	1,854 − 723	2.	4,752 − 541	3.	9,675 − 2,543	4.	3,788 − 1,436	5.	5,834 − 3,421
6.	2,803 − 441	7.	8,317 − 5,506	8.	4,296 − 2,077	9.	6,370 − 3,145	10.	7,927 − 2,445

11. $1,775 - 964 = \square$ 12. $5,724 - 4,391 = \square$

13. $7,841 - 3,457 = \square$ 14. $4,386 - 2,327 = \square$

SET 1 Subtract.

pages 118–119

1.	2.	3.	4.	5.
2,149 − 625	7,409 − 7,072	6,874 − 2,935	8,920 − 3,074	9,163 − 5,204

6.	7.	8.	9.	10.
4,825 − 1,689	1,453 − 955	5,305 − 3,429	4,407 − 2,370	5,976 − 1,789

11. $5,708 − 2,640 = \square$ 12. $9,457 − 5,108 = \square$ 13. $3,409 − 1,536 = \square$

SET 2 Subtract. Check by adding.

pages 120–121

1.	2.	3.	4.	5.
$1.47 − .84	$6.73 − 1.85	$15.29 − 9.57	$9.24 − 2.43	$60.68 − 16.91

6.	7.	8.	9.	10.
$20.77 − 13.21	$5.76 − 2.50	$79.91 − 61.32	$50.24 − 29.69	$84.80 − 53.92

11. $\$5.41 − \$2.64 = \square$ 12. $\$38.79 − \$8.38 = \square$

SET 3 Round to the nearest hundred and estimate each difference.

pages 122–123

1.	2.	3.	4.	5.
326 − 188	906 − 544	760 − 312	925 − 695	554 − 477

6.	7.	8.	9.	10.
481 − 360	840 − 623	372 − 147	891 − 759	749 − 380

11. $522 − 369 = \square$ 12. $864 − 478 = \square$ 13. $668 − 210 = \square$

SET 4 Add or subtract.

pages 124–125

1.	2.	3.	4.	5.
48 + 48	67 − 32	$7.65 + .31	841 − 73	601 + 386

6.	7.	8.	9.	10.
2,432 − 924	8,076 + 881	3,876 − 1,609	$68.37 + 16.76	5,404 − 2,083

11. $\$2.09 − \$.65 = \square$ 12. $2,498 + 5,650 = \square$ 13. $9,685 − 3,419 = \square$

14. $\$3.21 − \$1.23 = \square$ 15. $\$7.00 − \$5.61 = \square$

SET 1 Write each time, using numbers.   pages 134–139

1.   2.   3.   4.

5.   6.   7.   8.

Tell how much time has passed.

9. start   2:00   10. start   7:15   11. start   9:00
   end   4:00   end   7:50   end   12:00

12. start 6:00   13. start   8:05   14. start   5:00
    end   6:45   end   8:25   end   9:00

SET 2 Which unit would you use to measure the time?
         Choose minute or hour.   pages 140–141

1. brushing your hair   2. writing a sentence

3. singing a song   4. visiting a museum

5. making your bed   6. brushing the dog

7. watching a movie   8. taking a shower

SET 3 Use the calendar on page 142 to answer
         each question.   pages 142–143

1. What is the date of the second Sunday?

2. What is the date of the fourth Monday?

3. What is the date of the third Wednesday?

4. What is the date of the fifth Tuesday?

5. What is the date of the first Thursday?

SET 1 **Write the value. Use a dollar sign and decimal point.** pages 146–149, 152–153

1. 15 pennies

2. 3 quarters

3. 6 nickels

4. 7 dimes

5. 2 half dollars

6. 11 nickels

7. 1 dollar, 1 quarter, 2 dimes

8. 1 ten-dollar bill, 3 quarters, 1 nickel

9. 4 five-dollar bills, 1 quarter, 9 pennies

Compare. Use > or < for ●.

10. $8.69 ● $8.68

11. $1.80 ● $2.00

12. $3.28 ● $3.82

13. $6.00 ● $7.30

SET 2 **Use the pictograph to answer each question.** pages 154–155

The drama club put on the play *Winnie-the-Pooh.*
This pictograph shows how many students from
each grade saw the play.

NUMBER OF STUDENTS WHO SAW <u>WINNIE-THE-POOH</u>	
First graders	𝙭 𝙭 𝙭 𝙭 𝙭
Second graders	𝙭 𝙭 𝙭 𝙭 𝙭 𝙭
Third graders	𝙭 𝙭 𝙭 𝙭
Fourth graders	𝙭 𝙭 𝙭

Each 𝙭 stands for 2 children.

1. How many second graders saw
the play?

2. Which grade had the most
students who saw the play?

3. Which grade had the least
number of students who saw
the play?

4. Did more first graders or second
graders see the play?

EXTRA PRACTICE

SET 1 **Find each product.**

pages 168–177, 184–185

1. $\begin{array}{r} 2 \\ \times 5 \\ \hline \end{array}$
2. $\begin{array}{r} 5 \\ \times 4 \\ \hline \end{array}$
3. $\begin{array}{r} 3 \\ \times 9 \\ \hline \end{array}$
4. $\begin{array}{r} 4 \\ \times 9 \\ \hline \end{array}$
5. $\begin{array}{r} 6 \\ \times 3 \\ \hline \end{array}$
6. $\begin{array}{r} 3 \\ \times 4 \\ \hline \end{array}$
7. $\begin{array}{r} 5 \\ \times 7 \\ \hline \end{array}$

8. $\begin{array}{r} 6 \\ \times 6 \\ \hline \end{array}$
9. $\begin{array}{r} 6 \\ \times 9 \\ \hline \end{array}$
10. $\begin{array}{r} 4 \\ \times 5 \\ \hline \end{array}$
11. $\begin{array}{r} 2 \\ \times 3 \\ \hline \end{array}$
12. $\begin{array}{r} 3 \\ \times 3 \\ \hline \end{array}$
13. $\begin{array}{r} 2 \\ \times 4 \\ \hline \end{array}$
14.

15. $9 \times 2 = $ ■
16. $7 \times 6 = \square$
17. $8 \times 6 = \square$
18. $7 \times 2 = \square$

SET 2 **Find each product.**

pages 180–181, 186–191

1. $\begin{array}{r} 8 \\ \times 8 \\ \hline \end{array}$
2. $\begin{array}{r} 7 \\ \times 5 \\ \hline \end{array}$
3. $\begin{array}{r} 9 \\ \times 2 \\ \hline \end{array}$
4. $\begin{array}{r} 0 \\ \times 4 \\ \hline \end{array}$
5. $\begin{array}{r} 7 \\ \times 9 \\ \hline \end{array}$
6. $\begin{array}{r} 8 \\ \times 6 \\ \hline \end{array}$
7. $\begin{array}{r} 1 \\ \times 2 \\ \hline \end{array}$

8. $9 \times 9 = \square$
9. $7 \times 8 = \square$
10. $5 \times 9 = \square$
11. $9 \times 1 = \square$

SET 3 **Multiply.**

pages 182–183

1. $\begin{array}{r} 3 \\ \times 7 \\ \hline \end{array}$ $\begin{array}{r} 7 \\ \times 3 \\ \hline \end{array}$
2. $\begin{array}{r} 1 \\ \times 8 \\ \hline \end{array}$ $\begin{array}{r} 8 \\ \times 1 \\ \hline \end{array}$
3. $\begin{array}{r} 4 \\ \times 6 \\ \hline \end{array}$ $\begin{array}{r} 6 \\ \times 4 \\ \hline \end{array}$
4. $\begin{array}{r} 5 \\ \times 8 \\ \hline \end{array}$ $\begin{array}{r} 8 \\ \times 5 \\ \hline \end{array}$

5. $\begin{array}{r} 0 \\ \times 9 \\ \hline \end{array}$ $\begin{array}{r} 9 \\ \times 0 \\ \hline \end{array}$
6. $\begin{array}{r} 3 \\ \times 6 \\ \hline \end{array}$ $\begin{array}{r} 6 \\ \times 3 \\ \hline \end{array}$
7. $\begin{array}{r} 2 \\ \times 7 \\ \hline \end{array}$ $\begin{array}{r} 7 \\ \times 2 \\ \hline \end{array}$
8. $\begin{array}{r} 4 \\ \times 7 \\ \hline \end{array}$ $\begin{array}{r} 7 \\ \times 4 \\ \hline \end{array}$

9. $8 \times 2 = \square$
   $2 \times 8 = \square$
10. $6 \times 1 = \square$
    $1 \times 6 = \square$
11. $8 \times 3 = \square$
    $3 \times 8 = \square$

SET 4 **Answer each question.**

pages 204–209

1. How many groups of 6?

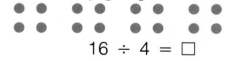

   $12 \div 6 = \square$

2. How many groups of 4?

   $16 \div 4 = \square$

Find each quotient.

3. $4 \div 2 = \square$
4. $12 \div 2 = \square$
5. $8 \div 2 = \square$
6. $10 \div 2 = \square$

7. $14 \div 2 = \square$
8. $18 \div 2 = \square$
9. $6 \div 2 = \square$
10. $16 \div 2 = \square$

11. $24 \div 3 = \square$
12. $9 \div 3 = \square$
13. $15 \div 3 = \square$
14. $27 \div 3 = \square$

SET 1   Divide.   pages 210–215

1. $12 \div 4 = \Box$ 2. $20 \div 4 = \Box$ 3. $32 \div 4 = \Box$ 4. $8 \div 4 = \Box$

5. $16 \div 4 = \Box$ 6. $24 \div 4 = \Box$ 7. $35 \div 5 = \Box$ 8. $10 \div 5 = \Box$

9. $25 \div 5 = \Box$ 10. $20 \div 5 = \Box$ 11. $15 \div 5 = \Box$ 12. $40 \div 5 = \Box$

13. $8 \div 1 = \Box$ 14. $5 \div 5 = \Box$ 15. $0 \div 7 = \Box$ 16. $9 \div 9 = \Box$

SET 2   Find each quotient.   pages 220–225

1. $7\overline{)7}$ 2. $7\overline{)42}$ 3. $6\overline{)18}$ 4. $7\overline{)35}$ 5. $6\overline{)48}$

6. $6\overline{)42}$ 7. $7\overline{)63}$ 8. $7\overline{)56}$ 9. $6\overline{)24}$ 10. $7\overline{)14}$

11. $30 \div 6 = \Box$ 12. $28 \div 7 = \Box$ 13. $36 \div 6 = \Box$ 14. $49 \div 7 = \Box$

SET 3   Divide.   pages 226–229

1. $8\overline{)32}$ 2. $9\overline{)72}$ 3. $8\overline{)24}$ 4. $9\overline{)63}$ 5. $8\overline{)40}$

6. $64 \div 8 = \Box$ 7. $9 \div 9 = \Box$ 8. $16 \div 8 = \Box$ 9. $81 \div 9 = \Box$

SET 4   Draw a bar of each length.   pages 242–245, 248–251

1. 5 centimeters   2. 7 centimeters   3. 3 centimeters

4. 9 centimeters   5. 1 centimeter   6. 10 centimeters

Choose cm, m, or km to measure each.

7. height of a giraffe   8. length of a truck

9. length of a grasshopper   10. distance an airplane travels

11. length of a highway   12. length of a comb

Compare. Use >, <, or = for ●.

1. 1 kilogram ● 1 gram   2. 5,000 grams ● 5 kilograms

3. 200 milliliters ● 2 liters   4. 7,000 milliliters ● 70 liters

EXTRA PRACTICE

SET 1 Read the Celsius temperature on each. pages 252–253

1.
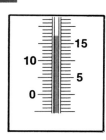

2.
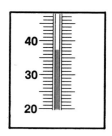

3.
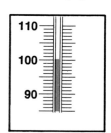

SET 2 Write a fraction for the red part. pages 262–263, 266–267

1.
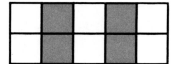

2.
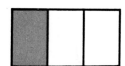

3.
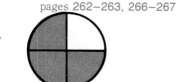

Complete the fractions.

4.
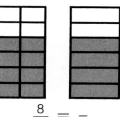
$$\frac{8}{12} = \frac{}{6}$$

5.
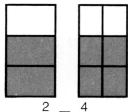
$$\frac{2}{3} = \frac{4}{}$$

6.
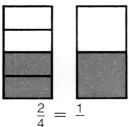
$$\frac{2}{4} = \frac{1}{}$$

SET 3 Compare the fractions. Write > or <. pages 268–269

1.
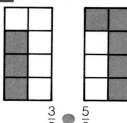
$$\frac{3}{8} \ \bullet\ \frac{5}{8}$$

2.
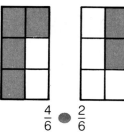
$$\frac{4}{6} \ \bullet\ \frac{2}{6}$$

3.
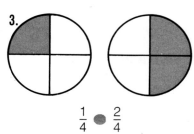
$$\frac{1}{4} \ \bullet\ \frac{2}{4}$$

SET 4 Use the chart on page 270 to write >, <, or =. pages 270–271

1. $\frac{1}{4} \ \bullet\ \frac{1}{3}$

2. $\frac{3}{4} \ \bullet\ \frac{4}{6}$

3. $\frac{1}{2} \ \bullet\ \frac{3}{5}$

4. $\frac{5}{10} \ \bullet\ \frac{1}{2}$

5. $\frac{1}{3} \ \bullet\ \frac{2}{10}$

6. $\frac{1}{5} \ \bullet\ \frac{1}{2}$

7. $\frac{2}{10} \ \bullet\ \frac{1}{5}$

8. $\frac{2}{3} \ \bullet\ \frac{1}{2}$

SET 1 **Complete.** pages 274–275

1. $\frac{1}{2}$ of 12 = ☐   2. $\frac{1}{4}$ of 16 = ☐   3. $\frac{1}{7}$ of 35 = ☐

4. $\frac{1}{6}$ of 54 = ☐   5. $\frac{1}{9}$ of 18 = ☐   6. $\frac{1}{6}$ of 42 = ☐

7. $\frac{1}{8}$ of 32 = ☐   8. $\frac{1}{5}$ of 30 = ☐   9. $\frac{1}{3}$ of 24 = ☐

SET 2 **Write the mixed number for the part that is red.** pages 276–277

1. 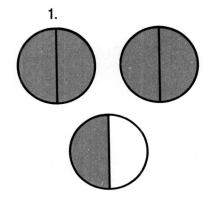   2. 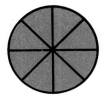   3.

SET 3 **Write a decimal for each.** pages 278–281

1. $\frac{8}{10}$ 2. $\frac{3}{10}$ 3. $\frac{5}{10}$ 4. $\frac{7}{10}$ 5. $\frac{1}{10}$

6. $2\frac{5}{10}$ 7. $6\frac{1}{10}$ 8. $4\frac{3}{10}$ 9. $8\frac{4}{10}$ 10. $9\frac{9}{10}$

11. two tenths   12. four tenths   13. six tenths

14. three and seven tenths   15. eight and one tenth

SET 4 **Add or subtract.** pages 282–283

1. $\begin{array}{r} 2.4 \\ +7.3 \end{array}$ 2. $\begin{array}{r} 6.8 \\ -1.5 \end{array}$ 3. $\begin{array}{r} 19.6 \\ +14.3 \end{array}$ 4. $\begin{array}{r} 21.4 \\ +\ 8.6 \end{array}$ 5. $\begin{array}{r} 25.6 \\ +\ 4.8 \end{array}$

6. $\begin{array}{r} 15.5 \\ -\ 9.5 \end{array}$ 7. $\begin{array}{r} 3.3 \\ -3.2 \end{array}$ 8. $\begin{array}{r} 82.7 \\ +10.6 \end{array}$ 9. $\begin{array}{r} 48.5 \\ -24.8 \end{array}$ 10. $\begin{array}{r} 71.1 \\ -38.7 \end{array}$

11. 8.5 − 3.7 = ☐   12. 23.9 + 12.7 = ☐   13. 67.2 − 38.5 = ☐

EXTRA PRACTICE

SET 1 Multiply.

pages 296–299

1. 7×5 2. 6×8 3. 9×3 4. 4×3 5. 8×7 6. 6×9

7. 30×5 8. 80×4 9. 70×6 10. 200×9 11. 800×8 12. 500×5

13. $6 \times 90 = \square$ 14. $8 \times 50 = \square$ 15. $9 \times 80 = \square$

16. $2 \times 400 = \square$ 17. $6 \times 600 = \square$ 18. $4 \times 700 = \square$

19. $7 \times 300 = \square$ 20. $3 \times 800 = \square$ 21. $6 \times 900 = \square$

SET 2 Multiply.

pages 300–301, 304–305

1. 34×2 2. 11×5 3. 58×0 4. 33×3 5. 96×1

6. 47×2 7. 13×5 8. 19×3 9. 35×2 10. 16×2

11. $2 \times 42 = \square$ 12. $4 \times 22 = \square$ 13. $3 \times 23 = \square$

14. $2 \times 27 = \square$ 15. $6 \times 15 = \square$ 16. $3 \times 29 = \square$

17. $6 \times 14 = \square$ 18. $4 \times 24 = \square$ 19. $2 \times 37 = \square$

SET 3 Multiply.

pages 306–309

1. 39×3 2. 53×8 3. 68×5 4. 87×7 5. 75×4

6. 62×6 7. 16×9 8. 92×7 9. 34×6 10. 57×2

11. 281×6 12. 423×4 13. 520×9 14. 913×5 15. 852×3

16. $7 \times 213 = \square$ 17. $2 \times 607 = \square$ 18. $6 \times 421 = \square$

19. $3 \times 646 = \square$ 20. $8 \times 141 = \square$ 21. $5 \times 109 = \square$

SET 1 Divide.

pages 318–323

1. $15 \div 3 = \square$ 2. $30 \div 6 = \square$ 3. $45 \div 5 = \square$ 4. $81 \div 9 = \square$

5. $28 \div 4 = \square$ 6. $48 \div 8 = \square$ 7. $56 \div 7 = \square$ 8. $42 \div 6 = \square$

9. $2\overline{)11}$ 10. $5\overline{)35}$ 11. $3\overline{)23}$ 12. $4\overline{)31}$ 13. $6\overline{)26}$

14. $4\overline{)29}$ 15. $2\overline{)19}$ 16. $6\overline{)57}$ 17. $7\overline{)35}$ 18. $9\overline{)75}$

19. $8\overline{)58}$ 20. $7\overline{)25}$ 21. $9\overline{)81}$ 22. $8\overline{)50}$ 23. $7\overline{)59}$

SET 2 Divide.

pages 326–329

1. $60 \div 2 = \square$ 2. $40 \div 2 = \square$ 3. $90 \div 3 = \square$ 4. $100 \div 5 = \square$

5. $50 \div 2 = \square$ 6. $88 \div 4 = \square$ 7. $72 \div 6 = \square$ 8. $52 \div 4 = \square$

9. $2\overline{)400}$ 10. $7\overline{)700}$ 11. $3\overline{)600}$ 12. $3\overline{)900}$ 13. $4\overline{)800}$

14. $3\overline{)57}$ 15. $5\overline{)75}$ 16. $4\overline{)64}$ 17. $5\overline{)85}$ 18. $4\overline{)84}$

19. $2\overline{)92}$ 20. $3\overline{)63}$ 21. $2\overline{)58}$ 22. $6\overline{)78}$ 23. $3\overline{)75}$

24. $6\overline{)66}$ 25. $6\overline{)84}$ 26. $6\overline{)90}$ 27. $3\overline{)96}$ 28. $4\overline{)60}$

SET 3 Divide.

pages 330–333

1. $37 \div 3 = \square$ 2. $66 \div 4 = \square$ 3. $54 \div 5 = \square$ 4. $87 \div 6 = \square$

5. $62 \div 5 = \square$ 6. $93 \div 9 = \square$ 7. $483 \div 4 = \square$ 8. $269 \div 2 = \square$

9. $698 \div 4 = \square$ 10. $713 \div 5 = \square$ 11. $546 \div 3 = \square$ 12. $987 \div 8 = \square$

13. $8\overline{)98}$ 14. $4\overline{)75}$ 15. $6\overline{)83}$ 16. $5\overline{)68}$ 17. $2\overline{)31}$

18. $7\overline{)93}$ 19. $3\overline{)58}$ 20. $7\overline{)794}$ 21. $6\overline{)650}$ 22. $4\overline{)598}$

SET 1   Draw a bar for each length.

pages 344–349

1. 4 in.
2. 5 in.
3. $1\frac{1}{2}$ in.
4. 6 in.
5. $2\frac{1}{4}$ in.

6. $6\frac{1}{4}$ in.
7. $3\frac{1}{2}$ in.
8. $7\frac{1}{4}$ in.
9. $9\frac{1}{2}$ in.
10. 8 in.

Choose ft, yd, mi, oz, or lb to measure each.

11. the width of a desk

12. the length of a baseball field

13. the weight of an apple

14. the distance a bus travels

15. the height of a person

16. the weight of a bicycle

SET 2   Complete.

pages 352–355

1. 1 pt = ___ c
2. 1 qt = ___ pt
3. 1 gal = ___ qt

4. 4 c = ___ qt
5. 2 c = ___ pt
6. 8 qt = ___ gal

7. 4 qt = ___ gal
8. 1 qt = ___ c
9. 2 pt = ___ qt

Read the Fahrenheit temperature shown on each.

10.
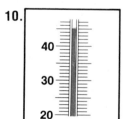

11.
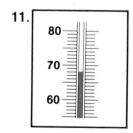

12.
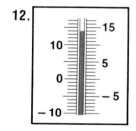

SET 3   Use the table to answer each question.

pages 356–359

1. How many times was red picked?

2. How many times was blue picked?

3. How many times was green picked?

4. How many times was yellow picked?

5. Which color was picked most often?

MARBLES PICKED FROM A BAG	
Red	Yellow
卌 |||	卌 卌 卌
Green	Blue
卌	卌 卌	

SET 1   Name each space or plane figure.

pages 368–373

1.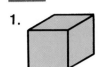

2.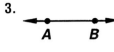

3.
A   B

4.
C   D

5.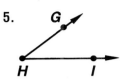
G
H   I

SET 2   Tell whether each pair of figures is congruent.

pages 374–377

1.

2.

Tell whether the dashed line is a line of symmetry.

3.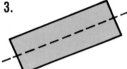

4.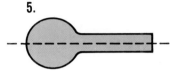

5.

SET 3   Find the perimeter of each figure.

pages 380–385

1.   12 m
4 m [   ] 4 m
      12 m

2.   7 cm
7 cm [   ] 7 cm
         7 cm

3.   15 cm
9 cm /   \
         17 cm

Find the area or volume of each figure.

4.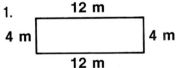

5.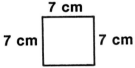

6.

pages 386–387

SET 4   Use the graph to answer each question.

1. What ordered pair gives the location of the star?

2. What ordered pair gives the location of the square?

3. What is located at (2,5)?

4. What is located at (5,3)?

5. What is located at (3,4)?

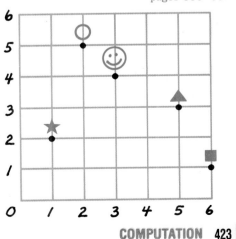

EXTRA PRACTICE

SET 1   Look at the picture. Solve each problem.

pages 12–13

1. Whose name has the fewest letters?

2. Which names have the same number of letters?

3. In all, how many letters are in the students' names?

4. How many more letters are in Robyn's name than in Sam's?

SET 2   Look at the picture. Solve each problem.

pages 24–25

1. How much do the balloon and the ball cost?

2. Which costs more, the boat or the crayon?

3. How much more does the balloon cost than the crayon?

4. How much do the boat, crayon, and ball cost in all?

SET 3   Read the problem. Tell whether you would add or subtract. Then solve each problem.

pages 44–45

1. Ride tickets are 13¢ for adults and 7¢ for children. How much do 2 children's tickets cost?

2. Mrs. Silbey bought a ticket for 13¢. She gave the cashier 15¢. How much change did she receive?

3. Mitchell had 10¢. He found a dime on the ground. How much money did he have then?

4. How much more is an adult's ticket than a child's ticket?

5. Gina had a dime. She bought a child's ticket. How much money did she have then?

6. Mr. Gallo took his son on the ride. How much did he pay for the tickets?

SET 1   Solve each problem.

pages 56–57

1. Glue costs 98¢ at the school store. Markers cost $1.05. Which costs more?

2. Guesses for "Beans in the Jar" had to be rounded to the nearest hundred. Marc thought there were 872 beans. To what number did he round his guess?

3. Stephanie has 1 dollar, 3 dimes, and 4 pennies. Carrie has 15 dimes. Who has more money?

4. Cheryl scored 3,125 points on the beanbag toss. Ben scored 2,986 points. Who scored higher?

SET 2   Tell what is missing in each problem.

pages 76–77

1. Ruth is 8 hours older than Paula. How old is Ruth?

2. Ed has 2 dimes and 3 nickels. Can he buy a bag of peanuts?

3. Mr. and Mrs. Carty took their two sons to a movie. Adult tickets cost $4.00. How much did Mr. Carty pay for tickets?

4. Marielle earns 14 stickers on Monday and 35 stickers on Tuesday. How many stickers did she earn during the whole week of school?

5. The Green Sox won 3 baseball games last week. How many did they lose?

6. Jon and Robert are twins. How old were they 3 years ago?

7. Sam's yard has 16 oak trees and some elm trees. How many trees are there in all?

8. Gene picked 42 apples. He made some apple pies. How many apples did he use in each pie?

SET 3   Solve each problem.

pages 90–91

1. The Book Fair sold 352 books on Monday and 447 books on Tuesday. To the nearest hundred, how many books were sold on both days?

2. The Book Fair sold 74 game books, and 139 puzzle books. How many books were sold in all?

3. Jesse bought a book about trains. Samantha's book about reptiles cost $2.25 more. How much did Samantha's book cost?

4. Mrs. Minkoff's class scored 987 points on field day. Mr. Jones' class scored 1,423, and Ms. Lee's class scored 2,021. Whose class scored the most points?

SET 1 Read the problem. Tell which fact is extra.
Then solve each problem.

pages 114–115

1. Danny had $10.00, Judy had
$15.25, and Jan had $6.75. How
much did Judy and Jan have
together?

2. Michael had 32 cows, 17
chickens, and 9 goats. How many
cows and chickens were there in
all?

3. Alyson picked 319 cherries. She
ate 38. Leon picked 287 cherries.
How many cherries did Alyson
have left?

4. A package sent overnight by
Super Express costs $25.00.
Quick Mail charges $10.75. How
much does it cost to send 2
packages by Quick Mail?

SET 2 Tell which facts are missing or which are extra. Make up
a fact if it is missing, then solve each problem.

pages 126–127

1. Shallah sold 116 raisin cookies
and 89 oatmeal cookies at the
fair. She also sold 320 cartons of
juice. How many more raisin
cookies were sold than oatmeal
cookies?

2. Adria sold 29 more raisin cookies
than oatmeal cookies. How many
raisin cookies did she sell?

3. Raisin cookies cost 35¢ and
oatmeal cookies cost 29¢. How
much money did Adam collect?

4. Jessica spent $4.89 and Dorothy
spent $2.50 at the fair. Ethel
spent $6.00. How much did
Jessica and Dorothy spend
altogether?

SET 3 Find and complete each pattern.

pages 144–145

1. ○△○△△○△△△ _ _ _ _ _ _

2. 100, 95, 90, 85, __, __, __

3. YYYY, YYYX, _____, YXXX, XXXX

4. 1, 10, 2, 9, 3, 8, __, __, __, __

5. ■ ○ ▶ ❑ ◐ ▼ ■ __ __ __ __

6. 9 + 6, 8 + 5, ____, 6 + 3, ____, 4 + 1

7. 20, 22, 25, 29, 34, __, __, __,

8. C, B, A, D, E, F, __, __, __

SET 1   You have 95¢ to spend. Use the information
in the table to solve each problem.   pages 158–159

Item	Price
Pencil	25¢
Eraser	40¢
Ruler	50¢
Package of paper	60¢

1. Can you buy both a ruler and paper?

2. Can you buy both a package of paper and 1 pencil?

3. Can you buy 2 erasers?

4. Can you buy 3 different items?

SET 2   Find the pattern and solve each problem.   pages 178–179

1. The zoo pandas are fed every 3 hours. The first feeding is at 10:15 A.M. What are the times of the next 3 feedings?

2. Thor works with the monkeys every other day beginning with Monday. What are the next two days that Thor works with the monkeys?

3. For the bird show, the parrots are lined up by color. The first bird is blue, the next two are red, the fourth bird is yellow, and the fifth bird is green. If this pattern repeats, what color will the tenth and eleventh birds be?

4. Scout patches are sold in the gift shop for $1.00 each. Two patches are sold for $.95 each. Three patches are sold for $.90 each. Follow the pattern. How much will each of four patches cost?

SET 3   Use the price list to solve each problem.   pages 194–195

1. Lois bought 2 popcorns and 2 juices. How much did she spend?

2. Carmen bought one of each item. How much did he spend?

3. Rita bought 1 popcorn and 1 juice. How much change did she receive from $1.00?

4. Which cost more, 4 fruits or 3 juices? How much more?

PRICE LIST	
Popcorn	60¢
Juice	35¢
Fruit	25¢

SET 1 Solve each problem.

pages 218–219

1. The storekeeper had 50 erasers. He sold 7 erasers to Ken and 5 to Maryann. How many erasers does the storekeeper have left?

2. Rainbow stickers were 25¢ each or 5 for $1.00. How many stickers can Michelle buy for $4.50?

3. Carrie bought 4 jars of paint for her art project. Each jar cost $1.50. How much change did Carrie receive from $10.00?

4. Sonia bought 3 coloring books for 59¢ each and 8 crayons for 15¢ each. How much did she spend?

5. Fresh corn was 3 ears for 50¢. How much did Mrs. Thorpe pay for a dozen ears?

6. Marbles cost 2 for 25¢. Luis had a dollar. He bought 6 marbles. How much money does he have left?

SET 2 Solve each problem.

pages 232–233

1. Mark Bird can build a deck in 3 days. How many decks can he build in 18 days?

2. Mark buys boards that are 8 feet long. He needs 72 feet of boards to make a deck. How many boards does he need to buy?

3. Each step from the deck to the ground costs $7. The Smythe's deck needs 9 steps. How much will the Smythes have to pay for the steps?

4. Nails are sold in boxes of 100 for $2.25. Mark needs 250 nails for a deck. How much will he spend on nails?

SET 3 Experiment to solve each problem.

pages 246–247

1. A teacher's desk is 1 meter wide. Will it fit through the door of your classroom?

2. A cat weighs about 4 kilograms. How many books would it take to make 4 kilograms?

3. There is a long chalkboard in the classroom. It took 19 children standing side by side to measure across the board. About how many meters would that be?

4. A "Super Pencil" at the school store is 55 centimeters long. How much longer is this than a regular school pencil?

EXTRA PRACTICE

SET 1 Use the table to solve each problem.

pages 254–255

Animal	Height in Centimeters
Ape	258
Dog	66
Giraffe	647
Cat	43
Canary	15
Horse	154

1. What is the difference in height between an ape and a cat?

2. Which two animals are the closest in height?

3. What is the sum of the heights of the dog, the canary, and the cat?

4. Which two animals together equal a height of 220 cm?

5. What is the difference between the tallest and shortest animal?

SET 2 Make a drawing to help solve each problem.

pages 272–273

1. Stuart had a piece of string 23 in. long. He cut the string into two pieces. One piece was 9 in. long. How long is the other piece?

2. Sam and Mitch each got a large glass of apple juice. Sam drank $\frac{3}{4}$ of his glass. Mitch drank $\frac{2}{3}$ of his glass. Who drank more juice?

3. Shirley bought 4 boxes of apples. Each box had 6 apples. How many apples did Shirley have?

4. Pat had 21 marbles. She shared the marbles with 2 of her friends. How many marbles does each child have?

SET 3 Use the table below to solve each problem.

pages 284–285

Item	Number Sold
Postcards	△ △ △ △
Tee shirts	△ △ △
Mugs	△ △
Posters	△
Pencils	△ △ △ △ △

△ = 100 items

1. How many mugs were sold?

2. What item sold the most?

3. How many items were sold in all?

4. How many more postcards were sold than tee shirts?

5. How many pencils and postcards were sold?

PROBLEM SOLVING **429**

SET 1   Solve each problem.

pages 302–303

1. Mr. Kou ordered 30 cans of punch for a party. He ordered 12 cans of grape and 6 cans of orange. The rest were cherry. How many cans of cherry did he order?

2. Ms. Noel started reading groups at 9:30 A.M. They lasted 1 hour and 45 minutes. Then she took the class to music for 45 minutes. What time was it then?

3. Sally put ribbon around the 4 sides of an art project. Each side was 20 cm long. How much ribbon did she need?

4. Mrs. Rosen bought 24 pencils at 2¢ each. She also bought 7 erasers at 5¢ each. How much did she spend in all?

SET 2   Use the picture to solve each problem.

pages 310–311

1. Alice sold 3 sub sandwiches. How much will she make?

2. Howard bought a peanut butter and jelly sandwich and a salad. He gave Alice $5.00. How much change did he get?

3. If Alice sells all of the fruit plates, how much will she make?

4. Alice sold 2 salads. Then she sold $\frac{1}{2}$ of the salads that were left. How many salads did Alice sell?

SET 3   Use the table to solve each problem.

pages 324–325

1. Who read the most books?

2. How many more books did Adam read than Jane?

3. What is the difference between the most books read and the fewest books read?

4. Marilyn read the same number of books in June. What is her total for the 2 months?

BOOKS READ IN MAY	
Student	Books Read
Adam	17
Bob	22
Jane	10
Ken	5
Marilyn	13
Marsha	26

SET 1   Use the table to solve each problem.   pages 334–335

SMITTY'S WEATHER CALENDAR					
Days	February	March	April	May	June
Sunny days	19	23	16	11	25
Rainy days	9	8	14	20	5

1. What month has the fewest days?

2. What month had the most rain?

3. Which month had 5 times as many sunny days as rainy days?

4. How many more rainy days were there in April than in February?

SET 2   Use a model to solve each problem.   pages 350–351

1. Sal finished the race in 36 seconds. Sam took 19 seconds longer than Sal. Jen took 24 seconds longer than Sam. How long did Jen take to run the race?

2. Jan and Dean collected shells at the beach. Dean found 24 shells. Jan found half as many shells as Dean. How many shells did Jan find?

3. Mako swam 18 laps in the pool. Ed swam twice as many laps. Mindy swam 7 laps less than Ed. How many laps did Mindy swim?

4. Judy made a large meat loaf. She cut it into fourths. She cut each fourth in half. How many pieces of meat loaf were there?

SET 3   Solve each problem.   pages 360–361

1. Guy went on a 5-day fishing trip. He caught 10 fish the first day, 4 fish 3 other days, and 6 fish the last day. How many fish did Guy catch in all?

2. If Guy had not fished on the last day, would he have caught more than 20 fish?

3. If Guy had caught twice as many fish on the first day, what would be his 5-day total?

4. If Guy had not fished on the third day, how many fish would he have caught?

5. Guy's father caught 1 less fish than Guy on each of the first and last days. How many fish did he catch on those two days?

6. His father caught 1 more fish than Guy on each of the other 3 days. How many fish did Guy's father catch in all?

EXTRA PRACTICE

SET 1 Use guess and test to solve each problem.

pages 378–379

1. Rachel has 25 blocks. All are rectangles or squares. She has 9 more squares than rectangles. How many of each does she have?

2. Emma has a quilt of 32 squares of cloth. The squares are either red or blue. She has 3 times as many blue as red squares. How many of each color are there?

3. Roy bought a kite for 37¢. He gave the clerk 13 coins. All were nickels or pennies. How many of each coin did he use?

4. Rex tossed 5 number cubes. All the cubes were either 4s or 5s. Rex's total was 22. How many 4s and 5s were there?

SET 2 Use the table to solve each problem.

pages 388–389

1. Gina bought 1 triangle and 4 squares. How much did she pay?

2. Matt made a design 11 cm wide. Which 3 shapes did he buy?

3. Aaron spent $2.65 on his design. Which 3 shapes did he buy?

4. Marcie bought 2 shapes. Her design was 8 cm wide. She spent $1.46. What did she buy?

PLASTIC SHAPES		
Shape	Cost	Width
△	$.59	3 cm
□	$.73	4 cm
○	$.96	5 cm

SET 3 Use the graph to solve each problem.

pages 388–389

SUNNY DAYS	
February	✳ ✳ ✳ ✳ ✳
April	✳ ✳ ✳ ✳ ✳ ✳ ✳ ✳
June	✳ ✳ ✳ ✳ ✳ ✳ ✳ ✳ ✳
August	✳ ✳ ✳ ✳ ✳ ✳ ✳ ✳ ✳ ✳
October	✳ ✳ ✳ ✳ ✳ ✳ ✳
December	✳ ✳ ✳ ✳ ✳ ✳

✳ = 3 days

1. Which month has more sunny days, April or October?

2. How many sunny days does June have?

3. How many more sunny days are there in August than in December?

4. How many sunny days are there in the 6 months in the graph?

Glossary

addends The numbers that are added.
Example: 7 + 8 = 15
The addends are 7 and 8.

addition An operation on two or more numbers to find the sum.
Example: 4 + 2 + 3 = 9
The sum is 9.

angle Two rays with a common endpoint.
Example:

area The number of square units needed to cover a region.

bar graph A graph with bars of different lengths to show information.

BASIC A computer language.

circle A closed figure. All the points of a circle are the same distance from a point called the center.

congruent figures Figures that have the same size and shape.

cube A space figure with six square faces.
Example:

customary system A measurement system that measures length in inches, feet, yards, and miles; capacity in cups, pints, quarts, and gallons; weight in ounces, pounds, and tons; and temperature in degrees Fahrenheit. *See* Table of Measures.

cylinder A space figure with two bases that are congruent circles.
Example:

decimal A number with places to the right of a decimal point.
Examples: 0.4, 1.8

degree Celsius (°C) A unit for measuring temperature in the metric system.

degree Fahrenheit (°F) A unit for measuring temperature in the customary system.

denominator The number below the bar in a fraction.
Example: $\frac{2}{5}$
The denominator is 5.

difference The answer in subtraction.
Example: 9 − 4 = 5
The difference is 5.

digit Any of the symbols used to write numbers: 0, 1, 2, 3, 4, 5, 6, 7, 8, and 9.

dividend The number to be divided.
Example: $6\overline{)36}$ or 36 ÷ 6
The dividend is 36.

divisible A number is divisible by another number if the remainder is zero after dividing.

division An operation on two numbers that results in a quotient.

divisor The number by which another number is to be divided.
Example: $7\overline{)28}$ or 28 ÷ 7
The divisor is 7.

edge The segment where two faces of a space figure meet.
Example:

END The last line in a BASIC computer program.

ENTER The function that instructs the computer to accept and process the information. It is also called RETURN.

equal (=) A symbol that means "has the same value as."

equivalent fractions Fractions that name the same number.
Example: $\frac{1}{2}$ and $\frac{2}{4}$

estimate To use an approximate rather than an exact answer.

even number A number that has 0, 2, 4, 6, or 8 in ones place.

face A flat surface of a space figure.

fact family Related facts using the same numbers.
Example: 2 + 3 = 5   5 − 3 = 2
3 + 2 = 5   5 − 2 = 3

factors The numbers that are multiplied to give a product.
Example: 3 × 5 = 15
The factors are 3 and 5.

flowchart A diagram that shows a step-by-step way to solve a problem.

fraction A number that names part of a whole or a group.
Examples: $\frac{1}{2}$, $\frac{2}{3}$, $\frac{6}{8}$ are fractions.

graph A drawing used to show information.

greater than (>) The symbol used to compare two numbers when the greater number is written first.
Examples: 7 > 3, 9 > 6

grouping property of addition The way in which numbers are grouped does not change the sum.
Example: 2 + (4 + 5) = (2 + 4) + 5

grouping property of multiplication The way in which numbers are grouped does not change the product.
Example: 2 × (3 × 5) = (2 × 3) × 5

input The numbers and commands entered in a calculator or a computer. A computer keyboard is an input device.

less than (<) The symbol used to compare two numbers when the lesser number is written first.
Examples: 3 < 7, 6 < 9

LET A statement in a BASIC computer program that assigns a value to a memory location named by a letter.

line The collection of points along a straight path that goes on and on in opposite directions. A line has no endpoints.

line of symmetry A line on which a figure can be folded so that both sides match.
Example:

line segment A part of a line having two endpoints.

metric system A measurement system that measures length in millimeters, centimeters, meters, and kilometers; capacity in milliliters and liters; mass in grams and kilograms; and temperature in degrees Celsius. *See* Table of Measures.

mixed number A number written as a whole number and a fraction.
Example: $3\frac{4}{5}$

multiplication An operation on two or more numbers, called factors, to find a product.
Example: 4 × 5 = 20
The product is 20.

number line A line that shows numbers in order.
Example:

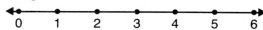

number sentence A fact written in horizontal form.
Example: 3 × 4 = 12

numerator The number above the fraction bar in a fraction.
Example: $\frac{2}{5}$
The numerator is 2.

odd number A whole number that has 1, 3, 5, 7, or 9 in ones place.

order property of addition The order in which numbers are added does not change the sum.
Example: 9 + 3 = 3 + 9

order property of multiplication The order in which numbers are multiplied does not change the product.
Example: $3 \times 2 = 2 \times 3$

ordered pair A pair of numbers that gives the location of a place on a map or a graph.

ordinal number A number used to tell order or position.
Examples: first, fifth

outcome A possible result in an experiment.

output The answer given by a computer or a calculator. A computer monitor is an output device.

perimeter The distance around a figure.

pictograph A graph that shows number information by using picture symbols.

place value The value of a digit determined by its position in a number.
Example: In 562, 5 means 5 hundreds, 6 means 6 tens, 2 means 2 ones.

plane A flat surface extending endlessly in all directions.

PRINT A command to the computer to show information on the screen.

product The answer in multiplication.
Example: $4 \times 8 = 32$
The product is 32.

program A list of instructions for the computer.

property of one The product of any number and 1 is that number.

quotient The answer in division.
Example: $24 \div 3 = 8$ or $3\overline{)24}$ with 8 above
The quotient is 8.

ray A part of a line that has one endpoint and goes on and on in one direction.

rectangle A figure with four square corners.
Example:

regroup To use 1 ten to form 10 ones; 1 hundred to form 10 tens; 12 ones to form 1 ten 2 ones; and so on.

remainder The number that is left over after dividing.
Example: $42 \div 8 = 5$ R2
The remainder is 2.

right angle An angle that has the shape of a square corner.
Example:

Roman numerals Symbols that the Romans used for numbers: I, V, X, L, C, D and M.

rounding Expressing a number to the nearest ten, nearest hundred, and so on.
Example: 43 rounded to the nearest ten is 40.

RUN An instruction that tells the computer to follow instructions one line at a time.

sphere A space figure shaped like a round ball.

square A rectangle with four equal sides and four corners.

subtraction An operation on two numbers to find the difference.
Example: $15 - 3 = 12$
The difference is 12.

sum The answer in addition.
Example: $8 + 7 = 15$
The sum is 15.

triangle A figure with three sides and three corners.

volume The number of cubic units that fit inside a space figure.

zero property of addition The sum of any number and 0 is that number.
Example: $3 + 0 = 3$

zero property of multiplication The product of any number and 0 is 0.
Example: $5 \times 0 = 0$

TABLE OF MEASURES

Metric

Length

1 centimeter (cm) = 10 millimeters (mm)
1 meter (m) = 100 centimeters
1 kilometer (km) = 1,000 meters

Mass

1 kilogram (kg) = 1,000 grams (g)

Capacity

1 liter (L) = 1,000 milliliters (mL)

Customary

Length

1 foot (ft) = 12 inches (in.)
1 yard (yd) = 36 inches, or 3 feet
1 mile (mi) = 5,280 feet, or 1,760 yards

Weight

1 pound (lb) = 16 ounces (oz)

Capacity

1 pint (pt) = 2 cups (c)
1 quart (qt) = 2 pints
1 gallon (gal) = 4 quarts

Time

1 minute (min) = 60 seconds (s)
1 hour (h) = 60 minutes
1 day (d) = 24 hours
1 week (wk) = 7 days
1 month (mo) = 28 to 31 days, or about 4 weeks
1 year (yr) = 12 months, or 52 weeks, or 365 days

Money

1 nickel = 5 cents (¢)
1 dime = 10 cents, or 2 nickels
1 quarter = 2 dimes and 1 nickel
1 half-dollar = 2 quarters
1 dollar ($) = 4 quarters

SYMBOLS

=	is equal to	10¢	ten cents
>	is greater than	$1.60	one dollar and sixty cents
<	is less than	6:45	six forty-five o'clock
. . .	and so on	°C	degree Celsius
		°F	degree Fahrenheit

Index

CREDITS

Cover: Computer Art/Ron Morecraft and Nancy Moore

All photographs by Silver Burdett unless otherwise noted.

All line art by Burmar unless otherwise noted

Sports equipment provided by Fitzgerald Sporting Goods Company, Morristown, New Jersey

CHAPTER 1 1: Sid Avery/Shostal Associates. 2: Roberta Collier. 4, 5: Elizabeth Miles. 6: Victoria Beller-Smith for Silver Burdett. 7: Courtesy Center Grove School, Randolph, New Jersey. 8: *r.* Dan De Wilde for Silver Burdett. 12: Ann Wilson. 14, 15: Roberta Collier. 16, 17: Bob Shein. 18: Courtesy Peripole Musical Instruments. 19: Roberta Collier. 20, 21: George Ulrich. 22, 23: Yoshi Miyake. 24, 25: Ann Wilson. 26, 27: Susan Swan. 29: Elizabeth Miles. 32: Ann Wilson.

CHAPTER 2 33: Hanson Carroll/Peter Arnold, Inc. 35: Michal Heron. 36: *border* Michal Heron; Gwen Connelly. 37: *border* Michal Heron. 38, 39: Yoshi Miyake. 40: *t.* Nadine Orabona/Tom Stack & Associates; *m.* Betsy Day. 41: *t.* Betsy Day; *l.* Jim Winter/Tom Stack & Associates; *r.* Don and Pat Valenti/Tom Stack & Associates. 44, 45: Lane Yerkes. 46, 47: Ann Iosa. 48: Eric Carle/Shostal Associates. 49: Gwen Connelly. 50: *r.* Yoshi Miyake. 51: Yoshi Miyake. 52–53: Tom Powers. 53: Peter Krempasky. 54, 55: Imagery. 56, 57: Jackie Rogers. 61: Tom Powers. 62: *b.* Sally Schaedler.

CHAPTER 3 63: © G.C. Kelley/Photo Researchers, Inc. 64, 65: Jerry Cable. 66: *t.* John Hamberger; *b.* E.R. Degginger. 68: *t.* Jerry Cable. 69: Jerry Cable. 70: Jeremy Guitar. 72: E.R. Degginger. 74: Jeremy Guitar. 76–79: Bob Masheris. 80: *t.* © Tom McHugh/Photo Researchers, Inc.; *b.* John Running/Stock, Boston. 81: Ann Wilson. 82: *t.* Ann Wilson; *b.* Charles Mueller/E.R. Degginger. 83: Ann Wilson. 84, 85: Elizabeth Miles. 86, 87: Lane Yerkes. 88, 89: Bob Masheris. 90: *t.* Nancy Munger. 91: Nancy Munger. 100: Sally Schaedler.

CHAPTER 4 101: Charles Gupton/Stock, Boston. 102: *r.* Len Ebert. 103: Len Ebert. 104: *t.* Michal Heron for Silver Burdett. 105: Dan De Wilde for Silver Burdett. 106, 107: Michele Noiset. 108: Gary Undercuffler. 110: Burt Dodson. 112: Robin Brickman. 114: Jackie Rogers. 115: *r.* Nancy Munger. 116, 117: Kim Mulkey. 118, 119: Michele Noiset. 120: Dan De Wilde for Silver Burdett. 122, 123: Bob Masheris. 124, 125: David Wenzel. 126: Sally Schaedler. 127: Susan Swan. 130: Susan Miller.

CHAPTER 5 133: NASA/Shostal Associates. 134: *r.* NASA. 136: *t.* NASA. 138: *t.* E.R. Degginger. 139: *b.* Tom Powers. 140: NASA. 142: George Ulrich. 145: Susan Swan. 147: *b.* Jeremy Guitar. 150: *b.l.* George Ulrich. 151: *l.* George Ulrich. 152: *l.* George Ulrich; *r.* Flip and Debra Schulke/Black Star. 153: *l.* George Ulrich. 154: *b.* NASA. 155: *b.* Jeremy Guitar. 155: *m.* Bookmakers. 156, 157: Tom Powers. 159: Lane Yerkes. 160, 161: George Ulrich.

CHAPTER 6 167: Doug Wallin/Taurus Photos. 168: Yoshi Miyake. 170: Steven Schindler. 171: Tom Noonan. 172: Yoshi Miyake. 174: Steven Schindler. 178: Nancy Munger. 179: *t.*, *m.* Bob Masheris. 180: Diane Patterson. 182: Mary Ann Zanconato. 184: Jane Kendall. 186: David Wenzel. 188: David Wenzel. 191: Tom Noonan. 192, 193: George Ulrich. 194: Mou-Sien Tseng. 195: *b.l.* The Granger Collection; *r.* Bob Greiser/Focus West.

CHAPTER 7 203: © Serraillier/Photo Researchers, Inc. 204, 205: Alan Eitzen. 206: *l.* Tom Heneghan/West Stock; *r.* Jan Palmer. 207: David Falconer. 208: *t.* Bill Stanley/West Stock; *b.* Mou-Sien Tseng. 210, 211: Carolyn Croll. 212: Barbara Todd. 214: Robert Jackson. 216: Barbara Todd. 218, 219: Vincent Modica/Stock, Boston. 220: Jeff Foott/Bruce Coleman. 221: Dick Garvey/West Stock. 222: Keith Gunnar/West Stock. 224: *l.* Dan De Wilde for Silver Burdett. 226: © 1987 Annie Griffiths/Woodfin Camp & Associates. 227: Michele Noiset. 228, 229: Susan Swan. 230: *t.* Tom Noonan. 231: Susan Swan. 232: Sally Schaedler. 232–233: Michele Noiset. 233: *b.* Carolyn Croll. 236: Bookmakers. 237: Tom Powers.

CHAPTER 8 241: Werner Müller/Peter Arnold, Inc. 242, 243: Len Ebert. 244: *t.* E.R. Degginger. 245: *t.* Robert Jackson; *b.* G. Ziesier/Peter Arnold, Inc. 246: *t.* Sally Schaedler; *b.* E.R. Degginger. 247: E.R. Degginger. 248: *r.* Alec Duncan/Taurus Photos. 249: *l.* © Sven-O-Lindblad/Photo Researchers, Inc.; *r.* Mohamed Amin/Bruce Coleman. 250: *r.* Laurie Marks. 252: *t.l.*, *t.r.* John Hamberger. 253: *b.l.* © William Bacon/Photo Researchers, Inc.; *b.r.* Stouffer Productions/Animals, Animals. 254: Charles E. Schmidt/Taurus Photos. 255: *t.* Imagery. 258: Ellen Appleby. 259: Susan Swan.

CHAPTER 9 261: Steve Leonard/Click, Chicago. 262: *t.* Kathleen McCord. 264: *t.* Lane Yerkes; *b.* Barbara Todd. 266: *t.* Lane Yerkes. 267: *b.* Lane Yerkes. 268: *t.l.* John Lawn; *t.r.* Craig Aurness/West Light. 269: *b.* John Lawn. 270: *t.* Michele Noiset. 272: Lane Yerkes. 274: Kathleen McCord. 275: Barbara Todd. 276–277: Lane Yerkes. 277: *b.* Laurie Marks. 278: *t.* Laurie Marks. 282: Hal Frenck. 285: *b.* Peter Krempasky. 288: John Lawn. 289: Diane Patterson.

CHAPTER 10 295: Don and Pat Valenti/DRK Photos. 296: *t.* John Colwell/Grant Heilman Photography; *b.* Tom Noonan. 298, 299: Michael Adams. 300: *t.* Sally Schaedler. 302, 303: Tom Noonan. 304: *t.* Don Patterson. 306: *t.l.* Don Patterson. 308: *t.* John Colwell/Grant Heilman Photography; *b.* Tom Noonan. 311: *t.* Peter Krempasky; *b.* Sally Schaedler. 314: *t.* Michael Adams. 315: Ellen Appleby.

CHAPTER 11 317: Rhoda Sidney/Leo deWys, Inc. 318: John Lawn. 319: Tom Powers. 320: Sally Schaedler. 322, 323: Tom Powers. 330: *b.* Pierer/Leo deWys, Inc. 331: Paul Anderson. 332–333: Tom Noonan. 333: *b.* Peter Krempasky. 334: Randy Chewning. 340: *t.* Lockheed-California Company. 340–341: After Image. 341: Chad Slattery/After Image; *b.* John Lund/After Image.

CHAPTER 12 343: Tom Kennedy/Black Star. 346: *l.* David Madison/Duomo; *r.* David Madison. 347: Joseph A. DiChello. 350: Daryl Moore. 353: Daryl Moore. 354: *t.l.* © 1987 Michal Heron/Woodfin Camp & Associates; *t.r.* Charles Baker/Click, Chicago. 355: © 1987 Michal Heron/Woodfin Camp & Associates. 356: *t.* Paul Anderson. 357: *b.* Paul Anderson. 358: Lane Yerkes. 359: Sally Schaedler. 360: *t.* Bookmakers; *b.l.* Richard Pelling/Focus on Sports; *b.m.* National Baseball Hall of Fame, Cooperstown, New York; *b.r.* Focus on Sports. 361: Randy Chewning.

CHAPTER 13 367: Imagery. 371: Don Dyen. 373: *b.* Sally Schaedler. 374: *t.* David Reinbold. 375: *b.* Susan Swan. 376: *t.l.* Barbara Todd; *t.r.* Dan De Wilde for Silver Burdett. 377: *t.*, *b.* Barbara Todd. 379: *t.* Kathleen McCord. 380: *r.* Lane Yerkes. 382: Sally Schaedler. 383: *b.* David Reinbold. 384: *t.* Sally Schaedler. 385: *b.* Don Dyen. 386, 387: Susan Swan. 388: *t.* Kathleen McCord; *b.* Bookmakers. 389: Kathleen McCord. 392: Diane Paterson. 393: Diane Paterson.

Extra Practice 419: Bookmakers. 423: Bookmakers. 424: Barbara Todd. 430: Susan Swan.

2 3 4 5 6 7 8 9 10—RRD—93 92 91 90 89 88 87 86